CISTERCIAN STUDIES SERIES: NUMBER ONE HUNDRED TWENTY-TWO

Roger De Ganck

TOWARDS UNIFICATION WITH GOD
BEATRICE OF NAZARETH IN HER CONTEXT
Part Three

CISTERCIAN STUDIES SERIES: NUMBER ONE HUNDRED TWENTY-TWO

Towards Unification with God

Beatrice of Nazareth in Her Context
Part Three

by

Roger De Ganck

Cistercian Publications
Kalamazoo, Michigan

The work of Cistercian Publications is made possible in part
by support from Western Michigan University to the
Institute of Cistercian Studies.

Available in Britain and Europe from
Cassell plc
London

Available elsewhere from
Cistercian Publications (Distribution)
St Joseph's Abbey
Spencer, MA 01562

Volume Three of a series of three:

The Life of Beatrice of Nazareth
(Cistercian Fathers Series, Number 50)

Beatrice of Nazareth in Her Context
(Cistercian Studies Series, Number 121)

Towards Unification with God
Beatrice of Nazareth in Her Context, Volume Two, Part Three
(Cistercian Studies Series, Number 122)

Library of Congress Cataloging-in-Publication Data
(Revised for vol: pt. 3)

Ganck, Roger de, 1908-
Beatrice of Nazareth in her context.

(Cistercian studies series ; no. 121–122)
Includes bibliographical references and index.
Contents: [pt. 1–2. without special title] —
pt. 3. Towards unification with God.
1. Beatrijs, van Tienen, ca. 1200-1268. 2. Theology—Middle Ages,
600-1500. 3. Asceticism—History—Middle Ages, 600-1500.
4. Vita Beatricis. I. [Ganck, Roger de, 1908-   . Beatrice of Nazareth ;
v. 2-3]
BX4705.B25868G36   vol. 2-   271'.97 [271'.97] [B] 90-35817
[BV5095.B42]
Printed in the United States of America

TABLE OF CONTENTS

This volume is numbered in consecutive pagination with Beatrice of Nazareth in Her Context.

PART THREE

INTRODUCTION

THE PSYCHOSOMATIC PHENOMENA we mentioned in Part Two of the previous volume provoke the question: What is real in all this? The somatic manifestations, not to say perturbations, call into question the psychic state of the *mulieres religiosae* and their so-called mysticism. It should be noted that they themselves did not speak about mysticism; much less did they consider themselves to be mystics. Their biographers occasionally use the term mystic, though not with the meaning the expression conveys today.[1] Nor should we expect to hear the *mulieres religiosae* speak about Christ-mysticism, eucharistic mysticism, trinitarian mysticism, *minne*-mysticism or about essence-mysticism. These terms belong to the scholarly terminology of later times, as also do such expressions as 'the dark night' or 'infused contemplation'.

Of the six *mulieres religiosae* under consideration in these pages, Ida of Leuven was the only illiterate. Though she had the opportunity to go to school and learn Latin, she turned it down and was not even able to read.[2] She is also the only one whose

---

1 Beatrice's biographer speaks of the mystical ring, *mysticum annulum* (76,27), which she received as a symbol at her consecration as a virgin. He says also that in reading the Bible she sought for the mystical meaning, *mysticum sensum* (85,30), the spiritual meaning of it. (See Henri de Lubac, *Exégèse médiévale*, II/l [Paris, 1959], 549–620: 'La topologie mystique', and Jean Leclercq, 'Les Traductions de la Bible et la Spiritualité médiévale', in W. Lourdaux and D. Verhelst eds, *The Bible and Medieval Culture*, (Leuven, 1979), 263–77; 277. Ida of Leuven's biographer mentions that when, as a small child she went with her mother to church, she saw for a short moment a brilliant light coming down and shining above the consecrated host. He calls it a *mystica visio* in the sense of a curious and unusual happening (*AA SS* April 2: 158, 2), which could as well have been a visual aberration. He speaks also of Christ as the mystical lamb, *agnus mysticus* (*ibid.*, 179, 29), just as he calls the Eucharist *mysticum sacramentum* (*ibid.*, 182, 40), but this has little to do with Ida as a mystic.

2 This is three times stressed in her biography: *AA SS* April 2: 158, 3; 183, 4; 188, 26.

biography was written by a confessor.[3] This lack of schooling fostered in Ida the tendency to be a one-way person, sincere and straightforward, but easily duped by her emotions,imagination and naïveté.[4] Ida of Nivelles, Alice of Schaarbeek, Ida Lewis and Beatrice on the other hand, were schooled and their biographies show no indication that they made themselves dependent on confessors, except for the sacraments. As for the talented Hadewijch, it has been said that she wrote her visions for a confessor, an opinion accurately corrected.[5]

Except perhaps for Ida of Leuven, all the *mulieres religiosae*, each in her own way, gave proof that they became adult and mature women who could stand on their own feet. What they wrote, said and did indicates that they were intelligent, emotional and sensitive women, without being sentimental. All of them, including Ida of Leuven, were strong-willed and generous. Mention has been made above of the way in which the *mulieres religiosae* conducted themselves in relation to clergy and laypeople.[6] Would that behavior be typical of all the *mulieres religiosae* we know of? As far as we can surmise, the answer would be affirmative. To use an idiomatic expression, even clergymen 'kissed the ground' on which some *mulieres religiosae* walked, among them Mary of Oignies and Lutgard. Hadewijch and at least four, if not all five, of the other *mulieres religiosae* considered here show that they respected the clergy without developing a subservient 'reverend Father'-mentality.[7] Unlike earlier and

3 Her biographer, himself quite credulous, based her *Vita* on the notes left by Ida's former confessor, an unidentified Hugh.

4 The troubles she had at home, for instance, were more than once provoked by Ida without her realizing, much less intending, it.

5 N. De Paepe, *Hadewijch. Strofische Gedichten*, 149–58.

6 See above, Chapter X, 294–301.

7 Among the six *mulieres religiosae* under consideration, only the biography of Ida of Leuven mentions once that she addressed her confessor as Reverend Father (*AA SS* April 2:181,7). An acceptable explanation may point to the biographer himself who had a great respect and admiration for Ida's former confessor. What was said at the beginning of this note is supported by what the *Vita* tells us about Ida's dismissal of an assistant chaplain who had said something that hurt her feelings. See *ibid.*, 183, 5–6.

contemporary women of the *Wandering*-movement they did not go around preaching and venting their discontent with some clergymen or with the structure and function of the hierarchical Church.[8] They were not like some of today's feminists who, while rightly battling misogyny, fall into the extreme of being anti-male. If the *Vitae* of the *mulieres religiosae*, mostly written by clerics, point a finger at clerics, the pointing was done by the biographers themselves in chiding some licentious, avaricious and power-hungry clerics who neglected their pastoral duties.[9]

The *mulieres religiosae* had knowledge of the Jewish faith through the Old Testament. The small number of contemporary Jews living in their country had a reputation for being business people or money lenders of dubious standing. Muslims were 'infidels' who made pilgrimages to the Holy Land hazardous. The stories they might have heard about them from crusaders in no way helped to make the Islamic religion understandable or acceptable to them. The Americas, the Far East and other as yet undiscovered lands were completely *terra incognita*, and so were the religions and mysticisms of these regions. The only religion with which the *mulieres religiosae* were deeply familiar was the Western Catholic faith, and with it a small awareness of the Eastern Orthodox branch, particularly the Greek Fathers of whom they had, through their mentors, some slight knowledge. The small part of the world which was theirs had its own cultural past which inevitably influenced them. The industrial, commercial, social and cultural evolutions in the burgeoning towns and

8 H. Grundmann, *Religiöse Bewegungen*, 503–13.

9 Such warnings and denunciations by biographers did not come out of the blue. Diego, bishop of Osma in Spain, and his companion Dominic Gusman, supported by Foulques, the Cistercian bishop of Toulouse, took the wind out of the anti-clerical diatribes of the Cathars and Valdenses by adopting their frugal lifestyle and ideals of poverty. (Christine Thouzellier, *Catharisme et Valdéisme*, 193–204). Innocent III (d.1216) fostered this tactic and convinced the Cistercians who were his first delegates in this area to adopt the new practice. (Achille Luchaire, *Innocent III*, Paris, 1905, rpt 1969, vol.2, 87–113); this proved beneficial as well for the poverty ideals of the *mulieres religiosae*.

cities of the thirteenth century have already been sufficiently discussed in the first chapter of the previous book.

In this restricted world they were born and raised as Christians. Their familiarity with the Bible in its Vulgate form 'gave them strong religious convictions which allowed them to draw immediate consequences for their behaviour'.[10] They did so *vehementer*, with an impetuous eagerness to enter into union with God: a union for which they knew they were made. They were not satisfied with a merely speculative and intellectual knowledge of God. In one of her visions Hadewijch was brought to the top of a very high mountain. A dueler or champion (*kimpe*) accompanied her up to, but not onto, the plateau where the Lord resided. On the way back the champion told her that when he lived on earth (apparently as a theologian) he had 'followed the strict counsel of the intellect'. He admitted that by withholding his affection from Christ's humanity he had wronged the Lord.[11] The *mulieres religiosae* certainly did not have to reproach themselves for such a lack of affection. Their greatest and most burning desire was to love God by experiencing him, to come to an experiential knowledge of him. To know *about* somebody or something is one thing, to know somebody *experientially* is something else, deeper and more complete, for experience touches the individual as nothing else can. Today experiential knowledge of the divine is called mysticism.[12]

In parts One and Two we have tried to indicate how man, created by and for God, has the capacity of participating in the divine. With the help of God's gifts and graces the *mulieres religiosae* strove ardently to free themselves as much as possible from all that could hinder the fulfillment of this capacity. From the incarnation of God's Son, from his life and death they learned

10 Jean Leclercq, 'Psycho-history and the Understanding of Medieval People', *CSt* 11 (1976) 268–89; 277.

11 Vision 8; VM, *Visioenen*, 1: 90–91, ll.117–23.

12 Instead of listing the superabundant literature about mysticism, we need only to refer to an anthology of writings about mysticism seen from different angles by several authors, and edited by Richard Woods, *Understanding Mysticism* (Garden City, NY.), 1980.

what they had to do to make themselves 'roomy' for God.[13] They eagerly followed Christ to become more purified, more totally open and free for God. In part Three an effort will be made to show what God did in and with them to make them even 'roomier' for union with him.

---

13 *Roomy* is taken from Thomas M.Tomasic's 'Neoplatonism and the Mysticism of William of St.-Thierry', *An Introduction to the Medieval Mystics of Europe*, Paul Szarmack ed., (Albany, NY, 1984) 69, where he translates *capax Dei* as: 'roomy enough to receive God'.

CHAPTER TWELVE

BURNING DESIRE

T HE DESIRE OF THE *MULIERES RELIGIOSAE* for God was not
mere wishful thinking, much less a cupidity, as *desiderium* implied in classical Latin. For them, it was an
affectively loaded longing and yearning to love God and to
become united with him.

Desire, obviously, knows many levels and shades. Hadewijch,
conscious of her responsibility as leader or at least as counselor of
a small group of *mulieres religiosae* warned them against desires
which were directed toward anything but God. She was particularly anxious to point out the harmfulness of cheap and misleading desires. 'Desire for God is sometimes sweet', she wrote.
'Nevertheless it does not always come from God, for it may well
up from the experiences of the senses rather than from grace, and
from nature rather than from the spirit'.[1] 'Under the cover of holy
desires most people go astray. They look for consolation in much
lower comforts that they can grasp. This is a great pity!'.[2] Hadewijch had in mind here religious or spiritual comforts rather than
material ones. She simply could not tolerate—either for her

---

1 Letter 10; VM, *Brieven*, 1: 86, ll. 10–13. Hadewijch could have borrowed
this sentence from Richard's *In Cantica Canticorum Explanatio*, PL 196:422C.
2 Letter 6; VM, *Brieven*, 1: 63, ll. 218–21.

friends', her own or for God's sake—that her friends would 'go astray'. As she wrote in another letter:

> Sweet feelings [about God] are quite inferior, for one is easily conquered by them and so the strength of desire diminishes. What they feel is so great to them that they cannot come to the knowledge of the [objective] greatness and the perfect being of Love (*Minne*). For when the heart and the lower feelings, which are easily satisfied, are touched according to our emotional inclinations, they think they are in the highest heavens. In these satisfactions they forget the real debt which is claimed at all times: the debt of [man's] love which Love demands.[3]

Like a muezzin calling from the top of a minaret, Hadewijch cries out the message: 'We must seek God and nothing else. In desires for devotion all those who are seeking anything other than God, err'.[4] She simply could not keep silent when desire deteriorated into sentimentality or what she called 'frivolous love'.[5]

Before Beatrice, in 1231, was able to integrate decisively her fear of sin with the unshakable conviction that love is the answer, it sometimes seemed to her that all the roads leading to the 'heavenly fatherland were beset with snares and traps from beginning to end. She feared that however carefully she made her way through them, the foot of her affection would still be caught in one or another of the snares'.[6]

To desire is not as easy as it looks at first sight. Desire implies an absence—the not having the object desired—and this is

3 Letter 30; VM, *Brieven*, 1: 253, ll. 37–48.
4 Letter 4; VM, *Brieven*, 1: 40, ll. 72–76. Hadewijch is here in line with Richard:'in the third degree of impetuous love nothing can satisfy the soul except this one love [for God], just as nothing else can please it: one unique love, one unique desire, one unique thirst, one unique endeavor'. See G. Dumeige, *Les quatre degrés*, 135, ll. 21–24.
5 Letter 12; VM, *Brieven*, 1: 106, ll. 108–119: 'affectien van lichter minnen'.
6 *Vita*, 134, 105. This image is appropriate for her time. If she had lived in the twentieth century, she would have had a broad choice of many man-made devices to trap people.

usually frustrating.[7] The presence or the having of what is desired was called by the *mulieres religiosae* not possession, but love. When they speak of possessing God, the expression is followed or preceded by the word love. In the christian context this love does not aim at a passing, but at a lasting, even an everlasting, union of lovers. Desire is voluntaristic and emotionally affective, though both qualifications are subject to a great variety of degrees. According to Augustine, William and Bernard, love and desire are a vehement, in the sense of impetuous will, *vehemens voluntas*.[8] Sometimes love and affect seem to be synonymous to William; at other times they are not.[9] What he called *affectus cordis* could be translated 'by the impulse, or energy, or commitment, or operation of love; when directed by illuminating grace, one can only go upwards'[10] or Godward. 'Among all the natural endowments of man' said Bernard, 'love holds the first place, especially when it is directed toward God, who is the source from which it comes'.[11] Beatrice affirmed Bernard's first phrase that 'among all the natural endowments of man, love holds first place' when she said that man's desire for God is natural: 'through keennesss of spirit, the soul clings more firmly and more promptly in simple desire for the Supreme Good' (122,44). The

7 *Vita*, 214,39. Beatrice was frustrated in her desire, *frustrata suo desiderio*, when she thought she could grasp the incomprehensible, but in fact could not, though she tried with increased desire, *elevato desiderio*.

8 For Augustine, see his *De Trinitate* 11,5; PL 42: 988, and 15,14; PL 42: 1089; for William his Cant PL 180: 499C; SCh 82:188: 'Vehemens autem voluntas vel quasi ad absentem, desiderium est, vel affecta circa praesentem amor est'. (A passionate will, directed as if to an absent person, is desire; drawn to someone present, is love). This sentence could be compared with what Bernard says in SC 79,1; SBOp 2: 272: 'O amor praeceps, vehemens, fragrans, impetuose, qui praeter te aliud cogitare non sinis, fastidis cetera, contemnis omnia praeter te, te contentus! (Oh headstrong, vehement, burning, impetuous love, which does not allow to think of anything but you; you loathe the rest, you spurn all else but yourself, contented only with yourself.)

9 In pre-scholastic times *affectus* was an expression with variegated meanings. See W. Zwingmann, 'Ex affectu cordis', *Citeaux* 18 (1967) 15: an expression with 'keine unbedingte eindeutige und immer verbindliche Festlegung'. See also Thomas X. Davis, *The Mirror of Faith*, CF 15 (Kalamazoo, 1979) 93–95.

10 D. Bell, *The Image*, 132.

11 Bernard, SC 7,2; SBOp 1: 31: 'Excellit in naturae donis affectio haec amoris, praesertim cum ad suum recurrit principium, quod est Deus'.

second part of Bernard's sentence is the equivalent of William's illuminating grace.

They knew that desire cannot be attributed to God anthropomorphically. God seeks man's love, not to be 'enriched' by it—to put it in human terms—but to help man toward his human consummation.[12] They were very thankful that God was there for them, even when they could have him only by desire. The upward movement of illuminating grace was for that very reason very important to them. Joris Reynaert, for instance, listed how often this term, or more accurately, its meaning is used by Hadewijch, who called it illuminated reason, *verlichte rede*. This term occurs twelve times in her letters and ten times in her other writings.[13] Beatrice's biographer did not use the expression, but spoke instead in terms of illuminating counsel,[14] or the guiding light of divine clarity,[15] or in other similar words. In her first *maniere* Beatrice describes the whole trajectory of the soul, from its creation, through illumination, toward consummation. In this *maniere*,

> the soul is actively drawn into the desire to attain and to remain in that purity, liberty and nobility in which it was made by its Creator according to his image and likeness, which the soul must intensely love and preserve.[16]

God is sought not by steps of the feet but by desires,[17] and these steps of desire are very important because they help expand a person's roominess for God. Hadewijch said that as humility makes the soul deep, so does desire make it wide: both virtues make one's capacity for God commensurate to his 'dimensions'. In her twelfth vision she described the ornaments embroidered on her heavenly robe:

12 Jacques Blanpain, 'Language mystique, expression de désir' dans les Sermons sur le Cantique de Bernard de Clairvaux', *Coll* 36 (1974) 45–68; 52.
13 *Beeldspraak*, 58, nn.18 and 19.
14 *Vita*, 27,66; 85,20; 97,123; 130,7; 201,4.
15 *Vita*, 52,91 ,68,37; 86,40; 163,56; 174,81 and so forth.
16 R-VM, *Seven manieren*, 4, ll. 14–24.
17 Bernard, SC 84,1; SBOp 2: 303: 'Non pedum passibus, sed desideriis quaeritur Deus'.

Humility bore witness that she was so deep and unfathomable that she could truly receive to the full the greatness [of
God's love] in her unfathomableness. Desire bore witness
how vast she was in her territory, *lantscap*,[18] and how
beautiful and splendid in her full wealth, so that she might
well gather in all the greatness of heaven.[19]

Beatrice also spoke of the vastness, the breadth and the amplitude of her desire for a love relationship with God.[20] 'Just as faith
leads to full knowledge, so desire leads to perfect love. And just
as it is said 'Unless you have believed you shall not understand,
so it may likewise be said without absurdity: Unless you have
desired you shall not perfectly love. Understanding is therefore
the fruit of faith, perfect love the fruit of desire'.[21] Beatrice
indicated that desire is the mark, the dynamic characteristic of
man's striving toward his ultimate goal. In her seventh *maniere*
she said that 'the soul knows God, loves him and so desires him,
that ... it desires to see, possess and have fruition of him'.[22]
William addressing God, says

the more clearly and truly these things [God's perfections
which make him adorable and lovable] declare you, and
affirm that you are worthy to be loved, the more ardently
desirable do they make you appear to me. But alas! This
experience is not one to be enjoyed with unmitigated pleasure and delight; rather it is one of yearnings, strivings and
frustration, though not a torment without some sweetness.
For just as the offerings I make to you do not suffice to

18. See J. Reynaert, *Beeldspraak*, 246–57: Het mystieke landschap.

19 VM, *Visioenen*, 1: 129, ll. 78–84.

20 *Vita*, desiderii latitudo, 96,114; 100,27; 204,71; desiderii amplitudo:
96,118.

21 Bernard, Letter 18,2; SBOp 7: 67: 'Sicut autem fides ducit ad plenam
cognitionem, sic desiderium ad perfectam dilectionem. Et sicut dicitur: *nisi
credideritis, non intelligetis*, sic dici aeque non absurde potest: Si non
desideraveritis non perfecte amabitis. Intellectus igitur est fructus fidei, perfecta
caritas desiderii'.

22 R-VM, *Seven manieren*, 31–32, ll. 52 and 59–60.

please you perfectly unless I offer you myself along with them, so the contemplation of your manifold perfections, though it does give us a measure of refreshment, does not satisfy us unless we have yourself along with it.[23]

A study of the meanings Hadewijch attaches to the term 'desire' leads one to conclude that desire completely affects the whole person, psychologically as well as somatically.[24] Hadewijch wrote to a friend that she should strive toward God's totality: 'Enlarge your mind by lofty desires toward the totality of God'.[25] Ida Lewis' biography puts it more metaphorically: 'putting on the little wings of love, she lifted herself up above herself. In this flight of desire, borne aloft by contemplative updrafts, she penetrated into celestial mysteries'.[26]

The dynamism of desire toward the totality of the other is mutual. For instance, in one of her letters Hadewijch wrote :'You should always look fixedly on your Beloved whom you desire. For he who gazes on what he desires becomes so ardently enkindled that his heart yields to the sweet burden of love'.[27] Of Ida of Nivelles it was said that, 'adhering to God through a more ardent love and a more impetuous desire [than others had] she very often attracted God into her and was herself totally attracted to him'.[28] Alice of Schaarbeek on her part, 'spurred by an impetuous desire, beautified herself inwardly and outwardly [in her behavior] in order to be admitted into the chamber of her Bridegroom'.[29] The *Liber amoris* mentions that [human] love took her javelins, namely the fiery javelins of desire, and while

23 Contemp 1,4; PL 184: 369AB; CF 3:40.

24 R. Vanneste, *Abstracta*, 93.

25 Letter one; VM, *Brieven*, 1: 18, ll. 52–53.

26 *AA SS* Oct.13: 113,18: 'Ascensiones in corde suo disposuit, et se supra se sublevans sumptis amoris pennulis, volatu desiderii, contemplativis tractibus sublimata, coelestium arcana penetrans'.

27 Letter 18; VM, *Brieven*, 1: 159, ll. 189–93.

28 *Quinque*, 247: 'Deo adhaerens Deum in se trahebat et a Deo in Deum tota trahebatur'.

29 *AA SS* June 2: 478, 4: 'Vehementer desiderii stimulo urgeri, ad Sponsi sui thalamum faciem ornavit, intus et exterius seipsam decoravit'.

she could not reach the throne of this lofty giant [God], she could at least shoot at him from afar'.[30]

The pull of all these desires made Beatrice aware that they stemmed from God's will,[31] and Hadewijch complained—as Beatrice would also say in her treatise—that 'the unattainable desire, which Love has always given me for the sake of fruition, has injured and wounded me in the breast and in the heart'.[32]

This desire has no end in sight. Beatrice's saying that 'the instability of the human condition never attains stability of desire in the haven of a quiet resting place' (102,37), is confirmed by Bernard,[33] and Richard as well.[34] About 1262, Thomas of Villers wrote two letters to his sister Alice, a Cistercian nun in Vrouwenpark, who had complained how flat her spiritual life seemed to be. The only honest answer he could think of was: 'to love him [God], to desire him, to long for him from the bottom of the heart in all affectivity and to do his will'.[35] The ordinariness of daily living, especially in a convent where there are few occasions for

---

30 John Morson and Hilary Costello, 'The *Liber amoris*', *Citeaux* 16 (1965) 114–35; 133, ll. 164–66. The text of this short treatise, not written by Guerric, as was formerly thought, but closer to Bernard in content, is preserved in a manuscript of the Cisterican abbey of Ter Duinen, now MS. 88/179 of the Seminary, Bruges.

31 H. Vekeman, '*Vita Beatricis* en *Seuen manieren van minne*. Een vergelijkende studie, *OGE* 46 (1972) 3–54; 35.

32 Letter 29; VM, *Brieven*, 1: 244, ll.52–55. Though it does not exactly correspond to what Hadewijch said, Richard's first degree of impetuous love, the one which injures and wounds, applies to some extent to her: 'Does not the heart seem deeply pierced when the burning sting of love penetrates the ardor of its desire?' See Gervais Dumeige, *Les quatre degrés*, 131, ll. 11–14. Jean Chatillon, 'Les quatre degrés de la Charité d'après Richard de Saint-Victor' *RAM* 20 (1939) 237–64; 240, made the observation that *affectus* is here taken in its larger sense of affectivity or deep emotion.

33 SC 84,1; SBOp 2: 303: 'There will be no end of desire nor therefore of seeking. Consider,if you can this fervor of seeking without want, and of desire without solicitude, for presence excludes the one, fulness the other'.

34. G. Dumeige, *Les quatre degrés*, 133, ll. 16–19: 'The second degree of impetuous love does not allow for any intermission. Its uninterrupted ardor burns the soul as with a high fever; not by day nor by night does the continuous intensity of its desire give it rest'.

35 E. Mikkers, 'Deux lettres inédites de Thomas, chantre de Villers', *Coll* 10 (1948) 161–73; 166, ll. 1–3.

change and few outlets to break the monotony of the regular, daily schedule, can be hard for a human being lacking a desire for God 'from the bottom of the heart'.

Beatrice and Hadewijch considered this steadfastness in ordinary daily living to be of greater importance than tears and psychosomatic manifestations, even when they experienced such phenomena. Near the beginning of her first *maniere* Beatrice mentions her longing for the Lord and expresses how 'the pious soul desires to serve him faithfully, to follow him vigorously and to love him truly'.[36] What Hadewijch desired most was 'not consolation or any other relief'. She looked forward not so much to a relaxation of tension, as to 'the certainty that she was accepted by *Minne*'.[37] In times of spiritual aridity 'the only way for man to keep his desire steady is to base it on former experiences. Thus the desire for God, of whom man is often aware through his feeling of an absence, will express or portray itself through past real or imagined satisfactions'.[38] And this is what Beatrice did: 'from the Bridegroom's chamber she brought back that vehement desire of her heart which could never be recalled from seeking heavenly things' (197,25). In such a case, as Beatrice herself wrote in her second *maniere*, 'the soul sets itself the task of serving the Lord freely and out of love alone, without any other motive...faithfully performing every service'.[39]

If Beatrice was to consider herself and her life meaningful even when she missed the presence of her Beloved, she *had* to develop and nourish a love of desire.[40] Several pertinent studies have shown the importance and meaning of desire for Hadewijch,[41] and for Beatrice.[42]

---

36 R-VM, *Seven manieren*, 3–4, ll. 11–13. See H. Vekeman, 'Minne in de "Seuen manieren van Minne" van Beatrijs van Nazareth', *Citeaux* 19 (1968) 284–316; 286.

37 35th Poem in Stanzas; VM, *Strophische Gedichten*, 226, ll. 71–72. See N. De Paepe, *Hadewijch. Strofische Gedichten*, 273.

38. J. Blanpain, 'Language mystique, expression de désir', *Coll* 36 (1974) 55.

39 R-VM, *Seven manieren*, 7–8; ll. 3–5; 12–13.

40 H. Vekeman, *Lexicografisch Onderzoek*, 2: 365.

41 R. Vanneste, *Abstracta*, 90–94; J. Reynaert, *Beeldspraak*, 447 q.v. begherte .

42 H. Vekeman, *Lexicografisch Onderzoek*, 2: 240–48.

The heart is evidently no less important to desire than to love. In the part of the biography related to Beatrice's journal, 'the desire of the heart' is a standard expression from beginning to end.[43] It has also a very important function in her treatise,[44] as it has in Hadewijch's writings.[45]

For Hadewijch as for Mechtild of Magdeburg desire is at once a source of suffering and delight.[46] Hadewijch herself wrote in the 44th of her Poems in Stanzas that 'compared to the pain of desiring Love (*Minne*) all other pains are to be scorned'.[47] In her seventh *maniere* Beatrice once more opposes her desire for God, *verlancnisse*, to *gevancnisse*, the prison of being on earth.[48]

Ida of Leuven's biographer speaks the same language:

There is a love of fruition distinct from the love of desire. The former is a perfect delectation, proper to the enjoyment of the Sovereign Good seen face to face. The latter in its longing for the Supreme Good is not wholly frustrated in the foretaste of celestial sweetness. It is nevertheless harassed by anxieties, because in the prison of human life, it is not blessed with the thorough and unobstructed possession and enjoying of what it loves, what it desires, what it has affection for.[49]

It would be surprising if the *mulieres religiosae* did not use the metaphor 'hunger and thirst for God' when speaking about their burning desire. They were already familiar with it through the

43 *Vita*, 40,62; 46,27; 49,10; 52,103; 52,110; 79,17; 105,5; 156,25; 157,29; 185,39; 185,50; 186,53; 189,111; 197,25; 198,58; 204,78; 209,31; 212,72; 223,21; 226,80, and this list is not complete.

44. H. Vekeman, *Lexicografisch Onderzoek*, 2: 267–72.

45 N. De Paepe, *Hadewijch. Strofische Gedichten*, 287–95.

46 Frances Gooday, 'Mechtild of Magdeburg and Hadewijch of Antwerp. A Comparison', *OGE* 48 (1974) 305–62; 323.

47 VM, *Strophische Gedichten*, 280, ll. 11–12.

48 R-VM, *Seven Manieren*, 32, ll. 69 and 62.

49 *AA SS* April: 179,31. The biographer took the distinction between *amor fruitionis* and *amor desiderii* from William's Contemp, PL 184: 370C: 'Est amor desiderii et est amor fruitionis. Amor desiderii meretur aliquando visionem, visio fruitionem, fruitio amoris perfectionem'.

Bible and their mentors: Hugh,[50] Richard,[51] Thomas the Cistercian,[52] Bernard,[53] and William.[54] It occurs as well in Yvo,[55] who seems to have influenced directly or indirectly both Hadewijch and Beatrice.[56] The Victorines seem to have been more thirsty and the Cistercians more hungry, at least in the texts quoted above. This observation can be perceived to some small degree in the *mulieres religiosae*. They spoke of hunger or of thirst, as did Ida Lewis who 'thirsted for love',[57] while Beatrice's biography mentions that, 'since she could not find what she desired in present things, her appetite, continually hungry and famished, sought satiety in eternal refection' (203,66). In other passages of her biography hunger and thirst are spoken of together: 'At times she would hunger and thirst with an appetite for eternal things' (205,85). She does not, however, seem to have suffered from

50 *In Hierarchiam* 6; PL 175: 1038D–1039A:'Love is always confident that by following the impetuosity of its ardent desire it can arrive at the Beloved. She is thirsty to enter into him, to be with him and, if it could be done, to be nearly what he is'.

51 Particularly in his *Four Degrees of Impetuous Love* (ed. G. Dumeige, 155, ll. 10–31), where he enumerates four kinds of thirst.

52 Cant; PL 207: 469AC. David Bell ('Contemplation and the vision of God in the Commentary on the Song of Songs by Thomas the Cistercian', *Citeaux* 29 [1978] 207–227; 213) has indicated how Thomas based his commentary on existing writings, in this instance on Richard.

53 Dil 4,11; SBOp 3: 127: 'For those who seek and long for God's presence, his memory is, at least, at hand. Not one by which they are satiated, but one by which they hunger more in order to become satiated'. See also Bernard's Conv 14,26–27; SBOp 4: 100–101; CF 25: 61–63.

54 In a tortuous sentence in his Cant, PL 180: 394A, William compares the working of God's love to that of the sun at creation in relation to the waters, 'So, God's love hovers over the faithful one, ac, ing and bestowing kindness upon him, drawing up to him the one who is following him by some natural hunger and who has, like fire, the natural ability of rising upward' [to union with God]: 'Sic amor Dei amori fidelis sui superfertur aspirando et benefaciendo rapiens eum ad se naturali quodam appetitu se sequentem, et instar ignis vim habentem naturalem sursum tendendi'.

55 See G. Dumeige, *Yves, Epître*, 61: 'desire could not satiate the man with only one desire: to desire. For desire is hunger for God'.(Non potuit satiari desiderio qui nonnisi desiderare concupivit. Fames enim animae desiderium). Yves borrowed, as he often does, the last part of this sentence from Bernard, SC 74,3; SBOp 2: 241.

56 B. Spaapen, 'Hadewijch en het vijfde visioen', *OGE* 45 (1971) 138–39.

57 *AA SS* Oct.13: 110,11: 'amore sitiens'.

'spiritual diabetes'.[58] In 1232, when she had already made an important and decisive turn in her spiritual life, Beatrice

> seeing herself unconstrained by any sinful impediment from progressing further without obstacles in the way of virtue, suddenly began to place herself totally at the service of love, only hungering and thirsting for the taste of love, only carrying out in act and in conduct the good-pleasure of Love.[59]

Hadewijch said in her own way in the 33rd of her Poems in Stanzas:

> Satiety and hunger, all in one
> Are the share of free love
> As is ever known by those
> Whom Love has touched by herself.
> This is satiety: when Love comes, one cannot bear her;
> This is hunger: when Love withdraws, one complains.[60]

Hungering is an expression used to indicate the pain of arriving at union with the Beloved, a union that originates with him. In Letter 31, Hadewijch wrote to a correspondant how Christ had told somebody (Hadewijch herself):

> Your soul's hunger disposes me to prepare everything for you, so that I, all that I am, shall be yours. Through your striving to satisfy your hunger for me, you grew up to full perfection and you became like to me: your death and mine

---

58 In his 'Four Kinds of Mystical Experience', in *Understanding Mysticism* (R. Woods ed.), 379–99; 394, W.H. Auden quotes a quip by the Anglican bishop C.D. Broad: 'A healthy appetite for righteousness, kept in due control by good manners, is an excellent thing; but to "hunger and to thirst" after it is often merely a symptom of spiritual diabetes'.

59 *Vita*, 196,2. The Latin text has *caritas* and it is not a bold guess that the original vernacular had *Minne*, usually translated in English as Love.

60 VM, *Strophische Gedichten*, 213, ll. 25–30.

shall be one, and therefore we shall live with one life, and one love will satisfy the hunger of us both.[61]

In fact, when the *mulieres religiosae* spoke about their hunger and thirst which needed to be satisfied, they could well have been aware that God himself is insatiable satiety, as Augustine said,[62] and that their own desire for satiety could never be fully satiated. Beatrice tried very hard nevertheless:

> Although she found her bodily strength quite unequal to her heart's desire, she so disposed all her actions and affections interiorly and exteriorly according to reason (*consilio rationis*), that no part of her might be empty and idle. She ceaselessly forced her mind to serve its Creator with holy affections, her mouth to serve him in divine praises, her hand in loving works, and the other members of her body in their proper actions. Thus, at least in some degree, she zealously satisfied her insatiable desire.[63]

But her combination of emotion and reason could only satisfy her 'to some degree', for the finite can never comprehend the infinite. As Hadewijch wrote:

> Those who strive and desire to give God love to the full and to content him in his sublimity, can never perfectly satisfy him .... For the sublime Love and the magnitude that God is, are never fulfilled or known by all that one can accomplish.[64]

Richard,[65] and Yvo,[66] had already spoken of insatiability, and Beatrice was well aware of it. She realized that 'sighing for

61 VM, *Brieven*, 1: 263, ll. 14–20. In his *Beeldspraak*, 210–13, n. 219 and 395, n.86, J. Reynaert refers to some passages in Hadewijch's writings where she speaks of hunger and thirst.

62 *Sermo* 170,9; PL 38: 931: 'Satietas insatiabilis'.

63 *Vita*, 181,185.

64 Letter 12, VM, *Brieven*, 1: 102, ll. 17–23.

65 G. Dumeige, *Les quatre degrés*, 139–41; J. Chatillon, 'Les quatre degrés', *RAM* 20 (1939) 253: 'what characterizes the fourth degree is its insatiability'.

66 G. Dumeige, *Yves. Epître*, 55–57.

eternal things, her insatiable appetite for Love, would be unable to rise and to attain what she unappeasedly desired' (221,74). This fact did not stop her from craving the impossible. She

continued more energetically and valiantly in the service of almighty God. With her mind more clearly enlightened by truth, she saw that the insatiable desire of her heart had been less than discreet because she had desired to devote much more strength in the service of her Creator, and to render him pleasing obedience with a stronger desire than any worldly creature could fulfill by its own power.[67]

In the preceding pages desire for God has often been qualified by such adjectives as 'vehement, impetuous, burning'. This aspect of the notions of desire and of love is metaphorically represented by the term *ardor*. An illustration of this combination of desire with the notion of burning heat is given in the biography of Ida of Nivelles. She mentions this experience:

Once it happened that for several days I was in the infirmary because of physical sickness and because of my powerful love and insatiable desire for the Divinity as well. My heart grew so passionate within me and my chest so inflamed as if from a fire which does not consume but illuminates and sets afire.[68]

Burning desires inevitably trigger emotions that could not but affect the *mulieres religiosae* psychically and somatically. All six women considered in this study experienced psychosomatic phenomena, each in her personal and emotionally different way. Some of these phenomena which occurred during Mass or which

67 *Vita*, 226,79.
68 *Quinque*, 254: 'Contingit me...infirmari in infirmitorio tam infirmitate corporis quam valido amore et insatiabili desiderio divinitatis. Cum autem hoc modo incalesceret cor meum intra me, et in praecordiis meis exardesceret ignis non consumens, sed illuminans et inflammans'.

were related to the Eucharist have already been reported above.[69]
To Hadewijch's psychosomatic experience mentioned there could
be added a remark she herself made which says much in her
favor. She realized that her strong desire to be one with God in
fruition could not be fulfilled at that time. 'For this', she wrote, 'I
was still too childish and too little grown-up; I had not as yet
sufficiently suffered for it or lived the number of years requisite
for such an eminent worthiness'.[70]

It would be well to keep in mind that psychosomatic phenomena were not always highly prized by the *mulieres religiosae*. In
several instances they asked to be delivered from them, as we
mentioned in Part Two. Though they usually said that they asked
the Lord to moderate 'his excesses', there is little doubt that the
mulieres religiosae did their own part in this process of restraint.
They burned with desire for union with God and it had therefore a
metaphysical point of reference. But they realized too, that to
attain union, they had to go through their own physical, psychic
and spiritual ascesis, and so they acted in their eagerness to make
themselves wide open for such union. For instance, when Ida of
Nivelles was once deeply centered in prayer, *orationi insistens*,
her soul suddenly began to 'melt' from the impetuosity of her
ardent desire, and finally she lost consciousness.[71] Her friend
Beatrice too experienced that 'the very vehement desire of hers
waxed so increasingly strong in her mind that sometimes she was
deprived of the use of her bodily senses and did not know what
went on around her'(159,76). Occasionally the *mulieres religiosae*'s desire and love did much more than make them faint.
Hadewijch, for instance, wrote in her seventh vision:

On a certain Pentecost Sunday I had an apparition at dawn.
Matins were sung in church and I was present. My heart and

---

69 Chapter XI, pp. 307–41 *et passim*.
70 Vision one; VM, *Visioenen*, 1: 9–10, l.9–12.
71 *Quinque*, 212: 'Dum quadam vice orationi insisteret, coepit ex ardentis
desiderii vehementia liquescere repente anima ejus, ita ut viribus corporis
destitueretur'. The melting, *liquescere*, is one of the metaphors used at that time
to describe the effect of a very emotionally experienced overflow of love.

veins and all my limbs trembled and quivered with eager desire.... On that day I was so fearfully and so painfully beset by desirous love that every one of my limbs threatened to break and each of my veins was in travail. The longing in which I then was, cannot be expressed by any language or by any person I know. Everything I could say about it would be unheard-of to all those who never strove toward *Minne* with the works of desire, and whom Love never acknowledged as hers.[72]

Through desire, Beatrice's heart 'was often dilated for long periods of time, and this, together with her enlarged arteries, would strike her with the shudder of death, since her desire prevented them from returning to their natural state and position' (157,48). In her fifth *maniere* she wrote that

when love acts vehemently and riotously in the heart, it becomes so excessive and exuberantly burning that the soul thinks its heart has been wounded in many grave ways, and that these wounds are daily renewed and aggravated by more bitter sorrows, and each time actualized anew. So it seems that its veins are opened and its blood is boiling out, its marrow is withered and its legs weak, its chest burns and its throat is dry, so that its face and all its members perceive the inner heat and experience the tumult that *Minne* is making. At this time it also feels an arrow piercing through its heart all the way to the throat and beyond, even to the brain, as if it would lose its mind.... By all these things the soul is wounded and its heart much damaged and its strength fails.[73]

Mechtild of Magdeburg wrote in terms similar to Hadewijch's in her *Book of the Flowing Light of the Godhead*. She even described one of her psychosomatic experiences in exactly the

---

72 VM, *Visioenen*, 1: 74, ll. 1–5; 10–20.
73. R-VM, *Seven manieren*, 19–21, ll. 33–49.

same words that Beatrice used in the text of the fifth *maniere* we have just cited.[74]

Ida of Leuven had the peculiar experience of a bodily distention or elongation as it is technically called. According to her biographer's understanding, 'the fervor of her love sometimes became so excessive that, while it inwardly inflamed her soul, it also caused the body to expand outwardly beyond its usual size and to swell to a monstruous bulk, forcing her to take off her belt and garters all together...a dilatation which stemmed from nothing else but the abundance of love'.[75]

74 Hans Neumann, ' Mechtild von Magdeburg und die mittelniederländische Frauenmystik', *Medieval German Studies* (= *Festschrift für Frederic Norman*), (London, 1965) 231–46; 242. Neumann is of the opinion that Mechtild, then still a beguine, had access to an intermediate copy from the Rhineland of the writings of Hadewijch and of Beatrice's treatise.

75 *AA SS* April 2: 186,17: 'Prae nimio quoque fervore dilectionis interdum illius animam interius inflammante, sic exterius ultra solitum excrescebat et monstruosa quadam grossitudine dilatabatur in corpore, quod cingulum vel corrigias ea de causa cogeretur omnino deponere ...sola caritatis opulentia pinguedine dilatatum.' This is the biographer's interpretation. Note 32 of Chapter X has given a medical explanation of the phenomenon.

CHAPTER THIRTEEN

DESIRED BURNING

W E HAVE ALREADY SEEN HOW MUCH the *mulieres reli-giosae* desired to be purified, free from defects and egocentricity in order to be free for union with God. This desire burned strongly enough to make them eager to go through a total purification. From their point of view, the *mulieres religiosae* kept their desire burning continually because they desired Somebody who burned with desire for them, as we have spoken of above and at length.

Each *mulier religiosa* could have made her own the saying of Beatrice that 'anticipating the Lord's vehement desire, she therefore knew for certain that she was bound to render him the return of his love'(204,69). As will become clear in this chapter, once the *mulieres religiosae* identified their desire with love, their burning desire was bound to turn into a desired burning.[1] The love-partner they accepted at his request and sought with boundless intensity was no other than the transcendent God himself.

The *mulieres religiosae* were well enough acquainted with Scripture and their mentors to know that this God is a devouring fire, *ignis consumens*, and a God of desire, *Deus desiderans*.

---

1 In *Beatrijs. Lexicografisch Onderzoek*, 2: 243, H. Vekeman made the correct observation that on the level of conduct and experience, desire and love are synonymous. The *mulieres religiosae*'s burning desire for God, turned into a desired burning, a desire to burn in his love.

Of the transcendent God as *ignis consumens*, Hadewijch wrote that he 'is terrible and implacable, devouring and burning unsparingly'.[2] Beatrice expressed the excruciating pain she felt because she could in no way raise herself up to the level of this *Deus desiderans*. As she wrote in her third *Maniere*:

> The soul's greatest sorrow is that it cannot satisfy *Minne* according to its own great desire. It knows well that it [the soul] is, necessarily, lacking in love. It knows well that such fulfillment surpasses human capacity and all her own strength. For what the soul desires is impossible and improper for any creature, namely that the soul alone could serve, love and know Love in accordance with Love's dignity, and moreover do this as much as and unspeakably more than, all men on earth and all spirits in heaven and all creatures above and below. With full will and strong desire the soul wills to supply what is so greatly lacking in its works, but it cannot satisfy this desire.[3]

Hadewijch would have had no problem in agreeing with Beatrice. In her Letter 22, she spoke of four ways leading to *Minne*. Over the fourth way towered the archway of desire, so great and high that no one who goes through it can ever be satiated. Desire ever outstrips its fulfillment. For this reason 'they consume without being nourished'.[4]

The *mulieres religiosae* did all they could to make themselves roomy for God,[5] in the conscious certainty that God's own desire

---

2 Vision 11; VM, *Visioenen*, 1: 118, ll. 128–30.

3 Third *maniere*; R-VM, *Seven manieren*, 10–11, ll. 17–33.

4 VM, *Brieven*, 1: 196, l.212. According to J. Reynaert's interpretation, *Beeldspraak*, 210, the relation between 'to consume' and 'not to be nourished' is like that between 'to desire' and 'not to be fulfilled'.

5 This is not a thought originating from the *mulieres religiosae*. In his excellent study 'Die Gottesgeburt. Die Lehre der Kirchenväter von der Geburt Christi im Herzen des Glaubigen', *ZKT* 59 (1935) 333–418, Hugo Rahner follows the evolution of this view from the Apostolic Fathers (Ignatius of Antioch, martyred between 98–117, who already said that the incarnation of God's Son took place to allow man to make room for him within his own heart : Dem Logos in sich Raum zu geben) through Origen, Ambrose, Augustine, the Victorines and Cistercians (394–409) till Meister Eckhart.

would step in to make their capacity for desire and love even roomier. They had arrived at a crossroad where they had to conform to a demanding God. As her *Vita* (205,83) has it,

> thus Beatrice lived, and of such things the life of her spirit consisted: at one time burnt up with the fire of love, she would be fervent and bubbling; at another, affected by the sweetness of heavenly delights, she would be gesturing and dancing; again she would hunger and thirst with an appetite for eternal things. In everything, however, she was quiet and patient, conforming herself in all ways to the divine good-pleasure in things both sweet and bitter, adverse and prosperous. For a long time she was in this exercise of love, experiencing the different affections in turn, now all together, now one by one.

In this passage the accent lies on conformity, a conformity which leads to transformation.[6] The need for conformity indicates that the *mulieres religiosae* did not have a claim of their own to union with God, except for God's own demanding love, which implies conformity. The components of Beatrice's text show up in Hadewijch's writings also. Because of the latter's strong and gifted personality, she expresses it more poignantly. Though few biographical data have come to us about her, nobody, happily, came along to weave her writings into a Latin biography and destroy the Flemish originals, as was the case with Beatrice. In her Poem 43 in Stanzas, Hadewijch challenged God whom she has called a devouring fire, and who challenged her to conform to him:

> O sublime Being, noble *Minne*
> When will you make my being so fair

---

6 Bernard, SC 62,5; SBOp 2:158; 'transformamur cum conformamur'. Erich Kleineidam says that Bernard added a new meaning to the classical Latin verb 'to conform'. See his 'Wissen, Wissenschaft, Theologie bei Bernhard von Clairvaux', *Bernhard von Clairvaux. Mönch und Mystiker*, J. Lortz ed., (Mainz, 1954) 28–67; 151: 'Bernhard prägt dafür einen neuen Ausdruck, den das klassische Latein nicht kennt'.

That I will be wholly conformed to your Being?
For I wish to be wholly conformed:
All my otherness would be yours
Everything that is yours would be altogether mine.
I wish to burn in your fire.[7]

It is evident that the wish 'to burn in your fire' has little to do with masochism on the part of Hadewijch or the other *mulieres religiosae*. Nor should we think that this desired burning is only of short duration. Desire 'must rule a long time in the heart'.[8] One has to go through it 'step by step'.[9] It is *Minne* who takes the lead, while 'the soul rests, acts and refrains from acting, without and within, in accordance with *Minne*'s will'.[10] It is thus that the soul grows, grows up, becomes grown up (*volwassen*) to arrive at its perfection: to be forever united with God.[11] To quote Beatrice: 'The soul desires to lead its whole life so as to work, grow and ascend to a greater height of love and a closer knowledge of God, until it reaches that full perfection for which it is made and called by God'.[12]

The refrain at the end of Hadewijch's Poem 43 in Stanzas, tells what to expect from this call to conformity with a God who is a devouring fire:

All who shudder before the greatness of Love
And in hope find strength in her greatness—
Love shall scrub them more than a [white] sheet.[13]

---

7 VM, *Strophishe Gedichten*, 274, ll. 43–49. Her text is a neat poetic rephrasing of Bernard's alliterative 'transformamur cum conformamur': we are transformed when we are conformed.

8 R-VM, *Seven manieren*, 3, 1.6.

9 First Poem in Stanzas, VM, *Strophische Gedichten*, 8, 1.84.

10 R-VM, *Seven manieren*, 25, ll. 33–34.

11 J. Reynaert, *Beeldspraak*, 271, n. 19 lists the many texts in Hadewijch's writings where she speaks of this process.

12 R-VM, *Seven manieren*, 4, ll. 19–24.

13 VM, *Strophische Gedichten*, 277, ll. 102–104.

Biographers, paying attention mostly to externals, do not give us much information about what went on within the *mulieres religiosae* they were writing about. Nevertheless, what they communicated does at least indirectly, and often directly, testify about the *mulieres religiosae* as we have already seen in the preceding pages and will witness even more later. As the most outspoken among them, Beatrice, and still more Hadewijch, tried to put into words what, according to their experience, this burning in Love's fire and this 'scrubbing' means in practice. In Letter 29 Hadewijch indicates that God's absolute primacy and priority require her to stand unwaveringly in full joy and grief for his sake and for hers:

> The city [or place] of Love which enlightened reason showed me, was so far above human thought that I understood that joy and grief in anything great or small were unbecoming, except in this: that I was a human being (*mensche*) and experienced Love with a loving heart, and that God was so great that I, in my humanity, could not come in touch with the Godhead and had to remain without fruition.[14]

She wrote in similar terms to some of her friends: 'If you wish to walk the way of Love, it is much better for you to seek exertion and to suffer for the honor of Love than to wish to feel it.... Do not care about honor or shame; fear neither the torment on earth nor that of hell'.[15] In another Letter she wrote: 'You must so exclusively leave all for all, and burn ardently in your soul and in your being and in all your works, that nothing else exists for you any more except God alone: no pleasure and no pains, nothing easy and nothing difficult; you must live in this condition without cessation'.[16]

Hadewijch did not advise others to do what she herself did not

14 VM, *Brieven*, 1: 244, ll. 44–52.
15 Letter 22; VM, *Brieven*, 1: 27, ll. 62–69; 71–73.
16 Letter 12; VM, *Brieven*, 1: 116, ll. 196–202.

do, even though she sometimes speaks in the third person, especially in her poems,

> A faithful loving heart
> Willing to suffer for Love
> Has to know experientially
> The sweet and the bitter, joy and sorrow:
> All that one has to do for Love's sake.[17]

Desire and burning should be considered together. The desire to be conformed to Christ and subsequently transformed and made ready for union was so penetratingly deep and painfully burning within her heart that Hadewijch wrote:

> He who loves performs great works. He spares nothing and he never becomes discouraged by any distress that happens to him, or any torment that befalls him. But in adverse situations he shows himself always ardent and cheerful. So it is in all things small and great, easy and difficult, whereby he may acquire virtues that are truly becoming of *Minne*.[18]

Beatrice spoke in the same vein. One day, when she was told by the Lord that her name was written in the book of the living, she asked why, and the third proof he gave her was that he had done so by 'the vehement attraction by which I provoked you to follow me... with continuous steps of virtue through things both sweet and bitter, harsh and smooth' (171,42). She begged 'with urgent desire of the heart to be tormented in her body' (185,42), but she did not stop there. Realizing how much she was obliged to God's mercy, she said, according to her biography (186,63):

> If perhaps I have offered less than I owed by exposing only my poor body for torments, I add also my spirit to be

---

17 Poem 5 in Stanzas; VM, *Strophische Gedichten*, 32, ll. 2–7.
18 Letter 30; VM, *Brieven*, 1: 252, ll. 14–21.

afflicted as much as it pleases you, by various kinds of temptations and spiritual troubles, certain as I am that with temptation you will also provide the way out so that I can bear the weight, however great.

Two weeks later she received the startling news that two dear friends had died, one of them Ida of Nivelles, the dearest and most intimate friend she had ever had. As her biography tells it (227,100), through these and other efficacious burnings, 'she was so consolidated and confirmed in true love, that the more she was vexed in body or mind by any corporeal or spiritual trouble... the more she would stand all hard and harsh things, not only most patiently but also very willingly without impatience or sorrow, bearing everything in equanimity'.

Yet, as her *Seven manieren* amply show Beatrice was not at the end of her purifying journey. In her fifth *maniere* she wrote that 'the more the soul is given from above, the more is demanded of it; the greater the things shown to it, with more desire it is drawn to approach more closely to the light of truth and purity and nobility and the enjoyment of Love'.[19]

In her sixth *maniere* she stressed that 'all those who desire to obtain Love', may not 'spare themselves in great labors and pains, in bearing troubles and in suffering contempt'.[20]

All this talk about suffering everything with equanimity implies that these women were at times deeply affected psychologically by depressions, which inevitably result from so many ups and downs. If they continued to integrate these depressions into their personal growth, it was thanks to their own efforts supported by their trust and conviction that God's love always has the last word. By considering all these vicissitudes as the means of coming closer to God, Hadewijch avoided becoming a victim of hidden depression. In her second Poem in Stanzas she made this lesson clear:

19 R-VM, *Seven manieren*, 22, ll. 70–75.
20 *Ibid.*, 27, ll. 62–67.

He who serves Love has to go through an arduous
   adventure
Before he gains insight into Love's procedure.
In order that he be totally loved by Love
He has to taste the bitter and the sour;
No moment of rest is allowed
Before Love binds him totally in love
And brings him to delightful fruition.[21]

Beatrice described 'Love's procedure' in her seventh *maniere*:

Love does not allow the soul to be appeased or to rest or
enjoy any peace. Love pulls it up and sets it down, soothes it
for a short while and then torments it, gives it death and then
brings it back to life; gives it health and then wounds it
again, makes it first demented and then wise. So Love draws
it to a higher state.[22]

In her Poem 34 in Stanzas, Hadewijch wrote similarly:

All of you who are magnanimous,
Who wish to content Love with love,
I urge you to be in Love's service
In all her comings and goings,
In her lifting up and in her knocking down.[23]

The experience of being thrown around in all directions at
times gave the impression that God, in his desire to make them
more capacious for intimate union, inflicted a 'wound of love' as
Beatrice called it. The text of Beatrice's fifth *maniere* cited
above,[24] is found in the following context:

The soul feels Love acting riotously within, sparing nothing,
uncontrollably seizing and consuming everything within the

---

21 VM, *Strophische Gedichten*, 15, ll. 30–36.
22 R-VM, *Seven manieren*, 30, ll. 24–31.
23 VM, *Strophische Gedichten*, 220, ll. 73–77.
24 Referred to in n. 19 above.

soul like a devouring fire which draws to itself and consumes everything it can get hold of. By all these things the soul is much wounded and its heart much damaged and all its strength fails. Yet the soul is nourished, its love is fed and its mind is lifted up and suspended. For Love so greatly surpasses all understanding that the soul cannot attain full enjoyment of it. Therefore out of pain the soul sometimes desires to break the bond without breaking the unity of love.... The soul is always more and more provoked and drawn around, but it is not satisfied nor satiated. What most afflicts and wounds it, also heals and soothes it most ; what wounds it most deeply is the only thing that gives it health.[25]

In his paradoxical love, God first gave the *mulieres religiosae* some taste of consolation, and then set them on fire and 'scrubbed' them thoroughly. They had to go through a heavy training program, incomparably more demanding than that of astronauts in the making.[26] All the physical, psychic and spiritual resources of the *mulieres religiosae* were tested to the limit by the love of the One who is Love. In such conditions Hadewijch's seemingly disrespectful complaint becomes understandable:

Suffering was sweet to me for the sake of *Minne*. But he [God] has been more cruel to me than any devil ever was. Devils could not stop me from loving him... but he himself deprived me of this sweetness.... And now, I am treated like one to whom something is offered in jest, and when one wishes to take it, one is slapped on the hand. 'God's wrath

25 R-VM, *Seven manieren*, 20–23, ll. 50–69; 75–80.
26. E. Arbman, *Ecstasy*, 2: 320 noted that 'in Christian mysticism, one finds it [the love for God] described as a deep, consuming passion, an ardent longing, a constant unassuageable hunger and thirst for a complete union with God as the highest goal, already here in this life and whatever it may cost in the form of voluntary, free and complete renunciation of all that is not believed to promote or to be completely compatible with an attainment of this supreme and incomparable spiritual goal, i.e.: of all other human, earthly and temporal good.'

on him who fancied it to be true!', he is told. And what he thought he had is held back.[27]

Experiences like this one fostered what the *mulieres religiosae* called *languor*.[28] According to Richard's third degree of impetuous love:

> the soul consummated and languishing by excessive love, can not think of anything else nor do anything else. It is power less to act otherwise. In this state of overwhelming love, resembling weariness, the soul remains so immobilized that it can move neither by thought nor by act, except to where its desire attracts it, or its feeling drives it.[29]

Beatrice's biographer (159,68) mentions that

> her affection sighed very much for eternal things; she was so wounded and languished so for love that this vehement desire caused her mouth and nose to bleed frequently and copiously. In short, the violence of its assaults so affected the frail dwelling of outer man that it cast her into a very great languor. This languor increased its hold on her body, and during the many remaining years of her life, fastened itself to her as her own passion.

On a later occasion, she had a very similar bodily experience. She had begun to listen to a sermon with eager longing when, as her *Vita* mentions (240,7): 'suddenly her heart seemed to her almost broken and wholly shaken by the very great ardor of love. Indeed it left its natural place and rose to her throat. It stayed there a long time trembling and throbbing.... Thus languishing

---

27 Letter 1; VM, *Brieven*, 1: 18–19, ll. 56–63; 78–82. This image could have been inspired by a similar metaphor used by Yvo. See G. Dumeige, *Yves, Epître*, 55–57.

28 Et. Gilson *Mystical Theology*, 104, n. 145 states that for Bernard the most pronounced languor is caused by the absence of the beloved; see Bernard's SC 51,3; SBOp2: 85.

29 G. Dumeige, *Les quatre degrés*, 137, ll. 12–37.

with love, sick in body but robust in soul, she remained in that state during the whole sermon'.

To use an expression of the late Jean Chatillon, it was impossible for her to do anything except what was motivated by her love.[30] 'Beatrice could not return God's love as fully as she desired, the weakness of human nature being incapable of this. She necessarily languished in the inconvenience caused by love' (204,71). Shortly afterwards, when Beatrice had learned to conform her will totally to God's will, 'she recognized from then on that the very great desire which had caused her body to languish was totally appeased' (226,73). This sentence is important, for it shows that languor is not an 'incurable disease' in an oversensitive person. Beatrice—like the other *mulieres religiosae*—was at times so deeply affected by languor that she broke down emotionally, without being psychologically sick. In her fourth *maniere* Beatrice uses an appropriate comparison to express her sensitivity in the state of languor: 'Just as a full vessel overflows and spills when it is suddenly moved, so at times the soul is very quickly moved and totally overcome by the great fulness of heart so that in spite of itself it must often spill over'.[31]

When the *mulieres religiosae*, affected by languor, aligned themselves with God's love, and viewed the relationship from his side, they could and did integrate their languor into a deeper and more intimate love-relationship with their God. Hadewijch, for instance, wrote in her second Poem in Stanzas:

> So greatly has the pain of love worn me out
> That I am now unfit for anything
> ...Yet, I will gladly suffer all things,

30 J. Chatillon, 'Les quatre degrés de la Charité d'aprés Richard de Saint-Victor', *RAM* 20 (1939) 237–64; 248. According to Chatillon, Richard did not share the opinion of Bernard, who considered languor as the state of the soul in the absence of the beloved, above n.28. Yvo, without saying so, borrowed this opinion from Bernard, [G. Dumeige, *Yves*, 57, ll. 13–16] stressing thereby this one aspect. What Gilson said in n. 28 above and Chatillon in n. 30 in relation to languor is correct but incomplete. In his sermon And 2,4; SBOp 5: 436, Bernard is in line with Richard.

31 R-VM, *Seven manieren*, 16, ll. 45–49.

> For Love has never revoked
> The promise she held out to me.[32]

Two of the Idas seem to agree with Hadewijch. During the last fourteen months of her life, Ida of Nivelles was gravely ill,

> as if pressured in a kettle, in preparation to be called from the darkness of mortality into the bright dwelling of the supreme city.... But this condition and pain never made her fainthearted, slothful or impatient, but she showed herself most ready to sustain more of this languor if it would be pleasing to God's eyes.[33]

Ida Lewis' biographer, obviously echoing Richard's Four Degrees, says that one Christmas day she was brought to bed by a high fever. But there is fever and fever. First he spoke of the fever which affects the body, then of one of this fever's causes, which he also called fever: 'vehemently assailed by continued and acute fevers of love, the daughter of love, languishing from love, thirsty for love, ... [was] delightfully agonizing'.[34]

To experience the alternate presence and absence of God is to know *vicissitudines*,[35] known by Hadewijch as *onghed023uricheit*, and by Beatrice in a slightly different idiom as *ongeduricheit*. As long as the soul dwells in an unglorified body the alternation of presence and absence is inevitable. The absence is the more painful, but also the more helpful of the two. To feel the absence of God or of *Minne* can have two aspects, depending on the point

---

32 VM, *Strophische Gedichten*, 17, ll. 64–65; 70–72.

33 *Quinque*, 286: 'Cumque quatuordecim mensibus infirmitatis hujus frixorio coactaretur, numquam ejusdem infirmitatis occasione pusillanimis, acediosa vel impatiens extitit. Sed semper se paratissimam exhibuit ad sustinendum multo validiorem infirmitatem si id placuisset in oculis Domini'.

34 *AA SS* Oct.13: 117, 33–34: 'Correpta vehementius amoris febribus continuis et acutis, amore languit amoris filia, amorem sitiens, amore debria...sicque delectabiliter agonizans'.

35 See Bernard's SC 32,2; SBOp 1: 227.

of view one takes. For Hadewijch, the first aspect is the awareness of not being able to cope with the inaccessible God and, out
of false humility, to despair of ever attaining to union with him.
People who take this stand live as if in hell.[36] But if they rise
courageously above this paralyzing despair, and with their inborn
noble pride (*fierheid*) dare to go through an arduous adventure, as
Hadewijch called it, they are said to pass from hell to purgatory:

> Those who go to God in his depths by way of purgatory, live
> in the land of holy grief; for what was given them in trust is
> soon consumed by their deep, longing passion. This causes
> the soul's longing to grow continually: she knows interiorly
> how much of God is lacking in her; that he has something
> that she does not have, nor that it can be fully hers.[37]

The awareness of God's infinity and of human inability ever to
match it, and the consciousness that one can never reach God's
fulness are things which cause fearful pain. Then one fears that

> Love does not love enough because her grip is so strong that
> Love continually oppresses and helps too little, and that one
> is the only one to love. This is [noble] distrust (*ontrouwe*),
> of a higher quality than any vested trust, I mean, a [vested]
> trust which gives some satisfaction without real [experien-
> tial] knowledge, a [vested] trust which is satisfied with the
> satisfaction of the moment. [Noble] distrust, however,
> expands consciousness so much that one thinks to be oneself
> insane: one's heart sighs, the veins stretch and tear continu-
> ally and the soul melts away. Although one loves Love so
> violently, nevertheless this [noble] distrust can neither feel
> nor trust Love, so much does desire dilate [noble] distrust.
> [Noble] distrust never allows desire any rest in any trust but,
> in the fear of not being loved enough, continually distrusts
> desire. [Noble] distrust is so lofty that it continually fears

36 See above chapter IX, p. 263, n. 47.
37 Letter 22; VM, *Brieven*, 1: 197–98, ll. 237–45.

either that it does not love enough or that it is not loved enough.[38]

Beatrice went through an equally painful process, though evidently within the context of her own personality. From her youth till she was thirty-one, her *Vita* discloses her frequent fear.[39] Her fear of sin meant chiefly her fear of not coming to union with God in heaven immediately at her death, without any delay. Ida Lewis suffered from the same fear, and went through a similar hell.[40] Once Beatrice overcame this neurotic fear, then love or *Minne* could take over and 'reign in her heart'. Then God's love and that of Beatrice took hold of her heart, and *Minne* reigned in a steadfast and exclusive way.[41]

To assume that once Love or *Minne* had taken over, pain and suffering would disappear, goes against all the evidence. As Beatrice, Hadewijch and Ida Lewis say, 'it seems to the soul as if it lives while dying and dies while living, or dies while feeling the pains of hell'.[42] To the saying: '*Minne* rewards, even though she comes late', Hadewijch responded

---

38 Letter 8; VM, *Brieven*, 1: 76, ll. 27–47. According to P. Dinzelbacher, the mystics of the Late Middle Ages were more afraid of not being loved [by God] than had the previous generations been. See his *Vision*, 167: 'die späteren fürchten mehr als die Hölle, von Jesus und den Himmlischen nicht geliebt zu werden'. Hadewijch's *ontrouwe* is a higher form of [total] trust outstanding by far the ordinary trust of people who are satisfied with the momentary satisfaction. Herman Vekeman elaborated on this subject in his paper 'Die ontrouwe maakt ze diep. Een nieuwe interpretatie van het vijfde visioen van Hadewijch', *De Nieuwe Taalgids* 71 (1978) 385–409.

39 *Vita*, 65,25; 70,82; 90,65; 106,16; 106,22; 110,55; 130,16; 131,34; 132,57; 133,72; 134,94; 144,59; 145,11; 149,91; 150,100; 152,18; 155,6l; 156,9; 168,65; 169,84; 169,73; 180,159. This list is not exhaustive.

40 *AA SS* Oct.13: 112, 14: 'Cumque cum Domino loqueretur... postulavit ut quicquid inconveniens hac in vita contraheret ex terrenae labis contagio, purgaretur a Domino funditus per poenitentiam in praesenti, ut, cum soluto carcere corporali de praesentis vitae periculis vellet ipsius animam evocare, nullis obstaculis praepedita, cum dilecto mansionem suscipiens ad ipsius cubiculum gaudens libere penitus evolaret'.

41 Sixth *maniere*, 25–28, ll. 31,32,51,61,69. See H. Vekeman, *Lexicografisch Onderzoek*, 2: 100–02.

42 For Beatrice, see R-VM, *Seven Manieren*, 12, ll. 47–48; for Hadewijch, Poem 10 in Couplets, *Mengeldichten*, 48, ll. 51–52; for Ida Lewis: *AA SS* Oct.13: 114,52.

This is my answer to that:
Those who follow her, suffer
Many a night by day.[43]

This suffering for and from *Minne* 'many a night by day', is also metaphorically described as hell. *Minne* is hell to the extent that she does not give herself, because hell is nothing else than the absence of *Minne*.[44] It made Beatrice say that 'all its [the soul's] life is hellish, misfortune and affliction because of the horror of this dreadful desire [for *Minne*] which it [the soul] can neither satisfy, nor appease, nor calm'.[45] In her 16th Poem in Stanzas, Hadewijch described the hellishness of this experience, by saying that this is the most appropriate term to express its torment:

As hell turns everything to ruin,
In *Minne* nothing else is acquired
Than disquiet and severe torment:
Forever in turbulence, overtaken again and again,
Wholly devoured and totally swallowed up
In hell's unfathomable nature.
To founder all the time in heat and cold
In the deep, utmost darkness of Love—
This outdoes hell's mercilessness.
One who knows Love & has experienced
    her comings & goings
Can understand why it is truly appropriate
That hell is *Minne*'s highest name.[46]

If *Minne* is hell, this is because it demands the ultimate surrender from the human Ego: the exclusion of all egocentricity. *Minne*'s comings are not for sale and cannot be controlled. God does not come at man's beck and call, nor does he go when the

43 Poem 9 in Stanzas; VM, *Strophische Gedichten*, 57, ll. 57–60. See also H. van Cranenbergh, 'Hadewijchs twaalfde visioen en negende strophische gedicht. Een proeve van tekstverklaring', *OGE* 36 (1961) 361–84; 379.
44 J. Reynaert, *Beeldspraak*, 163.
45 R-VM, *Seven manieren*, 12, ll. 49–52.
46 VM, *Mengeldichten*, 83, ll. 155–67.

enchantement is over. The comings act like bellows blowing the fire of love into the heart and when they depart, they leave the heart burning with an increased desire. God is not bound by anyone's expectations, but when he comes he should be received with open arms, as the *mulieres religiosae* so faithfully did. When he goes, the arms stay open till he comes again, if and when he wills. All this could be supported by texts from Beatrice and especially from Hadewijch, though given the purpose of this present work, this task is better left to a team of scholars in different disciplines, for the question is complex both religiously and psychologically.

In the thirteenth century the *mulieres religiosae* spoke of *Minne* and of God's 'absences' as hell, while the Spanish mystics of the sixteenth century used the expression 'dark night', which entered the modern vocabulary to describe such cases. Dark as such a night might be (including the off-and-on element), is a most excellent way to light, joy and fruition. Though usually experienced as painful and 'depressing', the *mulieres religiosae*'s burning love prevented them from utter despair and from seeking drastic ways to escape despair.[47] Christ's example was normative. From him they learned confidence, trust, courage and the desire to follow him whom they had heard say in Luke's gospel (22:15): '*desiderio desideravi*': I have earnestly longed to eat this passover with you before I suffer. In her fourteenth vision Hadewijch wrote that

> the tremendous power that he [Christ] then gave me, which I did not possess previously, was a new strength of his own being, a strength enabling me to live as he, the God-man did, with my sufferings according to his example and in union with him, as he was for me when he lived as man for

47 Kenneth Wilbers remarks:'it might be noted that no matter how profound the depression or agony of the dark night might be, the literature contains virtually no cases of it leading to suicide (in sharp contrast to existential or borderline depressions for example). It is as if the depression of the dark night had a 'higher' or 'purgatorial' or 'intelligent' purpose — and all this is exactly the claim of contemplatives. See his 'The Developmental Spectrum and Psychiatry', *Journal of Transpersonal Psychology* 16 (1984) 137–66; 148.

me. That was the strength to endure Love — as long as the fruition of Love would be lacking — that I should really endure the sharp arrows which Love shoots at me.... I received then such a strength that I could endure with equanimity everything that overcame me: joy and grief, laughter and weeping, disgraces and afflictions.[48]

When Beatrice had been in darkness and temptations for three unbroken years, she had a rapture during which she received a warning from the Lord:

She perceived two things, mercy and love, radiating from him toward her, and she immediately recognized with enlightened mind what they meant. In the ray of mercy which she saw, she deserved to be rebuked by the Lord for being so disturbed in this struggle, so burdened with fears and sorrows, especially since she saw him so prepared to help, so powerful to rescue. In the ray of love she recognized clearly that the Lord was propitious and merciful toward her, that his mercy was helping her, not beating her down or casting her off from the divine mercy under the pretext of this struggle. Rather it was exalting her, raising her up and lifting her to the summit of virtue.[49]

One Sunday, Ida Lewis did not experience her usual visitation by the Lord when she went to communion, and 'she remained a long time fearful and trembling'. When a nun of her community told her that this happened by way of trial, Ida gave an answer which shows how the emotions caused by this absence did not impede her from being at the same time detached from his absence, for she said: 'If I am not at fault because of this absence, God knows that I do not much desire to have this grace'.[50] On her part, Ida of Nivelles stated 'that she had such a confidence in the

---

48 VM, *Visioenen*, 1: 157–58, ll. 11–20; 163, ll. 95–100.

49 *Vita*, 149,80. This took place shortly before she was able to integrate her fear.

50 *AA SS* Oct.13: 122, 52: 'Si super hoc non sum culpabilis, novit Deus quod istam gratiam non multum cupio possidere'.

Lord, that if by accident or by being pushed, she were to fall into deep waters, she was certain that her life would be in no way in danger in the midst of stormy waters'.[51]

The *mulieres religiosae* expressed in a variety of ways the 'vicissitudes' they experienced, all showing how they were emotionally affected. One effect had to do with tears,[52] sighs and groans. In Beatrice's case, these were related to compunction,[53] supplication, thanksgiving, self-knowledge, fear and the state of exile.[54] Once she had become able to integrate her fear, then tears, sighs and groans virtually disappear from her biography,[55] even when she returned from an ecstasy and found herself back in exile.

51 *Quinque*, 289: 'Et in aquis vehementibus sine vitae suae periculo versari'. If she knew how to swim, Ida could not have reasonably considered this as an example of her imperturbable trust in the Lord.

52 Heinz G. Weinand, *Tränen. Untersuchungen über das Weinen in der deutschen Sprache und Literatur des Mittelalters*, (Bonn, 1958) who states that tears for 'earthly' reasons, including mourning ['Weltliche Tränen, 41–65] were more frequent than those for 'religious' or 'geistliche' reasons (28–40). Tears are more frequent in the East than in the West. See Irénée Hausherr, *Penthos. The Doctrine of Compunction in the Christian East*, ET by Anselm Hufstader, *CS* 53 (Kalamazoo, 1982) and Pierre Adnès, 'Larmes' in *DSp* 9 (1976) 287–303. The 'gift of tears' expectedly shows up in Joseph Strange's publication of Caesarius of Heisterbach's *Dialogus miraculorum*, (Cologne, 1851).

53 *Vita*, 44,64.

54 *Vita*, 56,58; 157,48. The sighing and groaning expressing her fear or her sorrow at being in exile are somewhat like the fifth kind of tears of the five mentioned by the Cistercian Adam of Perseigne. See Gaetano Raciti, 'Un opuscule inédit d'Adam de Perseigne: Le "Livre de l'Amour mutuel"', *Citeaux* 31 (1981) 296–341; 313–15. This *Liber* was written about 1195 for the nuns of Fontevrault. No inference is made that this *Liber de mutuo amore* was known by Beatrice.

55 To shed tears easily was considered unbecoming to men, at least in some circumstances. See H. Weinand, *Tränen*, 71. Beatrice's father, who seems to have had no formal education, 'never had enough of the edifying word [i.e. sermons, the usual instruction for laypeople at that time], but having received it in the soil of his heart, he... watered it sweetly and daily with the [metaphorical] abundant rainfall of his tears until it should bear fruit (12,87). He also went to communion 'with deeply felt devotion and abundance of [real] tears' (13,98). In a letter mentioned above (Chapter XII, n.35), Thomas of Villers told his sister that their brother Geoffrey Pachome, also a monk in Villers, admitted that he seldom had tears, but that his prayer of vehement desire was undoubtedly the equivalent of the weeping from the heart. See E. Mikkers, 'Deux lettres', *Coll* 10 (1948), 167, ll.47–48.

On other occasions some *mulieres religiosae* were so over-taken by their desire and love for God that they expressed it spontaneously not in tears but in laughter, as did Beatrice (57,91; 144,54), or in gestures and dancing. In the latter cases the techni-cal term is *tripudium*, which is more a jubilation and exultation, a leaping for joy than a mere enjoyment. It was understood in this sense by Hugh,[56] Bernard,[57] and Richard.[58] When Ida of Leuven came out of a vision in which she had seen Our Lady and her baby, 'she shouted in a high-pitched voice: "Oh! fairest son of the fairest mother". Being beside herself...she expressed her feelings with bodily gestures as if exceedingly drunk'.[59] Ernst Benz, referring to Francis of Assisi, Teresa of Avila and Mad-dalena de' Pazzi, states that people who have visions often give vent to their delight by jumping and dancing.[60] These physical movements and dancing are not connected only with visions, but can also happen in relation to the Eucharist, as in Beatrice's case (79,18; 193,21).

Her biographer took care to indicate that Beatrice could not help it when a *tripudium* occurred: 'whether she willed it or not, her mind's inner jubilation would betray itself outwardly either in laughter or dancing, a gesture or in some other disclosure'.[61] 'By such outward disclosures she showed her inner feelings, however hard she willed to resist' (79,18). He specified too that the psychologically releasing outburst of inwardly experienced de-lights had a spiritual character, *tripudium spirituale* (79,12). He

56 R. Baron, *Hugues de Saint-Victor. La contemplation et ses espèces*, 110.
57 SC 61,8; SBOp 2: 153.
58 *Benjamin Major*, PL 196: 174C, who relates the *tripudium* to ecstasy.
59 AA SS April 2: 166,33: 'Eja pulcherrime fili pulcherrimae matris, ad similitudinem ebriae vel amentis, altisonis et saepe repetitis vocibus exclamabat... verum etiam corporalium membrorum gestibus'.
60 *Die Vision*, 234: 'Die Erfahrung der himmlichen Freuden, des spontansten Ausdruck der Erfahrung des Erlöstseins, und der Befreiung kann gelegentlich dazu führen, dass der Strom der Freude auch den Leib des Visionärs ergreift und der Visionär seinen Zustand in einem Hüpfen und Tanzen zum Ausdruck bringt'.
61 *Vita*, 74,51. Herbert Grundmann in *Festschrift für Jost Trier*, (B. Von Wiese and K.H. Borck eds), (Meisenheim, 1954), 477–511 has published a study about *Jubel* where he described the shifts in meaning of the term jubilation in theological and mystical literature.

also relates *tripudium* to 'the consolation of divine grace' which 'would suddenly present itself, so inebriating and flooding her heart with a certain ineffable joy that... it would also outwardly bubble up in bodily form, stir her up to a *spiritual dance* in which she would excitedly strike parts of her body' (200,10). Another time 'affected by the sweetness of heavenly delight, she would be gesturing and dancing'.[62] Ida Lewis also 'could not contain the delights she felt inside her heart, but disclosed them by bodily movements'.[63] The two occasions when Alice of Schaarbeek had a *tripudium* have already been mentioned.[64] As a decaying leper, unable to stand on her feet, her hands totally crippled, the only *tripudium* left to Alice was song: *tripudiando cantare*.[65]

To have been excessively in love seems to be characteristic of the *mulieres religiosae*. If one were to look for another term to describe them, it would be to call them women madly in love with God, *mulieres amorosae*.

In addition to languor and *tripudium* the *mulieres religiosae* also speak of *orewoet*: Hadewijch several times, and Beatrice once in her treatise but several times in her *Vita*. The same term in its Latin equivalents occurs also in the biographies of other *mulieres religiosae*. Philologists have difficulty in determining the meaning(s) of *orewoet*. Ruusbroec, who was born twenty five years after Beatrice's death, also used the term, but after the fourteenth century the expression went out of use.[66] This disuse could be due to a shift in spirituality,[67] as manifested by the

---

62 *Vita*, 205,84. The biographer seems to have been highly appreciative of Beatrice's dancing. When he described her death, he made her dance into heaven (271,24): 'Thus happily she migrated with hymns, canticles and dancing into the choir of seraphs... there to enjoy without end the consolation of Christ'.

63 *AA SS* Oct.13: 112,13: 'Ut cor eruptans gaudia, quid haberet interius, corporis ex indicio signis manifestissime loqueretur'.

64 See above, p. 266, n. 55; p. 323, n. 67.

65 *AA SS* June 2: 482,31.

66 As noted by VM, *Strophische Gedichten*, 178.

67 See chapters 7–9 of François Vandenbroucke's part in *The Spirituality of the Middle Ages*, vol. 2 of A History of Christian Spirituality by J. Leclercq, Fr. Vandenbroucke and L. Bouyer (eds), ET by the Benedictines of Holme Eden Abbey, Carlisle (New York, 1968); Georgette Epiney-Burgard, *Gerard Grote et les débuts de la Dévotion moderne*, (Wiesbaden, 1970) and the article by

aberrant Flagellants,[68] and also in the prolonged ecclesiastical and secular turmoils of the time.[69]

In the next few pages it seems preferable to speak first of *orewoet* as used by Hadewijch and then by Beatrice and a few others. Joseph Van Mierlo,[70] Norbert De Paepe,[71] and particularly Joris Reynaert[72] are the three authors who have most extensively studied the meanings of *orewoet* in Hadewijch's writings. The Latin equivalents are as numerous as the shades of *orewoet*'s meanings: *aestus amoris*, ardent love; *insania* or *furor amoris*, madness of love; *languor animi, inertia spiritus*, or inertia caused by excessive love.[73]

Orewoet is nowhere strictly defined in Hadewijch's writings and has several meanings. In Poem 7 in Stanzas *orewoet* is experienced as a psychological state, as a fire in which the soul melts away and is thrown into the abyss of Love. Leonce Reypens made the observation that Hadewijch and Beatrice compared God as love to an inextinguishable fire, compelling them to love him more than can usually be done by a creature.[74] In her Poem 7 in Stanzas Hadewijch states:

> Love brings me to distress,
> Into many a new woe;
> My soul melts away
> In the fierce desired burning [*orewoede*] of love;
> The abyss into which she steers me

Bernard Spaapen about the doctrine of the popular book *The Imitation of Christ*, in DSp 7: 2355–68.

68 See E. Delaruelle, 'Pourquoi n'y eut-il pas de Flagellants en France en 1349?', *La Piété populaire*, 315–27.

69 E. Delaruelle, E.R. Labande and P. Ourliac, *L'Église au temps du Grand Schisme et de la crise conciliaire (1378–1449)*, vol 14 of *Histoire de l'Église* (A. Fliche and V. Martin, eds, Paris 1964) 727–941.

70 *Strophische Gedichten*, 177–78.

71 Hadewijch. *Strofische Gedichten*, 229–31.

72 *Beeldspraak*, 377–81.

73 See Reinhard Kuhn, *The Demon of the Noontide. Ennui in Western Literature*, (Princeton, NJ.,1976) 39–64; G. Dumeige, *Les quatre degrés*, 139–41, and the references in n.45 of Chapter X.

74 Leonce Reypens,'Ruusbroec-Studiën. Het mystieke "Gherinen"', *OGE* 12 (1938) 157–86; 181–82.

> Is deeper than the sea;
> For Love's new deep abyss
> Renews the wound in me.[75]

In Poem 31 in stanzas, *orewoet* is compared to a storm, to be fought against by the noble-minded, the *fiere*, who dare to 'challenge' God's Majesty:[76]

> From slothful hearts and ignoble minds
> The great good remains hidden,
> Which those well understand,
> Who live passionately [*orewoet*] for Love;
> For they perform many a valiant assault
> In storm and adventure:
> It is right that they should make headway
> In high service of Love.[77]

Orewoet is also a dynamic force with remarkable results in reversing extremes and in straightening out differences, as Hadewijch says in Poem 28 in Stanzas:

> The madness (*orewoet*) of Love
> Is a rich fief;
> Anyone who would recognize this
> Would not ask Love for anything else:
> It can unite what is divided
> And makes them one.
> I present the truth about this:
> She [*orewoet*] makes the sweet to be sour
> And the stranger a neighbor,
> And she makes the lowest great
> She makes weak the strong

75 VM, *Strophische Gedichten*, 45, ll. 39–47.
76 See Bernard's saying: 'amori cedat Majestas', [God's] Majesty yields to love, SC 59,2; SBOp2: 136.
77 VM, *Strophische Gedichten* 209, ll. 65–72.

And the sick wholly healthy,
She makes the sturdy crippled,
And heals the one who was wounded.
...
In the high school of Love
One learns the fierce burning [*orewoet*].[78]

The texts relating to Beatrice's *orewoet* or its Latin equivalents
can easily be followed in her *Vita*. When she had her first ecstasy
in Rameya (1217), she experienced a great madness in her
heart.[79] Some years later, as her biography (157,29) tells it:

this fervent desire [to be with Christ] had been growing for a
long time in her heart, but now it began to increase so
strongly that not only could she not apply her memory to
anything else day and night, but scarcely ever could she
recall her bodily eyes from looking upward.... But her
mind's conversation was in heaven and she noticed nothing
of what was taking place around her.

Her 'desire [to suffer in order to be wholly purified] increased
with the passage of time to such madness (*vesania*) that the
strength of her heart could scarcely bear it any longer' (185,40).
Around that time she went to communion 'with open heart and
enlarged veins, *as if* she were mad (*ac si demens*) with excessive
desire' (193,21). 'In her desire to die [to be with Christ] her spirit
grievously shook by its own power the whole vessel of her body
and Beatrice, unable to stand the spiritual joy which flooded her,
acted as though deranged'.(200,17)

This 'madness' seems to have been accompanied by visible
bodily effects. As the biography has it, Beatrice

was so touched interiorly by ineffable jubilation of heart that
not only could she not move a member, but she could not

78 *Ibid.*, 180–81, ll. 31–44; 51–52.
79 *Vita*, 58,96:'immensa cordis sui quam patiebatur insania'.

even open her mouth to speak. Rather, lying as if mindless, she seemed as though dead (*velut amens, jacens ut mortua*), bereft of all use of the outer senses. Occasionally also, affected by the sweetness of heavenly joy she became pale and trembled in her whole body as though seized by a strong fever or paralysis. Not without reason either, since she was burning with the fever of incomprehensible desire.[80]

On December 26, 1232, Beatrice

understood by the raging impetuous struggles that a new and unfamiliar madness was rising within her. Its inflooding was like that of a wave of the sea impatient of all restraint, passing beyond its bounds by its great impetus.... Finally it so violently affected her whole frail body that the disease seemed to stimulate a kind of frenzy which she bore out of the most fervent fire of love (*caritatis incendium*) and sheer desire for heavenly things. Beatrice understood that the spirit within her was thriving with more purity according to the stronger assault of the forementioned violence and the more vigorous impetus of the desire which she suffered.[81]

Her spiritual 'violence' deeply affected her both physically and psychically. She felt obliged

to abstain from good things, fearing that from the quality of words proceeding from the abundance of the heart, the mad love she sustained within might be detected. She prayed for this discreetly, but in vain. For even if she was silent or spoke no word, the unusual sweetness of her manners openly and outwardly showed to those more discreet and better practised in love what she was feeling within.[82]

80 *Vita*, 203,57: 'quasi validissima febre, paralisive correpta'.
81 *Vita*, 219,5: The whole paragraph defines better than Hadewijch does at times the *vesania*, the *orewoet*, as a fiery storm of love (frenetice passionis insania, ...ex ferventissimo caritatis incendio) with its psychological impact.
82 *Vita*, 220,42: 'amoris insaniam deprehendi posse metuerit'. The attack lasted for some six weeks (221,58).

After that, this spiritual insanity (*spiritualis insania*) became quiet, and changed into a wonderful sweetness of love....

> As long as she lived, she could not be fully freed from this paralyzing passion (*paralytica passio*), but at certain and irregular times, and especially when she thought or spoke or even heard others speak of the supreme Good, her very lively spirit would become excited. Immediately she would tremble in all the members of her weak body, and equally in head and heart. Or this would happen also when her insatiable appetite for love, sighing for eternal things, would be unable to rise and attain what she desired unappeasedly.[83]

In order to avoid the impression that Beatrice's great sensitivity and strong emotions led her to madness, the biographer took care to affirm that her madness was one not of the mind but of the heart, *viz.* that Beatrice was madly in love (58,97; 157,29; 185,41; 220,43). Her madness was only apparent, indicated by 'as if', *ac si*, which the biographer added to forestall any misinterpretation (193,21; 200,16 and 21; 203,57; 219,22). Her madness was a spiritual insanity (221,61), or what William and others called a holy insanity.[84] Indeed, the use of the noun 'madness' or of the verb 'to go mad' should not mislead us. As Herman Vekeman rightly pointed out, Beatrice's insanity was the insatiability of love, *insatiabilitas amoris*, rather than insanity of love, *insanitas amoris*.[85] She felt an extreme, unquenchable, burning desire for union with God. Following Leonce Reypens' Latin translation of *orewoet* in Beatrice's treatise as *amoris tumultus*, we have rendered *orewoet* as 'tumult of love', that is, the vicissitudes of which Bernard spoke.[86]

---

83 *Vita*, 221,61. The whole passage is related to 'storms'. Vekeman, '*Vita Beatricis* en *Seuen manieren van Minne*', *OGE* 46 (1972) 42. Her *paralytica passio* deserves a more extensive medical and psychological scrutiny.

84 Nat am 3,6; PL 184: 383C; CF 30:58: 'sancta insania'.

85 *Lexicografisch Onderzoek*, 2: 375.

86 See R–VM, *Seven manieren*, 20, ll. 45–46: *orewoed van minnen*, and *Vita*, 255,361–62: *amoris tumultus*.

After this elaboration on *orewoet* in Hadewijch and Beatrice, the other *mulieres religiosae* might seem insignificant in comparison. Such a conclusion would, however, be erroneous and is disproved by the many references given in the preceding pages.[87] To collect them here to show that these *mulieres religiosae* also frequently had experienced an *orewoet* would be unnecessarily repetitious. What the *mulieres religiosae* experienced compares well with other 'emotional ardours of a more intense type', which Herbert Thurston discussed at some length.[88]

To indulge in a final reference and to conclude fittingly this chapter, we mention an experience of Ida Lewis. One Christmas, reflecting on what she had read in Augustine about the Trinity, 'her soul was suddenly steeped in great delight and her mind became boiling hot'; the onslaught made her 'afraid of *almost* losing her senses and becoming insane from the extraordinary joy she experienced in her heart'.[89] By her burning desire and desired burning, Ida Lewis, like the other *mulieres religiosae*, showed herself madly in love with her God.

---

87 See, for instance, above n. 68 and 71 of Chapter XII, related to Ida of Nivelles.

88 *The Physical Phenomena*, 209–21: 'Incendium amoris'

89 *AA SS* Oct.13: 122,52: 'Tantis repente gaudiis, exaestuante spiritu, fuit ipsius anima delibuta, quod pene timuit ne sensum perderet, et prae mirabili cordis laetitia semet amittens penitus insaniret'. In Letter 25 (VM, *Brieven*, 1: 216, ll. 34–39) Hadewijch expresses something nearly similar to what Ida said.

CHAPTER FOURTEEN

ECSTASIES AND VISIONS

T HE *MULIERES RELIGIOSAE* COULD NOT be other than physically and psychically affected by the demanding efforts of their ascetical lives, their burning desire, and desired burning. To assess their psychic state in relation to their ecstasies and visions is no simple matter. Hastily made or clear-cut judgments can easily lead to misinterpretation. Factors imperfectly known and altogether unknown at times require us to abstain from positing a humanly satisfactory and definitive conclusion,[1] especially in the case, as we shall see, of a person who is 'beyond the spirit', in a realm where our human conceptualization cannot penetrate.

Natural scientists should be given every opportunity to observe ecstatics and visionaries and to make their diagnoses. Yet, however helpful their findings and conclusions, they cannot go beyond what is observable, material, and open to analysis. The experiences of mysticism are, no doubt, not rational, but suprarational; not contrary to reason but beyond reason in ways that we cannot understand positively but which we may defend

---

1 Frits Staals, *Exploring Mysticism. A Methodological Essay* (Berkeley-Los Angeles-London, 1975) 134: 'We have since Descartes been led to suppose that methodical doubt is the hallmark of the unprejudiced search for truth. Many people assume that such a doubt should be resorted to as early as possible, if not immediately'.

negatively against the charge of contradiction. Empirical sciences cannot pierce the mysterious encounter of God with man.

Also to be taken into consideration is the pathological element. Frits Staals correctly pointed out that 'what mystical and pathological states have in common, is that both are distinct from the normal state. Beyond that we know little'.[2] What little can be known is, nevertheless, worth exploring. What can be observed, analyzed and determined is not so much what God does within a mystic, but rather how the mystic reacts to what goes on within himself.

Ernst Benz' observations about visions and sickness still stand: ecstasies and visions affect people differently. For some they act as a physical tonic. Others experience physical healing and subsequently an increased capacity for enduring pain, often in empathy with the sufferings for others. This happened, for instance, to Alice of Schaarbeek. Others experience sickness and strength successively. This seems to have been the case with several *mulieres religiosae*, some of whom considered sickness as a blessing.[3] As David Knowles observed:

Ecstasies, raptures and the like have in themselves no spiritual value.... We are considering the alienation of the mind, often accompanied by symptoms of trance or lifelessness, which are recorded or have in recent times been observed in mystics real or supposed. In themselves, they resemble very closely some of the phenomena of morbid psychology, and may often in fact be no different from these. Experience and

2 F. Staals, *Exploring Mysticism*, 133, where the author adds : 'It can be argued that particular exercises and the nonordinary states of mind to which they give access must *eo ipso* be pathological. But a gymnast may also acquire nonordinary skill: by the same argument many sports must be pronounced pathological'. F. Staals seems to be of the opinion that this argument is applicable to the Far Eastern mysticism he is particularly interested in. As far as Christianity is concerned the first part of the cited text is valid, but the reference to a gymnast who acquires nonordinary skill is not, since the nonordinary element of christian ecstatic states belongs to a totally different realm, we believe.

3 E.Benz, *Die Vision*, 17–34: Vision und Krankheit.

observation, however, show that what may justly be called an influence of a supernatural kind, an awareness of the nearness of God, may have a reflex effect on a spiritually immature person.... It is an equally great error to regard as marvellous and supernatural what is in fact a symptom of physical or psychological weakness, and to attach importance to nothing but material things and label all visions as morbid, or hallucinations. The visible signs of themselves tell nothing of their cause, and a low conception of the supernatural, and a materialistic denial of its existence, are equally far from a true presentation of the fact behind the appearances. The practical problem remains of distinguishing between fraudulent, self-deceiving, morbid and entirely sincere personalities. It is a difficult problem, but no more difficult than any judgment of character based only on appearances.[4]

Hereditary or personal predisposition should also be considered. Whatever the psychic state in which people begin life's journey, 'they can learn to be sick in an healthy way, and mystics are among the most successful'.[5] This optimistic view, not about chronically deranged persons or the incurably psychically disordered, but about ailing mystics has some truth in it, though even some mystics may, in fact, have been psychologically

---

4 David Knowles, *The Nature of Mysticism* (New York, 1966) 55–56.

5 Joseph Bernhardt, 'Heiligkeit und Krankheit', *GL* 23 (1950) 172–95; 187.

6 A case in point is the Cistercian nun Lukardis of Oberweimar (d.1309) whose biography has been published in *AB* 18 (1899) 305–67. H. Thurston (*The Physical Phenomena*, 129), after analyzing her stigmata and her behavior concludes that 'hysterical though she was, no one can read the account [of her biography] without realizing that she was a deeply religious person'. Another case, not as acute as that of Lukardis, is Elisabeth of Spaalbeek (d.1304, not 1275 as Thurston has it), another stigmatic. The account by abbot Philip of Clairvaux, published in *CCH*, Part one, vol.1 (Brussels, 1899) 362–78, brought Thurston (*The Physical Phenomena*, 77) to the conclusion that Elisabeth behaved in strange ways.'The very vividness of the dramatic realization of the trance state led her quite unconsciously to maltreat herself' (*ibid.*, 34). Thurston admits however (*ibid.*, 58) that it would be unreasonable to doubt that the narrative reproduces facts with all desirable accuracy'.

unbalanced.[6] Kenneth Wapnick approaching the psyche of mystics from yet another angle, states that

> the entire mystic path may be understood to be a strengthening process whereby the mystic gradually develops the 'muscles' to withstand the experience of the 'inner world'. It is a strengthening that is responsible for the long periods of suffering and fallowness that are often the mystic's fate, as well as the mystic's faith in the positive outcome of his experience.[7]

Much of the analysis depends also on the position stressed by an author. The psychiatrist Jerome Kroll made the pointed remark: 'I do think it matters whether we allow ourselves to become armchair analysts ready to attribute all kind of illnesses to mysterious psychological mechanisms. In this sense it is unsatisfactory...to dismiss many visionaries under the label of hysteria'.[8] If the temperament of some mystics had an inclination toward neurosis, this could easily become heightened through the inordinate vehemence of their striving to become free from all obstacles to their union with God. Even one otherwise competent scholar can slip into error by making too hasty an evaluation.[9]

Seen through twentieth-century eyeglasses, ecstatics and visionaries appear to walk on thin ice. This obliges us to look first at the terminology used to describe their experiences. Before scholasticism, and even afterwards, this vocabulary was extensive and at times confusing. Within the limits of this chapter we need only refer to the studies about the mentors of the *mulieres*

7 Kenneth Wapnick, 'Mysticism and Schizophrenia', *Journal of Transpersonal Psychology* 1 (1969) 49–68; 63. He concludes his study by saying that 'the mystic provides the example of the method, whereby the inner and the outer may be joined; the schizophrenic, the tragic result when they are separate'.

8 Jerome Kroll, 'Carol Hauselander's Childhood Neurosis', *Vox Benedictina* 2 (1985) 74–80; 80.

9 Stephanus A. Axters, *Inleiding tot een Geschiedenis van de Mystiek in de Nederlanden*, Verslagen en Handelingen van de Koninklijke Academie voor Taal-en Letterkunde (Ghent, 1967) 165–305; 175–76, touches the problem of neurosis in regard to Beatrice, Hadewijch and Ivette of Huy. In fact, the references do not indicate neurosis, but the aftereffects of an ecstasy.

religiosae: Augustine,[10] Hugh,[11] Richard,[12] William,[13] and Bernard.[14] The Victorines, being teachers of college students, had a pronounced tendency to outline mystical experiences more systematically than did the Cistercians who, generally speaking as monks to monks, had more the heart in mind than the systematization of phenomena.[15]

Robert Javelet has described ecstasy in the twelfth century,[16] while Ferdinand Jetté studied it from the thirteenth till the

10 Pierre Courcelle, ' La première expérience augustinienne de l'extase', *AM* 1: 53–57; André Mandouze, 'L'Extase d'Ostie', *ibid*.: 67–84.

11. Roger Baron, *Études sur Hugues de Saint-Victor* (Paris, 1963) especially 17–25: Diffinitiones magistri Hugonis; *Id.,Hugues de Saint-Victor. La contemplation et ses espèces*; Robert Javelet, 'Sens et Réalité Ultime selon Hugues de Saint-Victor', *Ultimate Reality and Meaning* 3 (1980) 84–113.

12 Jean Chatillon, 'Les quatre degrés de la Charité d'après Richard de Saint-Victor', *RAM* 20 (1939) 237–64; *Id.*, 'Les trois modes de la Contemplation selon Richard de Saint-Victor', *Bulletin de Littérature Ecclésiastique* 41 (1940) 3–26; G. Dumeige, *Les quatre degrés*; Robert Javelet, 'Sens et Réalité ultime selon Richard de Saint-Victor', *Ultimate Reality and Meaning* 6 (1983) 221–43.

13 The latest and best publication is David N. Bell's *The Image and Likeness*, *CS* 78 (Kalamazoo, 1984). The bibliography mentions the many other studies on William. On p.197, n. 92 the author refers also to the use of *ecstasis* and *excessus* in the Bible.

14 E. Gilson, *The Mystical Theology*, 152. R. Javelet, however, has reservations: He is of the opinion that what Gilson described as the high-point or peak-experience of Bernard's mysticism is a *sublevatio*, not the higher *alienatio*. See Robert Javelet, *Psychologie*, 145–47; *Id.*, 'Intelligence et amour chez les auteurs spirituels du xiie siècle', *RAM* 37 (1961) 273–90; 288, n. 55.

15 David Knowles, *The Evolution of Medieval Thought* (London, 1962) 141–46: 'The School of St Victor and St Bernard', wherein unfortunately he omits other Cistercians. Incidentally, next to them, Peter Cantor and his friend Alan of Lille, both teachers in Paris could be mentioned, not because they became *fin de carrière* Cistercians (Peter died in Longpont in 1193, and Alan in Cîteaux in 1203) but because both made efforts to bring a more precise terminology to theological, philosophical and literary matters. For Peter Cantor, see John Baldwin, *Masters, Princes and Merchants*, (Princeton, 1970) 2 vols. (Baldwin's attention goes chiefly to Peter's *Verbum* abbreviatum); Gillian R. Evans, 'The Place of Peter the Chanter's *De tropibus loquendis*, *AC* 38 (1983) 231–53. Of the many publications about Alan, see the reference to M-T d'Alverny in note 27 of Chapter V. Between pages 24–25 d'Alverny inserted a plate from manuscript J19767 of London's British Museum, where magister Peter Cantor and magister Alanus appear together. It is, however, difficult to evaluate what influence they could have had on the *mulieres religiosae*.

16 DSp 4: 2113–20.

fifteenth century, and included Hadewijch and Beatrice.[17] Mystical states have been well described in Ernst Benz' *Die Vision*, and even more systematically and phenomenologically (but not theologically) by Peter Dinzelbacher in *Vision*. In English some definitions have been given by David Knowles,[18] are sporadically spoken of in *Understanding Mysticism* (Richard Woods ed.), and treated more extensively by Evelyn Underhill.[19] The terminology differs from one generation to the next, from one author to another,[20] and in the same author from earlier till later writings,[21] all of which makes the terminology confusing and complicated.

Ecstasy, borrowed from the Greek *ekstasis*, is the term preferred in modern English to indicate a person's movement from an ordinary state of consciousness to another, accompanied by an overpowering emotion. Two different words for *ecstasy* have traditionally been used: *excessus* and *raptus*. In fact, the terms were so close as to be used almost interchangeably. But between *ecstasis* and *excessus* some medieval writers made a clear distinction, one we shall study a little later (see below, pp. 418f).

Bernard and William, for instance, following a scriptural

---

17 *Ibid.*: 2131–33.

18 *The Nature of Mysticism*, (see note 4), particularly chapter 6: Visions and ecstasies.

19 Richard Woods, ed., *Understanding Mysticism* (Garden City, NY., 1980) Evelyn Underhill, *Mysticism. A Study in the Nature and Development of Man's Spiritual Consciousness*, 10th ed. (Cleveland–New York, 1963).

20 P. Dinzelbacher made pertinent observations in this regard. See his *Vision* 78–89: Die Typisierung der mittelalterlichen Visionen. Ernst Arbman's *Ecstasy* in 3 vols is interesting enough, but his definitions at times embrace too many different aspects.

21 Though, according to E. Gilson (*Mystical Theology*, 94) Bernard did not attempt a systematic classification of mystical states—probably because of the strongly marked individuality of mystics—G.B. Burch (*The Steps*, 95–97) made the observation that it was not until his *Hum* (written before or in 1125; SBOp 3: 4) that Bernard took the possibility of mystical experiences for granted. In 1137 he spoke in his *SC* 23 for the first time of his personal experience, and near the end of his life, in *SC* 74 he expressed it more emphatically. To Burch's last reference another one could be added (*SC* 85,13–14; SBOp 2: 315–16) where he says that a rapture (*raptus*) is an experience beyond description. The most intimate contact with God is, according to C. Mohrmann (SBOp 2: xxii), called by him *adventus*.

vocabulary rarely made use of the term ecstasy,[22] and preferred *excessus* (*mentis*). To express a prophetical or mystical ecstasy, Jerome likewise spoke of *excessus*. Augustine sometimes used the term ecstasy, at other times *excessus*.[23] For Cassian, writing in Latin of eastern teaching, *excessus* had a mystical meaning, and it is Cassian rather than the proposed Maximus the Confessor[24] who is responsible for Bernard's preference for *excessus* over ecstasy.[25] In his use of *excessus* William seems to be more dependent on Augustine.[26] The classical trichotomous approach to human anthropology should also be taken into account, with its distinction between the inferior aspect of the soul (*anima*) and its superior aspects, the rational (*animus*) and the spiritual (*spiritus*) soul, in relation to the body (*corpus*). The *anima* vivifies the body; the activity (*vis*) of the superior rational soul is to direct the body while the same superior aspect as spirit is turned upward to God.[27] Whatever the origin and meaning of the mystical terminology used by their mentors, it was these intermediaries the *mulieres religiosae* and their biographers seem to have followed, but not always closely.

Though God is free to communicate himself when and as much as he wills, he usually acts with man's consent in the sense that he expects man's cooperative receptivity. When a person goes through the trial of purification from egocentric tendencies and grows in virtues within himself and in relation to his neighbors—

22 E. Gilson, *Mystical Theology*, 237, n. 156; D. Bell, *The Image*, 197.

23 Christine Mohrmann, 'Observations sur la langue et le style de Saint Bernard', SBOp 2: xxi.

24 As advanced by E. Gilson, *Mystical Theology*, 26.

25 L.T. Lorié, *Spiritual Terminology in the Latin Translations of the Vita Antonii*, Latinitas Christianorum Primaeva 11, C. Mohrmann and H.H. Janssen eds. (Nijmegen, 1955) 153–54. Owen Chadwick, *John Cassian*, 2nd ed.(Cambridge, 1960) 104–09 supports Lorié's view. Bernard's use of *excessus* has been treated by Michael Casey, 'In Pursuit of Ecstasy: Reflections on Bernard of Clairvaux' "De diligendo Deo"', *MnS* 16 (1985) 139–156.

26 D. Bell, *The Image*, 197.

27 This is how it is explained by Richard in his *De exterminatione mali* 3,8; PL 196: 1114CD. For Bernard's description, see his *SC* 30,9; SBOp 1: 216, and W. Hiss, *Die Anthropologie Bernhards von Clairvaux*, 94–7 for more references. Hadewijch too used this trichotomy (R. Vanneste, *Abstracta* 63, n. 1) as did Beatrice: Herman Vekeman, *Lexicografisch Onderzoek*, 2: 285–86.

in part by learning from mistakes—God sometimes touches him in his interior senses. Insights, inspirations, stimulations, and a whole string of similar terms are encountered in the biographies of the *mulieres religiosae* as manifestations of the illuminating grace which these women accepted and wholeheartedly responded to. Such *touches* made them wider and deeper, more sensitive and responsive. Through this *dilation* as it is called, they gradually became ready for *sublevatio* or *elevatio*, the preparedness to receive that *mystical touch* called in the vernacular of their day *gherinen*.[28] The *gherinen*, so to speak, opens the door to God's activity; God now steps in with such an abundance and with such affluence that the *mulieres religiosae* (and other people similarly affected) went, not out of their minds, but out of their spirits: their conceptualizing perception was sharply reduced: indeed from one point of view it was almost annihilated but from another it was transfigured and transformed.[29]

In an *excessus*, it is God who leads and man who is led,[30] i.e. he opens himself to a cooperating passive reception. So understood, this could be spoken of as an interaction. According to Etienne Gilson:

> Ecstasy designates a state in which the corporeal senses cease to exercise their functions. In this sense ecstasy

28 L. Reypens, 'Ruusbroec-Studiën, I, Het mystieke 'gherinen', *OGE* 12 (1938) 158–86, where he speaks also (158, n. 2 and 3) about Hadewijch's and Beatrice's *gerenen*, another idiomatic form of Ruusbroec's *gherinen*.

29 This phenomenon was later technically called 'infused'. The *mulieres religiosae* or their biographers used *infusio*, the noun, and the verb *infundere*,'to pour in', but not as a technical term. Infusion meant to them an abundant inpouring of grace, an unaccustomed deeper level of consciousness or an exceptionally blazing love.

30 The use of drugs or 'Instant Mysticism' as E. Bernz calls it (*Die Vision*, 81) is an absurdity because a man-made neurochemical component has nothing to do with the essence of a true mystical experience. What they might have in common are the somatic effects. For a more extensive study of the 'numerous parallels and similarities between mystical and drug-induced states', see Frits Staals, *Exploring Mysticism*, 155–67: 'drugs and powers', and the papers in J. White (ed.) *The Highest State of Consciousness* (New York, 1972).

belongs to the genus *excessus*.[31] It is an *excessus* [as ecstasy] which takes the mystic out of external sensibility. If the *ecstasy* is complete it takes the mystic, not only out of the external senses, but also of the internal senses. The term *excessus* takes on a mystical sense only when it indicates the passage from a normal human state, even where this is attained by the aid of grace to a state which is more than human. The two most important *excessus* are, that which liberates man from his external senses (ecstasy properly so called), and that which takes him beyond thought itself (*abductio interioris sensus*). We see therefore that strictly speaking, we should distinguish ecstasy from *excessus*, taken absolutely, but the terms are too closely connected to allow us always to observe the precaution.[32]

Excessus in this final sense of taking somebody 'away', beyond thought itself, the *abductio interioris sensus*, is technically known as *alienatio*. When the *alienatio* is so violent that it sweeps the soul immediately to God, the term *abalienatio* is used. In this case the adverb 'hastily' (*raptim*) stresses the unexpectedness of the experience.

The term *rapture* (*raptus*) implies 'that the soul has no part of its own to play in the operation; the mystic state is effected without its co-operation'.[33] Rapture is a brusque interruption of God's grace, ravishing the soul for a short time into ecstasy. The passive element is often stressed by the use of passive verb forms such as 'to be pulled into' (*trahi*), 'to be lifted up' (*attolli*), 'to be seized' (*captari*), 'to be abducted' (*abduci*), all of which indicate that it is God's grace which is at work, and not man's efforts. These terms are often used in different combinations. The

31 In classical Latin the verb *excedere*, followed by *hominem*, meant a man who died by leaving his body. See Du Cange, *Glossarium novum ad Scriptores Medii Aevi*, ed. P. Carpentier (Paris, 1766) vol.2: 306. In Christian terminology it means to rise for a short while beyond the external and internal senses, *viz.* to go beyond one's usual perceptional processes.

32 E. Gilson, *Mystical Theology*, 237, n. 156. Most authors agree with Gilson on this point.

33 E. Gilson, *ibid.*, 106.

physical result of an ecstasy, its effect on the body, is often described by the term sleep (*somnus*) and even death (*mors*), as we shall see below.

Seen in context, Gilson's definition of *raptus* as 'a ravishment in which the ravished soul has no part of its own to play in this operation' is correct. We should keep in mind, however, that ravishment is a grace given to produce a deep loving union with God. Like any grace, it implies consent, at least at the moment when the enraptured soul realizes what is happening and allows God's grace free reign without resistance. A case in point is the short and incomplete biography of Beatrice of Zwijveke. She had a vision of Christ showing the marks of his passion in his humanity. But since her physical and psychic strength had already been taxed by an earlier vision of the same kind, she restrained herself and tried to lose sight of the apparition. But immediately she was again enraptured (*rapta*) and now saw Christ's face expressing his love for her and at the same time showing her that he was upset (*irascens*) because she was inclined to withhold her consent.[34] Such cases, however rare, are helpful in clarifying God's intervention in a rapture.

Our biographers use *excessus* (as ecstasy and as *excessus*), and carefully indicate that the *mulieres religiosae* did not bring these experiences on themselves.[35] Of Ida of Nivelles it is said that 'God's hand came over her and, melting like wax before the fire [of God's love], she became wholly alienated and enraptured in spirit'.[36] On another occasion she was 'at once abducted into an ecstasy of mind'.[37] Ida Lewis was also 'enraptured in ecstasy'

---

34 L. Reypens, 'Nog een dertiendeeuwse mystieke Cisterciënsernon', *OGE* 23 (1949) 246, ll. 106–09: 'Et vidit in spiritu eandem quam viderat visionem et tunc, deficientibus viribus corporis, se abstraxit et oblivi voluit. Et tunc statim iterum rapta fuit et faciem cristi quasi iracundam vidit, more alicuius aliquem diligentis et irascentis quia eius insequi amorem omittat'. Such 'withholding of consent' is only possible at the beginning of a *raptus*, see Carl Albrecht, *Psychologie des mystischen Bewusstseins* (Bremen, 1951) 66.

35 Alice of Schaarbeek's short biography does not mention ecstasies explicitly. She is said to have had some visions, but her biographer does not connect them with a preceding ecstasy.

36 *Quinque*, 244: 'a sensibus corporeis penitus alienata in spiritu rapta est'.

37 *Ibid.*, 280: 'statim in mentis excessu abducitur'.

(*mentis exstasi*): she 'endured' (*patiens*), or was 'pulled up' (*tracta*), or 'called out' to ecstasy (*evocata*).[38] In a rapture, Ida of Leuven's 'mind was led beyond bodily boundaries to the contemplation of heavenly things'.[39] She could be enraptured in ecstasy (*in exstasi rapitur*), or lifted up into an ecstasy of mind (*per mentis excessum sustolitur*), or snatched away in an 'egress' of mind (*in egressu mentis eripitur*).[40] Occasionally 'the Lord himself took her up and forthwith she leapt into an ecstacy of mind',[41] or 'the activity of her outer senses being lulled to sleep, she was raised up into a rapture of mind'.[42] Ida's biographer sometimes uses a repetitious sentence to mark her ecstasies: 'enraptured in ecstasy, deprived of the burden of her [physical] senses, she was lifted up to explore celestial things'.[43] Ida seemed to have appreciated her ecstasies very much, perhaps too much.[44]

Beatrice was 'caught beyond herself in ecstasy of mind'.[45] At times the suddenness is stressed,[46] or ecstasy is combined with *abalienatio*.[47]

38 *AA SS* Oct. 13: 120,42; 118,36; 121,49; 122,50. Though the four references speak about ecstasy, her biographer uses the term *excessus* also.

39 *AA SS* April 2: 173,11: 'Tandem raperetur, et corporalium sensuum officio consopita, mens extra metas corporeas ad contemplanda caelestia...duceretur'.

40 *Ibid.*, 179,30; 181,36; 177,22.

41 *Ibid.*, 188,25: 'in excessum mentis extemplo prosiliit'.

42 *Ibid.*, 182,40: 'in excessum mentis elevata, prosiliit, sopito sensuum exteriorum officio'.

43 *Ibid.*, 189,27: 'in excessu mentis eripitur et exuto sensualitatis onere, spiritus ad indaganda caelestia sublevatur'.

44 Ida's biographer mentions that she felt frustrated (*ibid.*, 179,31) 'not being able, there and then, to enjoy the supreme Good, which is God, as readily as she wished': 'eo quod amor suus et desiderium ipso summo bono, quod Deus est, eodem adhuc in tempore pro voluntatis suae libito minime frueretur'.

45 *Vita*, 149,45: 'she was rapt on high in ecstasy of mind'; *Vita*, 163,38; 203,56; 206,15: 'she could not discern or consider anything happening around her, since her bodily senses withdrew inside'.

46 *Vita*, 55,27: 'she immediately leapt up, seized in an ecstasy of her mind'; 236,30: 'snatched up immediately in ecstasy of mind'.

47 *Vita*, 172,53: 'stripped of her bodily senses, she was suddenly caught up to heaven through the ecstasy of contemplation, transported to that sublime choir of the Seraphim, caught up there by the divine spirit in mind, not in body, with her soul, not her flesh'.

The texts cited here do, in fact, mention two kinds of ecstasy: in and beyond the spirit, or as Hadewijch put it: 'in' and 'buten den gheeste'.[48] Writing at a time when vernacular languages were in their infancy as literary vehicles, the talented Hadewijch and Beatrice made great contributions to the formulation of a precise mystical terminology in their mother tongue.[49] In her sixth vision, for example, Hadewijch clearly expresses the two ascending and the two descending movements of a 'complete' ecstasy. She was first taken up in the spirit and from there beyond the spirit. From this latter state she was brought back into the spirit and then to her ordinary bodily consciousness.[50] Beatrice too knew these distinctions. In her fifth *maniere* she writes that 'Love draws the soul outside itself and above itself...in the fruition of Love'.[51]

Ida of Nivelles' biographer says that after a rapture (*raptus*) she felt her spirit return to her body.[52] On one occasion, when Ida Lewis was in ecstasy, a nun tried to open her eyelids, but they closed quickly again, and this has to be taken as a sign that she was at that moment *in* the spirit, not *out* of the spirit, for in the latter case her forced eyelids would have stayed open.[53] Ida of

48 Hadewijch's 'in the spirit' (*in den gheeste*) is the equivavalent of Bernard's *ecstasis* and of Richard's *in spiritu*; her 'beyond the spirit' (*buten den gheeste*) is the equivalent of Bernard's *excessus* and of Richard's *sine spiritu*. For Bernard, see E. Gilson, *Mystical Theology*, 237, n. 156; for Richard, see his *Benjamin major*, 12; PL 196: 182B. Robert Javelet (DSp 4: 2120) says that Richard's *sine spiritu* is not an absolute loss of consciousness, but an *abalienatio*, a radical change on the level of consciousness, '*changement d'axe radical de conscience*'.

49 For the importance of such a contribution, see Alois M. Haas, *Sermo mysticus. Studien zur Theologie und Sprache der deutschen Mystik*, Dokimion 4 (Freiburg/Switzerl., 1979) 19–36: Mystische Erfahrung und Sprache.

50 VM, *Visioenen*, 1: 65–70, ll. 10–103. See J. Reynaert, *Beeldspraak*, 252–53.

51 R-VM, *Seven manieren*, 17, ll. 16–18. We opt with H. Vekeman (Lexicografisch Onderzoek, 2: 345, for the reading *gebruken* (of manuscript H) instead of *gebreken* (of manuscript B) preferred by R-VM.

52 *Quinque*, 224: 'reversa ad seipsam, visumque fuit ei quod sensiebat spiritum suum sua viscera regredientem'. The whole episode has been deftly described in the already mentioned study of P. Dinzelbacher: 'Ida von Nijvels Brückenvision', *OGE* 52 (1978) 179–94.

53 *AA SS* Oct,.13: 121,49: 'Vidit quod quotiens studuerat ipsos [oculos] aperire, virgo rapta statim recludere properarat'. See Ernst Arbman, *Ecstasy*. vol.2: (Stockholm, 1968), 169.

Leuven's biographer, who does not seem to have been too familiar with this kind of terminology, tried to smooth out the problem
by applying to Ida Paul's saying that 'she was caught up—
whether still in the body or out of the body—I do not know, God
knows'(2 Cor: 12,2).[54]

Hadewijch usually says in a short sentence that 'she was taken
up in the spirit'.[55] At times, however, she completes this sentence
by saying that she was taken up in an ecstasy and withdrawn from
her exterior senses: 'When I had received the Lord [in the Eucha-
rist] he then received me into himself, so that he withdrew me
from my senses and from every remembrance of alien things'.[56]
Or she would say: 'From within I was then wholly withdrawn in
the spirit',[57] or: 'I was taken up in the spirit out of myself'.[58] She
puts it equally clearly when she says she was 'taken beyond the
spirit'[59]

It must not be assumed that an ecstasy *in* the spirit is always
followed by an ecstasy *beyond* the spirit. In some cases we have
only the affirmation of the seer or her biographer that she had
been rapt into ecstasy, but we lack specific details. In other
instances the visions look more like apparitions than visions
related to an ecstasy. If ecstasies occurred in public, as they did
when they were connected with the Eucharist, the context shows
that we may infer but not assume an ecstasy beyond the spirit.[60]
Feigned ecstasies by some persons cannot be excluded. The
major feature of an ecstasy in the spirit is that in such an ecstasy
there is room for imagination and phantasy, while there is none in
an ecstasy as *excessus*, beyond the spirit.

54 *AA SS* April 2: 166,32; 173,12.

55 VM, *Visioenen*, 1: Vision 5: 58, l. 1–2; vision 6: 65, l. 9–10; vision 9: 95, l.
7; vision 11: 110, ll. 1–2; vision 13: 140, ll. 1–3.

56 *Ibid.*, vision 1: 10, ll. 15–18. This text reminds one of Bernard's saying: 'I
try to express with the most suitable words I can muster, the ecstatic ascent of
the purified mind to God, and the loving descent of God into the soul': *SC* 31,6;
SBOp 1: 223.

57 Vision 4, *ibid.*, 48, l. 78.

58 Vision 12, *ibid.*, 125, l. 1–3.

59 VM, *Visioenen* 1: vision 5: 62, l. 63; vision 6: 69, l. 82; vision 9: 98, ll. 67–
70; vision 13: 153, l. 257.

60 See Chapter XI: Christ in the Eucharist.

Their biographers tell us that during their ecstasies the *mulieres religiosae* became totally oblivious to everything that went on around them.[61] Beatrice could not move (203,53) or speak, even when she tried (215,45: *casso labore*) and she was deprived of her bodily senses (172,53), as too, were Ida of Nivelles, Ida Lewis, and Ida of Leuven.[62] In most cases physical unconsciousness was accompanied or followed by catalepsy. The inner senses were sharpened—something biographers express by saying that they saw 'not with the bodily but with the spiritual eyes, with eyes of the mind, not of the body'.[63] During a rapture after communion Ida Lewis' face turned red.[64] A nun of her community asked her why her face sometimes became pale, at other times purple during an ecstasy. She replied that those who are rapt to see the wonderful mysteries of the Trinity become pale in the face, whereas those who fly into ecstasy (*volant ad exstasim*) to see Christ in his humanity become red.[65]

Among the writings by or about ecstatics, very few examples emerge which do not require a distinction or at least a clarification between ecstasy and *excessus*. A provisional definition by Peter Dinzelbacher states that an ecstasy is a phenomenon indicating the withdrawal of the soul from the body.[66] At first sight, this description seems close to the *excessus* of classical Latin: the separation of soul and body at death. The cases of Barontus

61 *Vita*, 163,35; 203,56; 206,15; 215,45; 222,11; 223,28; 236,30; — Ida of Nivelles, *Quinque*, 211,244, 250; — Ida Lewis, *AA SS* Oct.13: 117,32; 121,45; 121,46; — Ida of Leuven, *AA SS* April 2: 173,11; 189,27.

62 Ida of Nivelles, *Quinque*, 281; — Ida Lewis, *AA SS* Oct,.13: 117,32; 121,49; — Ida of Leuven, *AA SS* April 2: 180,35; 182,45.

63 Beatrice, *Vita*, 149,80; 172,55; — Ida of Leuven, *AA SS* April 2: 173,61; 181,9; In the first instance, the biographer says that this happened often, *saepius*, even very often, *saepissime*. When in ecstasy in the spirit, Ida of Nivelles tastes and sees (*Quinque*, 271) as did Beatrice (206,15). This aspect will have to be looked at again below, when visions are treated.

64 *AA SS* Oct.13: 117,32: 'Faciem mirabiliter habens omnino rubeam et praeclaram'.

65 *Ibid.*, 121,49: 'Qui secundum Trinitatis magnalia tracti seu rapti sunt, colorem pallidum, sed qui volant ad exstasim humanitatis dulcia delibando, colorem rubeum consequuntur'.

66 *Vision*, 50: 'Als Ekstase soll hier vorläufig nur das Phänomen des Austritts der Seele aus dem Körper bezeichnet werden. Die zurückgelassene Leib zeigt dabei als Symptome meist Unsensibilität und oft Starre'.

(678/9) and of Tundal (1149), referred to by Dinzelbacher, have several near-duplicates in Caesarius of Heisterbach's *Dialogus miraculorum* and similar *Legendaria*: the soul leaves the body, but a short time afterwards rejoins it for a shorter or longer period and usually for a special moral purpose. Ida of Leuven's biography mentions also such a case.[67]

Most medieval authors used the terms *vision, sleep* or *somnus* nearly interchangeably. This metaphor goes back to the Bible and the Fathers of the Church. In the Middle Ages this use is characterized by coupling the terms together as *in visione somnii* or *in somnii visione*.[68] When our *mulieres religiosae* or their biographers relate sleep to an ecstasy or an *excessus* rather than to ordinary sleep or a dream related to a vision, they could have been influenced by such mentors as Bernard,[69] Richard,[70] or William.[71]

67 See above, Chapter X, n.128.
68 P. Dinzelbacher, *Vision*, 48–50.
69 SC 52, 2–3; SBOp 2: 91–92; 'The heavenly bridegroom is plainly shown as passionately defending the repose of his beloved, eager to embrace her within his arms as she sleeps, lest she be roused from her delicious slumber by annoyance or disquiet.... Let me explain if I can what this sleep is which the bridegroom wishes his beloved to enjoy, from which he will not allow her to be wakened under any circumstances, except at her good-pleasure.... This sleep of the bride, is not the tranquil repose of the body that for a time sweetly lulls the fleshy senses, nor the dreaded sleep whose custom it is to take life away completely. Further still is it removed from that deathly sleep by which a man perseveres irrevocably in sin and so dies. It is a slumber which is vital and watchful, which enlightens the heart, drives away death, and communicates eternal life. For it is a genuine sleep that yet does not stupify the mind but transports it'.
70 Sleep, as *torpor* corresponds to the *alienatio* of the mind, by which the mind becomes removed from what it is accustomed to. As if taken by sleep it wanders away from human things to the contemplation of things divine.' *Benjamin major* 4,22; PL 196: 165D. See G. Dumeige, *Les quatre degrés*, 193: *alienatio* is equivalent to *excessus* and 'sleep'.
71 D. Bell, *The Image*, 203–4: 'If then, the soul in ecstasy is truly asleep *in somno quietis*, it is a curious sort of sleep, for the soul is both aware and unaware of itself at the same time. In fact, says William (following Augustine), ecstasy is inebriation as well as sleep.... Rather then, than saying simply that in ecstasy the *intelligentia* is asleep...we might more accurately say that rationality is transfigured, transformed and perfected'. William's texts are referred to in Bell's footnotes.

The outstanding *mulieres religiosae* having their minds and hearts turned in toward God in his being and his doings, preferred to speak of the sleep of contemplation, *somnus contemplationis*,[72] which they considered a sleep of love, *somnus amoris*.[73] Ida of Nivelles' biography several times mentions this special kind of sleep: 'At once, forsaken by her bodily faculties, she was raised up in an *excessus* of mind...and as usual fell asleep'.[74] Talking about her swoons when she went to communion the biographer says that 'she went frequently from the refectory of the salutary Eucharist to the spiritual dormitory wherein, alienated from her bodily senses, she slumbered quietly and went happily to sleep in the arms of her bridegroom'.[75] 'Enraptured in an *excessus*, she dropped to the floor and could not be moved at all'; 'she fell asleep' through a spiritual inebriation 'in the arms of her Bridegroom'. For, as the biographer comments further: 'love made her melt like wax, and by this *excessus* she was sent upward to heavenly things. But the same love drew her down from above and put her back among the tribulations on earth, there to apply herself to be compassionate and to commiserate with the troubles of her neighbors'.[76] Ida Lewis, enraptured in an *excessus*, often fell into a spiritual slumber.[77] The frequency of this phenomenon and the trouble it caused impelled her 'to ask the Lord to have this sleep taken away from her'.[78] Ida of Leuven's biography mentions that a Praemonstratensian, waking up from the sleep of

---

72 Beatrice, *Vita*, 163,48; 180,152; 207,38. — Ida of Leuven, *AA SS* April 2: 169,43.

73 Beatrice, *Vita*, 75,75; — Ida of Nivelles, *Quinque*, 212, 243, 266.

74 *Quinque*, 257: 'more solito obdormivit'.

75 *Ibid.*, 274: 'ut a refectorio salutaris Eucharistiae, transiret ad dormitorium spirituale, in quo a sensibus corporis alienata, inter sponsi sui brachia quiete et felicissime sopiretur'.

76 *Ibid.*, 281: 'per excessum rapta...inter sponsi sui brachia somno spiritualis inebrietatis obdormivit.... Charitas enim eam interius ad cerae similitudinem liquefactam per excessum ad superna emittabat. Et eadem charitas illam deorsum retrahebat ut posita in tribulationibus compati studeret et misereri'.

77 *AA SS* Oct .13: 118,36: 'mentis exstasim patiens, excessu rapta spiritus ...saepius in somnis spiritualibus obdormivit'.

78 *Ibid.*, 120,41: 'Rogavi Dominum ut haec a me dormitio tolleretur'.

contemplation, went to her whom he had seen while he was rapt in an *excessus*.[79]

'During a sermon, Beatrice was so overcome with heavenly delights that she fainted... wholly occupied in interior delights as if asleep, all her bodily members being quite still' (163,48). 'She lay with great pleasure in the arms of her bridegroon and slept the sweet sleep of love' (75,75). At another occasion, 'God's bride, Beatrice, awoke from the sleep of contemplation and received back the use of her bodily senses'.[80] Hadewijch was inclined to compare spiritual sleep to the apostle John's reclining on Jesus' breast at the Last Supper. In Letter 18 she wrote to a friend: 'You should contemplate your dear God cordially, yes, much more than cordially...so that you can rest with St. John, who slept on Jesus' breast. And this is what they do who serve Love in liberty : they rest on that sweet, wise heart'.[81]

It would be superfluous to elaborate on what the *mulieres religiosae* and their biographers tell at this point. When they speak of sleep related to an ecstasy or an *excessus* it is clear that they have in mind a *spiritual* sleep, a captivation by God's love, to which they surrender in order to slumber eagerly and happily in the arms of their Beloved. No wonder that when they came back to themselves they sometimes reported having a feeling of floating in air. On one occasion, Beatrice 'seemed to herself to be floating in air' (58,120). Ida of Leuven was so 'overcome' with spiritual delights that 'she could not even feel her feet leaving their prints on the ground, as if her whole body was flying through the air'.[82] Another time, coming out of a rapture 'she had the impression that instead of walking, she was gliding, her feet and legs raised above the dusty ground, with no footprints left for anyone to see'.[83]

79 *AA SS* April 2: 169,43: 'experrectus...a somno contemplationis'.

80 *Vita*, 180,152. This happened after an *excessus*, followed by a vision which the biographer interpreted as a vision of God, face to face.

81 Letter 18, VM, *Brieven*, 1: 159, l. 177–78; 182–85.

82 *AA SS* April 2: 176,21: 'Ac si toto corpore volatisset in aëre'.

83 *Ibid.*, 181,36: 'Ita quod pedes incedentis et poplites a terrae pulvere sublevatis, ut sibi certissime videbatur, aspiceres, et terrenae substantiae quodcumque vestigium imprimere non putares': a considerably milder levitation than

A brief word should be added about the metaphorical 'death of contemplation', *viz.* contemplation as mystical death. This metaphor became widely used and misused in later centuries.[84] Richard treated this aspect most explicitly and succinctly in his *Benjamin minor* in which Benjamin, symbolizing a higher state of contemplation, is born, and Rachel, symbolizing a lower state of contemplation, dies.[85] Bernard proved to be the most influential transmitter of this image to later writers.[86] While the *mulieres religiosae* or their biographers spoke at times of 'the sleep of contemplation',[87] they were less eager to speak of the 'death of contemplation'. There is one indirect reference in Beatrice's biography,[88] and one in that of Ida Lewis.[89] Hadewijch seems to have known this metaphor and its use by the minnesingers of the twelfth and thirteenth centuries.[90]

those mentioned by H. Thurston, *The Physical Phenomena*, 1–31. See also E. Arbman, *Ecstasy* 2: 234–74: The Ecstatic Levitation and Its Psychology.

84 A. Haas, *Sermo mysticus*, 392–480: mors mystica. The author summarized his study in 'mort mystique', DSp 10 (1980) 1777–90.

85 *Benjamin min*or, 74; PL 196: 52A–53D, using a reference to Psalm 67:28.

86 In his *SC* 52,4–5; SBOp 2: 92–93 he wrote: 'It is not absurd for me to call the bride's ecstasy a death, but one that snatches away not life but life's snares...In this life we move about surrounded by traps, but these cause no fear when the soul is drawn out of itself by a thought that is both powerful and holy, provided that it so separates itself and flies away from the mind that it transcends the normal manner and habit of thinking. For since the ecstatic soul (*excedente anima*) is out of the awareness of life, though not from life itself, it must by necessity be cut off from the temptations of life. How good the death that does not take away life but makes it better; good in that the body does not perish but the soul is exalted.... This kind of ecstasy (*excessus*), in my opinion, is alone or principally called contemplation'. See also the comments on this text by Watkin Williams, *Monastic Studies* (Manchester, 1938) 181–82.

87 Beatrice, *Vita*, 75,75; 163,48; 180,152; 207,38; — Ida of Nivelles: *Quinque*, 212,243,257,281; — Ida Lewis: *AA SS* Oct.13: 118,36; — Ida of Leuven: *AA SS* April 2: 169,43, to give a few examples.

88 *Vita*, 238,18: 'because of her excessive love she thought she was letting go of this life'.

89 *AA SS* Oct.13: 121, 45: 'Having an ecstasy she remained totally as if dead': 'manens prorsus ut mortua'. The context refers explicitly to her 'vehement desire to contemplate the grandeur of heaven'.

90 J. Reynaert, *Beeldspraak*, 321–32: Het doodsmotief, particularly 327–30, where he briefly refers to Richard, Bernard and courtly love. In relation to Mechtild of Magdeburg and Margaret Porrete, A. Haas too points to the minnesinger in connection with *mors mystica*, dying of love. See his *Sermo*

As we have seen so far, the first ecstacy leads to a second; *ecstasis* yields to *excessus*.[91] This distinction, and Hadewijch's description of the two upward and the two downward steps of her ecstasies, have been helpful, and yet not totally satisfactory. God's ways are not man's ways, and his ways cannot be categorized in human terms.[92] When we are summarizing human experiences we are, David Knowles points out, dealing with

the experience of individual human beings, none of whom exactly resembles his neighbor in situation, qualities, and eternal destiny. Any kind of classification of behaviour and experience must therefore be a step removed from reality; the individual will not conform exactly to the rules, and the rules are not an exact measurement of the individual. This, if true in purely natural, human matters, is a hundred times more so when it is a question of God's dealings with the soul on a higher, spiritual level.... Hence we must perpetually be on our guard to avoid both the Scylla of artificial, neat cataloguing and the Charybdis of vague and disordered narratives of experiences and feelings in which no distinction is made between the human and the divine.[93]

mysticus, 446–49 and DSp 10: 1782. Some other references could be gathered from Peter Dronke's *Medieval Latin and the Rise of European Love Lyric* (Oxford, 1968), vol.2, s.v. death for love, and from Fr. Willaert, *De Poëtica van Hadewijch*, 498 q.v. *doet*.

91 A. Haas, *Sermo mysticus*, 34: 'Wenn es sich mit dem mystischen Sprachen so verhält, dass es die Norm menschlichen Redens durchbricht ...dann lädt alles dazu ein, anzunehmen, dass hier gewissermassen der Schritt von den vielfältigen Erfahrungen des Menschen zurückgetan wird zur Einen Erfahrung, die sie alle trägt'.

92 A.Haas, *ibid.*, 35: 'Die mystische Rede [ist]...ein Erfahrungszeugnis, das unmittelbar über den lebendigen, seinsspendenden Gott abgelegt wird. Aber dieses Zeugnis kann nicht reinster Seinsoptimismus sein, da es — wenigstens christlich — ins Kreuz hinein führt. Man wird daher auch die mystische Erfahrung nicht so kategorisieren dürfen, dass sie als allzeit *notwendige* und beschwörbare Legitimation und Rechtfertigung für theologisches und philosophisches Reden gebraucht werden könnte. Das hiesse, sie verzwecklichen, sie missbrauchen; denn sie ist wesentlich ausserkategorial, eben gnadenhaft'.

93 D. Knowles, *The Nature of Mysticism*, 60–61. See also E. Benz, *Die Vision*, 37 and 475–76.

An ecstasy is a phenomenon transcending our human capacities to observe and catalogue. It may also be considered a weakness in the ecstatic, who is unable to endure the overwhelming action of God as he seeks union with a creature made to his image and likeness.[94] Scholars and experts have noted that before falling into ecstasy some ecstatics were often afflicted with an acute attack of fever,[95] or an excessive bodily heat,[96] or some other physical symptom.[97] It is to be expected that the burning desire of our *mulieres religiosae* could easily have fostered such effects. Deep desire pressed to the limit, the vicissitudes connected with the alternation of God's presence and absence, and the violence of an *orewoet* inevitably weakened them physically. A few examples from our *mulieres religiosae* suffice to show that they did not and could not escape such weakness before they grew stronger.

One Trinity Sunday Hadewijch received communion in bed because, as she says,

I felt such an attraction within my spirit. I could not control myself outwardly to the extent of being able to move among people. This attraction which I had inwardly was to be one with God in fruition.[98]

In her sixth vision she said that 'because of my longing I was again strongly moved and then I was taken up in the spirit'.[99] One Christmas night, she was in a different mood: 'I was downcast and was taken up in the spirit'.[100]

On one occasion, Ida of Nivelles was in the infirmary because of physical sickness and at the same time her heart was burning

94 D. Knowles, *The English Mystical Tradition*, 2nd ed., (London, 1964) 12, and Karl Rahner, 'Über Visionen und verwandte Erscheinungen', *GL* 21 (1948) 179–213; 199–200.

95 P. Dinzelbacher, *Vision*, 51: 'Der Übergang in die Ekstase, der, wie so häufig, eine Erkrankung vorausgegangen ist (Fieberanfall)'.

96 H. Thurston, *The Physical Phenomena*, 209–21.

97 E. Benz, *Die Vision*, 231–32.

98 Vision one; VM, *Visioenen*, 1: 9, ll. 1–9.

99 *Ibid.*, 65, ll. 8–10.

100 Vision 11; VM, *Visioenen*, 1: 110, ll. 1–2. In *Visioenen*, 2: 67–68, VM collected the different circumstances preceding her visions.

with a powerful and insatiable desire for the Trinity; suddenly a man of venerable countenance appeared to her and gave her a spiritual taste of the Trinity.[101] At another time she was praying with ardent desire, and suddenly her soul began to melt. Her bodily strength failed and she passed into an *alienatio*.[102]

Beatrice felt ecstasy approaching. Halfway through a sermon 'her spirit began to be marvellously touched and moved inside by the divine Spirit. The union and bond were so strong and indissoluble that her soul, active in every part of her body, immediately diffused this sense of internal embrace throughout the members of the body', and she slumped down inert into the lap of the nun sitting next to her (161,13). Near the end of 1231, Beatrice had risen from her sick bed, her health not yet fully recovered. She was attending mass in the stalls reserved for the infirm when 'suddenly the most kind Lord of mercies pierced her soul with the fire of his love as with a fiery javelin', and she heard him speaking to her. Reflecting on what she had heard, 'she was suddenly caught up in heaven through an ecstasy of contemplation' (170,4). 'Occasionally also, affected by the sweetness of heavenly joys she became pale and trembled in her body as though seized by a strong fever or paralysis... finally, exhausted by all this, her whole strength so gave way that she collapsed on her sick bed, broken and failing in almost every part of her body'(203,57). At another time 'in the spiritual washing [by Christ's blood] she was wonderfully and superhumanly kindled and set on fire by love... more than human strength can stand, and she was enraptured' (238,13).

Ida Lewis' raptures were usually connected with the Eucharist.[103] Because of the great intensity of love she felt, Ida of Leuven was 'filled with an unabating delight, at times for a week or for a fortnight or even forty days and nights'. To cool off when

---

101 *Quinque*, 254: 'Ecce subito astitit mihi vir quidam venerabilis aspectu...et dixit mihi: ego libentissime...divinitatis meae favum cordi tuo ad cumulum instillabo. Quo dicto sumpsit liquorem de ore suo emanentem et stillavit in os meum'.

102 *Ibid.*, 211: 'in mentis transiens alienationem'.

103 *AA SS* Oct.13: 117,31; 118,36; 121,46.

she judged that her delight was more than human strength could stand, she once ran to the river with a linen cloth which she plunged into the stream, then drew out and twisted around and around, repeating this over and over again.[104] It was her experience 'that as the inflow of delight intensified, her bodily strength correspondingly ebbed'.[105] Ida's biographer mentions too that 'after a long and heavy illness, she was rapt into an ecstasy'.[106] By contrast, Ida of Nivelles' biography tells us that 'she said that the more the burden of her infirmity brought her down, the more her unencumbered spirit lifted up and passed over into God'.[107] This was the way God let the *mulieres religiosae* experience their littleness and his infinity, their impotence and his omnipotence. The ecstasies and *excessus* which he gave them were his doing, not theirs. He stirred in their hearts an ongoing growing love for him, and they responded wholeheartedly to him. At the same time they knew that their closeness to and union in love with him in no way shortened the distance between the infinite and the finite. They experienced both his 'Godness' and their own 'human-ness'.

Having now treated what occurred prior to ecstasy or vision, we will in the next few pages focus on ecstasy in its highest degree, that is the *excessus* beyond the spirit, Augustine's *visio intellectualis*. Ecstasies of this kind were relatively frequent in the Late Middle Ages. In *Vision*, Peter Dinzelbacher places them in the category of *mystical ecstasies* which attain union, an immediate contact with or direct experience of God. They occurred without mental images, they cannot be described, and they took place within the soul.[108] Hadewijch claimed she was then beyond

104 *AA SS* April 2: 186,18: 'volens per modicum temporis, et ad horam ab hac sua se delectatione subducere,...cucurrit ad fluvium.

105 *Ibid.*, 'illa suis deliciis affluente, corporali quoque robore plus ob hoc in se solito decrescente'.

106 *Ibid.*, 178,26: 'post infirmitatem diuturnam et validam, in excessu mentis erepta'.

107 *Quinque*, 287: 'quanto magis corpus ejus infirmitatis pondere praemebatur, tanto liberius spiritus suus elevabatur et transibat in Deum'.

108 P. Dinzelbacher, *Vision*, 53–56. That they take place in the soul is consistent with Dinzelbacher's definition of an ecstasy. See above, n. 66 of this chapter.

the spirit, as did other *mulieres religiosae*, even if some of them do not mention the fact as explicitly and clearly as did Hadewijch.

It would have helped us to avoid misunderstandings and misinterpretations if the distinction between *ecstasis* and *excessus* had survived to the present day. But since ecstasy has gained citizenship at the expense of *excessus*, it is preferable to keep the term ecstasy without forgetting its technical difference from *excessus*. We will talk now about ecstasy as *excessus* or *alienatio*. There are known cases when such a ecstasy took place without any premonition or preparedness. It came as a totally unexpected interruption. God is always free to act when and as it pleases him, yet this presupposes that he makes the ecstatic pleasing to himself, preparing him/her to consent freely, to be made ready or open (*capax*) for such an encounter and all its consequences. The ordinary road to this extraordinary ecstasy passes along a life of *ascesis* and the inculcation of virtues needed to purify the ego from all that is egocentric and to make it ready to attain the fulness of its beauty. By this the soul cooperates in God's 'stepping in' (*ingressus*) and for its own enrapture outside itself (its *egressus*). During an *excessus*, the exterior and interior senses are both transcended and the possibility of union with God and fruition of him becomes a reality. David Knowles describes thus this mystical experience:

> A mystical knowledge of God, which is never entirely separable from an equally immediate and experiential union with God by love has three characteristics. It is recognized by the person concerned as something utterly different from and more real and adequate than all his previous knowledge and love for God. It is experienced as something at once immanent and received, something moving and filling the powers of the mind and soul. It is felt as taking place at a deeper level of the personality and soul than that on which the normal process of thought and will take place, and the mystic is aware, both in himself and in others, of the soul, its qualities and of the divine presence and action within it, as

something wholly distinct from the reasoning mind with its powers. Finally, this experience is wholly incommunicable, save as a bare statement, and in this respect all the utterances of the mystics are entirely inadequate as representations of the mystical experience, but it brings absolute certainty to the mind of the recipient. This is the traditional mystical theology, the mystical knowledge of God, in its purest form.[109]

A mystical experience is not merely a psychological phenomenon but is always trans-psychological, since it remains in ontological continuity with supernatural realities. Ontological continuity does not prevent psychological discontinuity. On the contrary, if this ontological continuity is real, mystical knowledge can only add a new psychological grasp of the divine reality, without supplementing the knowledge of faith.[110] Ecstasy (as *excessus*) has a negative character: it includes the cessation of conceptual thought. This state is not total unconsciousness, but rather an enlargement, an intensification, or even a higher form of intellectual activity, and this is its positive aspect. Since the testimony of the mystics as to their inmost states cannot be checked, it is undoubtedly permissible for a psychologist to interpret what they do say in conformity with the psychological theory which he judges to be the most acceptable.[111]

From an ecstasy in the spirit, the ecstatic is moved beyond all imagery (*Entbilderung*) to a new way of knowing devoid of images and concepts.[112] The possibility of inspecting and investigating what goes on beyond imagery is denied us. In this sense, David Bell, borrowing a phrase from Augustine, correctly speaks of a 'Doctrine of Ignorance'.[113] Wherever the *excessus* may have

109 D. Knowles, *The English Mystical Tradition*, 2–3.

110 Augustin Léonard, 'Recherches phénoménologiques autour de l'expérience mystique', *SVS* 54 (1952) 430–94; 456.

111 Joseph Maréchal, *Studies in the Psychology of the Mystics*, ET by A. Thorold, rpt (Albany, NY., 1964) 186–95.

112 Carl Albrecht, *Das mystische Erkennen* (Bremen, 1958), 29.

113 D. Bell, 'A Doctrine of Ignorance: Annihilation of Individuality in Christian and Muslim Mysticism', *Benedictus*, Studies in Honor of St Benedict

taken the ecstatic, he is still with us corporally and his behavior can be observed. The impossibility of conceptualizing what went on 'beyond the spirit' when the *mulieres religiosae* had an *excessus* is balanced by a knowledge of their daily living where they behaved as do people with a healthy psychic balance.

Among Christians are those...who are capable of receiving not only the gift of faith and the powers to love and serve God, but a new supernatural knowledge of love, the beginning of God's own knowledge of himself and love of himself which is the life of the Blessed Trinity and of the blessed in heaven, who see God as he is and know even as they are known. In them grace does more than co-operate with their human efforts; it operates itself directly in the powers which receive with free consent.... Moreover, it is the universal teaching of all the great masters that the mystical life is the pure gift of God, which cannot be deserved or expected by anyone, whatever his virtue.[114]

In a mystical experience of the sort we are speaking of, both whom and what are experienced are extremely important: God himself and a sharing in his fruition or *ghebruken*, as the *mulieres religiosae* called it. The ineffability of their mystical experiences notwithstanding, mystics tried as best they could to express the inexpressible. Unable to use ordinary language or the terminology proper to empirical knowledge, they created their own vocabulary—strange to our modern minds—by using paradoxes, oxymorons, negations, antitheses, tautologies, and repetitions, all devices of speech indicating that an overwhelming mystical experience cannot be verbally expressed.[115] Leaving aside the

of Nursia; Studies in Medieval Cistercian History 8 [R. Elder, ed.] (Kalamazoo, 1981) 30–44.

114 D. Knowles, *The English Mystical Tradition*, 7–8.

115 R. Vanneste, *Abstracta*, 10–11; A. Haas, *Sermo mysticus*, 28. This could sometimes bring some writers—including Hadewijch, all her orthodoxy notwithstanding—to use equivocal sayings at times. See J. Reynaert, *Beeldspraak*, 404–05.

vocabulary used by their mentors, [116] we allow the *mulieres religiosae* to speak for themselves.

As usual, Hadewijch is quite informative. In her fifth vision she states: 'And he took me up, out of the spirit in that highest of wonders beyond reason. There I had fruition of him as I shall eternally'. In her sixth she says:

I then fell—from myself and all I had seen in him [in the vision]—beyond the spirit and, wholly lost, fell upon his breast, the fruition of his nature, which is love. There I remained, engulfed and lost, without any comprehension at all of knowledge, or sight, or understanding, except to be one with him and to have fruition in this union. I remained in it less than half an hour.

In the ninth: 'Love came and embraced me, and I went beyond the spirit and remained lying until late that day, inebriated with unspeakable wonders'. In the tenth: 'And the Voice [who had spoken to her in the vision] embraced me with an unheard-of wonder, and I swooned in it, and my spirit failed me to see or hear more. And I lay in this fruition half an hour'. In the thirteenth: 'The fruition overcame me as before, and I sank into the fathomless abyss and went beyond the spirit whereof one can never speak at all'. In the fourteenth:

Once I lay for three days and as many nights entranced in spirit at the countenance of our Beloved. This has often lasted for that length of time, and also for the same length of time entirely beyond the spirit, lost to myself and all people (*menschen*), [I was] in fruition of him. To know how he gives himself there, to be beyond the spirit and to be in him this surpasses all other gifts and favors; then one is not less than he himself is... and I saw the place to which I was destined, in order that I might taste [Christ] Man and God as one, which no one can do unless he

116 For an overview of the mentors, see R. Javelet, *Psychologie*, 140–60.

were as God,[117] and were wholly as the one who is our
Minne.[118]

Hadewijch described the ineffability of her mystical experience
in one of her letters as well:

And in this unity in which I was taken and in which I was
enlightened, I understood this [God's] Essence (*Wesen,
Being*) and knew it more clearly than one can know anything that is knowable on earth by speech, reason or sight.
What is terrestrial cannot understand heavenly speech. For
all that is on earth, one can find words and Flemish
(*Dietsch*) enough. But for what I mean to say, there is no
Flemish, nor any other language. I know the language as
much as anyone can know it, but for this, as I said already, I
have none because as far as I know none is adequate.[119]

After Beatrice had her first mystical experience in 1217, she
said that 'God's prodigality could in no way be understood by one
who had not previously experienced it (56,70). In November

---

117 The sentence 'he were as God' (*ware al alse god*) is the equivalent of
'Deus sicuti est', an expression dear to the mentors of the *mulieres religiosae*
(for Bernard: E. Gilson, *Mystical Theology*, 235, n. 114; for William: D. Bell,
The Image, 219–20; for Richard: G. Dumeige, *Les quatre degrés*, 159–67,
particularly paragraphs 32 and 37). In some of his publications in *RAM* and
OGE, L. Reypens was mistaken in the opinion that Hadewijch, Ruusbroec and
some other mystics thought that beatific vision is possible already on earth. N.
De Paepe (*Hadewijch. Strofische Gedichten*, 144, n. 66) and B. Spaapen ('Hadewijch en het vijfde visioen', *OGE* 44 [1972] 119) accepted Reypens' position.
This opinion has been rectified by Paul Mommaers in his overview of the
spirituality in 'L'Ecole néerlandaise', *RAM* 49 (1973) 477, and by Albert
Deblaere, 'Témoignage mystique chrétien', *Studia missionalia* 26 (1977) 117–
147; 139–40 with references. Hadewijch knew very well that a 'vision of God' is
not identical with the beatific vision. See VM, *Visioenen*, 1: 152, ll. 24–43.
118 Vision 5: VM, *Visioenen*, 1: 62, ll. 62–65; vision 6:*ibid.*, 69, ll. 82–89;
vision 9: *ibid.*, 98, ll. 69–71; vision 10: *ibid.*, 105, ll. 70–74; vision 13: *ibid.*, 153,
ll. 255–58; vision 14: *ibid.*, 165–66, 145–57; 162–65.
119 Letter 17; VM, *Brieven*, 1: 144–45, ll. 108–22. P. Mommaers, 'Der
Mystiker und das Wort. Ein Einblick auf Hadewijch und Ruusbroec', *GL*, 57
(1984) 4–12, tried to show how difficult it is for mystics to communicate their
experiences comprehensibly.

1231 she had her first 'complete' mystical experience, which the biographer understood to be a vision of God face to face.[120] Beatrice took it as a confirmation of her ultimate destination (173,61) of which she had now received a foretaste. In reflecting on what she had heard after a colloquy with the Lord, 'she was suddenly caught up to heaven through the ecstasy of contemplation, stripped of her bodily senses' (172,53). Then she 'was transported to that sublime choir of the seraphim, the closest to the divine essence, caught up there in mind by the divine Spirit'.[121] 'With her soul, not her flesh' (172,56) taken up to heaven, and as the biographer (173,69) states:

> she deserved to see by the clear light of contemplation the divine essence in the fulness of its glory...and with ardent praise she rested in him with supreme beatitude, incomprehensible to human senses, clinging firmly to him in an embrace of unthinkable delight.

Around Christmas 1232

Beatrice conceived a great desire to know the Holy and Undivided Trinity. Although the Trinity is wholly incom-

120 *Vita* 174,75. Beatrice's biographer appeals to Augustine (whom he seldom quotes) and to Haymo. There can be no doubt that this is Haymo of Auxerre (d. about 865–866), not Haymo, the bishop of Halberstadt (see Henri Barré, 'Haymo d'Auxerre', DSp, 7: 91–97). The biographer's quotations are taken from Haymo's *Expositio ad Epistolam II ad Corinthios*, and they are, in fact, mostly verbatim quotations from Augustine. Among Augustinian scholars there is little agreement touching Augustine's position in this matter. E. Hendrikx, *Augustinus Verhältniss zur Mystik* (Würzburg, 1936) 178–81, denies that Augustine believed in the possibility of a beatific vision on earth (except in two questionable instances). M. Korger, 'Grundproblemen der Augustinischen Erkenntnislehre', *Recherches Augustiniennes* 2 (1962) 33–57 thinks that Augustine never denied the face-to-face visions of Moses and Paul, the representatives of the Old and New Testament. D. Bell (*The Image*, 87), who reviewed the whole problem arrived at the conclusion that 'what Augustine says depends on time and text, and I think there can be no doubt that he underwent considerable indecision and vacillation on this important question'.

121 *Vita*, 172,55: 'divino spiritu mente rapta'. The biographer does not show any indication that he ever read Hadewijch's writings.

prehensible to human understanding, she aspired to the unattainable with great confidence, not rashly like some who seek things too high for them and search into what is deeper than their understanding, but with humble heart, devout mind and fervent love. Not in vain either, for... it happened that the light of heavenly truth aglittered like lightning into her opened heart. There in a moment of time she merited to lay hold of what she sought; what she could not explore by vigor of mind, the divine Spirit breathed into her through heavenly grace, not to store away in her mind but in order to enjoy (*ad fruendum*) for the briefest moment. When she called upon all the keenness of her senses to grasp the truth laid open to her, and was ready to commit to memory what in a moment and in the wink of an eye she had perceived of the most high Trinity, the light of knowledge was suddenly withdrawn. What she thought she held in her mind, escaped her heart, passing like a flash of lightning. She did not acquire it until the most high God took pity on the fervent desire of his chosen one, and again illuminated her interiorly with a ray of the aforementioned knowledge.[122]

When she had remained a short time in this sweet contemplation [of the Trinity], she quickly came back to herself, and thought to recall to mind and to commit to memory by the sharpness of her interior sense what she had learned in mind only by the revelation of divine wisdom. But warned by the Lord to rest from this vain labor, she reverently acquiesced and obeyed. The divine reply asserted her that what she less prudently presumed she understood by human sense, escaped not so much hers as all human understanding, and could be grasped only by the grace of heavenly revelation.[123]

Her friend, Ida of Nivelles, coming out of a vision in which she had seen the Trinity present at the eucharistic consecration, could

122 *Vita*, 213,4.
123 *Vita*, 217,98.

find no words to express what she had seen.[124] Ida Lewis'
biographer reports that a nun who saw her in ecstasy had no doubt
that Ida had been enraptured by the ineffable delights of
heaven.[125] Ida herself said: 'when I come back [from an ecstasy]
I can in no way explain what I experienced'.[126] At another time,
coming out of an ecstasy, the same Ida told the nun who took care
of her: 'I am not amazed that people should wonder about me. I
myself am not amazed. What I wonder about greatly are the
unheard-of, ineffable, and marvellous things the divine mercy
allows me to become acquainted with and to experience so
abundantly'.[127]

After Ida of Leuven returned to herself after an ecstasy, she did
not know whether it had happened in or out of the body, but she
could describe her vision to some extent. Yet she felt 'utterly
unable to express the delectation she had experienced. No full
justice could be done by words to make intelligible what transcends all human senses'.[128] On another day, after she had gone
to communion, 'the Most High enlightened her so abundantly
with the graces and gifts of the Holy Spirit that no mind could
ascend to it nor any intellect grasp it, to express it in words or
understand it with the heart'.[129]

Ida Lewis lodged an understandable complaint. One day, called
to the parlor after an ecstatic experience, she said: 'How

124 *Quinque*, 271:'nec tamen omnino effari potuit divinum illud et inscru-
tabile mysterium quod intuebatur'.

125 *AA SS* Oct.13: 120,42: 'Illa vero cognoscens et intelligens absque nebula
dubii quod fuisset virgo laudabilis rapta mentis in exstasi ad illas ineffabiles
paradysi delicias'.

126 *Ibid.*, 120,41: 'ad me reversa, bona quae habui non possum aliquatenus
explicare'.

127 *Ibid.*, 121, 45: 'miror et ego plurimum super ineffabilibus et mirabilibus
inauditis, quae divina misericordia largiente, me permittit ...agnoscere tam
largius et sentire'.

128 *AA SS* April 2: 166,33 : 'ad se reversa, visionem aliquatenus explicare
praevaluit, delectationis dulcedinem...nullis postea verbis exprimere potuit,
quippe quae cunctis humanis sensibus supereminens, ad plenam sui declara-
tionem qualiumcumque verborum intelligentiam non admisit'.

129 *Ibid.*, 175,16: 'tam copiosa gratiarum et charismatum Sancti Spiritus
affluentia perlustravit Altissimus, quod ad id verbotenus exprimendum intel-
ligendumve corde tenus nullus omnino consurgeret animus, nullus caperet
intellectus'.

extremely difficult it is to come back to oneself and to have to talk about alien things immediately after having tasted and savored the sweetness of the Lord'.[130]

Unable to express the ineffable, incapable of explaining the 'doctrine of ignorance', the *mulieres religiosae*, each in her own way, experienced God to the extent that he allowed. Hadewijch spoke of fruition; Beatrice of delight and fruition; Ida of Nivelles mentioned the inexpressible marvels she had seen; Ida Lewis the unheard-of, ineffable realities she had experienced, Ida of Leuven spoke of degustation, and Alice of Schaarbeek was described as pregnant (*gravida*) with God.

Our ignorance of such experiences is only intellectual, and not wholly black and desolate. When 'in the spirit', the visionaries' imagination, feelings and phantasies could play tricks, as they do in our dreams, but this could not happen when they were 'beyond the spirit'. We need not expect fool-proof guarantees about what they experienced beyond the spirit. The *mulieres religiosae* who had the experience have told us that what is beyond the spirit is beyond conceptualization, theirs as well as ours. All these women repeatedly said that the ineffable can only be experienced. All we have is their affirmation and our own knowledge that beyond is beyond. Yet their avowal was confirmed by their way of living and their behavior, the normality of their personalities, and their concern for their neighbors,—all of which militate against the suspicion of egocentricity, fraud, or other kinds of deceit. An open and willing heart already believes that union with God can be and has been experienced by some persons and to some extent. God's inexpressible Otherness is turned toward us, lovingly radiating the unitive love which burns within him and to which he invites us.[131]

---

130 *AA SS* Oct.13: 114, 23: 'Declaravit quanti sit ponderis spiritualibus, Dei dulcedine degustata, confestim ad se regredi, deque rebus forensecis posse loqui'.

131 A. Haas, *Sermo mysticus*, 34–35: 'Die Vereinigung mit Gott, die Erfahrung werden darf, ist ja sachlich auch nichts anderes als die Erfahrung von Gottes Andersheit gerade noch in seiner gnadenhaften, liebenden Zuwendung, wenn auch der unitive Aspekt gewisslich darin dominiert'.

In earlier times ecstatics had visions very early in life, at about ten years of age or less.[132] The *mulieres religiosae* were a little older, but relatively young, when they began to have mystical experiences. Hadewijch wrote that 'since I was ten years old I have been so overwhelmed by passionate Love that I should have died during the first two [following] years, if God had not given me forms of strength other than people ordinarily receive'.[133] She stated explicitly in her sixth vision that she was at the time nineteen. [134] Ida of Nivelles received her first 'visitation' before she entered Rameya at sixteen.[135] Beatrice had her first mystical experience when she was seventeen, at the end of her stay in Rameya.[136] Ida Lewis was fourteen when she had her first *tripudium*,[137] and some two years later she began having mystical experiences.[138] The biographical information we have on Alice of Schaarbeek does not allow us to pinpoint her first mystical experiences exactly. She entered Ter Kameren at a young age, and her biographer mentions how rapidly she advanced in virtuous living even before she was stricken with leprosy,[139] and more quickly afterwards.[140] Ida of Leuven may have been born in 1210; she entered Roosendaal when she was perhaps twenty-two in order to escape the attention she had already attracted by several mystical experiences.[141]

---

132 P. Dinzelbacher, *Vision*, 222.

133 Letter 11; VM *Brieven*, 1: 93–94, ll. 10–15.

134 VM; *Visioenen*, 1: 65, ll. 1–2.

135 *Quinque*, 204: 'Ut merito credendum sit lacrymas illas ex fonte gratiae coelestis emanasse. Haec prima fuit visitatio'.

136 *Vita*, 55,27.

137 *AA SS* Oct.13: 112,13: 'Ut cor eruptans gaudia, quid haberet interius, corporis ex indicio signis manifestissimis loqueretur'.

138 *Ibid.*, 113,18. She went every Sunday to communion; this practice supposes that she had already made her profession at a date not specified by the biographer.

139 *AA SS* June 2: 479,9: 'Cum ipsa virtutum augmento in annis cresceret et tamen discretione virtutum numerum annorum superaret'.

140 *Ibid.*: Once she realized what her leprosy meant,'delectata est et consolata'. *Ibid.*, 479,11: 'Tanta jubilatione, tanta mentis exultatione... cor dilectae (Alice), quod prae nimio animi tripudio, quod sentiret. quidve secum ageretur, penitus ignoraret'.

141 J. Van Schoors, *Ida van Leuven*, diss. (Leuven, 1983) 92.

At the time of the *mulieres religiosae* movement, more women seemed to experience ecstasies and visions than did men. In the thirteenth century the ratio is about fifty-fifty, but in the fourteenth century the women outnumbered the men, particularly in Germany.[142] Statistics could lead us to unwarranted conclusions. Numbers are not as important as the depth, character and personality of the persons involved. Alongside the Helfta nuns, Clare Sciffi and Angela of Foligno, such Flemish women as Hadewijch, Beatrice, the three Idas, and Alice of Schaarbeek undeniably stand out among the *mulieres religiosae*, each in her own unique way. In the early Middle Ages social movements normally affected women of the nobility, while in the twelfth and thirteenth centuries more middle-class women were involved. As we have seen, the *mulieres religiosae*'s 'nobility' lay primarily in their conviction that they were created to the image and likeness of God. Women's exclusion from ministry, from other exterior activities and higher education may also have led them to pursue the way of the 'inner path', but not with the intentionality some modern feminists posit.

In the thirteenth century there was a documented *mulieres religiosae* movement in Belgium, as there was one in the neighboring Rhineland (the two movements were, *de facto*, interrelated), in Saxony, Switzerland and Italy.[143] To speak of a 'Flemish *ecstatic* movement' seems farfetched. One could be impressed by the prologue of the biography of Mary of Oignies (1173–1213), written shortly after her death by her admirer, James of Vitry, later cardinal, and addressed to Fulco, or Foulques, the Cistercian bishop of Toulouse. James mentions, also in his *Historia Occidentalis*, many exceptional phenomena occurring at that time in Belgium:

142 P. Dinzelbacher, *Vision*, 222–28.
143 See A. Mens, *Oorsprong*, 113–21; Herman Grundmann, 'Die geschichtlichen Grundlagen der Deutschen Mystik', *Altdeutsche und Altniederländische Mystik* (K.Ruh ed.), (Darmstadt, 1964) 80; Hans Neumann, 'Mechtild von Magdeburg und die mittelniederländische Frauenmystik', *Medieval German Studies* (London, 1965) 242.

I call upon your holiness as a witness, for with your eyes you have seen the wonderful operations of God and the distribution of graces among various persons.... You have seen some women so dissolved by such a special and wonderful affection of love for God that they languished with desire, only rarely able to rise from their beds for many years, having no other cause for their infirmity than him for whom their souls were melting with desire.... Other women were rapt outside themselves with such an inebriation of spirit that, resting in that holy silence almost all day long... [they were] alienated from anything exterior. No shout could awake them; they did not feel any bodily injury, even if they were vehemently pricked.

I saw another woman who was kept by her Spouse for nearly thirty years with such jealousy in the cloister that there could be no going outside of it for her, even if a thousand men tried to drag her with their hands. For many times she tried to leave, even with some people drawing her, but the attempt was in vain and consequently quickly abandoned.

I saw another who was rapt outside of herself frequently, as often as twenty-five times a day. While I was present, she was rapt, I think, seven times. She remained immobile until her return to herself, in whatever position she had been when the rapture seized her; neither did she fall, however much she was bent over because her familiar spirit supported her. Sometimes her hand remained immobile in the air just as it was when the rapture seized her. When she returned to herself, she was filled with such joy, that she was impelled to show her interior joy with a bodily clapping of the hands.

I know one of these holy women who was longing so vehemently to be refreshed with the flesh of the true Lamb. The true Lamb himself did not let her languish any longer, but gave himself to her, and thus refreshed, she grew strong again. I saw another one in whom the Lord worked so marvellously that although she lay dead for a long time, her soul came back to her body and she lived again before her body was buried in the ground. She obtained from the Lord the grace to suffer purgatory while still living in this world. Therefore she was afflicted by the Lord for a long time so that sometimes she rolled herself in fire, and sometimes she stayed for a long time in icy water in winter, and sometimes also she was forced to enter the tombs of the dead. Finally after this penance she lived in such peace and deserved such great graces from the Lord that often she was rapt in spirit and conducted the souls of the deceased to purgatory, or through purgatory to the heavenly realms without any harm to herself.[144]

James of Vitry's report shows that many extraordinary phenomena were happening as it also indicates that James took for granted a supernatural cause for all these occurrences, some of them quite bizarre. All that has so far been said about the *mulieres religiosae* does not point to a widespread *ecstatic movement* in Belgium. Ecstatics formed a very small minority among the thousands of *mulieres religiosae* at that time. It is true that Beatrice and Ida Lewis are presented in an ecstatic posture in the legendary 'family tree' of Humbelina, painted in 1643.[145] Ida of

144 *AA SS* June 5: 542–72; n. 5–8 and Reypens, *Vita*, 221–23. For brevity's sake the stories about the (here) superfluous biblical texts are omitted. James of Vitry well-meant credulity can be easily followed in G. Frenken, *Die Exempla des Jacob von Vitry* (Munich, 1914) particularly in James' *Sermones communes*, 93–149. See also Thomas Fr.Crane, *The Exempla or Illustrative Stories from the "Sermones Vulgares" of Jacques de Vitry* (New York, 1870, rpt 1971) wherein he lists what he called James' 'popular tales'.

145 The painting (made in 1643 and perhaps (?) a copy of an older one) is preserved in the monastery of Mariënlof in Kerniel, Belgium. The plates of this legendary 'Tree of Humbelina', showing Beatrice and Ida Lewis in an ecstatic posture, can be found in *OGE* 10 (1936) between pages 26–27, and *ibid.*, 57 (1983) facing p.321 respectively. Both have their arms extended, and forearms and hands lifted upward. In his poorly edited version of Beatrice's *Seven Manieren*, her biographer writes that 'hence, with her heart lifted up, her hands and her eyes too were lifted up to heaven under the impulse of her heart, as if even those bodily members aspired to the heavenly fatherland' (260,536). For contemporary sketches, see François Garnier, *Le language de l'Image au Moyen Age. Signification et Symbolique* (Paris, 1982) 223–26: Bras écartés.

Leuven too was described as standing in an ecstatic posture.[146] But do a few ecstatics give us sufficient authority to speak of a native ecstatic movement as several Flemish scholars still do? It seems more appropriate to speak of an ecstatic phenomenon than of an ecstatic movement.[147]

An ecstasy might last a short time (*modicum*) or 'half an hour', a biblical (Rv 8:1) more than temporal expression used by Bernard,[148] William,[149] and others. In 1231, when Beatrice had her ecstasy beyond the spirit, it could have lasted no more than a few, perhaps five, minutes (176,12 and 180,154). Hadewijch spoke once of a short time, and twice of half an hour.[150] In her fourteenth vision, however, she says that within twenty-four hours she was rapt in spirit three times, frequently for three days and nights, and that she was equally as long rapt beyond the spirit.[151] Ecstatics could hardly have been able to evaluate the time they were beyond the spirit, since all conceptualization, including that of time, had ceased. Nor could bystanders have been able to tell how long an ecstasy beyond the spirit lasted. Neither they nor the ecstatics themselves had the means to use a time clock.

---

146 *AA SS* April 2: 173,12: 'ad caelestia contemplanda cor suum cum manibus' (elevavit).

147 This stress—especially by prominent philologists as N. De Paepe [*Hadewijch. Strofische Gedichten*, 134 and 334] and H. Vekeman [*TNTL* 88 (1972) 179]—on a 'ecstatic movement' in what is now called Belgium could well be partly a reaction against nineteenth-century German scholars who corralled German and Flemish (*Diets*) medieval writers and texts under the heading *Deutsch* (German). Today German philologists now distinguish between *altdeutsche* (Old German), *altniederländische* and even *altflämische* (Old Dutch or Old Flemish) *Mystic* (Mysticism). Belgium and what is now 'The Netherlands' were the Low Countries (*Lage Landen*). The southern part, which is roughly equivalent to Belgium, was in the forefront of spirituality during the twelfth, thirteenth and fourteenth centuries, while the northern part, roughly equivalent to the modern Netherlands, began to become conspicuous during the second part of the fourteenth century.

148 Grad hum 7,21; SBOp 3:32; CF 13:49. Consciousness of time is practically absent. See C. Albrecht, *Psychologie des mystischen Bewusstseins*, 78: 'Die Wegmarken für das Zeitgefühl fehlen'.

149 Contempl 4,10; PL 184:372D.

150 Vision 5; VM, *Visioenen*, 1: 62, l.65; vision 6: *ibid.* 69, l. 89; vision 10, *ibid.*, 165, l.74.

151 Vision 14; VM, *Visioenen*, 1: 164, ll.125–26; *ibid.*, 165, ll. 145–49.

Bystanders could, however, determine the length of time ecstatics were unconscious: Ida of Nivelles remained so several hours, from communion till vespers the next day.[152] Ida Lewis was unconscious from communion for the rest of the day or for half a day.[153] Ernst Arbman estimated 'the length of ecstatic absorption' at a short period of half an hour, though he cites cases in which an ecstasy lasted three or more days.[154] Peter Dinzelbacher came to the conclusion that visionaries fall into two categories. Visionaries of the older generations remained unconscious for various periods, some lasting even a month, with several days being the average. In the second category (that of the *mulieres religiosae*), the average was several hours, but the individual instances ranged from a very short time to two or three days at most.[155] At any rate, though a vision may follow an ecstasy in the spirit, when the ecstatic moves 'beyond the spirit', we again face the wall of ignorance.

Although the *mulieres religiosae* were unable to recount what they experienced during an ecstasy, they remembered it, sometimes painfully, and would contrast it with the miseries of the exile in which they found themselves afterwards.[156] However, this was not always the case. Beatrice's biographer relates that she 'quickly returned to herself, and retained the sweetness of contemplation, but only in memory, not experiencing it' (237,52). Hadewijch stated that she tasted what she had experienced, without mentioning the duration of this taste.[157] At times the aftertaste and its duration are explicitly mentioned. Ida of Nivelles retained an aftertaste for one month,[158] or even two.[159] On one occasion related to the Trinity, Ida Lewis had an aftertaste lasting ten

---

152 *Quinque*, 271, 257.

153 *AA SS* Oct. 13: 118,36; 121,46.

154 E. Arbman, *Ecstasy*, vol.2: 85–95.

155 P. Dinzelbacher, *Vision*, 141–45: Der Visionär und die Zeit.

156 See above, Chapter X pp. 284–85.

157 Vision 3, VM, *Visioenen* 1: 44, ll. 23–24. See also her letter 18, VM, *Brieven*, 1: 156, ll. 112–15.

158 *Quinque*, 251–53, already mentioned in Chapter X p. 325, n. 72.

159 *Ibid.*, 257–58.

days.[160] Beatrice remained dazzled for a whole week after she received her consecration as a virgin (77,50). For one month she enjoyed the aftertaste of her first mystical experience (59,130), and the one in November 1231 (182,102) left an aftertaste for two months. The aftereffects related to the Eucharist have been related above in Chapter Eleven.

The ecstatic *mulieres religiosae* were more than once annoyed by the quite understandable curiosity of the people with whom they lived. As we mentioned in part two of this study, they were also sometimes belittled and mocked by people who had chosen the same life-style, held the same faith, and were shaped by the same religious, cultural, economic and social environment. Biographers were often aware that the remarkable information they intended to communicate would be greeted with disbelief, if not sarcasm.[161] It is still fashionable, even in scientific circles, to look down on ecstasies and visions as if all of them were due purely to imagination and subjectivity. Scientific objectivity can also become subjective.[162] Hadewijch seems not to have been far off the mark when she writes that 'when people hear something they cannot understand, they begin by doubting it'.[163] All this does not dispense us from from asking with David Knowles:

160 *AA SS* Oct.13: 117,33.

161 Thomas of Cantimpré said as much in his *Vita Margarete de Ypris*, re-edited by G.Meersseman in *AFP* 18 (1948) 106–30; 119, ll. 37–38. More such cases are mentioned by P. Dinzelbacher in 'Das Christusbild der heiligen Lutgard von Tongeren', *OGE* 56 (1982) 217–77; 221, n. 13. In his fabulous *Bonum universale de Apibus* and in several other biographies, however, the same Thomas does indeed tell some unbelievable stories. Ida of Nivelles' biographer attacks sceptical readers, who would not take seriously what he wrote about her (*Quinque*, 241, 243, 248, 281 and the prologue omitted by C. Henriquez, but published in *CCH*, Pars I [Brussels, 1889] 223). *Legendaria* such as Caesarius of Heisterbach's *Dialogus miraculorum* and Conrad of Eberbach's *Exordium Magnum Cisterciense* and similar collections help little to evoke trust in genuine biographers. It should be stressed, however, that their intention was to tell not 'true', but rather morally edifying stories.

162 See, for instance, *Les Visions mystiques*, (Nouvelles de l'Institut Catholique de Paris, n.1, February 1977) (Paris,1977), (reviewed by P. Dinzelbacher, *OGE* 55 [1981] 285–87), and the remarks by the same author in the introduction of his study on Lutgard, *OGE* 56 (1982) 217–21.

163 Letter 22; VM, *Brieven*, 1: 191, ll 89–90.

What is the nature of what are called visions, locutions, raptures and the like? ....The best answer is based on two principles, the one theological, the other philosophical. The first is, that God suits his gifts to the various degrees of advancement that souls have reached. The second, which in reality is another version of the first, is that whatever is received, depends for the manner of its perception upon the capacity and potentiality of the individual soul [*quidquid recipitur, secundum modum recipientis recipitur*]. In other words, it is the imperfect human organism that receives perceptibly, but inadequately, the divine gift to the soul, and it receives it in such a way as to scale it down to its own capacity.[164]

As we have said already, the *mulieres religiosae* were 'madly in love with God'. It is obviously from this point of view that the ecstasies and the visions of the *mulieres religiosae* should be regarded. Two parties—the human and the divine—are involved and affect each other, and the human party stays within the realm of observation. As D. Knowles commented:

When, partly by its own efforts, assisted by grace, and partly by the direct action of God upon it, a soul has freed itself from all inordinate love of, and advertence to, anything apart from God, the divine agency, the Holy Spirit, may take possession of its faculties and 'infuse' love and knowledge to which the recipient opposes no barriers; he has strength to bear this infusion, this contact with God, and the purity to accept it. He becomes to a greater or less extent united in will and love with God. As one so united he is, far more truly than before, a fully developed personality, since he not only realizes to the full his natural potentialities, but also liberates God's action upon it, the *potentia obedientialis*, the capacity of the creature to receive powers of a supernatural kind in obedience and submission to God. On the empirical level, the mystical life is usually distinguished by an

164 D. Knowles, *The English Mystical Tradition*, 12.

awareness, on the part of the individual concerned, of the existence of the soul at a deeper level than that of ordinary mental consciousness, and often also of the indwelling of God, the Three Divine Persons, within it.[165]

In ecstasies in the spirit, visions and allocutions occur in a sense-perceptible way: Christ is seen as a child or a man; Mary appears sometimes with, sometimes without her baby, sometimes grieving for the way people behave; saints and other celestial beings are seen as if present in a spatio-temporal sense, — even though Christ is no longer a baby, or Mary a mother with her baby in her arms, nor are the saints moving or speaking as if they were still in their earthly corporeal state. For that reason such visions are at least to be presumed to be imaginative visions. According to Karl Rahner, 'the imaginative vision, which presupposes infused contemplation, is only the radiation and reflex of contemplation in the sphere of the senses, the incarnation of the mystical process of the spirit'.[166] Once the imagination comes into play, illusions and delusions can, and sometimes do, appear at the horizon.[167]

Another problem is caused by scholars who do not always use the same terminology,[168] or mean the same thing when they speak of visions.[169] Though Peter Dinzelbacher's definition of a vision is exacting, it helps us to avoid confusion in this matter, more by way of precision than of elimination. A 'complete' vision requires five characteristics: it is an experience in which — 1. someone in a supra-natural way — 2. is transposed from his

---

165 *Ibid.*, 18.

166 K. Rahner, *Visions and Prophesies* (Quaestiones disputatae 10) , ET by Ch. Henkey and R. Strachan, 3rd ed. (New York, 1964) 57 and 62–63.

167 K. Rahner, *ibid.* 66–69, lists cases where visionaries show 'plenty of historical falsehood, theological error or distortions, and subjectivity extending to bad taste'.

168 E. Arbman, for instance, (*Ecstasy*, 1: 225) prefers to call an apparition a 'waking vision'.

169 L. Reypens counted some thirty visions in Lutgard's biography, 'Sint Lutgarts mystieke opgang', *OGE* 20 (1946) 11, while P. Dinzelbacher (*OGE* 56 [1982] 222) says, in accordance with his definition, that Lutgard seems never to have had visions, but plenty of apparitions.

surroundings into another place — 3. The person transported in this way beholds this place and all that it contains as a describable image — 4. The transportation occurs in an ecstasy (or in a dream), — 5. in which something hitherto unknown to him is disclosed.[170]

If any of these five characteristics is missing, there is no vision in the strict sense. The amazingly numerous medieval texts wherein one or more of the five characteristics are missing should for that reason be called not visions—even if the texts use the term vision, —but apparitions or something else. Hadewijch had several visions in the strict sense,[171] as did Beatrice,[172] and Ida of Nivelles.[173] Sometimes visions were 'requested',[174] as were apparitions.[175]

Classification of visions is often another source of confusion.[176] Because the visions of the *mulieres religiosae* took place in a religious context, they are usually divided in accordance with Augustine's threefold visionary scale.[177] The ascent begins with ordinary corporeal objects, and leads from there to the mental or imaginative images of those objects. This second level is called the *spiritual* and covers a wide area, ranging from simple dream-visions to the Revelation of Saint John the Divine, but the

170 P. Dinzelbacher, *Vision*, 29: 'Von einer Vision sprechen wir dann, wenn ein Mensch das Erlebnis hat, aus seiner Umwelt auf aussernatürliche Weise in einen anderen Raum versetzt zu werden, er diesen Raum beziehungsweise dessen Inhalte als beschreibbares Bild schaut, diese Versetzung in Ekstase (oder im Schlaf) geschieht, und ihm dadurch bisher Verborgenes offenbar wird'.

171 Visions 1,3,5,8,11,12,13. The fourth and sixth visions take place in too abstract surroundings. See P. Dinzelbacher, *Vision*, 130.

172 *Vita*, 172,53; 215,46; 223,28; 236,30; R-VM, *Seven Manieren*, 30–31, ll. 30–36.

173 *Quinque*, 211, 266–68, and her 'Brückenvision', *ibid.*, 221–23.

174 Beatrice, *Vita*, 52,107, though Ida of Nivelles told her that she might anticipate it (51,74).

175 Ida of Nivelles, *Quinque*, 251–53, 254–55; — Alice of Schaarbeek, *AA SS* June 2: 482,30; — Ida Lewis, *AA SS* Oct.13: 117,33.

176 See Dinzelbacher's *Vision*, 78–89: Die Typisierung der mittelalterlichen Visionen. Visions can be looked at from the aspect of literature, theology, psychology, history, sociology or other diciplines and under the same terms studied from divergent aspects.

177 From his *De Genesi ad litteram*, 12,15 onward; PL 34: 458 and ff.

constant basis which runs throughout is that these are all conceptual formations on the imaginative level. The third level is the
intellectual, which is extra or rather supra-conceptual, and therefore above and beyond *corporalia* and corporeal images.[178]

Visions of some *mulieres religiosae* prove to be full of vivid
detail. Ida of Leuven had a 'vision' with her physical eyes — in
fact, an hallucination: 'She saw the sky opening and a great flood
with an abundance of sunrays gushing down, passing through her
in and out. She reported later that she had seen all this with her
bodily eyes'.[179] Spiritual visions, which some authors prefer to
call imaginative, are the most frequent. They include the visions
seen 'in the spirit'. They are an echo of the visionary's interior,
spiritual striving toward God,[180] or what Beatrice called an impetus or reflex 'of the vigor from the desire for eternal things'.[181]
Ida of Leuven was certainly not a feminist in the modern sense,
nor was it possible in her day even to think about women being
ordained to the priesthood. Yet, one day 'rapt into ecstasy she saw
herself standing behind the celebrating priest, herself dressed as a
priest in vestments priceless beyond all telling. Thus fittingly
attired and unseen by the priest, she was refreshed by the reception of the sacrament of the Lord's body and blood'.[182]

Most of the time when Hadewijch, Beatrice, the three Idas, and
Alice of Schaarbeek saw Christ in an imaginative vision, they
conversed with him, frequently calling him 'the Beloved' (*dilectus*), often prefixed by 'sweet'.[183] As for their visions of the

---

178 D. Bell, *The Image*, 67.
179 *AA SS* April 2: 165,26.
180 K. Rahner 'Über Visionen', *GL* 21 (1948) 199.
181 *Vita*, 219,11: 'vis fortitudinis ex eternorum desiderio... cuius impetus...fortis fuit et validus'.
182 *AA SS* April 2: 183,5. In fact, this has little to do with the priesthood. The
celebrating assistant chaplain had made cutting remarks to Ida, who refused to
meet him when he asked three times to see her in order to apologize. When Ida
had digested her hurt and felt able to be reconciled with him, she stood next to
him in priestly dress at communion time during Mass and told him so later since
he had been unaware of Ida's 'vision'. If Ida lacked education, she certainly had
imagination.
183 *Suavis* or a similar word expresses not precisely 'sweetness', but rather
tender familiarity and affection. For a more extensive explication, see

Trinity, they could not 'see' the Trinity directly, but they spoke instead of the divine attributes: God's beauty, power, goodness or simply the Godhead.[184] Hadewijch's visions are rather symbolic than allegorical, though occasionally the latter also occur.[185]

In the description of their visions, the *mulieres religiosae* used images gathered from daily living and stored in their minds by ordinary observations and impressions. Their familiarity with the Bible, readings, the daily liturgy, the available iconography, and their own reflections and meditations naturally filtered into their visions. A few examples make this clear.

On a Christmas night, Ida Lewis heard a voice saying:'this is my Son, the Beloved', and Ida of Leuven heard the same just before she went to communion on the feast of Epiphany.[186] After an intense prayer Beatrice, 'caught up beyond herself in ecstasy of mind, saw with the eyes of the mind the heavens opened and Jesus standing at the right hand of the power of God'.[187] Enraptured in the spirit, Ida of Nivelles had a vision of a fortified castle built on top of a high mountain and it was revealed to her that this was the place of blessedness (*locus beatitudinis*, viz. heaven). At the bottom of the mountain there were several narrow paths leading up to the top. People went up, some quickly, some slowly, and all arrived by great effort at the top. Looking around, Ida saw at the left side of the mountain's base a deep valley of misfortune, with a large and broad street running along it. Many people, well dressed, having great fun and enjoying themselves went down

P. Dinzelbacher's *Vision*, 155–65: Verbale Kommunikation. See also above Chapter XI, n. 69. The opposite of sweetness is not sourness but dryness as M.A. Ewer noted in *A Survey of Mystical Symbolism* (London-New York) 1933, 53 and 150 and quoted in J. Reynaert's *Beeldspraak*, 206, n. 86.

184 See, for instance, J. Reynaert, *Beeldspraak*, 144–51 for Hadewijch, or Beatrice's *Vita*, 43, 40; 55, 29; 164, 58; 213, 5; 217, 89; 223, 36.

185 VM, *Visioenen*, 2: 87; P. Dinzelbacher, *Vision*, 174.

186 See below, nn. 200 and 201.

187 *Vita*, 149,80. This text refers to Acts 7:56 relating the deacon Stephen being stoned to death. A breviary of Spermalie, a community of Cistercian nuns in Sijsele near Bruges, preserved in Bruges' seminary MS 54/100 and written about 1270 has an illuminated letter H, showing a kneeling nun in front of the stoned Stephen. Plate 14 of '*Vlaamse kunst op perkament* (Bruges, 1981) is a colored miniature of this scene.

that street leading to hell.[188] In some of her letters, Hadewijch wrote about the one way leading to God and the many ways leading to perdition.[189]

Some visions are manifestly inspired by the liturgy,[190] some others by spiritual readings,[191] or a meditation:

It happened on one Christmas day that Beatrice had begun to apply the whole of her heart's intention to fervent meditation and to treat carefully in her heart the holy mystery of the Lord's incarnation. Behold, she was rapt on high in ecstasy of mind, and her spirit was raised up by the divine spirit to see an admirable vision. She looked and the all-powerful and eternal Father was emitting from himself a great river, from which many brooks and brooklets branched forth here and there, which offered a drink of water springing up to eternal life to those who willed to approach them.[192]

Visions could also have been influenced by iconography: Beatrice of Zwijveke 'saw the heavens opening and Jesus offering himself for us on the altar, and the Father showing the wounds in

188 *Quinque*, 244–46. The biographer, not Ida, compares the ones who went up the mountain to members of religious orders. This vision is based on Lk. 13: 23 and parallels.

189 J. Reynaert, *Beeldspraak*, 250 with references.

190 Some examples are mentioned in Chapter XI on the Eucharist. Some appearances are related to religious feasts.

191 Ida of Nivelles' 'Brückenvision', for instance, is marked by Gregory the Great's *Dialogi de vita et miraculis patrum Italicorum*. See P. Dinzelbacher, 'Ida von Nijvels Brückenvision, *OGE* 52 (1978) 182.

192 *Vita*, 215,48. The river symbolized Christ, the brooks the marks of his passion and the brooklets the gifts of grace. Beatrice intended to stress 'the holy mysteries of the Lord's incarnation'. At the end of this vision she followed the river to its source and she understood the mystery of the Trinity, three persons existing in the essence of the one God. Beatrice's vision could also be related to Richard's commentary on the Apocalypse (*In Apocalypsim* 7,7; PL 196: 875B–77C): 'De fluvio aquae vivae et ligno vitae, et fructu ejus' (about the river of living water, the tree of life and its fruits).

Jesus' hands, feet and side'.[193] Ida of Leuven yearned to see the infant Christ and to join the Magi in offering gifts and adoring him.[194] 'In her body or out of it, I do not know, God knows, she was transported to a certain house [the biographer expressed his belief that this helicoptering was done by angelic hands] where she found Mary and the Infant. She fell to her knees and adored him in the manner of the Magi as she had so long wished to do'.[195]

The description of visions occasionally gives a good insight into the visionary herself. One shows Ida of Nivelles, a mature, emotional woman, another the uneducated Ida of Leuven, an imaginative, sentimental young woman. The texts also indicate the biographers' inability to picture the scene, though both were credulous men.

While an abbot was celebrating mass for Ida of Nivelles in a church near Liège, an immense light illumined her interiorly. Suddenly Mary stepped forward, holding her baby in her arms, and gave him to Ida saying: 'Take him, put him on your lap and enjoy yourself, hugging and kissing him'. Meanwhile Mary sat on a nearby chair and watched their intimacy tenderly and merrily. Finally, when the delightfulness of the embraces and kisses had run its course (*jucunditate expleta*) Mary received her baby back from Ida and disappeared.[196]

As Ida of Leuven attended mass one day, she was rapt into ecstasy between the epistle and gospel. Mary came with her baby and put him on Ida's lap. Ida hugged him closely to herself with 'embraces of arms and eyes', while Mary stood watching quietly,

193 L. Reypens, 'Nog een dertiendeuse mystieke Cisterciënsernon', *OGE* 23 (1949) 246, 1.126–28. This vision occurred to her seven times between the Tuesday after Easter and Pentecost. In *Lexikon der christlichen Ikonographie* vol.1 (Rome, 1968) 529, plate 6, W. Braunfels has such a miniature taken from a missal of about 1130 from Cambrai, and it is also reproduced on plate 22 of N. Perella's *The Kiss*, referred to below, Chapter XVI, n. 2.

194 *AA SS* April: 166,31.

195. *Ibid.*, 166,32. This *desired* vision is painted in a miniature of a missal from Flanders, made about 1253, which is now preserved in the Boston Public Library. The reproduction is published in *Vlaamse kunst op perkament*, plate 64, and its artistic composition explained on pp. 160–61.

196 *Quinque*, 257–58.

as if she had transferred her entire right over her son to Ida. Here
the story takes an odd turn. Ida saw Elisabeth, the mother of John
the precursor, standing on her other side with a bathtub, various
utensils and lukewarm water to give, together with Ida, the baby a
bath. The baby cupped his hands and clapped on the water as
playing children will, toying with the waves, splashing the floor
and sprinkling his own little body. Ida chuckled loudly, and when
the bath was over she lifted him out of the water, dressed him,
laid him on her bosom, playing with him familiarly in maternal
fashion. This scene did not last long, for at the *Sanctus* before the
canon of the mass, the child's mother asked to have him back.
Ida, however refused, hugging him more tightly than before,
nestling him in her arms to hide him. The ensuing struggle
between Mary and Ida lasted till the consecration of the mass,
when Mary was able to retrieve her baby and disappear with him.
Whenever Ida told this story, she would naively downplay her
role to avoid vainglory. 'Drunken people', she said 'and those out
of their minds sometimes tend to see things happening differently
from how they happen in reality. This is mainly because of an
obstacle to their discernment which does not allow their reason to
function properly'.[197]

At times visual and auditory sensations are combined with
other phenomena. A priest was talking with Ida's abbess in the
monastery's parlor when he suddenly swooned, regained his
composure after a few moments, and said to her: 'If I had a bow
and an arrow I would shoot her'[198] When the astounded abbess
asked him what he meant, he replied: 'Ida [of Nivelles] went to
communion and, as usual, was taken up to heaven'. He himself
then became enraptured, he continued, and was taken up to
heaven where he found

197 *AA SS* April 2: 177,22–23. The loquacious, story-loving biographer does
not seem to have had any more discernment than Ida herself. This is all the more
regrettable, as Ida deserved better, her own sentimentality notwithstanding.

198 This is typical of thirteenth-century society. In the reports of seventeenth-
century visions, angels no longer fought devils with arrows but with firearms.
See E. Benz, *Die Vision*, 11.

Ida standing in the presence of the King of glory, who said to her: 'My daughter, give this man some of the abundant grace which I granted you'. Immediately and cheerfully Ida went to the priest and kissed him with a holy kiss (*osculo sancto osculata est eum*), not mouth to mouth, but spirit to spirit.

Now returned 'to the land of the living', the priest told the abbess that never in his whole life had he experienced such an abundance of divine knowledge as in this *vision*. Wanting to verify the priest's story, the abbess inquired about it and was told that, indeed, Ida had been enraptured as the priest had stated.[199]

During a Christmas night, Ida Lewis had an apparition of an ineffably beautiful person holding in his arms a child radiating beauty and loveliness, and he said to her: 'This is my beloved Son'. Totally engulfed by divine light she saw (*vidit*) a certain aspect of the Trinity: the Father personally cohering to the Son. Ida began to ask God about someone who was on her mind. Coming back to herself she wondered how she had been able to stand this experience.[200] One Epiphany, Ida of Leuven was sitting at her place awaiting communion time in restful silence,

and she saw clearly in a mental sight, not in a bodily vision, how her own heart and soul looked like a vast canvas, stretched out far and wide covering a vast area, to gather the incoming grace that would be poured upon her. And in a whisper the Triune God told her of his impending coming, and without delay he fulfilled the promise.

Ida went to communion, interiorly hearing the Father's voice saying: 'This is my Beloved Son in whom I am well pleased'.[201]

199 *Quinque*, 266–68: this vision combines a double rapture, an audition in the form of a request, followed by the execution of a kiss 'spirit to spirit'.

200 *AA SS* Oct.,13: 117,34: this vision combines an apparition, a vision, (the text mentions that she saw 'quaedam mysteria Trinita*tis*'), a dialogue and the realization that she was psychically worn out.

201 *AASS* April 2: 184,9: a vision caused by her intense expectation of the impending communion, the voice telling her of the blessings of the Eucharist, and a text taken from the Gospels.

Visions are not always combined with apparitions. According to Peter Dinzelbacher:

> An apparition is a supersensible eidetic perception which befalls someone who does not lose the simultaneous perception of his natural surroundings, *viz.* without the loss of his ordinary consciousness. An apparition is therefore describable and often accompanied by revelations or an injunction.[202]

If we apply this distinction to the literature, we discover that some of the *mulieres religiosae* combined visions and apparitions; some did not. On page 233 we cited a passage from Hadewijch's seventh vision in which she described how Christ had come from the altar to give her communion under both species. She continued: 'all this was seen, tasted and felt outwardly, as one can outwardly taste, see and feel in the reception of the Sacrament. So can the lover and the beloved receive the fullest satisfaction of seeing and of hearing, the passing of the one into the other.[203]

Here Hadewijch is talking not of a vision but about an apparition, expressing her burning desire to see, to taste, to feel a deep intimacy with Christ, the God-Man, and the interpenetration of both. Beatrice had a nearly similar 'appearance of the Lord standing at the altar with outstretched arms in an inexpressible desire for her approach'. When she had received communion, 'the Lord pressed Beatrice's heart to his own, and absorbed her spirit wholly to himself' (193,29).

Several apparitions have already been mentioned above. A few vignettes will serve to illustrate them, even though biographers do not always distinguish visions from apparitions.

---

202 P. Dinzelbacher, *Vision*, 33–34: An apparition is 'eine übersinnliche eidetische Wahrnehmung...die einem Menschen ohne Verlust der gleichzeitigen Wahrnehmung seiner natürlichen Umwelt widerfährt, das heisst ohne Verlust des Tagesbewusstseins, ohne Ekstase oder Traum'.

203 VM, *Visioenen*, 1: 78–79, ll. 88–94. See also James Walsh, 'Guillaume de Saint-Thierry et les sens spirituels', *RAM* 35 (1959) 27–42; 29–32.

When in 1249 Alice of Schaarbeek felt herself near the end of her life, she hoped soon to enjoy fruition of her long-desired lover (*sperans frui diu desiderato*). The Lord appeared to her in the middle of the night to tell her that she would die on this very day, but one year later, adding that 'she would suffer during that year more pain than she had already suffered during the course of her worsening leprosy, but she would be of greater help to many people, living and dead'.[204] In an experience previously recounted,[205] Alice desired one Good Friday to see Christ on the cross. According to the biographer Christ complied with her desire. He appeared crucified to her and told her to look attentively at all that he had done and suffered for her redemption and that of the human race.[206]

During vigils on a certain Marian feastday, Our Lady appeared to Ida Lewis and gently put the baby on her lap. Ida, however, had to intone a psalm and, according to the Order's regulations, she had to stand to do this, her arms and the sleeves of her cowl hanging down. 'If I do it as prescribed' Ida thought, 'I cannot keep the child in my arms'. So she told him: 'Lord, take care of yourself, because I am going to intone as prescribed'. Whereupon the child clasped his arms around her neck, and hung there till she had completed the intonation, which she sang much better than she usually did. When she had performed the rite she sat down again and he resumed his place on her lap.[207]

204 *AA SS* June 2: 480,22 (above, Chapter X, p. 360, nn. 126,127). Since the text speaks of a nocturnal apparition, it is possible that we are dealing here with an apparition in a dream, a *Traumerscheinung* in Dinzelbacher's *Vision*, 44. It could also have been a premonition coming from her unconscious. A few lines earlier (*AA SS* June 2: 480,21) the biographer said that 'experiencing charity's violence within her (in se patiebatur charitatis violentiam), Alice had developed in her heart a strong desire to suffer for the sake of mankind's salvation'.

205 See above, chapter IX, n. 26.

206 *AA SS* June 2: 482,30.

207 *AA SS* Oct.13: 118,37. 'Contigit...quod ad ipsam pertinuit ut cantaret secundum ordinem versum suum. Quid tunc agere potuit, lacertorum amplexibus illigatum sic tenens puerum, quem prae caeteris omnibus diligebat? Cogitansque secum interius, haesitavit diu quid faceret, dicens ita: "Si tenuero puerum sic inter brachia, versumque sic cantavero, statutum Ordinis non servabo, quia cucullae manicas in articulis statuta jubent Ordinis declinari".

To express the effect of Ida of Nivelles' intercessory prayers, her biographer resorted to a double apparition. The child Jesus appeared to a God-fearing man who had asked to be freed from an annoying temptation. The child told him: 'Not yet. First I have to go to my friend Ida of Nivelles in Rameya'. The man could see the child appear to Ida who wept for joy. To show her how pleased he was by the demonstration of her affection and love, the child held a golden basin in his hand to collect her tears and to wash her face with them. Moreover, two angels appeared with a towel to dry her wet face. The man was so touched by this apparition (called here a vision) that he was relieved of his temptation. He did not know Ida, but went to Rameya to tell her the story of what he had seen.[208] Deceased persons appeared to Ida of Nivelles, Alice of Schaarbeek and Ida Lewis, and the devil appeared to Ida of Nivelles and Ida Lewis.[209] Ida of Leuven had a fantastic and frightening dream-vision of the devil.[210]

In persons of vivid imagination, visions and apparitions can easily be self-induced: it is even possible that hallucinations and

Cumque tempus versum expostulans jam instaret, bonitatis Dei circumfulta fiducia tali, protulit confidenter: "Cogitetis de vobis, Domine, quia cantans perfruar ordine". Cumque versum, ut debuit, incepisset, collo puer adhaerens virginis, illam secum firmiter vinciens, se cum illa ligavit firmius brachiolorum vinculis excellenter praedulcibus et amandis. Ipsa vero versum quem inchoaverat multo melius solito cantavit. Postea residens secundum ordinem, reponens super gremium puerum venerabilem, consolationes quam plurimas hic ab ipso recepit dulciter et devote'. The biographer intended to stress Ida's obedient performance of the rite as prescribed.

208 *Quinque*, 258–61. If anyone doubts this story, the biographer commented, he can verify its authenticity by asking the nun Christine of Rameya, to whom the man also told the story afterwards. It is too early to look for a contemporary iconographic source of inspiration for this story. Goswin of Bossut, the presumed biographer (S. Roisin, *L' Hagiographie*, 55–59) had the well-furnished library of Villers at his disposal, and although it is difficult to assess what he might have found there, he certainly did not lack imagination.

209 Ida of Nivelles put the devil to flight whenever and wherever he appreared (*Quinque*, 232–38). His dealing with Ida Lewis is mentioned in *AA SS* Oct.13: 123,55: Ida Lewis disdained him and had no fear of him, or only a little: 'respuit eum nec timuit, nisi parum'.

210 *AA SS* April 2: 160,8.

real visions occur in the same person.[211] As described by Ernst Arbman in his usual heavy style:

> an hallucination is an experience having the form of genuine sense perception or becoming aware, but without coverage in a corresponding external reality having been provoked without any stimulation of the corresponding external organs of sense.... Most common are visual and auditive hallucinations, which is to say that also other senses of the body may not be subject to similar affections.[212]

On one occasion, Ida of Leuven saw her own soul in the form of a vast temple or church[213] in which a solemn celebration was being prepared. She described at length the decoration of this temple, the function of the ministers and the number of singers assembled to intone the introit of the high priest, Christ himself. But Ida paid so much attention to the awesome grandeur of the setting, the beauty of the decorations and the attire of the ministers that, contrary to what usually happened on such occasions, she paid barely any attention to Christ.[214] The same Ida, still living in her city, one day went to communion. It seemed to her (*sibi videbatur*) as if the substance [of the Eucharist] had undergone a change. It became a fish that lodged between the middle of her throat and the middle of her belly, extending head downward with its jaws wide open to draw in the whole of her spirit and absorb it, transferring her spirit into its own innermost belly, as a fish would do with mouth wide open to gulp down its food.[215]

211 K. Rahner, 'Über Visionen', *GL* 21 (148) 207.

212 E. Arbman, *Ecstasy*, vol 1: 12.

213 Such visions, though infrequent, did take place. See Dinzelbacher, *Vision*, 52.

214 *AA SS* April 2: 180,34. In regard to a 'celestial' liturgy, see Josef Jungmann, *The Place of Christ in the Liturgical Prayer*, ET by Peeler (London, 1965) 239–63, and E. Lucchesi Palli, in *Lexicon der christlichen Ikonographie*, vol.3. (Rome, 1971) 103–106: 'himmlische Liturgie'.

215 *AA SS* April 2: 164,24. This passage follows the text wherein her desire to go to communion and to 'devour God' was spoken of above, Chapter XI, n. 40. To express the idea of God as the one who devours, the biographer compares this 'experience' with the story of Jonah being swallowed up by a sea monster.

Ida of Nivelles' biographer reports that she frequently had an apparition of the devil in the form of a monkey, a dog or some other animal. It has been suggested that this was an hallucination,[216] but this is unlikely. Ida had no fear at all of the devil and despised him.[217] Probably a better interpretation is that she had had abundant opportunities to see the devil represented ridiculously as an ape or a dog in illuminations, [218] gargoyles, corbels, and stained windows. The ungullible Ida, distrusting a spiritual vision, was then given a second vision, confirming that the first was not due to her fantasy.[219] But possible hallucinations should not distract us from a more important consideration.

When we speak in this context of revelations, it is evident that God's self-revelation in his spoken word in the Bible and his revelation in the incarnation of his Son are not meant. Former generations of visionaries had a tendency to use the terms 'vision' and 'revelation' for the same phenomenon. At the time of the *mulieres religiosae*, writers occasionally used vision as equivalent to revelation but more frequently, revelation was used to indicate a communication addressed to *mulieres religiosae* for their own benefit or that of others.[220] It is in this later sense that revelation is here understood.

Beatrice received one revelation as a command (127,47), another (*revelavit ei Dominus*) as an insight that her temptations were a blessing in disguise (144,43). She received a revelation, too, when she was made aware that she would not die yet, but should use her remaining time to grow to fuller maturity (174,81; 239,34). Consciousness, welling up from her unconscious after a dream, is called a 'nightly revelation', and helped her perceive

216 St. Axters, *Inleiding to een Geschiedenis van de Mystiek in de Nederlanden*, 79.

217 *Quinque*, 235 and 237, and note 209 above.

218 See Lillian Randall, *Images in the Margins of Gothic Manuscripts* (Berkeley-Los Angeles, 1966) with many reproductions of this kind. The author remarked also (p. 8) that 'there was a constant interchange, both commercial and cultural, between England and the provinces of particular interest in the present context, Artois, Hainaut, Picardy, Flanders, Brabant and Liège'.

219 *Quinque*, 229; L. Reypens, *Vita*, p. 219, l. 49, a sentence which Henriquez omitted in his *Quinque*.

220 P. Dinzelbacher, *Vision*, 46.

new ways of improving her conduct.[221] The 'revelations' attributed to Bartholomew and to Beatrice, about the foundation of
Nazareth, (228,14; 228,20) were not true revelations, but are
called that by the biographer to make his mistaken point.[222]

Ida of Nivelles' extrasensory perception of the sins committed
by others and the clairvoyance of Ida of Nivelles, Ida Lewis and
Ida of Leuven were used to manifest their hidden defects to other
people, and were accompanied by an exhortation to change while
they still had the time.[223] Revelations were sometimes called
inspirations. According to Arbman

what chiefly characterizes inspiration... is its sudden and
immediate appearance in the consciousness; it comes without conscious effort and apparently without preparation,
often completely unexpected. Hence the referring of it to an
extra personal origin, or power outside the subject's own
consciousness'.[224]

This revelation as inspiration is often called by biographers 'a
revelation of the Spirit of the Lord' or something similar. Quite
frequently this revelation/inspiration was heard in a whisper, a
faint murmur,[225] an expression which goes back to Gregory the
Great and which was familiar to the mentors of the *mulieres
religiosae*.[226] Of one of the many whispers Beatrice heard, her
biographer states that 'sometimes he [the Lord] would instruct

221 *Vita*, 199,65: 'novas vitae normas...revelationibus divinus spiritus inti-
mavit'. Ida of Nivelles' biography mentions also that 'the sublimity of the divine
revelations helped her 'to absorb with deftness and delight what she greatly
desired to derive from the inmost sweetness of the truth': *Quinque*, 280: 'ex
divinis revelationibus summa cum facilitate et jucunditate hauriebat, quod de
intima veritatis suavitate ardenter desiderabat'.
222 Roger De Ganck, 'The Three Foundations of Batholomew of Tienen ',
Citeaux 37 (1986) 49–75.
223 See above, Chapter X.
224 E. Arbman, *Ecstasy*, vol.1: 245.
225 *Susurrium*. See, for instance, the biography of Ida of Nivelles, *Quinque*,
221, 224,231; and that of Ida of Leuven, *AA SS* April 2: 174,15; 175,17; 184,9.
226 J. Reynaert, *Beeldspraak*, 200, referring to Gregory's commentary of
Jb 4:16.

her...with certain signs inwardly within the soul, not with the
sound of his voice, but with a gentle whisper of his inspiration'
(74,25). Both the revelation/inspiration and the whisper, or any
other inner speeches [227] were directed to an intellectual understanding. Beatrice, for instance, 'suddenly heard the divine voice
speaking to her soul, and she *understood* the Lord speaking these
words to her in a slight whisper' (162,25). This example, which
could be multiplied by others found in her *Vita*, as well as in that
of the other *mulieres religiosae*, points to someone who reveals
and speaks in whisperlike ways. The inspiration calls forth a
response in the form of tasting, seeing, feeling. Hadewijch said
that 'when one is ravished with Love, all that is seen in the spirit
is understood, tasted, seen and heard through and through'.[228]
The same sensory perceptions are mentioned by biographers, but
not always together as we have just seen Hadewijch do. Beatrice
saw and heard only 'David with the singers of the heavenly
Jerusalem magnificently praising the Majesty of divine power on
the lute and harp'.[229]

Several biographers seem to have liked to discern fragrant
scents emanating from their subject, as did the biographer of Ida
Lewis,[230] and of Ida of Leuven.[231] Even Alice of Schaarbeek, the
decaying leper, is said to have 'spread a sweet odor far and
wide'.[232] Fragances are not attributed to Hadewijch and Beatrice,

227 Ida of Nivelles' biographer stipulated that she 'heard in her heart' (audivit
in corde, *Quinque*, 229), or 'as is heard in the heart' ('sicut auditur in corde',
Quinque, 228), or as Beatrice's biography has it: 'by the revelation of the divine
wisdom' (217, 100), or 'by revelation of the divine spirit' (217,96) to give only a
few examples of this hagiological topos.

228 Vision 11, VM, *Visioenen* 1: 112, ll. 39–42. In the original each verb is
preceded by the prefix *dore*, through, which makes it truly through and through.

229 *Vita*, 55,31. For this heavenly music, see E. Benz, *Die Vision*, 418–440:
die himmlische Musik, and R.Hammerstein, *Die Musik der Engel. Untersuchungen zur Musikanschauung des Mittelalters*, Bern, 1962. For a longer
treatment of the tasting, seeing and feeling, see E. Benz, *Die Vision*, 413–17: das
visionäre Wort; J. Reynaert, *Beeldspraak*, 199–202; P. Dinzelbacher, *Vision*,
155–65: Verbale Kommunikation.

230 *AA SS* Oct.13: 113,9; 114,22; 115,26.

231 *AA SS* April 2: 183,4; 187,21 to give only these references.

232 *AA SS* June 2: 479,11:'odor suavitatis'.

except in biblical citations where odor and fragrance are mentioned.[233]

A final word should be said about the divine light which is as inaccessible to human eyes as is sunlight to a blind man. The inner sense of sight, called the inner eye, seems able to perceive this light to some extent.[234] Interiorized persons, deeply in touch with God through an intense inner life and an uncommon love, at times experience the brilliance of divine light. On one occasion, Hadewijch was taken up in the spirit and, as she wrote: 'Then he showed me again that ineffably beautiful countenance which was in appearance like a great fiery flood, wider and deeper than the sea'. [235] Another time, Hadewijch became aware of heat waves radiating from that light. As she was listening to a sermon about Augustine: 'at that moment I became inwardly so enkindled, that it seemed to me that everything on earth would have been burnt up by the flame which I felt within myself'.[236]

Some *mulieres religiosae* became so inflamed interiorly that their bodies, and especially their eyes, radiated so brilliant and diffusive a light that people who saw it could not control their astonishment. Such an externally visible radiance is technically known as *gloriole*. Ida of Leuven seem to have held the numerical record, at least within the circle of the *mulieres religiosae* here under consideration.[237] Similar light phenomena are reported of Ida Lewis,[238] and Ida of Nivelles. By her own radiance the latter could see and even read in the dark.[239] One day a lady who frequented the monastery church of Alice thought that it was on fire. In fact, when she entered, she saw Alice of Schaarbeek

---

233 Beatrice's biographer uses it as a figure of speech when she became a novice (25,33). Anyone interested in studying the 'odour of sanctity' from the second century A.D. on, can find information in H. Thurston, *The Physical Phenomena*, 222–32.

234 E. Benz, *Die Vision*, 329.

235 Vision 8; VM, *Visioenen*, 1: 84, ll. 30–33.

236 Letter 25, VM, *Brieven*, 1: 216, ll. 35–39.

237 *AA SS* April 2: 165, 26; 168, 37–39; 173, 21–22; 182, 22–23.

238 *AA SS* Oct.13: 107,1; 109,6; 123,53; 117,35. In the last reference her biographer says that the light she radiated was stronger than that of seven suns.

239 *Quinque*, 246–49; 254–56. Her biographer took it for granted. 'For us', he wrote,'such a phenomenon is not that incredible: God, the supreme light of all lights, by his light made Ida inwardly and outwardly luminous', *ibid.*, 256.

shining as if she were on fire.[240] Beatrice's biographer is more moderate. Only once does he mention a *gloriole* related to her:

From the fire with which she was burning inside, a spiritual fire arose also from her bodily eyes, and emitted from both her eyes a ray of wonderful brightness for those sitting around her to see. And while I speak with all due reverence for the saints, whoever examines the wonderful brightness shining on the faces of both the humble Beatrice and of Moses,... whose face seemed to have horns because of its brightness,[241] such a person will very rightly compare the two in regard to merit also.[242]

240 *AA SS* June 2: 479,14. On an Easter Sunday , being in church when the responsory '*surrexit Dominus de sepulchro*', (the Lord has risen from the grave) was being sung, Alice saw the heavens opened, looking like a grave from which there streamed forth such a brilliant clarity that the whole monastery seemed to be on fire (*ibid.*: 400,18). J. Reynaert, *Beeldspraak*, 122, n. 113 refers to a similar phenomenon related to Juliana of Cornillon.

241 *Vita*, 241,19. See Ruth Mellinkoff, *The Horned Moses in Medieval Art and Thought* (Berkeley-Los Angeles-London, 1970) illustrated by 130 plates. The author points out also that the bishop's miter (chapter 8: 94–106) can be traced back to the time when the horned Moses appeared in English art in the eleventh century. Beatrice's biographer could well have been inspired by art and by the symbolic meaning of the radiating horns: communion with God, shining outward. Though the same meaning was in the mind of the other biographers, they were inclined to give it a phosphoric, and sometimes a pyromaniacal, stress. For a more detailed description of luminous phenomena, see H. Thurston, *The Physical Phenomena*, 162–70: The Luminous Phenomena of Mysticism; E. Benz, *Die Vision*, 326–41: Das himmlische Licht; J. Reynaert, *Beeldspraak*, 55–91: Lichtmetaforiek, and Klaus Hedwig, *Sphaera Lucis. Studien zur Intelligität des seienden im Kontext der mittelalterlichen Lichtspekulation* (Beiträge zur Geschichte der Philosophie und Theologie des Mittelalters [L. Hödl and W. Kluxen eds] N.S. 18, (Münster/Westf., 1980) 237–55: Mystik des Lichtes.

242 *Vita*, 241,19.

CHAPTER FIFTEEN

MINNE

A S WE TREAT THE LOVE-RELATIONSHIP between God and the *mulieres religiosae*, we must keep in mind that several of the expressions used in this regard are metaphors meant to enhance the liveliness of what is being conveyed.[1] It should be evident that terms such as embraces, liquefaction, inebriation and similar expressions are employed metaphorically and not literally to indicate the fervor and intimacy of the relationship.

Biographers, writing in Latin, used the nouns *amor*, *dilectio*, and *charitas* and the related verbs to speak about love; such words are often equivocal in meaning. Gregory the Great, however, wrote that *charitas* is *dilectio* when expressing a special relation.[2] For Augustine *amor* is a neutral term used for any type of love; *dilectio*, however, is the love of conscious preference and is to be preferred when we speak of loving God.[3] The immediate mentors of the *mulieres religiosae* also use *amor*, *dilectio*,

---

1 Angus Fletcher, *Allegory. The Theory of a Symbolic Mode*, 4th ed. (Ithaca-London, 1975) 75–84.

2 *Homilia 17 in Evangelium*, 1; PL 76: 1139A.

3 D. Bell, *The Image*, 57 and the references given there; Isabelle Bochet, *Saint Augustin et le désir de Dieu*, (henceforth cited as *Augustin et le désir de Dieu*), (Paris, 1983) 277–80.

charitas, sometimes with equivalent meanings. Examples could be cited from Hugh,[4] Richard,[5] Bernard,[6] and William.[7]

Hadewijch and Beatrice in her short treatise use the noun and verb *Minne(n)*, (love, to love), which has a variety of meanings and nuances. It is, however, striking that in his Latin translation of her *Seven manieren van Minnen* Beatrice's biographer renders *minne* by *dilectio* (253,222), *amor* (257,389) and *caritas* (259, 472) a carelessness which indicates that he did not fully understand what Beatrice meant by *minne*.[8]

Though the *mulieres religiosae* were not acquainted with depth-psychology as we are today, they, like their mentors, showed pronounced, careful attention to a healthy development of their love, the deepest need of any human being. For love does not merely happen to be there. As William put it: 'Love is naturally implanted in the human soul by the author of nature'[9].

---

4 R. Baron, *Hugues de Saint-Victor. La contemplation et ses espèces*, 109, n. 38: 'il faut signaler la synonymie partielle de *amor, dilectio, charitas*'.

5 J. Chatillon, 'Les quatre degrés de la Charité d'après Richard de Saint-Victor, *RAM* 20 (1939) 239, n. 2: 'pour parler de l'amour Richard emploie simultanément et pratiquement, sans en distinguer les mots: *amor, charitas* et *dilectio*'; G. Dumeige, *Les degrés de la violente charité*, 115: 'il emploie indifféramment ici *amor, dilectio, charitas*, alors que d'autres ouvrages les distinguent plus soigneusement'. See for instance, Ferdinand Guimet, '*Caritas ordinata* et *amor discretus* dans la théologie trinitaire de Richard de Saint-Victor, *RMAL* 4 (1948) 225–36.

6 P. Delfgaauw, *Saint Bernard*, 69, n. 9: 'la distinction *amor, dilectio, caritas* n'est pas rigoureuse chez St Bernard'; Robert Dresser, 'Gradation: Rhetoric and Substance in Saint Bernard', *Goad and Nail*, Studies in Medieval Cistercian History (R. Elder ed.), CS 84, (Kalamazoo, 1985) 71–85; 83,n. 21: 'He [Bernard] employs *dilectio, amor*, and *caritas* synonymously and at random'.

7 D. Bell, *The Image*,149–58; 157: William too speaks of *amor, dilectio* and *caritas*. As the author points out: 'The careful delineation that constitutes *amor* or *dilectio* may be useful but is often not essential.

8 Moreover, he says (257,418) that 'love is the supremely well-ordered mother of virtues'. This statement, which is not in the original, could have been taken from Richard's *Explicatio in Cantica*, PL 196: 486C: 'charitas enim mater est virtutum', a sentence formulated also by Leo the Great, Gregory the Great and others (see J. Reynaert, *Beeldspraak*, 358). Hadewijch too knew this description, for she wrote in her *Poem 2 in Stanzas* (VM, *Strophische Gedichten*, 14, l. 20) that 'Love is the mother of all virtues'.

They knew fairly well that a balanced maturation of their personality was intrinsically connected with their relationship to God,
self, neighbor and nature. Each of these relationships had to
receive its due, if they cared for their psychic balance and spiritual growth.[10] These four relationships comprise what is technically known as well-ordered charity, *caritas ordinata*.[11]
According to Ida of Nivelles love takes pre-eminence among all
virtues.[12] Hadewijch advised a friend to take care of well-ordered
charity,[13] and Ida Lewis was praised because she was able to
establish a well-ordered love in her heart.[14]

Since we are better informed about Hadewijch and Beatrice
than any of the other *mulieres religiosae*, the following pages will
pay particular attention to the use of love or *minne* in their
writings. In and through *minne* one comes not only into contact,
but into union, with God. This union is expressed in different
ways, which will give us the opportunity in the next chapter to
listen to what other *mulieres religiosae* had to say about their
experiences.

Well-ordered love is love for God, self, neighbor, and nature,
in that order. Well-ordered love does not mean that its four
objects are equal, but that they are ordered, *viz.* that love for self,

---

9 Nat am 1,2; PL 184: 381A; CF 30:49: 'Amor ab auctore naturae naturaliter
est animae humanae inditus'.

10 When Beatrice, for instance, had a sudden insight 'beyond the spirit' of the
Trinity, she tried 'to recall to mind and to commit to memory by the sharpness of
her interior sense what she had learned in mind only by the revelation of the
divine wisdom'. She had to be recalled from becoming too attached to her
vision, for the text goes on to say: 'But she understood by revelation of the Holy
Spirit that her Creator's good-pleasure was rather that in the future she should
intend to help her neighbors in their needs with loving affection' (217,108).

11 For the mentors of the *mulieres religiosae* and other immediate prede-
cessors, see R. Javelet, *Image*, 1: 409–27: Caritas ordinata. In this connection
see also J. Reynaert, *Beeldspraak*, 358–59. For texts related to nature and
animals, see above C.69–69B

12 *Quinque*, 277: 'charitas virtutum omnium obtinet principatum'. As the
context shows *charitas* means here love for neighbor, as it does often in
Hadewijch (VM, *Brieven*, 2: 64) and as *charity* still does in contemporary
English; and *charities* for organized care of those in need.

13 Letter 2; VM, *Brieven* 1: 31, l. 173: 'rechter caritaten behoert in ordenen'.

14 *AA SS* Oct.13: 113,18: 'caritatem in se promeruit ordinari', which is a text
of Sg 2:4.

neighbor and nature are directed toward God and are included in that love. Augustine, speaking of man's ultimate development and realization, said that he will reach it when he has fruition of God alone, *solo Deo fruendum*.[15] At first sight such a phrase might make us wonder. But what Augustine meant to convey is that love of self, neighbor and nature finds fulfillment, not in loving God exclusively, but in loving God above all, a love in which the other objects of well-ordered love are included.[16] God's own love is embracingly all-inclusive. His love for us is included in his exclusive love for himself. In this sense we may say that God loves us exclusively. For 'to love us for himself exclusively is identical with what in him is to love himself exclusively'.[17] Pondering the total love of God, William wrote:

> When you [God] love us, you cannot but love us for your-
> self, since the truthful rule of ultimate justice permits even
> us to love nothing outside you.... To someone who loves
> God, it is possible for his love to reach the point of loving
> neither you nor himself for himself, but you and himself for
> yourself alone. By this he is refashioned to your image, after
> which you created him.[18]

15 *De doctrina christiana*, 1,22,20; PL 44:26.

16 E. Gilson, *Introduction*, 217–20. In harmony with Augustine, Bernard says that once the likeness to God has been restored in the soul, then what she loves in loving herself is a divine likeness: 'Now to resemble God is to love God for God's sake, since God is this love itself'. 'Impossible then', says Gilson, 'to ask St.Bernard to define the supreme degree of love in any other way than that in which he defines it: to love oneself no longer save for God. It is impossible to eliminate the love of self, not merely because along with it there would disappear the created being from whom it is altogether inseparable, but also because God loves us, and we should cease to be like him if we ceased to love ourselves. It is equally impossible to strike out the clause "save for God", for since God loves neither himself nor us save for himself, we should cease to be like him were we to love ourselves otherwise than he loves us, that is to say only for himself': *Mystical Theology*, 117–18.

17 E. Gilson, *Mystical Theology*, 118.

18 Contem 4,9; PL 184: 372B: 'Cum autem nos amas, nonnisi propter te nos amas, cum verissima summae justitiae regula etiam nos nil amare permittit extra te. Et certe possibile est amori Deum amantis...eo proficere ut te nec se amans

Or putting it differently: one cannot love God perfectly if one does not love him for his sake. At the same time this love for God's sake is the best way to love oneself and neighbor perfectly. What has been said about *caritas ordinata*, well-ordered love, should be taken very seriously. It is very important to realize firstly, that God has to love himself for his own sake. Secondly, that he created man in the only way he could create him in accordance with his loving plans: for his own sake; only by accepting this can man find fulfillment of himself. Thirdly, that man in his necessarily given freedom preferred to love neither himself nor God for God's sake, but loved each for his own sake. And fourthly, that God's Son came to teach man by his word and to show him by his deeds how man should love God, self and neighbor for God's sake. In the next chapter we will see in what various ways the *mulieres religiosae* expressed their effective desire to love nature, neighbor, self and God for God's sake, using images and metaphors comprehensible only in the context of their love for God as they lived it: for his sake. Such a love is not easily attained, but requires a lifelong striving to dissolve self-centeredness and to grow toward love of God for his sake. Once Beatrice had learned 'to transfer her whole will over to the divine good-pleasure' (226,93), she became aware of

> that indissoluble bond of love by which she was bound to the supreme Good. This bond was so consolidated and confirmed in true love that, the more she was vexed in body or mind by any corporeal or spiritual trouble, the more sweetly was she refreshed by this supreme Good. Thus she would stand all hard and harsh things, not only patiently but also most willingly, without impatience or sorrow.[19]

Hadewijch expressed the demanding, exacting experiences of such a love by saying:

propter se, et te et se propter te solum amet; et per hoc reformetur ad imaginem tuam ad quam creasti eum'. William here joins Bernard's fourth degree of loving God. See Dil 10,28; SBOp 3: 142; CF 13: 119.

19 *Vita*, 227,99.

Minne cries out with a loud voice without stay and without delay in all the hearts of those who love: 'love ye Love'. This voice makes a noise so great and unheard-of that it sounds more fearful than thunder. This word is the bond with which Love fetters her prisoners. It is the sword with which she wounds those she has touched. It is a rod with which she chastises her children. This word is the mastery by which she teaches her disciples.[20]

For Hadewijch, listening to *Minne*'s teaching meant standing in front of her:

Those who fall down in adoration before that Countenance receive grace; those who contemplate the Countenance standing receive justice and are enabled to fathom the deep abysses that are so terrifying to know for those unacquainted with them.[21]

Hadewijch compared this stand to the one taken by the patriarch Jacob who triumphed over the angel and won his blessing at the end of the struggle, although the angel hurt him in one foot and made him limp. Likewise, someone who does not love God alone above all still walks on two feet. Someone who does love God alone and above all and experiences God as Jacob did when he was blessed, will be hurt in one foot and limp. Allegorically the spritually healthy person will be limping—that is, psychologically crippled—since he can no longer give his total affection to earthly things.[22]

---

20 Letter 20; VM, *Brieven*, 1: 173–74, ll. 103–12.

21 Vision 12; VM, *Visioenen*, 1: 127, ll. 44–48. According to H. van Cranenburgh [Hadewijchs twaalfde visioen en negende strophische gedicht, *OGE* 35 (1961) 366], to fall down in adoration means activity in virtuous service; the standing means to be united with Christ, confirmed in love and capable of gazing into the depths of the divine abyss without breaking down.

22 J. Reynaert, 'Hadewijchs "Hoghe Geslachte" ', *Hoofheid en devotie in de Middeleeuwse Maatschappij*, 165 and n. 25. Reynaert rephrases Hadewijch's twelfth letter [VM, *Brieven*, 1: 109, ll.178–88] and refers to Hugh's *Miscellanea*, PL 177: 698A, as the most probable source of Hadewijch's allegorical interpretation of the limping Jacob, being hurt in his foot, instead of in his hip, as the Bible has it.

Both for Hadewijch and for Beatrice this confrontation implies the strength to carry — while still in the misery of this 'exile' the burden of loving service in good works and, at the same time, to overcome by *minne* the fear of the awesome God, as the two following quotations make clear.

> Love so powerfully possesses him whom she loves, that his mind cannot wander away for any instant, nor [can] his heart desire, nor his soul love [anything not included in this total love]. Love renders his memory so unified with her that he can no longer think of saints, nor of people in heaven or on earth, nor of angels, nor of himself, nor of God, but of Love alone in an ever-newly possessed presence.[23]

In her seventh *maniere*, Beatrice wrote that 'the soul knows him [the Beloved], loves him, and so desires him that it cannot pay attention to saints, men (*menschen*), angels or creatures except in that common love for him by which it loves everything'.[24] Like Hadewijch, Beatrice in her sixth *maniere* stresses love's totality, exclusive of all that is not included within it: 'then Love makes the soul so bold and free that in all its actions and omissions, in its work and rest, it fears neither men nor the demon, neither angels nor saints, nor God himself'.[25]

Beatrice's biographer, who read her treatise in accordance with his own thought-patterns, found these words about not fearing God too strong, at least for the simpleminded to whose comprehension he adapted her *Vita*. He, therefore, wrote in his

---

- 23 Letter 20; VM, *Brieven*, 1: 174, ll. 113–22. See in this regard, E. Heszler, 'Stufen der Minne bei Hadewijch', *Frauenmystik im Mittelalter*, (P. Dinzelbacher and D. Bauer eds), (Ostfilden, 1985) 99–122; 117. R. Vanneste (*Abstracta*, 60) pointed out that the presence, *ieghenwordicheit* , Hadewijch speaks of here has to be understood in its supreme meaning: that of union. He refers to Bernard's Pre 20,60; SBOp 3:293. 'Praesens igitur Deo est qui Deum amat, in quantum amat. In quo minus amat, absens profecto est' (He who loves God is present to him the more he loves him. Inasmuch as he loves him less, to that extent is he absent from him).

24 R-VM, *Seven manieren*, 31–32, ll. 52–55. For the 'common love' see above Chapter VI. The quotation has already been cited on page 205.

25 *Ibid.*, 27, ll. 52–55.

Latin translation of the sixth *maniere* that 'she feared neither man nor demon, nor the angelic or even the divine judgment'.[26]

Bernard called such passionate love 'pure love'. The first characteristic of pure love lies in the *exclusion* of every other affection:

> I put it as St Bernard puts it [says Étienne Gilson], but what he means to say is rather that pure love is *inclusive* of all other affections. The reason is this. The purity of love is one and the same thing with its intensity.... That is why the reference to *ardent* recurs so incessantly in his writings.[27]

This is also the reason why ardent love recurs so incessantly in the writings and biographies of the *mulieres religiosae*, as can be seen in chapters twelve and thirteen. It is also the reason why the *mulieres religiosae* spoke so gladly of the seraphs, 'the sublime spirits which Sacred Scripture calls seraphim, that is, the fiery ones, because of their sublime fullness of divine love, and who, it says, cling more closely than the others to the divine presence' (182,197). In her seventh *maniere*, Beatrice expressed her desire to share in the seraphs' fruition of God's love; this was her way of asking, in a veiled allusion, for the closest union with God.

> All that the soul is, all its will, its love are all there in that secure truth and pure clarity and noble sublimity and magnificent beauty, and in the sweet society of the heavenly spirits who overflow with superabundant love and who are in clear knowledge, possession and fruition of their love.

26 *Vita*, 258,462. If the biographer had been able to read Gilson, he might perhaps have felt more comfortable with Beatrice's sixth *maniere*. See Gilson, *Mystical Theology*, 146: 'When a soul thinks of punishment she can think of it in no way if not as deserved; when she no longer sees that she deserves it, that is not because she knows herself guilty, but pardoned, because she no longer thinks of it at all.... None but pure love has power to lay hold, without shame and without fear of this subsistent Beatitude, in whose possession the very notions of promise, of hope, of trust, or of punishment become void of meaning'.

27 E. Gilson, *Mystical Theology*, 141.

Then the soul's longed-for dealings are with the heavenly spirits, especially with the ardent seraphim; its delightful rest and enjoyable dwelling is with the great Godhead and the lofty Trinity.[28]

On a vigil of the feast of Michael the Archangel, Ida of Leuven was rapt in ecstasy and 'lifted up by the Lord into the choir of the hierarchies, *viz.* the seraphic choir, the highest and closest to the Trinity'.[29] For Hadewijch, too, seraphs are linked with fruition of God,[30] and in her thirteenth vision, seraphs are said to be in the service of man who is kin to the God-Man, a kinship which the seraphs do not share.[31] Alice of Schaarbeek's biographer was of the opinion that when she died, 'the Lord assigned her a place with the cherubim and seraphim, to be set on fire and to burn [in love], because she had desired him more ardently than others'.[32] Here too, the *mulieres religiosae* are in line with their mentors.[33] Though this talk about seraphs is not of primary importance, it is nevertheless worthy of mention, for that was precisely what the *mulieres religiosae* had in mind and heart: to be so fiery in their love for God that fruition of him might be their portion.

In Part One we provided many quotations and references to show how deeply the *mulieres religiosae* understood that God's gratuitous love began with creating them to his image and

28 R-VM, *Seven manieren*, 31, ll. 37–49.

29 *AA SS* April 2: 188,25: 'in chorum altissimae hierarchiae, supremum videlicet Seraphicum, illum scilicet individuae Trinitatis vicissimum ...elevavit'.

30 Vision 5; VM, *Visioenen*, 1: 61, ll. 61–62.

31 VM, *Visioenen*, 1: 145, ll. 113–14. See B. Spaapen, 'Hadewijch en het vijfde visioen', *OGE* 16 (1972) 138–40.

32 *AA SS* June 2: 482, 33: 'quia ceteris ipsum desiderabat ardentius, inter Cherubim et Seraphim, ut ardeat et accendatur, sibi locum assignavit'.

33 Bernard: Edmond Boissard, 'La doctrine des anges chez St Bernard', *AC* 9 (1953) 114–35; — William: Med 4,10; PL 180,217D; CF 13: 44. 'The blessed Seraphim, for whom their nearness to your presence and the clearness of their sight of you has earned them the name of the burning ones, *ardentes*'; — Richard: *Les quatre degrés*, G. Dumeige, 165, ll. 3–5. 'The angelic spirits who are called seraphs, the *ardentes*, that is. Their name says what they are, since no one of them shuns his [God's] heat'. See also the lengthy elaboration on the seraphs by Alan, in d' Alverny, *Alain de Lille. Textes inédits*, 129–32.

likeness, as he intended from all eternity, and—as we showed in Part Two—how the signs of his love reached a visible and tangible climax in the human birth, life, death and resurrection of God's Son.

In creating man, God made him lovable; in re-creating him through his Son's humanity, he made him more lovable and able—if he consented—to love him in return with enhanced motivation. Augustine pointed out that 'in order that we might receive the love by which we might love, we were loved while we did not yet have it.... For we would not have that with which we might love him unless we received it from him by his first loving us'.[34]

God's love for man, the source and cause of the love man owes to God, is strikingly expressed by William: 'Love's birthplace is God. There love is born, there nourished, there developed. There it is a citizen, not a stranger, but a native. Love is given by God alone and it endures in him, for it is due to no one else but him and for his sake'.[35] What William intimates is that God's love is gratuitously given, without any claim on our part, except the claim God gave us by creating us, as Bernard expressed it.[36]

In the preceding pages we have met with several instances where Hadewijch and Beatrice out of their own conviction spoke of the reciprocal love they owed to God.[37] Beatrice realized that 'she had been created by a *loving* God to his image and likeness' (138,165). This God 'anticipated her with his most vehement love

34 *De gratia Christi* 27; PL 44: 374. This is, as D.Bell noted (*The Image*, 60, n.168), based on 1 Jn 4:10 and 4:19, and a most important concept for the Cistercians in general and William in particular. E. Gilson, *Mystical Theology*, 22–25 showed it in relation to Bernard. Not unexpectedly Yvo borrowed it from the latter. See G. Dumeige, *Yves. Epître*, 65, ll.12–13.

35 Nat am 3, PL 184: 382B; CF 30: 53. 'Primum ejus [amoris] locus Deus est. Ibi natus, ibi provectus, ibi civis est, non aliena sed indigena. A Deo enim solo amor datus et in ipso permanet, quia nulli nisi ipsi et propter ipsum debetur'.

36 Dil 1,1; SBOp 3: 120. 'Dilexit ergo [nos] Deus et gratis'. Bernard follows here Augustine's saying that 'God loves us gratuitously', *Ennarationes in Psalmum 104*, 40; PL 36:1404.

37 They repeated in their own way what Augustine called 'enjoined love' (*praeceptum caritatis*; PL 35: 1531), and Bernard 'the debt of love' (*debitum caritatis*: Dil 5,15; SBOp 3: 131).

and therefore she knew for certain that she was bound to render him the return of love' (204, 69) by clinging 'closely to the creator of all things through loving affection' (264,36).

As love for God intensifies, it can with the help of God's grace, arrive at a certain parity with God's love: then a dialogue ensues between gratuitous and due love. Inasmuch as it is freely given, due love is gratuitous also.[38] This statement reflects the saying of Bernard that '[God's] love affects the soul spontaneously and effects a spontaneous response'.[39]

A spontaneous response, however, does not happen automatically. Even when God's love affects a soul spontaneously, the latter is assumed to be sufficiently far advanced that God's love elicits a cooperative effectiveness. Beatrice expresses this clearly in her sixth *maniere*:

When the Lord's bride has proceeded further and mounted higher in godliness, she experiences another *maniere* of loving in greater closeness and higher understanding [of love]. She feels that *Minne* has conquered all her adversaries within her, corrected her defects, [MSS. H and W add: subdued her senses, has adorned her nature, has amplified and exalted her state of soul] and gained dominion over herself without [further] obstruction. She also feels that love [now] possesses her heart securely and that she can undisturbedly have fruition in it and must have free, spontaneous correspondence and interaction with this love.[40]

According to Hadewijch:

we must seek everything by means of itself: strength by means of strength, discernment by means of discernment,

38 R. Javelet, *Psychologie*, 166: 'Un movement ascensionnel [assure] ...par grace...une certaine parité avec cet Amour divin qui en a l'initiative afin que le dialogue de l'amour gratuit et l'amour dû puisse être libre. Etant libre, l'amour dû est aussi amour gratuit'.

39 Dil 7,17; SBOp 3: 134. 'Sponte afficit et spontaneum facit'. Though William phrased it differently he too had recourse to the same affect-effect relation: Nat am 2,4; PL 184: 382D-383A; CF 30:56.

40 R-VM, *Seven manieren*, 23–24, ll. 2–14.

riches by means of riches, love by means of love, the all by means of the all, and always like by means of like. This alone can content the Beloved and nothing else can... we must continually dare to fight her [Love] in new assaults: with all our strength, all our discernment, all our wealth, all our love, with all these together. This is how to behave with the Beloved.[41]

To satisfy the Beloved, one must court him, says Hadewijch, and this is how it is done:

As long as we do not possess him, we have to serve him with all the virtues. But if we apply ourselves to the Beloved himself, all the things for which our service was previously carried out must be excluded from without and forgotten from within. As long as we serve in order to attain Love, we must attend to service. But when we have the Beloved with love, then we must exclude all the rest and have fruition of Love with all the promptings of our heart and with our whole being, and stand ready to receive the excellent wisdom the loving soul can win in love.[42] To that effect the [intellectual] faculties and the dispositions of the heart must always stand ready, and toward it the eyes must always gaze, and all the streams of the sweet flood [of Love] shall flow through and into each other. So must love live in Love.[43]

The last sentence of this quotation indicates that the response of the *mulieres religiosae* to God's love implies their total orien-

41 Letter 7, VM, *Brieven*, 1: 71–72, ll. 4–8, 10–13.
42 Hadewijch is here in agreement with William's Nat am 2,5; PL 184: 383B; CF 30: 57. 'If, in accordance with the dignity of its origin, the will progresses into love, then according to the natural order of its capacities it grows from love (*amor*), into *caritas*, and from *caritas* into wisdom': (voluntas...libera constituta, si secundum dignitatem naturalium suorum erigitur in amorem, secundum naturalem virtutum suarum ordinem de amore in charitatem, de charitate proficit in sapientiam). R. Javelet, (*Image* 1: 412) remarked that this growth is equivalent to the three liberties Bernard spoke of. See above, chapter four, p. 111.
43 Letter 21, VM, *Brieven*, 1: 178, ll. 35–50.

tation toward union with God. Hadewijch here echoes Bernard's statement, which, if not original, became nearly proverbial about how God should be loved: 'You wish to hear from me why and how God should be loved? My answer is that God himself is the reason why he is to be loved. As for how he is to be loved, there is no limit to that love'.[44]

In her second *maniere*, speaking from her heart, Beatrice also echoes Bernard, though the pulse of her heart seems to be faster:

'To her [the soul] it is enough that she serves him [the Beloved] and that the Lord allows her to serve him lovingly without measure and beyond measure and beyond human sense and reason, faithfully performing every service'.[45] She sounds even more passionate in her fifth *maniere*:

the soul is so tightly fettered by this bond [of love] and is so overcome by the immeasurableness of love that it cannot maintain measure according to reason, or moderation by restraint, or remain calm according to good judgment.[46]

The only valid and acceptable answer to God's love is a love without superficiality, 'parsimony or measure';[47] God's love is

44 Dil 1,1; SBOp 3: 119. 'Vultis ergo a me audire quare et quo modo diligendus sit Deus. Et ego. Causa diligendi Deum, Deus est; modus, sine modo diligere'. One's neighbor, and oneself, may be loved, but with some measure (*quidam modus*) Div 96,5; SBOp 6/1: 360. See P. Delfgaauw,'La nature et les degrés de l'amour de S.Bernard', *AC* 9 (1953) 243–52; 238; ET in *MnS* 1 (1963) 85–109; 90 and K. Knotzinger, 'Hohes Lied und bräutliche Christusliebe bei Bernhard von Clairvaux', *Jahrbuch für mystische Theologie* 7 (1961) 9–90; U. Küsters, *Der Verschlossene Garten*, Studia humaniora 2, (Düsseldorf, 1985) 65. This book treats the history of the Song of Songs'interpretations. The allegories used by the commentators in their treatises or sermons were at times unconsciously transformed by some *mulieres religiosae* into experiences of the 'really-seen-kind', as by Gertrude the Great, for instance. In his *Hohelied - Studien*, 149, n. 1, Fr. Ohly refers to J. Leclercq, *AC* 9 (1953) fasc. 1–2 120, n. 2, where texts about love without measure are quoted from a letter by Augustine, from Origen and from Gregory the Great. Gregory of Nyssa has it also. See J. Daniélou, *La vie de Moïse*, *SCh* 1 bis (Paris, 1955) 3. ET by Abraham Malherbe and Everett Ferguson, *The Life of Moses* (New York–Kalamazoo, 1977) ¶ 7, p. 31.
45 R-VM, *Seven manieren*, 8, ll. 8–13.
46 *Ibid.*, 22, ll. 64–69.
47 Hadewijch, Letter 30; VM, *Brieven*, 1: 172, l. 76.

given not by halves, but totally; Hadewijch's response to this love
could not be half-hearted, but had to be total. She wrote: 'Whoever loves ardently runs faster and more quickly attains God's
perfection, which is God himself, and to God's totality which is
God himself'.[48] Hadewijch knew very well that the totality of her
love for God, affected by him, was effected by her cooperation
with him. In her short sentence one can hear the emotional power
uniting these two lovers in one love: 'Without any bounds, *Minne*
took my heart totally to herself'.[49]

A loving response worthy of God's love does not look for
reward. A spontaneous, total response of love does not desire any
reward other than the fruition which God himself has built into
his own spontaneous love. As Augustine said: 'The reward of
God is God himself'.[50] Bernard's statement about loving God
without looking for a reward also became proverbial: 'Love seeks
no reason or fruit beyond itself. Its use is its fruit. I love because I
love; I love in order to love'.[51]

Hadewijch considered the search for God's love without regard
for reward to be an important part of the spiritual discipline
required to attain pure love. As she wrote in her second Letter:

One must not be sorrowful because of suffering nor long for
repose, but renounce all for all and entirely renounce repose.

48 Letter 13, *ibid.*, 1: 116, ll. 69–73.
49 Poem 30 in Stanzas; VM, *Strophische Gedichten*, 196–97, ll. 69–70.
50 *Ennarationes in Psalmum* 2, PL 36: 928. 'Praemium Dei, ipse Deus est'.
Or, as he said it in *Ennarationes in Psalmum* 118, 22,2: PL 37: 1563: 'Praemium
dilectionis ipse dilectus' (the Beloved himself is love's reward). Unlike *merces*
(wages), a reward implies something that cannot be demanded, something that
comes as a gift, even though it may be hoped for.
51 SC 83,4; SBOp 2: 300.'Amor praeter se non requirit causam, non fructus.
Fructus ejus, usus ejus. Amo quia amo. Amo ut amem'. To distinguish the
uniqueness of this love from any other, he adds that 'love is indeed great if it
returns to its beginning, if it goes back to its origin, if it flows back to its source
that it might continually flow again' (Magna res amor, si tamen ad suum recurrat
principium, si suae origini redditus, si refusus suo fonti, semper ex eo sumat
unde iugiter fluat). Earlier Bernard wrote in his Dil 7,17; SBOp 3: 133. 'God is
not loved without reward, although he should be loved without regard for
reward' (Non enim sine praemio diligitur Deus etsi absque praemii sit intuitu
diligendus). G. B. Burch, *The Steps*, 72–73, rectifies a misinterpretation by
Pierre Rousselot, in his *Pour l'histoire de l'amour au moyen âge*, 52–54, related
to this text.

Rejoice continually in the hope of acquiring love; for if you desire perfect love for God, you must not desire any repose whatever, except love.[52]

Her hope of acquiring love was based on her great trust in God's love: 'Love is noble and generous; she withholds no man's reward'.[53] Or, as she says elsewhere: in her striving toward perfect love for God, she had not the least doubt that 'Love rewards to the full, though she often comes late'.[54]

Beatrice's appreciation of God's love was so high that she was ready to strive for it, even if—as she put it paradoxically—there were no reward. 'The soul sets itself the task of serving the Lord freely out of love alone, without any motive and without any reward of grace and glory'. We would, however, be mistaken if we took her statement as an expression of total disinterestedness. It only appears to be so. To the text we have just quoted she added the simile: 'as a noble maiden serves her lord out of great love and without remuneration'.[55] To serve the Lord without remuneration was her ideal, because he loved her and she loved him. And this love-relationship itself was a matchless remuneration.

By loving God, man shares in his blessedness and finds in him his own completion. As Bernard put it: 'When God loves us, he desires nothing but to be loved in return, since he loves for no other reason than to be loved. For he knows that those who love him are blessed in this very love'.[56]

Nothing but God can satisfy man's immense need for fulfillment, for it is God who gave the human person the gnawing urge to strive toward God. 'God is love and no created thing can satisfy a creature made to God's image and likeness, except

---

52 VM, *Brieven*, 1: 24–25, ll. 8–13.
53 Letter 10; *ibid.*, 1: 88, ll. 40–42.
54 Letter 7; *ibid.*, 1: 72, ll. 18–19.
55 R-VM, *Seven manieren*, 7–8, ll. 3–8.
56 SC 83,4; SBOp 2: 301. 'Nam cum amat nos Deus, non aliud vult, quam amari: quippe non ad aliud amat, nisi ut ametur, sciens ipso amore beatos, qui se amaverint'.

the loving God (*caritas Deus*), who alone is greater than this creature'.[57]

Hadewijch expressed her full agreement when she wrote in her seventh Letter: 'Love is the only thing that can satisfy us, nothing else'.[58] Between God and the soul there is a deep, intimate and fruitive relationship: 'The soul is a bottomless abyss in which God suffices to himself, and his own self-sufficiency ever finds fruition to the full in the soul, as the soul, for its part, ever does in him'.[59] But there is a condition, for she wrote that 'God penetrates us just as deeply as we long for him'.[60]

Whoever aims at the fulfillment of his personality foregoes the selfish self in order to relate wholly to God.

He who wishes to understand and know God in his name and in his essence (*Wesen, being*), must belong completely to God; yes, so completely that, free from [his selfish] self, God is all to him.... Therefore, let him lose himself if he wishes to find God and to know what God is in himself.[61]

One is tempted to see in the preceding quotations from Hadewijch's letters a reflection of William's doctrine of *amor-intellectus*, love-understanding.[62] 'How can [the soul]... participate in the knowledge that God has of himself? There is knowledge because there is possession, penetration, indwelling of the one in

---

57 Bernard: SC 18,6; SBOp 1: 107. 'Deus caritas est, et nihil est in rebus quod possit replere creaturam factam ad imaginem Dei, nisi caritas Deus qui solus maior est illa'.

58 VM, *Brieven*, 1: 71, ll. 8–10.

59 Letter 18; VM, *ibid.*, 154–55, ll. 69–73. This text is reminiscent of William: 'You [God] love yourself in us, and us in your self, when we love you through you' (Te teipsum in nobis amas, et nos in te, cum te per te amamus): Contem 11, PL 184: 375B; CF 3: 35.

60 Letter 24; VM, *ibid.*, 212, ll. 89–90. William says the same thing but phrases it in reverse: 'One possesses you [God] insofar as he loves you' (quia habet te quis, in quantum amat te): Contem 11, PL 184: 376A; CF 3: 56.

61 Letter 22; VM, *ibid.*, 188, ll. 1–4, 6–8.

62 See Jean Déchanet, '*Amor ipse intellectus*: la doctrine de l'amour-intellection chez Guillaume de Saint-Thierry', *RMAL* 1 (1945) 349–74.

the other'.[63] David Bell, in reviewing this question, made the suggestion 'that the whole *amor-intellectus* doctrine can be reduced to two simple questions and two simple answers: how can we know God? Become what God is! How can we become what God is? Love Him!'[64] Having precisely this in mind, will and heart, the *mulieres religiosae* did their utmost to do just that.[65]

In her seventh *maniere*, which is also one of higher *minne*,[66] Beatrice has a paragraph which corresponds closely with William's *amor-intellectus* doctrine:

> The soul seeks its Beloved in his Majesty; it pursues him there, and gazes on him with heart and mind. She knows him, loves him, and so desires him *(kintene, mintene, beghertene)* that she cannot pay attention to saints or men *(menschen)* or angels or creatures, except with that common love in him by which she loves everything. With all the yearning of her heart and strength of mind, she desires to see and possess him and have fruition of him.[67]

What then is this *Minne* that Beatrice speaks of in her short but dense treatise of six hundred printed lines? Though God is *Minne*, and Christ is *Minne*, *Minne* itself is neither God nor Christ. All Beatrice's labors and sufferings, her ups and downs are accepted and integrated in the service of *Minne*. Beatrice 'felt' that her will had become *minne*, because God's will had become her will; she 'felt' that she herself had become *minne*, as she wrote in her

63 J. Déchanet, Introduction to William's *Exposition on the Song of Songs*, CF 6 (Spencer, MA) 1970, xxv.

64 Chapter six of D. Bell's, *The Image*, 217–49 pays attention to *Amor ipse intellectus est*, particularly on p. 237.

65 The references to Bernard and William suggest that they were the mentors most frequently followed by the *mulieres religiosae*. But even to speak of 'following' could be misleading, since these *mulieres religiosae* spoke or wrote also from their own experience and reflections. Not everything they said and did has to be based on what they heard or read, but it is nevertheless useful to note literary similarities.

66 R-VM, *Seven manieren*, 28, ll. 2–3.

67 *Ibid.*, 31–32, ll. 50–60.

fourth *maniere*: 'The soul feels ...that its will has become *minne*, that it [the soul] has wholly become *minne*'.[68]

Seen in its lexicographical context, *minne* is a polyvalent term, unrolling the script of God's love for Beatrice and of her own groping and growing love for him as it becomes deeper and stronger. When she observed the expression and expansion of his love toward nature and her neighbor, she realized that these too had to be included in her response in return. To encompass the manifold aspects of God, his love for himself, for his creation, and for Beatrice in particular, and the equally manifold aspects of her reciprocal love for this God, his creation, and herself, she personalized *minne*, in the sense that *minne* represents a syntactical, not an autonomous, personal entity. Within the realm of this personification, especially with reference to God, *minne* has all the attributes of a love-partner.[69] With her whole being Beatrice responded affectively and effectively to *Minne*.

Realizing that God is the Absolute and the Inaccessible who cannot be loved as he loves himself, she, Beatrice loved him and all the expressions of his creative love with all the love of which she was capable: a total love from her total being.

She had seen God's love at work in his creation, she had been aware of his presence within herself, she had marvelled above all at the incarnation of God's Son, the life and death of the God-Man. She understood that to love God in return she had to follow Christ in his love for his Father and in his love for man made to God's image and likeness. The Eucharist gave her strength to become purified through and through, until she recaptured the beauty and dignity in which she had been created. Her beauty and dignity were now enhanced through a painfully, faithfully carved-out Christlikeness. In the literary form she gave it in her treatise, *minne* is not interchangeable with God. But in her experiential living in love with *Minne* for *Minne*'s sake, Beatrice never forgot that this love was a relationship between God and herself, what-

---

68 *Ibid.*, 14–15, ll. 23–26.

69 The polyvalence of Beatrice's *minne* is shown at its best in H. Vekeman's 'Van Seuen Manieren van heiliger Minne. Exstase en traditie in een cultus van de Minne', *TNTL* 88 (1972) 172–99.

ever the extension and the inclusiveness of this relation were. At the end of her seventh *maniere* she called God her Bridegroom,[70] though in the whole of her treatise the term bridegroom is stamped all over with the term *minne*. As Vekeman put it: 'Beatrice's mysticism is a personal synthesis influenced by Cîteaux and the *mulieres religiosae* movement'.[71]

In the works of Hadewijch, the prolific writer and gifted poet ess, the feminine term *minne* occurs over two thousand times,[72] and its meanings have been differently interpreted. M.H. Van der Zeyde suggested that in *minne* we see an amorphous form.[73] Joseph Van Mierlo insisted that Hadewijch's *minne* is in reality the equivalent of God or Christ.[74] Nobert De Paepe, studying the use of *minne* in Hadewijch's *Poems in Stanzas*, came to the conclusion that she personalizes *minne* as an entity or figure (*gestalte*) outside God—personal without being a person—and that this expresses how Hadewijch experienced subjectively her love-relationship with God.[75] T.M. Guest tried to improve on De Paepe's suggestion, but her construction of *minne* as an autonomous being does not seem to reflect Hadewijch's meaning.[76] G.Kazemier, taking into account the influence of courtly love poetry on Hadewijch, suggests that we see in *minne* a feminine figure, characterized by the fickleness of the troubadour's lady.[77]

70 R-VM, *Seven Manieren*, 38, ll. 164–65.

71 H.Vekeman, 'Panorama du mysticisme moyen-néerlandais', *Septentrion* 10 (1981) 24–31; 27: 'La mystique de l'amour chez Beatrijs est une synthèse personnelle des influences exercées par Cîteaux et le movement féminin'.

72 Frances Gooday, 'Mechtild of Magdeburg and Hadewijch of Antwerp. A Comparison', *OGE* 48 (1974) 321.

73 See her *Hadewijch. Een studie van de mens en de schrijfster* (Groningen-The Hague-Batavia, 1934) 19.

74 In his 'De "Minne" in de Strophische Gedichten', *VMKVA* 1941, 687–705. In 'Hadewijch. Une mystique flamande du treizième siècle', *RAM* 5 (1924) 278, VM says that Hadewijch's *Minne* refers especially to our Lord.

75 *Hadewijch. Strofische Gedichten*, 261.

76 T.M. Guest, ' Hadewijch and Minne', *European Context. Studies in the History and Literature of the Netherlands presented to Th. Weevers*, P.K. King and P.F. Vincent eds, (Cambridge, 1976) 26–27.

77 'Hadewijch en de Minne in haar Strofische Gedichten', *TNTL* 87 (1971) 241–59; 251–52. In her treatise Beatrice uses some expressions which also appear in courtly poetry. How far she, too, was influenced by the latter remains

In his turn Joris Reynaert made a thorough investigation of the meanings of *minne* in Hadewijch's *Poems in Stanzas*. In the thirteenth century the German minnesingers and the French trouvères and troubadours shifted their lyric focus decidedly from service of the *Frau* (woman, lady) to that of *minne*. This shift is exemplified in a great number of nouns and verbs which Hadewijch integrated, along with twelfth-century mystical literature, into her concept of a personified *minne*.[78] In her other writings, Hadewijch's *minne* has the same polyvalent meaning as in her *Poems in Stanzas*.[79] Frank Willaert came to the conclusion that by personifying *Minne*, Hadewijch depersonalized her with the result that the personification encompasses both the concrete and the abstract.[80] It is therefore necessary to look at the context of *minne* on every occasion when Hadewijch uses the term. Taken out of context, some sayings about *minne* could seem to contradict others. There is the further fact that some of Hadewijch's contemporary writers and poets already complained about the overuse of the term *minne*. Thus it is difficult to see how clearly and neatly *minne* covers the multifaceted aspects of *caritas ordinata*, well-ordered love.[81]

Neither Hadewijch nor Beatrice intended to write theology. What they had in mind was to express their personal experience of a God in love with them as they themselves were madly in love with him. What Hadewijch, Beatrice and the other *mulieres religiosae* produced is not theoretical, abstract theology, but experientially lived theology, not bookish theology, but theology from the heart. That in Hadewijch's letters in particular *Minne* often refers to God or to Christ is certainly true. Equally above doubt is the fact that in many other places, especially in her poetry, Hadewijch personifies *minne* to express how, according to her experience, she was mercilessly purified by *Minne* in order to

---

to be seen, for a number of these expressions could well have become part of the common spoken language.

78 J. Reynaert, *Beeldspraak*, 333–61.

79 Briefly treated by J. Reynaert, *ibid.*, 361–62.

80 Frank Willaert, *De poëtica van Hadewijch*, 347–57.

81 See J. Pieper, *About Love*, 6 and another example in J. Reynaert, *Beeldspraak*, 364, n. 113.

attain *Minne*. But once she had perceived that *Minne* was signal-
ing her to follow Christ totally, she bore up under *Minne* who
treated her so willfully.

Hadewijch and Beatrice certainly had the right to use literary
ways and forms which they felt appropriate to express their
religious experiences. The argument that *Minne* should be identified theologically with God or Christ has validity. To maintain
philologically that *minne* is more or less personified has equally
some valid claims. But in fact, neither theology nor philology
may claim that Hadewijch's *minne* is exclusively theirs.

Chapter Six leaves us in no doubt that the *mulieres religiosae*
several times expressed their burning desire to die, not in order to
be with a personified *minne*, but to be with God and their Saviour
Jesus Christ. At the end of her seventh *maniere* Beatrice, repeating Paul's saying (Ph.1:32) wrote:

> I long to be dissolved and to be with Christ. In just that
> way the soul vehemently desires and is grievously impatient
> to be freed and to live with Christ.... Only because of holy
> and eternal love does the soul ardently and impetuously long
> and languish to arrive at the eternal land and its glorious
> fruition.[82]

In a touching sentence Christ told Hadewijch in her third
vision:

> If you become for me the one who, in perfect love, follows
> me in the way in which I was as Man, then you shall
> experience the fruition of me as the Minne *who* I am [as
> God]. Until that day you shall live following me in *what* I
> am [as Man]: active love, and you shall be love as I am
> Love. During your [earthly] lifetime till your birth to life in
> death, you shall not live for anything else than [this active]
> love. You accepted me in my unity [as God-Man] and I

---

82 R-VM, *Seven manieren*, 33, ll. 77–87.

acknowledged you. Go forth and live *what* I am [as Man] and return bringing to me full Godlikeness and have fruition of me as *who* I am [as God].[83]

Minne was as present in the biographies of the other *mulieres religiosae* as it was in the lives and writings of Hadewijch and Beatrice, even if the vernacular term *minne* is not used in biogra phies written in Latin. There is no evidence that the biographers themselves personalized *minne* or gave a polyvalent meaning to it. What the biographers wrote came to them mostly through the secondary sources they had used. But they had a satisfactory knowledge of patristic and monastic writers and were familiar with the Bible and the many commentaries on the *Song of Songs* in circulation at their time.[84] This explains a great deal of their familiarity with the metaphorical interpretations of the commentaries on the *Song* and their own expertness in handling metaphors as they wrote the biographies. Their usual tendency to moralize is a somewhat weakening factor in the presentation of their work, but it does not affect *minne*. They all intended to present love as the uniting factor between God and the *mulieres religiosae*.

Growth in love is far from an easy process. Beatrice, for instance, 'carefully tended the garden of her heart. She walled it in by self-control and put a solicitous guard at the gate. She carefully weeded out the seeds of vices and sowed various virtues'.[85] Thus prepared, she was ready to be led into the cellar or wine cellar [depending on the verse used: Sg 1:3 or Sg 2:4], where the smell and aroma of the stocked fruit of virtues

83 VM, *Visioenen*, 1: 43–44, ll. 15–25. Hadewijch here contrasts the *who* of Christ in the fruition of his divinity with the *what* of Christ in his activity as man. In her second vision (which is, in fact, one with the third; see N. De Paepe, *Hadewijch.Strofische Gedichten*, 151–52) Hadewijch stated that before this vision she had been thinking for about two years about *what* and *who* minne is. See VM, *Visioenen*, 1: 39, l. 20.

84 Fr. Ohly estimates in his *Hohelied-Studien*, 305–06, that in the twelfth century more than thirty commentaries on that short book were written, *viz.* more than during the preceding thousand years.

85. *Vita*, 118,4. Hadewijch was likewise 'solicitous to take care of her garden, pulling out the weeds and sowing virtues'. Letter 10: VM, *Brieven*, 1: 91, ll. 109–10.

[the moral sense],[86] and the fragrance of the Bridegroom [the mystical sense] affected her so much that she became inebriated:

Seeing herself unconstrained by any sinful impediment from progressing further without obstacle in the way of virtue, suddenly [she] began to place herself totally at the service of love, only carrying out in act and in conduct the good-pleasure of love. What else could she relish except love, she who had been brought so often into the wine cellar, who had been inebriated so often with the nectar of love and satisfied with heavenly delights, who had so often drawn from the Savior's fountains the taste of love.[87]

In *Poem 12 in Stanzas*, Hadewijch also spoke of inebriation by drinking from the underground veins of Love's fountain:

Those who give themselves to *Minne* to satisfy her,
What great wonder shall happen to them!
With love they shall cleave to her in oneness
And with love be drawn into the secret veins
Into the channels where *Minne* pours herself totally
    into them
And inebriates her friends even to drunkenness
Amazing them with her passionateness.[88]

Stabilized in virtuousness, intoxicated in the wine cellar, Beatrice went to the next phase: detachment from all that is not God:

As the daughter of love, she could only relish what she tasted of love, and the more she was inebriated within by its honey-sweet smell, the more ardently she thirsted for it. The more magnificently she was refreshed by this sweetness, the

---

86 For this moral sense, see H. de Lubac, *Exégèse médiévale* I: 43–118 and E. Gilson, *Mystical Theology*, 101–103.
87 *Vita*, 196,3.
88 VM, *Strophische Gedichten*, 76, ll. 51–58.

more her insatiable appetite increased in its desire. Since she
could not find in present things what she desired, her appetite, continually hungry and famished, sought the satiety of
the eternal refection.[89] With the wings which love, like a
mother, had fitted for her, Beatrice transcended not only
herself but every human and angelic creature and arrived
under the guidance of love at the uncreated Good. There,
without being repulsed in any way, she entered into the
Bridegroom's chamber (*sponsi thalamum*), and sought him
as he was feeding and resting at noon (Sg 1:7). Here she
deserved to be honored by him more festively with heavenly
joys, according to the greater purity of mind and affection
with which she flew to the sweet secret chamber of her
Lover and Beloved.[90]

Ida Lewis also found inebriation in the wine cellar of
minne: In her desire to enjoy inwardly the delights of [the
contemplative] Rachel, she made her heart ready for the
flight. Lifting herself up above herself with the little wings
of love, she penetrated by the flight of her desire...into
celestial secrets.... Led inside the wine cellar with the
Beloved, filled with celestial nectar, her heart decked out
with flowers, her mind dripping with honey and her spirit
overflowing with milk, she was able to put love in order
within herself.[91]

89 *Vita*, 203,63.
90 *Vita*, 196,12. This is probably based on Bernard's Hum 7,14; SBOp 3: 32,
see the paraphrase by E. Gilson: *Mystical Theology*, 102–04. The inebriation-
metaphor is quite ancient. The patristic use has been well covered by H. Lewy,
Sobria ebrietas. Untersuchungen zur Geschichte der antiken Mystik (Giessen,
1929). A. Solignac gave an overview of 'ivresse spirituelle' in the Middle Ages
and later centuries in *DSp* 7: 2322–37. See also G. Dubois, 'Spiritual Inebriation', *Liturgy* 12 (Gethsemani, 1978), n.2, 3–24 and R. Javelet, *Psychologie*, 44,
n.148. After Gregory the Great, Ambrose and Augustine, the twelfth century is
represented by Bernard, William and the Victorines.
91 *AA SS* Oct.13: 113,18: 'Ad Rachelis delicias se medullitus transferens,
ascensiones in corde suo disposuit, se supra se sublevans sumptis amoris
pennulis, volatu desiderii...coelestium arcana penetrans,... introducta cella vin-
aria cum dilecto, delibuta coelesti nectare, corde florigens, mente melliflua,

We find the same theme again in the biography of the leper, Alice of Schaarbeek: 'God preferred to dwell within the chamber of her mind as in the chamber of the bridegroom, desirous to inebriate his spouse with the sweetness of his fragrance'.[92]

We have already seen instances of *mulieres religiosae* so over whelmed with love for Christ that when he came to them in the Eucharist they lost consciousness and fainted from blissful inebriation.[93] It might be thought that these inebriations were self-induced. Of Ida Lewis, for example, it is simply said that she was 'again inebriated with delightful nectar'.[94] Ida of Nivelles could barely attend the choir-offices, because 'her soul was inebriated with such a sweetness'.[95] But let there be no mistake: this inebriation was not the result of subjectively stirred up feelings. The kind of inebriation of which the *mulieres religiosae* or their biographers spoke was one of love for God. Spiritual inebriation comes by a free gift of the inebriating God, and on the part of the one inebriated, a free acceptance of the intoxicating nectar of divine love. Ida of Nivelles' biographer says explicitly that when on a Christmas day she was finally able to go to communion, she was 'divinely inebriated by an abundant sweetness'.[96] When she saw Christ in the refectory as a twelve-year old boy enjoying her presence, 'she was greatly comforted by this vision and felt inebriated because she had been allowed by her Beloved to drink from the goblet filled with seasoned wine...until she lost her

lacteo spiritu, caritatem in se promeruit ordinare'. Alluding to Sg 4:11, the biographer made it a delightful flight.

92 *AA SS* June 2: 479,9:'Intra cubiculum mentis suae, quasi in thalamo secum morari, et suaviter odoris sui sponsam cupiens inebriari'.

93 See above, chapter XI, pp. 228–31. Psychologists, who look at these phenomena from their point of view arrive, at times, at a different interpretation. See Mela Escherich, 'Das Visionenwesen in den mittelalterlichen Frauenklöster', *Deutsche Psychologie* 1 (1916) 153–55. Escherich's somewhat outdated view has been corrected by Pierre Adnès, 'Goût spirituel', DSp 6: 626–44.

94 *AA SS* Oct. 13: 118,36: 'iterum jocunda nectare debriata'.

95 *Quinque*, 246: 'tanta suavitatis dulcedine anima ejus inebriata est'.

96 *Ibid.*, 253: 'abundantia suavitatis divinitus inebriata fuit'. As a reminder of the meaning of *suavitas*, sweetness, see chapter XI, n. 69.

bodily strength'.[97] When Christ whispered to Beatrice that he pledged himself to her forever and affirmed that from then on they would be united, 'her spirit began to be inwardly inebriated with such delight, that her bodily senses withdrew inside to enjoy the spiritual sweetness of this favor' (163,34). On one Epiphany day, Beatrice saw the Lord standing at the altar with out-stretched arms, waiting for her. When she approached and he applied his own heart to hers, she was so overwhelmed that she lost consciousness. Brought to bed, 'she rested with the Lord all day in tranquil peace of conscience, in exultant jubilation, drunk with inestimable sweetness of mind'(194,44).

Ida of Leuven, who often lost consciousness when she went to communion, also became inebriated in instances not related to the Eucharist. One day, on her way to church to listen to a sermon,'she went there with a quick step, totally inebriated with the sweetness of love'.[98] 'Sometimes the fullness of heavenly grace filled her mind with such an inebriation that any place she sat to rest seemed to her like the kingdom of heaven...so oblivious had she become of her human condition'.[99]

This inebriation usually brings with it forgetfulness of all else, including the human condition, as Bernard was fond of saying.[100] William expressed this effect by saying that 'under the touch of the Holy Spirit, the soul becomes intoxicated...and so drunk that it forgets its low miserable condition, its lost likeness, and

97 *Ibid.*, 248: 'ex dulci visione sibi ostensa magnifice confortata est et tamquam a dilecto suo poculum ex vino condito accepisse, vehementer inebriata...vires corporis amisit'.

98 *AA SS* April 2: 172,6: 'audiendi verbum Dei...festinante pede, tota caritatis inebriata dulcedine'. Spirituel inebriation does not always produce physical unconsciousness.

99 *Ibid.*, 172,2: 'Interdum ipsa coelestis gratiae plenitudo mentem illius intantum inebriando perfudit, ut ubicumque sedendo quiesceret, ipsum in quo residabat loculum, regnum extitisse coelorum, humanae conditionis eo tempore prorsus immemor existimaret'.

100 E. Gilson, *Mystical Theology*, 139, n. 208: 'ardent love is love at that degree of intensity which brings forgetfulness of the infinite Majesty of God, and a bold desire to enter into union. Bernard frequently compares this ardent love with an inebriation'. See also *ibid.*, p. 238, n. 164.

actually presumes to reach out to the unutterable perfection of God'.[101]

Cellar and wine cellar, used so repeatedly, became a *topos* in mystical terminology. This metaphor, like so many others, was flexible enough to admit of several variants. Ida of Nivelles' biographer connected her charismatic gifts with the wine cellar:

> It should be known that the measure of her revelations depended on the magnitude of her love. She was frequently brought by the Beloved into the wine cellar. There she received the goblet filled with the seasoned wine of his divine love. She became inebriated and carried away. From the divine revelations she drew with the greatest ease and delight that which she ardently desired from the intimate sweetness of truth.[102]

As was her custom after she had gone to communion, Ida Lewis withdrew to a solitary, secluded place and 'with a contemplative heart, remained there for a long time, savoring the sweetness of mind and the delight of soul with a sober inebriation'.[103]

'Sober inebriation' was not invented by the biographers. Augustine had already said 'that sober inebriation does not overturn the mind, but ravishes it upward and brings about a forgetfulness of earthly things'.[104] Bernard put it in his own way: 'This sober inebriation is filled with truth, not with strong drink, not

---

101 D. Bell, *The Image*, 203–04 and the references in n. 121.

102 *Quinque*, 280: 'Sciendum est ergo quod ex magnitudine charitatis ejus pendebat modus revelationis. Cum enim frequenter a dilecto suo introduceretur in cellam vinariam et ab eo poculum ex vino amoris divini conditum acciperet, statim prae ebrietate in mentis excessum abducebatur, et ex divinis revelationibus summa cum facilitate et jucunditate hauriebat, quod de intima veritatis suavitate ardenter desiderabat'. Ida's charismatic gifts have been mentioned above, Chapter X, pp. 301–304, in connection with her great desire to help her neighbors in need.

103 *AA SS* Oct.13: 120,43: 'se sequestrans, ibi mansit diutius, contemplativo pectore, suavitatem spiritus animaeque delicias ebrietate sobria degustando'.

104 *De agonia Christiana* 10, PL 40: 296. 'Talis [sobria] ebrietas non evertit mentem, sed tamen rapit sursum, et oblivionem praestat omnium terrenorum'. See above, n.90.

steeping in wine, but burning for God'.[105] Sober inebriation, in the context of love for God, affirms *minne*'s objective, which is none other than union with God. The *mulieres religiosae* realized that *minne* remains unfulfilled, unfinished, as long as it has not pierced through to union with the Beloved. As we will see in the next chapter, only then can love be satisfied and enjoyed.

---

105 Dil 11,33; SBOp 3: 147. 'Hinc sobria illa ebrietas vero, non mero ingurgitans, non madens vino, sed ardens Deo'. C. Mohrmann wrote this sentence in rhythmical form in SBOp 2: xxviii.

CHAPTER SIXTEEN

UNION NOW

'I T IS LOVE WHICH UNITES GOD to man and man to God', wrote Yvo in his letter to Severin, a letter known to Hadewijch and Beatrice. He continued:

This union is not only that ineffable unity by which our [human] nature is united with the eternal Word in the unity of [one] person, effected indeed by that love [God's] with which he loved us before the world was made, but [this unity also means] the one the apostle [Paul in 1 Co 6:17] spoke of: "Whoever adheres to God is one spirit with him". Indeed, this unity is one of love by which a man after God's own heart is united with him by conforming in all his desires to the supreme and eternal will by the lime (*glutinum*) which will not be dissolved and the bond (*vinculum*) which will not be broken.[1]

---

1 G. Dumeige, *Yves.Epître*, 77, ll. 19–25: 'Deum etiam homini et hominem Deo unit caritas, non solum illa ineffabili unitate qua nostra natura Verbo unitur eterno in unitate persone quam effecit utique illa caritas qua *ante mundi constitutionem* nos dilexit, sed etiam illa quam ait apostolus: *Qui adheret Deo unus spiritus est*. Profecto unitas hec amoris est qua homo secundum cor Dei, totis votis superne et eterne voluntati conformis, unitur Deo *glutino* quod non dissipabitur et vinculo quod non disrumpetur'. For the translation of *glutinum* as *lime*, see below, n. 48.

Though Yvo was not an original thinker but a compiler (chiefly from Bernard's writings), he expresses clearly what union with God is all about. The union between God and man is exemplified in the union of God and man in the God-Man. It is difficult to judge if Yvo is here aware of a theological question: was man created in view of the incarnation or vice-versa?[2] Independently of Yvo's opinion, the *mulieres religiosae* were deeply impressed by the incarnation: in his overflowing love for himself, God desired so much to have man as a love partner that he made his

2 The *mulieres religiosae* were not challenged by this question, certainly not with its later treatment by the scholastic Thomists and Scotists spoken of above, chapter VI, n. 48. No explicit study has yet been made about what stand the *mulieres religiosae* took or could have taken in this matter. Many passages in the preceding pages could be quoted and assembled to indicate that, indeed, they saw the incarnation in its double aspect: the self-communication of God's immeasurable love in the incarnation of the Son, the summit of the whole of creation; and the healing salvation of man, who wronged his God and himself by misusing his God-given freedom. When Hadewijch, for instance, insisted on man's need to practice virtues, she finished this sentence by saying that the end to which God created us was *his* own honor and praise and *our* own bliss in eternal glory (Letter 6, VM, *Brieven*, 1: 67, ll. 321–23. Italics added). It could be shown that Beatrice was of the same opinion. Her treatise offers several indications of it, as can be deduced from the text itself and from H. Vekeman's *Lexicografisch Onderzoek*, 2: 364–67: 'Het minne-klimaat in de 12de en 13de eeuw'. Beatrice's *Vita* too could prove very helpful, particularly from the time she had her first complete mystical experience in 1231. It would be more difficult to pinpoint this topic in the four other *mulieres religiosae* of whom we have only biographies written by clerics more interested in the edifying and stimulating lives of their subjects than in the theological positions undergirding their behavior and experiences. The *mulieres religiosae* unacquainted with the speculative questions arising in and discussed exclusively in theological circles, knew, nevertheless, the content of their christian belief quite well, as the preceding pages should have made clear. Moreover, it should be said that in several instances religious experiences were chronologically ahead of intellectual theology; both are orthodox though in different ways. At times, the former reach a depth which becomes all too easily obscured by the accumulation of verbose discussions. With the above mentioned bibliography (Chapter VI, n.48) at least the following publications should also be consulted: S. Otto, *Gottes Ebenbild in Geschichtlichkeit*; K. Rahner, *Theological Investigations*, 5, ET by K.H. Kruger (Baltimore-London, 1966) 157–92: 'Christology within an Evolutionary View of the World'; Helmut Riedlinger, 'Vom Weg des Glaubens zum Herrn der Zukunft', *Jesus. Ort der Erfahrung Gottes* (B. Casper ed.), (Freiburg-Basel, 1976) 237–47, and Piet Fransen, *Hermeneutics*, (cited in full in n.5 of Chapter XVII), particularly the section on Ecclesiology, 321–81.

love manifest, first in creating man and then re-creating him in and through his Son incarnate; then he made this encounter of the divine and the human in Christ the motive for man to strive wholeheartedly for Christlikeness and through this to share in Christ's divine Sonship. God thus opened the way for a union so deep and so intimate that it became almost unbreakable. This was the goal the *mulieres religiosae* kept continually in mind and heart.

The term 'bond' seems quite appropriate. Hadewijch spoke frequently of union as a bond,[3] and so too did Beatrice.[4] When the latter had her first vision beyond the spirit in 1231, 'the presence of the deity so wholly absorbed her within itself that she sought it alone in preference to all other joys, understanding that she was more closely united and joined to it with the bond of love'(174, 76).

'Bond' however, is only one of the many terms used to express union, and in its Latin form, *vinculum*, it is not commonly used by the biographers. But they liberally employ other words with similar meanings to draw attention to union, and to show in a variety of ways the solidity and depth of such union.

Most of the Latin words are clear enough and do not need any commentary. We find such terms as *accubitus*,[5] *adhaesio*, *copulatio*, or the less crude *copula spiritualis*,[6] *glutinum*, or

3 Hadewijch's several references to the bond as the expression of union with God have been treated by J. Reynaert, *Beeldspraak*, 41–53: Band van Minne. The author treated the similarities and dissimilarities between the bond of courtly lyricism and the bond in a religious context. The bond of love is graphically and touchingly expressed in plates 12 and 19 of Nicolas J. Perella's *The Kiss Sacred and Profane. An Interpretative History of Kiss Symbolism and Related Religio-Erotic Themes* (henceforth cited as *The Kiss*), (Berkeley-Los Angeles, 1969).

4 Her *Vita* mentions the *vinculum* or similar terms several times, as does the vernacular of her *Seven manieren*.

5 Reclining on a couch, as opposed to *concubitus*, a lying together, which has more erotic, indeed sexual overtones.

6 The verb *copulari* used by Ida of Leuven's biographer in his opening statement (see above Chapter VIII, n.93) evokes an erotic image as a symbol for a spiritual experience. See Jacques Blanpain,'Langage mystique, expression du désir dans les Sermons sur le Cantique des Cantiques de Bernard de Clairvaux', *Coll* 36 (1974) 51: 'Dans le symbole matrimonial, c'est l'union connue par

conglutinatio. Verbs are equally graphic: *adhaerere, inhaerere, confoederari, conglutinari, conjungere* (to connect together), *consimilari, copulari, jungere, sociari, consociari.* In many instances spoken of below, union in all its different expressions starts with *liquescere,* a melting caused by the vehemence of ardent love; the *mulieres religiosae* melted into their God.

Man's creation to God's image and likeness provides the basis and the goal of his being and living: union with God. As image he has an inborn dynamic capacity for God. By striving for likeness with his divine Archetype, he can, with the renovation offered to him by Christ and under the guidance of the Holy Spirit, arrive at union with God, a union he was created for, a union without which his life would have little, if any meaning. Unshakeable, complete and everlasting union is only possible 'in the time of glory' as Beatrice expressed it.[7] Here, 'in the time of grace', 'we should love God to the very best of our ability. Not only is it the very least we can do, since Christ loved us to the very end, but it is also the only way in which we can recover our lost likeness, our lost dignity'.[8]

Union in the time of grace has already been discussed in the last section of Chapter Six,[9] and save for a few aspects related to the recovery and perfecting of the likeness, we need not reiterate that material here. In the preceding pages we met several instances where the *mulieres religiosae* expressed their conviction that God's grace was absolutely necessary to reach the goal for which God created them. They were no less convinced that

l'expérience humaine ou imaginée par le désir qui exprime l'idéal de la relation avec Dieu'. This is probably what the biographer had in mind, for he says that frequently Ida's 'soul was called out of the dwelling place of her body by the bridegroom and the lover of virgins': *AA SS* April 2: 172,5; 'ipse sponsus virginum et amator, illius animam ex cunctis sui corporis habitaculis evocatam, ad se familiariter accersivit, ibique eam sanctissimis amplexibus honorando...saepe repetita vicissitudine'.

7 R-VM, *Seven manieren,* 38, ll. 167–68.

8 D. Bell, *The Image,* 159, referring to William's Ep frat, PL 184: 348B-C; SCh: 230. The author substantiates the relation likeness/love by an observation made by R. Javelet (*Image,* 1: 413) about twelfth-century spiritual writers: 'to love consists in a return to an ever more perfect likeness by grace'.

9. Chapter VI: liberating grace and unitive grace pp.168–212.

the response required by God's love had to be made by their freely choosing love. They also knew that both love and grace admit of degrees, since they are rooted in freedom and its use. William can be considered their spokesman when he writes:

When he is effected to the likeness of his Maker, man is affected to God, that is, [he becomes] one spirit (*unus spiritus*) with God, beautiful in Beauty, good in Goodness, and this [occurs] in due proportion, according to the strength of faith, the light of understanding, and the measure of love. He is then in God by grace, what God is by nature.[10]

When one has learned to set one's house in order or, to use the classical expression, when with God's help one has reached *caritas ordinata*, well-ordered charity,[11] and wills what God wills, then through this conformity of will one is made one spirit with God.[12] Conformity expresses unequivocally the true nature of unity with God. To say it, Bernard used three words: *unior cum*

10 Cant, PL 180: 505C; SCh 82: 216,94. 'Cumque efficitur ad similitudinem facientis, fit homo Deo affectus; hoc est cum Deo unus spiritus; pulcher in pulchro; bonus in bono; idque suo modo secundum virtutem fidei, et lumen intellectus et mensuram amoris, existens in Deo per gratiam, quod ille est per naturam'. The translation is taken from D. Bell, *The Image*, 174, where Bell (n. 27) made the observation that *unus spiritus* derives from 1 Co 6:17 and *unitas spiritus* from Eph 4:3. Referring to William's expression of being by grace what God is by nature (Ep frat, PL 184: 349B; SCh 223: 354,264), Paul Verdeyen remarked that this expression was taken over by Hadewijch and Ruusbroec: 'De invloed van Willem van Sint-Thierry op Hadewijch en Ruusbroec', *OGE* 51 (1977) 3–19; 17.

11 See above, Chapter XV, n. 11.

12 William, Cant; PL 180: 514B; SCh 82: 276,130: 'Ordinante in ea rege caritatem, incipiat etiam velle quod Deus vult. Et tunc per similitudinem voluntatis unus cum Deo spiritus fit. D. Bell (*The Image*, 212–13) remarks that William speaks of *unus spiritus* in relation to ecstasy and to (non-ecstatic) dwelling together of charitable individuals as, for instance, in Nat am PL 184: 406A; 'gratia...qua habitantes in unum seipsis in Deo et Deo in seipsis fruuntur' (the grace...whereby dwelling together in unity, they enjoy each other in God and God in each other). VM, *Brieven*, 2: 110 pointed out that Hadewijch understood William correctly in her letter 26 (VM, *Brieven*, 1: 218, ll. 30–34]. The ET in CF 30: 106 missed this nuance by translating: 'that grace...whereby they dwell in unity among themselves in God and enjoy God in themselves'.

conformor,[13] when I conform myself [to God], I am united [with him]. Likeness and union are interrelated from the beginning. Likeness, given to man at his creation, is an existential relationship with the divine Archetype and an inchoative union with It. When set in motion, vigorously pursued, and finally perfected, likeness attains union.[14] Hadewijch, as we mentioned above,[15] 'saw God's bride [Hadewijch herself] clad in a robe of total conformity of will', or, as she wrote in her thirteenth Letter: 'This is always its [the soul's] desire and prayer, to be in oneness with Love, as one reads in the Canticle: 'dilectus meus mihi et ego illi' (my Beloved is mine and I am his; Sg 2:16). Thus there shall be one single gathering in the one will of a unique love'.[16]

'The one will of a unique love' is the oneness of wills in one mutual love. To stress that this oneness does not by some identification end up in pantheism,[17] Bernard wrote:

As to God and man, each subsisting separately in his own substance and his own proper will, if they abide mutually in

13 SC 71,5; SBOp 2: 217.

14 E. Gilson, *Mystical Theology*, 131 and R. Javelet, *Image*, 1: 436.

15 Chapter VI, section E, n. 160.

16 VM, *Brieven*, 1: 113–14, ll. 11–16. For the evolution of the *mulieres religiosae* in their ascent to union, see St. Axters, 'De "unio mystica" voor de Brabants-Rijnlandse mystiek van de dertiende en de veertiende eeuw', *Mededelingen van de Kon. Academie voor Wetenschappen, Letteren en Schone Kunsten van België*, Klasse der Letteren 11, n. 6 (1949) 3–27; 5–10.

17 P. Rousselot (*Pour l'histoire de l'Amour au Moyen Age*, 49–55) objected to Bernard's use of the term *annihilation*. In no way does Bernard jeopardize an individual's personality. As Gilson remarked (*The Spirit of Medieval Philosophy*, ET by A. H C.Downes, [London, 1950] 289–303; *Mystical Theology*, 239–40, nn.179–81), the question is about the possible annihilation of not the person, but of the false self (the *proprium*). When the likeness has been restored, self-love ceases to have any meaning. By arriving at well-ordered love, man participates fully in God's love for himself. W. Hiss (*Die Anthropologie des Bernhards*, 107–10) met objections coming from psychoanalytical quarters, while E. Gilson in his paper 'Maxime, Erigène, S.Bernard', *Aus der Geisteswelt des Mittelalters*. Studien und Texte Martin Grabmann zur Vollendung des 60. Lebensjahres von Freunden und Schülern gewidmet (A. Lang, J. Lechner, M. Schmaus eds), vol.1, (Munich, 1935) 188–95 proved incorrect Adolf Harnack's accusation of pantheistic tendencies in the teachings of Bernard and others in relation to man's creation to God's image and likeness.

each other, we understand [that] they are not one by confusion of two substances but by the accord of two wills. In that
then consists their union: a communion of wills and their
accord in charity.[18]

Hadewijch's saying: 'and so the soul becomes with him [Christ
as God] all that he himself is',[19] has been questioned as having a
heterodox ring.[20] But Hadewijch seems to be in good company.
When William is speaking of this third and highest degree of
likeness, he states that 'it makes man one with God, one spirit'.[21]
Étienne Gilson comments that this sentence became 'a very great
scandal to certain theologians, but we know that we have to do
with a *unitas similitudinis*, a unity of likeness'.[22] William does,
indeed, speak of unity of similarity or a unity of likeness in his
Exp Rom,[23] and he adds that the *unitas similitudinis* brings about
a *unitas spiritus*, a unity of spirit, for the *idem spiritus*, the same
spirit, who is *donans* (Giver) and *donum* (Gift), is at once both
God's love for himself and for us. To quote Gilson once more:

Let us go further, to the even greater scandal of the same
theologians: not only does it make us will what God wills,
but it makes it impossible for us to will anything else. And,
indeed, *in the measure in which the likeness reigns in us*,
how could we possibly will evil, since charity, by which we
will, is in us as the gift of the love by which Goodness loves
Itself. The Holy Spirit does not here affect us from without;
by grace it is indeed Charity itself, that is the Holy Spirit
himself, who is in us this *unitas spiritus*, and is unity

18 SC 71,10; SBOp 2: 221: 'Atqui Deum et hominem, quia propriis extant ac
distant et voluntatibus et substantiis...in se alterutrum manere sentimus,id est
non substantiis confusos, sed voluntatibus consentaneos. Et haec unio ipsis
communio voluntatum et consensus in caritate'. The translation is taken from
Gilson, *Mystical Theology*, 125.
19 Letter 19, VM, *Brieven*, 1: 165, ll. 60–61.
20 See above, Chapter VI, p. 130, n. 33.
21 Ep frat PL 184: 394A; SCh 223: 352,262.
22 E. Gilson, *Mystical Theology*, 212–13.
23 PL 180: 638D; CF 27: 173.

between us and God as he is unity between the Father and the Son. In virtue of this gift, in short, the man who has become a man of God, does not merit to become God, but, in a manner which we can neither conceive nor express, what God is by nature he becomes by grace: *quod Deus est ex natura, homo ex gratia.*[24]

To express their unification with God, the *mulieres religiosae* had recourse to a great variety of images and metaphors, though we should always keep in mind that unification never becomes identification. They became one with God by oneness in love through participation, or whatever other term is used in this regard. Human language being what it is, Hadewijch and, to a lesser degree, Beatrice spoke about God as an abyss and about his other 'dimensions', such as depth, breadth[25] and so on. Because of the limitations of human speech, Beatrice spoke at the beginning of her seventh *maniere* of God's 'dimensions' attracting her as an irresistable magnet:

The soul is drawn through eternal Love (*Minne*) alone, and into the eternity of Love, and into the incomprehensibility and vastness and inaccessible sublimity and the deep abyss of the Divinity, which is wholly perfect in all things and

24 Et.Gilson, *Mystical Theology*, 214, where he adds that 'William's critics...having failed to understand that the perfect likeness he describes is the very likeness of the beatific vision, or the brief ecstasy [as *excessus*] which carries simply the human soul above its human condition, they do not see that what they take for pantheism is nothing but a description of a mystical and beatifying union of the soul with God'.

25 For Hadewijch, see R. Vanneste, *Abstracta*, 34–40, and J. Reynaert, *Beeldspraak*, 254–58. Some of Hadewijch's references to abyss have already been quoted in these pages. For Beatrice's use of abyss in her *Seven manieren*, see H. Vekeman, *Lexicografisch Onderzoek*, 2: 332. In her sixth *maniere* she says that like 'a fish swimming in the depths, and like a bird flying boldly in the vastness and the height of the sky, so the soul feels its spirit moving freely in the breadth and depth and vastness and height of *minne*' (R-VM, *Seven manieren*, 25–26, ll. 35–42]. Her *Vita* too, especially the third book, speaks *passim* of God's abyss and the other dimensions. This trait is very common among mystics, as Louis Dupré pointed out in *Transcendant Selfhood. The Loss and Rediscovery of the Inner Life*, New York, 1976,96: 'omnipresent are the images of depth. Almost equally common is the image of height'.

remains incomprehensible above all things, which is immutable, perfect Being.[26]

In fact, this process of being drawn or pulled into points to
union with God which happens only when charity is well-ordered.
Gilson, commenting on a text of Bernard, says that according to
the latter, the soul has

to empty itself of its illusory personality of self-will. A
disfiguring mask falls away, revealing the true countenance
of a soul whose nature is to have been made to the image of
God. Such expressions [as *deficere a se tota videtur* or *a
semetipsa liquescere*] have always a positive meaning as
well, which is indicated by St.Bernard when he adds to his
commentary: 'a semetipsa liquescere, atque in Dei penitus
transfundi voluntatem' (to melt away from one's [selfish]
self and flow wholly into the will of God). This transfusion
into the will of God is unity of spirit itself...unity of spirit,
because, since the soul is a likeness of God, the more it
conforms to God's will so much the more does it become
itself.[27]

While in God himself there is not a *union* of wills, but a *unity*
of will between the divine persons,[28] between God and man there

26 R-VM, *Seven manieren*, 29, ll. 7–13. The multiple use of 'and' in this
sentence, not only indicates that the written expression of Beatrice's mother
tongue was in its initial stage, but intimates also that she experienced God's
'dimensions' as really breathtaking. The original has *getrect*, translated by
Reypens as *trahitur* and retranslated from there into *drawn*. Moreover the text
here quoted is preceded by another, also beginning with *getrect*: 'The soul is
pulled into *minne* above what is human, above human sense and reason, and
above all the works of our heart. [The soul] is drawn (*getrect*) by eternal love
into the eternity of Love'. (R-VM, *Seven manieren*, 28–29, ll. 4–8]. Beatrice
opposes here the temporality of the human to the eternity of the divine. See H.
Vekeman, *Lexicografisch Onderzoek*, 2: 228.

27 Dil 10,28; SBOp 3: 143; E. Gilson, *Mystical Theology*, 128–29.

28 Bernard, SC 71,9; SBOp 2: 221: 'Si quis tamen inter Patrem et Filium
dicat esse consensum, non contendo, dummodo non voluntatum unionem, sed
unitatem intelligat voluntatis'.

has to be union of wills if there is to be union.[29] To express the result of such a union of wills the Greek branch of Christianity has used the bold expression 'deification'.[30] Bernard, who, according to Gilson, seems to have taken the expression from Maximus the Confessor, wrote that to be 'transformed by God [into union of wills and *caritas ordinata*] is deification'.[31] Hugh preferred to speak of deiformity,[32] while William avoiding the term deification,[33] speaks of *deificus* (being made Godlike).[34]

Bernard, immediately after saying that 'sic affici, deificari est', has recourse to three images to make clear that he does not mean that the soul becomes God when it attains deification.[35]

As a small drop of water mingled in much wine *seems* to be wholly lost and to take on the color and the taste of the wine; as a kindled and glowing iron becomes most *like* fire, having put off its prior form; and as the air, when flooded with the light of the sun is transformed into the very brightness of light, so that it *seems* to be not so much illuminated as to be the light itself, so it must needs be that all human affection in the saints will then, in some ineffable way, *melt* away from itself, and flow wholly into the will of God. Otherwise how will God be all in all, if something of

29 Bernard, SC 71, 10; SBOp 2: 221: 'Unio ipsis communio voluntatum et consensus in caritate' (this union is for them [God and man] a communion of wills and an agreement in charity).

30 Vl. Lossky, *Orthodox Theology*, 73: 'Certainly man was created by the will of God alone; but he cannot be deified by it alone. A single will for creation, but two to make the image into a likeness'. This theme has been extensively treated by M. Lot-Borodine, 'La doctrine de la "déification" dans l'Eglise grecque jusqu'au XIe siècle', *Revue d'Histoire des Religions*, n. 105–6 (1932) 5–43; 525–74; n. 107 (1933) 8–55.

31 Dil 10, 28; SBOp 3: 143.

32 *In Hierarchiam* PL 175: 1006AB; *ibid.*, 8,8: 1074D.

33 Jean Déchanet, Ep frat, SCh 223,407: William ' évite toujours ce mot'.

34 D. Bell, *The Image*, 109, n. 89.

35 C. Mohrmann, *Etudes sur le Latin des Chrétiens*, vol. 2: (Rome, 1961): 'Le style de saint Bernard', 347–67; 364: " Sic affici, deificari est". Mais cette parole concise ne lui suffit pas; tout de suite l'idée se concrétise dans une triple image dans un climax de toute beauté'.

himself remains in man? The substance indeed will remain, but in another form, another glory, another power.[36]

Of the three metaphors: the small drop of water mingled with much wine, the glowing iron, the air flooded with light, the first one was particularly attacked by Gerson (1363–1429), chancellor at the university of Paris, because according to him it implied that this mingling led to a mystical union with God by amalgamation.[37]

Bernard intentionally weakened the metaphors by presenting them as being 'seemingly' so and adding at the end that the substance will remain.[38] The 'melting' or *liquefactio* (or its corresponding verb) became a favorite expression in mystical terminology to express union with God on earth. Walter Schubart considered man's melting into God as the highest human goal.[39] Peter Dinzelbacher remarked how helpful it would be to study

36 Dil 10,28; SBOp 3: 143: 'Quomodo stilla aquae modica, multo infusa vino, deficere a se tota videtur, dum et saporem vini induit et colorem, et quomodo ferrum ignitum et candens igni simillimum fit, pristina propria exutum forma, et quomodo solis luce perfusus aer in eandem transformatur luminis claritatem, adeo ut non tam illuminatus quam ipsum lumen esse videatur, sic omnem tunc in sanctis humanam affectionem quodam ineffabili modo necesse est a semetipso liquescere, atque in Dei penitus transfundi voluntatem. Alioquin quomodo omnia in omnibus erit Deus, si in homine quidquam supererit? Manebit quidem substantia, sed in alia forma, alia gloria, aliaque potentia'. The translation is taken from Gilson, *Mystical Theology*, 132.

37 See Jean Pépin in his thorough paper: "'Stilla aquae modica multo vino, ferrum ignitum, luce perfusa aer''. L'origine de trois comparaisons familières à la théologie médiévale', *Divinitas* 11 (1967) 331–75. The first metaphor is not from Maximus the Confessor but, as Pépin suggests (374), from some other unknown source where all three metaphors appear together. Bernard's sentence became proverbial, if not in his time, certainly later and for several centuries to come. Gerson attacked the first metaphor, with Ruusbroec in his mind.

38 The 'drop of water' was used in another context as well. To signify the two natures of Christ, the Greek tradition introduced into the rite of the Eucharistic celebration the adding of a little water to the wine. This rite, rejected by the Monophysites was not yet prescribed in the Latin rite in Bernard's time. See Pépin, 'Stilla aquae', 368–69. That Bernard had this rite in mind when he used the metaphor is possible, but only possible.

39 Walter Schubart, *Religion und Eros* 2nd ed. (Munich, 1966) 152: 'Das höchste Ziel ist...völliger Verschmelzung mit der Gottheit', if it is well understood.

visionaries and their visions with the help of behavioral sciences. He added that in the thirteenth century the longing for self-realization by means of encountering another form or shape (*Gestalt*)—one thinks spontaneously of the concept of *minne* in Hadewijch and Beatrice—could run parallel to the encounter with and the melting into Christ in the visions of women mystics.[40] The *mulieres religiosae* do, indeed, speak of their *liquefactio*, the melting they experienced and which they found already described by their male mentors.[41]

Keeping its own individuality, a purified soul melts into God in an intimate oneness of love. If we are to understand the *mulieres religiosae*, we need to see that they understood how their burning desire and desired burning would lead them to a love of the highest possible intensity. Only such love could make them go deliberately and eagerly through the process of melting away all selfishness, and flowing by God's grace into God, in accordance with the intensity of their purified desire. This process is ulti-mately what *caritas ordinata*, well-ordered charity, means.

In her seventh vision, where she first described how Christ had appeared to her and embraced her, Hadewijch interrupted her narrative to describe how Christ melted away and she had the impression that she and Christ were one:

40 P. Dinzelbacher, *Vision*, 234: 'Dabei dürfte sich, um ein Beispiel zu nennen, etwa für das 13.Jahrhundert eine Parallele ergeben zwischen dem (u.a. in der naturwissenschaftlichen Bewegungslehre zu konstantierenden) Sehnen nach Selbstverwirklichung durch Begegnung mit einer anderen Gestalt und der Christusbegegnung und-verschmelzung in den Visionen der Mystikerinnen'. Such collaboration with behavioral sciences is certainly to be hoped for, but without neglecting the contribution of other scholars well-versed in sociology or mystical theology, whom R. Javelet in his *Image* is fond of calling 'les spiri-tuels', the spiritual masters of the twelfth century.

41 See, for instance, Hugh in his *In Hierarchiam* 2, PL 175: 944CD, and similar texts of Richard (*De Trinitate* 6, 14; PL 196: 978D; G. Dumeige, *Les quatres degrés*, 167–69) and the compiler Yvo (G.Dumeige, *Yves. Epître*, 79 and 85). Bernard and William are referred to by R. Javelet, *Psychologie*, 110, n. 364. E. Gilson speaks extensively of liquefaction in the *Mystical Theology* of Bernard, as does D. Bell of William in *The Image*. See also J.C. Franklin, *Mystical Transformations: The Imagery of Liquids in the Works of Mechtild of Magdeburg* (Madison, NY.-London, 1978).

Soon, after a short time, I lost that manly beauty [Christ] outwardly in his visible human form. I saw him completely come to naught and fade and totally melt away so that I could no longer perceive him outside me, and could not distinguish him within me. Then it was to me as if we were one without difference.[42]

Bernard's three metaphors were received by the women with different emphases depending on many factors or were expressed with slight variants. To stress the unifying effect of *minne*, Hadewijch says that *minne* is 'that burning fire that devours everything'.[43] When Ida of Nivelles 'was once in accordance with her custom dwelling on the contemplation of heavenly things...the hand of the Lord came upon her, and as wax before a fire, so she totally melted interiorly before the divine fire...and was rapt in spirit'.[44] Earlier, when she was still a novice, absorbed in prayer, Ida's soul began suddenly to melt from the vehemence of her ardent desire, 'and passed over into an *alienatio* of mind...and was [thereby] taken up into heaven'.[45] Near the end of her life 'love gripped her so excessively that inwardly she melted as wax does, and it lifted her on high'.[46] When asked by another nun how

---

42 VM, *Visioenen*, 1: 78, ll. 81–88. According to R. Vanneste (Abstracta, 70–74) what took place is a melting away of the appearing Christ and the melting away of Hadewijch's self-consciousness into a deep union with Christ. As she says at the end of her seventh vision 'after that I wholly melted away in him [Christ] and nothing remained any longer to me of myself [in my self-consciousness]. This is the meaning of 'we were one without difference'. Angela de Foligno (d.1309) and Teresa of Avila (d.1582) had a very similar experience. See Paul Lachance, *The Spiritual Journey of the Blessed Angela de Foligno according to the Memorial of Frater A.*, Studia Antoniana 24 (Rome, 1984) 355.

43 Letter 6; VM, *Brieven*, 1: 61, l. 175. For some more examples of this kind of melting by the *ignis consumens*, the consuming fire, see J. Reynaert, *Beeldspraak*, 114–16.

44 *Quinque*, 244: 'Quadam vice cum beata virgo secundum consuetudinem coelestium insistens contemplationi...facta est super eam manus Domini, et sicut cera a facie ignis, sic tota interius a facie ignis liquefacta divini...in spiritu rapta est'.

45 *Ibid.*, 211: 'Dum adhuc esset novitia, et quadam vice orationi insisteret, coepit ex ardentis desiderii vehementia liquescere repente anima ejus...et in mentis transiens alienationem, sursum erecta raperetur in coelum'.

46 *Ibid.*, 281: 'Charitas enim eam interius ad cerae similitudinem liquefactam per excessum ad superna emittebat'.

she felt when she experienced union with God, Ida Lewis responded: 'Like a little drop of water absorbed in a flask filled
quite full of wine, so is it then'.[47] At the end of the first book of
her *Vita*, Beatrice's biographer spoke of her melting away in
relation to the Eucharist. 'She showed her heart's desire [for
communion] more by the melting of her heart, the abundance of
tears or her unrestrained laughter'(79,15). After communion she
was so overwhelmed that she had to go to bed. 'But why wonder
at this?', wrote the biographer. 'Just as wax melts before the fire
and our God is a consuming fire — so her spirit melted before the
deifying sacrament.... Thus she used to melt with enormous
gratitude as often as she approached this sacrament to communicate' (80,27). Some years later, after the consecration at Mass
'her soul began to feel his presence within her with immense
fervor and devotion'. The text continues, using both the metaphor
of fire and that of a little drop of water: 'at his presence she
melted as though before a strong fire, and she was immediately
and wholly absorbed like a drop of water flowing down into that
ocean of love'(206,10). Connected or not with the metaphor of
melting, the little drop of water can be 'mingled with much wine'
(Bernard), or with a flask filled quite full of wine (Ida Lewis), or
flow into the ocean of love (Beatrice's *Vita*): three variants of
what happened to that little drop of water.

A passage in Ida of Nivelles' biography makes the transition,
or rather the combination, of liquefaction with *glutinum* (lime).[48]

---

47 *AA SS* Oct.13: 121,48: 'Sicut aquae stillula in utre vino plenius adimpleto,
ita tunc est'. The biographer tried to explain on his own what she meant. What
he says makes sense, but is not in harmony with the union expressed by the
mentors of the *mulieres religiosae*. 'She said so', he writes, ' as if to say: I am
not even visible in God, because the littleness of the creature can in no way be
compared with the lofty greatness of the Creator'. (Hoc dixit quasi diceret: In
Deo non appareo, quia modicitas creaturae comparari non praevalet excelsae
magnitudini Creatoris).

48 Just as 'enjoyment' is too weak to express the fulness of *fruitio* in mystical
terminology, as will be explained hereafter, so 'glue' falls short in rendering the
strong bond with God expressed by the term *glutinum*. In its mystical denotation,
glutinum is something which unites two things so thoroughly that separation is
extremely difficult. To translate *glutinum* as 'cement', as is sometimes done,
sounds fine to our ears, but less suited to thirteenth-century people used to see

One day, Ida of Nivelles suddenly saw a hand appear to give her the Eucharist. Without expressing any surprise at such an experience, 'she melted inwardly because of such an overwhelming sweetness so that she felt as if she were one spirit with the Lord, since her spirit was united to the divine spirit by a strong lime'.[49] The term *glutinum* goes back to the Vulgate translation of Is 41:7 and travelled through the Christian centuries as *glutinum amoris*, or *glutinum caritatis*, the lime of love.[50] Hadewijch and Ida of Nivelles' biography have several references to the 'lime of love'. Hadewijch, for instance, wrote in her sixteenth letter: 'If two things are to become one, nothing may be between them except the lime by which they are united together. That bond of lime is *minne* whereby God and the blessed soul are united in blessedness'.[51] Ida of Nivelles' biographer reports that 'she said...that her soul was so fastened to the Holy Trinity with the lime of the

masons employing mortar to build houses solid enough to defy centuries. In some modern publications *glutinum* is at times translated as "glue" (within quotation marks to indicate its specialness). Hadewijch used the actual word *lime* when she spoke of *glutinum*. To keep as close as possible to her time, it seems advisable to keep the term 'lime' for *glutinum*, keeping in mind that 'lime' means here a very strong bonding agent. In his dissertation: *'Minne' in 'Die Gheestelike Brulocht' of Jan van Ruusbroec* (Washington D.C., 1979. Facsimile edition by University Microfilms International [Ann Arbor,-London, 1981] 37, n. 12), James Wiseman made the observation that *ghebruken* is the Middle Dutch verb, etymologically related to the Latin *frui* (to enjoy). When used substantively it can be translated into English as "enjoyment", "bliss", "blissful repose", or, somewhat archaically but with etymological correctness as 'fruition'. According to Eric Partridge, *Origins. Etymological Dictionary of Modern English*, 2nd ed. (New York, 1959) 238, s.v. Frui 3, fruition means 'full use and enjoyment, hence a successful realization'. Even if enjoyment is more familiar to us, to stay close to the *mulieres religiosae*, it seems preferable to keep 'the full use and enjoyment' of *frui* together and to express the successful realisation of enjoyment as fruition.

49 *Quinque*, 220–21: 'Ecce subito apparuit ei manus, quae Sanctam Eucharistiam tradidit ei...tanta dulcedine interius liquefacta est ut spiritum suum valido glutino divino spiritui conjunctum, quasi unum cum Deo spiritum esse sentiret'.

50 The Latin expression appears in the writings of Augustine, Jerome, Richard, Thomas the Cistercian (for references, see D. Bell, 'Thomas the Cistercian', *Citeaux* 28 [1977] 262), of Bernard (SC 71,8; SBOp 2: 220; Div 4,3; SBOp 6/1: 96 and alibi) and of Yvo (G. Dumeige, *Yves.Epitre*, 75, 13).

51 VM, *Brieven* 1: 132, ll. 28–32. More references are given by J. Reynaert, *Beeldspraak*, 51–53.

most ardent love that her spirit became one spirit with the Lord'.[52] Beatrice's biography speaks of a *caritatis glutinum ineffabile*, an ineffable lime of love, but the context speaks this time of a spiritual friendship she had with a man.

> In that blaze of love with which Beatrice was burning interiorly, a certain friend of hers, most dear to her, was presented to the gaze of her heart. Their two spirits, unspeakably joined together in love (*caritatis ineffabili glutino*), were so strongly united in Christ, that the two were made one spirit with him.... The Lord showed to his beloved [Beatrice]...that he took delight in the union of her spirit with that of her friend; that he took delightful complacence in it.[53]

Man, in his need for love, and the *mulieres religiosae* in their burning desire for union with God, have been ingenious in finding images to express their needs and desires. One of them is the *Liebespfeil*, the dart causing the wound of love. The best known artwork representing the *vulnus amoris*, the wound of love, is Bernini's sculpture, to be found in the church of Santa Maria della Vittoria in Rome, of Teresa of Avila with her heart pierced by a seraph.[54] The Septuagint Greek version of Sg 4:9 reads 'being wounded by love'. This is, at least, what we find in Rufinus' translation of Origen's commentary on the Sg: 'quia vulnerata caritatis ego sum' (I am the wounded [victim] of love;

52 *Quinque*, 271: 'dicebat quia...sic ejus anima Sanctae Trinitati glutino ardentissimi ardoris impressa est, ita ut spiritus ejus unus cum Domino spiritus efficeretur'.

53 *Vita*, 239,20. There are no clues in the biography which allows us to guess who this friend may have been. What is said in the quotation about a deep and intimate spiritual friendship is nothing new. See Gerda Walther, *Die Phänomenologie der Mystic*, (Olten-Freiburg/Br., 1955) 209–10, and especially N. Perella, *The Kiss*, 61–63, quoting texts from Cicero, Ambrose, Augustine, Aelred of Rievaulx and of Bernard's threnody on the death of his brother Gerard (SC 26,9; SBOp 1: 177). Some expressions used by Beatrice's biographer are close to those of Bernard.

54 Described at length by Robert T. Peterson, *The Art of Ecstasy* (London, 1970).

literally: I am love's wounded one). Origen was the first consciously to transpose the theme of wounding by love's darts from the pagan Eros to the Christian God.[55] The *vulnus amoris*, the wound of love he spoke of, implied the idea that the soul 'suffers' this wound happily. This concept of *vulnus amoris*, or *vulnus caritatis*, has been expressed by Jerome, Augustine, Hugh, Richard in the first of his 'Four degrees of violent love', and Baldwin of Ford in his excellent and lengthy description of the *vulnus amoris*.[56]

We saw the *mulieres religiosae* concretizing the *vulnus amoris* as we watched them striving toward union with God. In several places Hadewijch speaks of this 'wound of love' in its various aspects.[57] Beatrice's text in her treatise about the wound of love has already been quoted,[58] and her *Vita* refers to it also: one day, when she was attending mass 'the most kind Lord of mercies suddenly pierced her heart with the fire of love as with a fiery javelin, and with a great thrust mightily penetrated it as with a pointed flaming sword' (170,14). Some time later, once more pierced with love's dart, 'she could not hide the wound she bore within, with her conscience only as witness. As the daughter of love, she could only relish what tasted of love, and the more she

---

55 Origen's works in their Latin translation were on the shelves of the libraries of Clairvaux, Signy and Morimond. See H. de Lubac, *Exégèse médiévale* vol.1: 226–27). He had already called God an archer: *Deus sagittarius est.* See Leo Pollmann, *Die Liebe in der hochmittelalterlichen Literatur Frankreichs*, Analecta Romania 18, (F. Schalk ed.), (Frankfurt/Main, 1966) 36. Gregory of Nyssa called God a 'crossbowman': H. von Balthasar, *Présence et Pensée*, 129.

56 For references, see N. Perella, *The Kiss*, where on pp. 109–111 the author elaborates on 'the wound of love'. See also E. Benz, *Die Vision*, 395–97: Der himmlische Liebespfeil. References to Cistercians are not made in these two publications, but are easily found in their commentaries on The Song. For Baldwin of Ford's description, see PL 204: 477–84, ET by D Bell, in *Spiritual Tractates* VIII, CF 38, 214–26, especially 216–17. A twelfth-century manuscript (Lille 112, probably from the former Cistercian abbey of Loos), says that God's sword is his love (*Dei gladius amor suus*). See J. Leclercq, 'Caelestinus de Caritate', *Cîteaux* 14 (1963) 202–17; 211.

57 See J. Reynaert, *Beeldspraak*, 47–49. Her sayings in this regard have to be seen in their context, too complex to be explained here.

58 See above, Chapter XIII, nn. 19–20.

was inebriated within by its honey-sweet smell, the more ardently she thirsted for it'.[59]

Of Ida Lewis it is said that 'pierced by the sword of love, she was in no small way wounded by the darts of love'.[60] In another place, her biographer speaks of the 'impetuosity of love wounding and piercing her heart'.[61] Ida of Leuven too was 'wounded by the sweet arrow of love', unable to eat 'nourished as she was during that time by the food of love'.[62] At another time, addressing Christ in her prayer, she said: 'you pierced my heart and my soul with the arrow of your love'.[63] The arrowhead (*spiculum*) was for Ida the intensity of love wounding her heart: 'ablaze with the fire of love she [was] stricken by the delightful wound of love'.[64]

Swords, javelins, darts, arrows—no matter what weapon is spoken of to express metaphorically the cause of 'the wound of love', the main point in each case in that it is Christ or God or *Minne* who is said to hurl the wounding arrow. No less remarkable is the fact that this shooting of flaming missiles, far from being destructive, was aimed at *mulieres religiosae* who had already gone through the burning fire of physical and spiritual asceticism, and were able and more than willing to be involved in loving intimacy with a God whose love was highly exacting. The contexts in which the shootings occur show also that the weapon hit the target: hearts already prepared for the *vulnus amoris*, the wound of love. Trouvères, troubadours and minnesingers also

59 *Vita*, 203,60. As can be seen, this one sentence combines several aspects of love and union. A. Sartorius, in his *Verteutschtes Cistercium bis-tertium*, Prague, 1708, has an engraving by C. Liska of Beatrice being transfixed by an arrow. The plate, is reproduced in Reypens' edition of the *Vita*, facing p.171. Sartorius' origianl Latin text was published by the author (Prague,1700).

60 *AA SS* Oct. 13: 110,11: 'caritatis transfixa gladio, vulnerata non mediocriter amoris jaculo'.

61 *Ibid.*, 117,33: 'Amoris impetuositas, cor ejus vulnerans et transfigens'.

62 *AA SS* April 2: 167,35: 'Dulcique vulnerata amoris spiculo... solo per id temporis amoris nutrita ferculo'.

63 *Ibid.*, 176,20: 'Tu cor simul et animam amoris spiculo transfixisti'.

64 *Ibid.*, 175,16: 'amoris incendio conflagrata, caritatis delicio vulnere sauciata'.

spoke and wrote about their wound of love,[65] and affirmed that this wound could only be healed by their beloved lady's kiss.[66] There is no need to treat here of what the immediate mentors of the *mulieres religiosae* said about the kiss. 'The twelfth century abounds in treatises that seek to explain the complex stirrings and movements of the heart, and the passionate investigations into the psyche of man tend to be focused on the phenomena of love precisely because the center of the inner life of man is recognized to be love'.[67]

We have already seen how Ida of Nivelles, out of love for her neighbor, tried to pull a woman out of purgatory but was unable to do so.[68] Standing on the other side of the stream which separated them, the Lord told her to leave the woman alone because she clung stubbornly to her own will and refused to pass over the dangerous looking narrow bridge leading to safety. Because Ida was united with the Lord's will and had complete trust in him, she was able to pass over the bridge. When she

65. Peter Dronke, *Medieval Latin and the Rise of European Love-Lyric* 1: 298 and *passim*; N. Perella, *The Kiss*, 117. Many of them were influenced by Bernard and other Cistercians. The bibliography is extensive. For brevity's sake it may suffice to refer to Maur Cocheril, *Graal* in *DSp* 6: 672–700, and to Alois Haas, *Sermo mysticus*, 37–66, for Bernard's influence on Wolfram of Eschenbach. Reciprocally trouvères, troubadours and minnesinger influenced Cistercians, *mulieres religiosae* and others. See L. Pollmann, *Die Liebe in der hochmittelalterlichen Literatur Frankreichs*, 36–53. For Hadewijch in particular, see N. De Paepe, *Hadewijch. Strofische Gedichten*, and J. Reynaert, *Beeldspraak*, where this topic is frequently touched upon. It is interesting to notice that several trouvères and troubadours became Cistercians: Fulco, later the bishop of Toulouse, Bertrand of Allamanon, Bernart of Ventadour, Bertran de Born, Helinand of Froidmont and William of Digulleville. See Jérôme du Halgouët,'Poètes oubliés', *Coll* 20 (1958) 128–44; 227–42. For the famous Serlo of Wilton, see P. Dronke, 1, 239.

66 N. Perella, *The Kiss*, 117–18.

67 *Ibid.*, 51–83: 'Medieval Mystics', where a large place is given to Bernard, William and Aelred (for Richard, see G. Dumeige, *Les quatre degrés*, 104–05). Perella affirms on p. 51 that 'one might say that in their descriptions of divine love the mystics at least are interested primarily in recording an experiential knowledge of God and secondarily in the psychological life of man. The point is, however, that they excel in portraying the latter because they are talking about an *experience*; in the matter of affective mysticism, speculation and experience are one'.

68 See above, chapter X, n. 162.

reached the Lord in the field on the other side of the stream, he embraced and kissed her and they had a celebration. Her biographer made the remark that Ida 'often used to embrace and kiss him with ardent love in the secret chamber of her heart', for she was the mystical bride of the Lord.[69]

In one of her letters Hadewijch wrote:

I spoke of the Beloved's kiss; that is to be united with him apart from everything else: to accept no other satisfaction except what one receives in the delight of union with him. The embracing means his comfort given to our loyal confidence in him with unfeigned charity. This is the embracing and kissing of the Beloved as far as it can be expresssed in words. But how much sweetness is found in the interior experience and fruition of the Beloved, all those who were ever born in human shape could not fully explain it to you.[70]

---

69 *Quinque*, 223. The text is given in accordance with the emendation published in *OGE* cited at the end of this note. 'Dominus... monuit dilectam suam [Ida] ut miseram [the other woman] relinqueret voluntati suae....Tunc se committens ponti virgo Christi et sine impedimento transiens, quanto magis gressum in anteriora porrigebat, tanto magis pontem latiorem inveniebat. Et cum pervenisset ante conspectum dilecti sui, ipse gratiosus et speciosus forma prae filiis hominum, sicut totus affluit dulcedine et misericordia, gratiosum ei complexum et osculum exhibere dignatus est et diem festum agere cum ea, quem ipsa frequenter intra secretum cordis sui cubiculum consueverat osculari et amplexari cum ardenti caritate et lachrymarum affluentia'. See Peter Dinzelbacher, 'Ida von Nijvels Brückenvision', *OGE* 52 (1978) 189–91, where he elaborates on parallel accounts of this scene at that time. The 'celebration', *diem festum agere*, is a biblical expression.

70 Letter 27; VM, *Brieven* 1: 222, ll. 38–48. J.Reynaert, *Beeldspraak*, 308 made the observation that 'as far as it can be expressed in words' (*in redene*) as VM proposes, can also mean that the kisses and embraces are related to union with Christ in his humanity. Hadewijch's sentence has some resemblance to the so-called proem of William's Contemp (PL 184: 366B) which is unlikely to have come from William's pen (Jean Déchanet, 'Le pseudo-prologue du *De contemplando Deo*', *Citeaux* 8 [1957] 5–12). How far this 'some resemblance' to the proem could apply to Hadewijch has been treated by J. Reynaert, *Beeldspraak*, 317–20, where he refers to Bernard's SC and William's Cant.

This quotation from Hadewijch speaks of kisses as expressing a unitive experience and the delight it entails.[71] Embraces, which usually go together with kisses, mean trusting abandonment to Christ, the loving Beloved. Two persons who are deeply in love have complete trust in one another; they kiss and embrace to express their love for and trust in one another. The *mulieres religiosae* were no exception. When Beatrice was embraced by Christ,[72] this embrace was explicitly identified with union:

> In that divine embrace and union she again deserved to receive the divine pledge and promise about keeping faith with her, and she on her part, again promised to keep firmly the same faith, which she would never more violate in the future. And she obligated everything she could, that is, body and soul, as a pledge that she would not void the faithfulness she had promised to the Lord by seeking anything contrary to his will.[73]

When Beatrice was swayed by 'the great spiritual delight which she had received, and by what she sensed and tasted in the liquefaction which she experienced' (206,14), she avoided human company. On such occasions 'she fled to her usual private place. There she gave herself up with freer zeal to meditation,...and in the sweet arms and kisses of her Bridegroom she rested in the sleep of contemplation' (207,35).

Stress is frequently laid on Christ's love for his bride. Ida of Leuven's biography has Christ saying to her: 'How is a bride-

---

71 William, also speaking about kisses, refers explicitly to this unitive experience. 'A kiss is a certain outward loving union of bodies, the sign and incentive of an inward union...Christ offers his kiss to the faithful soul, his bride, and imprints it upon her, when he grants her her own personal joy and pours forth within her the grace of his love, drawing her spirit to himself and infusing his own into her so that reciprocally they both may be one spirit' (osculum amica quaedam et exterior conjunctio corporum est, interioris conjunctionis signum et incentivum...Ipsum osculum fideli animae sponsae suae porrigit et imprimit...privatum ei et proprium commendans gaudium, gratiam ei sui amoris infundit; spiritum ejus sibi attrahens, et suum infundens ei, ut invicem unus spiritus sint). Cant PL 180: 483C; SCh 82, 113–14, 30.

72 See above Chapter V, p. 204, n. 258.

73 *Vita*, 166, 38.

groom to meet his chosen bride more eagerly, than that he should delightedly embrace her when she rushes to him, and that he draw her to his breast and clasps her with amorous affection?'[74]

A few secondary remarks could be added. When the *mulieres religiosae* speak of embraces and kisses, the accent lies not so much on the terms as on what these terms express: longing love and appreciation of being united to the Beloved. We should therefore not be surprised if in some instances embraces are mentioned without the kisses. It is unlikely that this was done intentionally in order to escape the impression of eroticism. As we have seen above,[75] the *mulieres'* mutual exchange of affection does have erotic overtones. But their attention went to Christ who in his human condition expressed the immeasurable love he had for them as God and as man. The illiterate Ida of Leuven, whom we would call a 'feeling type', knew very well that these embraces were not physical but spiritual. In a prayer to Christ, she said: 'You, my Lord, you know that my heart's only trouble is simply the fire of love seething to approach you, the excessive desire for fruition of you, the sweet dwelling together drawing the inner appetite to spiritual embraces'.[76]

Alice of Schaarbeek, still young, 'applied herself to embrace in her inner depths the love of God'.[77] She found that love in a way she had not expected. Blind and her leprosy far advanced, 'she lived continuously enfolded in the divine embraces except for the

74 *AA SS* April 2: 179,31: 'Quis sponsus electae suae sponsae propensiori valebit occurrere familiaritatis officio, quam ut occurrentem sibi delectabiliter amplexetur et ad pectum suum affectu stringat et applicet amoroso?'.

75 See above, Chapter VIII, pp. 237–42, and J. Reynaert, *Beeldspraak*, 307, n.27, where he cites a passage from H.A. Hatzfield, 'Linguistic Investigations of Old French High Spirituality', *in Publicationss of the Modern Language Association* 61 (1946) 332–378 saying that about 1300 mystical beguinal vocabulary in France tried to water down erotic language .

76 *AA SS* April 2: 176,20: 'Tu nosti, mi Domine, nullum aliud extitisse mei cordis incommodum, quam tui amoris adurens incendium ad te appropinquandi, nimis insatiabile desiderium te fruendi, dulce contubernium ad spirituales amplexus internum alliciens appetitum'.

77 *AA SS* June 2: 478,4: 'Dei amorem intimis visceribus studuit amplecti'.

times devoted to suffering for the deceased'.[78] Beatrice too spoke
of embraces of love with God. One day

> when Beatrice was sitting with the others listening to the
> sermon preached to the community, her heart suddenly
> seemed to her almost broken and wholly shaken by the very
> great ardor of love. Indeed it left its natural place and rose to
> her throat. It stayed there a long time trembling and throb-
> bing, and as a result she became quite unwell. Thus lan-
> guishing in love, sick in body but robust in soul, she
> remained during the whole sermon delightfully refreshing
> herself with the Beloved, resting in his embraces and
> kisses.[79]

Biographers do not talk only about *amplexus* (embraces) and
amplecti (to embrace). To emphasize the embrace they also speak
of *complexus* or use the verb *complecti*, to embrace one another.
Even this, at times, they reinforce by accentuating the unifying
force of these embraces. The texts say now that, by embracing
one another, they are connected to one another (*subjungere*),[80] or
are united together (*comprehendere*), used in the text referring to
Alice at note 78 above.

This reciprocity stresses the genuineness of the love on both
sides, and points also to the unique intimacy and familiarity
between Christ and the *mulieres religiosae*. Alice of Schaarbeek's biographer renders well Christ's affection for her and hers
for him. As we have noted earlier, when she entered the new
cabin built to segregate her from the community, Christ appeared
and came toward her with outstretched arms, embracing her as he
said: 'It is good that you have come, my daughter, so long
desired; welcome!'.[81] Similarly in Ida of Nivelles' biography

---

78 *Ibid.*, 482,31: 'erat anima ejus...in divinis amplexibus semper compre-
hensa, exceptis dumtaxat illis horis quibus pro defunctis fuerat deputata'.

79 *Vita*, 240,6.

80 Literally *subjungere* means being connected together to one another. The
'together', however, is redundant in English.

81 *AA SS* June 2: 479,12: 'Bene venisti, carissima filia, bene venisti, diu
desiderata'.

Christ is reported as saying: 'In the holy familiarity of love, it is fitting that I should go and celebrate with my friend Ida of Nivelles'.[82] Ida Lewis' biographer writes that one day Our Lady appeared to her, clasping (*amplectans*) her child in her arms and giving him to her. Ida was delighted to respond to this familiar intimacy. 'Loving her lover, as a bride loves her bridegroom, she took him joyfully, happily, and tenderly into the inmost recesses of her heart'.[83]

All true lovers find joy and rest in mutual embraces. The genuineness of the *mulieres religiosae*'s humanity shines through when they speak about embraces. Alice of Schaarbeek, whose lot was far from enjoyable, prompted her biographer to state that although her sufferings were infernal, 'it looked more as if in some way she was always reposing in Jesus' embraces'.[84] One day, after receiving communion, Ida of Nivelles, 'alienated from her bodily senses, was peacefully and most happily lulled to sleep in the arms of her Bridegroom'.[85] At another time, expressing to the Lord her concern about a difficulty her friend Beatrice was in, she asked him for a sign of her salvation. She was told: 'Tell her for me not to be distressed in her conscience, and remind her that she received so many blessings that she fell asleep in the arms of love near the door of the church, unable to move from that place'.[86]

Years later, Beatrice herself wrote in the fifth of her *seven manieren* that 'it [the soul] desires to rest in the sweet embrace of love, in desirable happiness and in the delight of possessing it'.[87]

82 *Quinque*, 259: 'Oportet me sancta familiaritate amoris diem festum agere cum amica mea Ida de Nivelle'.

83 *AA SS* Oct.13: 118, 37: 'Apparuit ei regina virginum... amplectans puerum...gaudens et hilaris, amans amantem, sponsa sponsum, laeta suscepit dulciter in medullis intrinsicis cordis sui'.

84 *AA SS* June 2: 481, 25: 'Attamen semper quasi in amplexu Jesu jacuit quodammodo'.

85 *Quinque*, 274: '...transiret ad dormitorium spirituale, in quo a sensibus corporeis alienata, inter sponsi sui brachia quieta felicissimeque sopiretur'.

86 *Ibid.*, 212: 'Inter brachia amoris obdormivit et de loco se movere non' [potuit].

87 R-VM, *Seven manieren*, 18, ll. 12–14.

Ida of Leuven's biographer says the same of her: 'deliciously wounded by love...she rested happily in the arms of her Beloved'.[88] Hadewijch did not think differently. Her insistence, of which we have spoken above,[89] on accepting suffering without seeking relief was aimed at striving toward *Minne* in complete trust. Finding *Minne*, one finds fruition in her, and all efforts to find rest will be stilled in the fruitive union with *Minne*: 'In that fruition of *Minne* there never was and never can be any other work than that one fruition in which the one almighty Deity is *Minne*'.[90]

When Beatrice was consecrated as a virgin, the presiding bishop put a ring on her finger as a symbol of her betrothal to Christ: 'betrothed by the engagement ring, she received at the same time the pledge not only of a transitory but of an everlasting fidelity'.[91] At least, this is the way she understood the matter, for the ceremonial itself used the expressions *sponsus* and *sponsa*, bridegroom and bride. Beatrice, and the other *mulieres religiosae* probably did not know the origin and evolution of the term

88 *AA SS* April 2: 175,16: 'Caritatis delicioso vulnere sauciata... feliciter inter dilecti sui brachia requievit'.

89 See above, Chapter XII, p. 375.

90 Letter 17; VM, *Brieven*, 1: 143, ll. 74–77. See also Esther Heszler, 'Stufen der Minne bei Hadewijch', *Frauenmystik im Mittelalter*, 115: 'Deshalb ist "rusten" [to rest] ein häufig gebrauchtes Synonym für die Einung'. Some more information can be found in Carl Albrecht, *Psychologie des mystischen Bewusstseins*, 221–26: Die allumfassende Ruhe.

91 *Vita*, 76,30. Of the six *mulieres religiosae* here studied, Beatrice is the only one of whom such a consecration is mentioned. Her *Vita* also notes (74,39) that 'sometimes she foresaw him [Christ] in spirit as her Bridegroom and Lord, and herself as his chosen bride, having in her ring the pledge of perpetual grace and comeliness, already endowed with her future dowry'. Alice of Schaarbeek's biographer says that in order to purify her thoroughly from all stain and to prepare her for his coming, the Lord acted as a bridegroom does: the ring he gave her was her leprosy, symbolizing his special predilection for her. He intended to come to her and to dwell in the bedroom of her mind as in his chamber. See *AA SS* June 2: 479,9: 'Causa visitationis et more sponsi, sponsae suae arrham tribuentis in signum perfectae dilectionis, ut soli Deo liberius posset vacare, et inter cubiculum mentis suae, quasi in thalamo secum morari'. H. Thurston, *The Physical Phenomena*, 130–40 gives information about visible and invisible engagement rings in later times. See also the important paper by Réginald Grégoire: 'Il matrimonio mistico', *Settimane di studio del centro italiano sull' alto medioevo* 24/2 (1977) 701–817.

'spiritual marriage'. It began with Origen who gave 'spiritual marriage' a mystical meaning. Ambrose of Milan, writing about the consecration of virgins, usually spoke of *nuptiae*, a wedding, and at times also of *sponsalia*, a betrothal.[92] Three centuries after Beatrice, the Spanish Carmelite school, or at least Teresa of Avila, would draw a clear distinction between a spiritual betrothal and a mystical marriage as the two highest degrees of union with God on earth. These terms have since become technical expressions.[93] Repeated betrothals [and marriages] were not unknown.[94] Beatrice's *Vita* too speaks of a repeated betrothal. Some fifteen years after her consecration as a virgin, Christ proposed a renewal of the betrothal to her. During an appearance, he showed his heart for an instant,[95] and he told her in Latin: 'to enter a covenant, a pact, so that in the future we may not be divided, but truly united' (165,14). This time there is no mention of an engagement ring, nor should we expect one, since these repeated promises are only re-affirmations of a commitment well on the way to its fulfillment.

The *mulieres religiosae* were more interested in union with their Beloved and all the requirements for union than in the outward symbol itself, which, nevertheless, they appreciated greatly. They were so convinced that their nobility as human beings was based on their creation in God's image and likeness that, in order to heal the damaged image and to restore the lost likeness, they desired wholeheartedly to be so thoroughly purified in body, heart and mind so as to obtain a stable love-relationship with their God.[96] The road toward this purification is

---

92 *De institutione virginum* 17; PL.16: 334.

93 Pierre Adnès, 'Mariage mystique', *DSp* 10: 388–408.

94 P. Adnès, *ibid.*, 395 speaks of repeated mystical marriages, but most of the examples he provides point rather to repeated 'spir itual betrothals'.

95 See above, Chapter VI, p. 206, n. 258.

96 Speaking of Bernard, E. Gilson (*Mystical Theology*, 99) says: In the measure in which the purification has been brought about, the soul has recovered its lost likeness. It has already become again such that God is able to recognize himself in it once more; so recognizing himself, he begins to dwell in it with complacence, for he cannot love himself without at the same time loving that which, by way of image and likeness is, as it were, another self. Loving it, or,

undoubtedly long, intricate and arduous. Reviewing her life, Ida Lewis' biographer wrote that 'the Lord having a predilection for his bride, chosen from among thousands, claimed her wholly for himself and would not let her be delivered to worldly delusions'.[97]

As we have seen in Chapter Ten, the *mulieres religiosae* set out to follow Christ eagerly through all the vicissitudes inevitable in the process of becoming like him: no more selfishness, but plain and total conformity to their Archetype who became man to help them regain their dignity and make it bloom. In her lengthy *Poem 12 in Couplets*, Hadewijch says that by serving others and being obedient to the Father as Christ was, the soul, through a complete purification, regains its original God-given beauty and becomes acceptable as his bride.[98]

God created man for union with him. The *mulieres religiosae*, eagerly seeking this union, were more than willing to work with him to effect this union. As Gilson, summarizing Bernard, said:

> Like always desires its like; man therefore desires this God whom he represents [as his image], and God covets, so to speak, this soul in whom he recognizes himself [all *proprium* or unlikeness gone and the likeness restored]. How should the betrothed not ardently desire to become the bride, and how should the bridegroom not desire to enter into union with his betrothed whose beauty is the work of his love?.[99]

what comes to the same thing, loving himself in it, God would now unite it with himself. That, precisely, is the meaning of the expression St. Bernard so often employs when he says that the soul has now become God's "betrothed". With him the metaphor always indicates a well-defined state, that of a soul which God can henceforth seek to make his spouse because he recognizes himself in it, and because nothing now remains in it to which his love cannot be given'.

97 *AA SS* Oct.13: 109,5: 'Istam enim ut electam ex millibus sibi Dominus vindicans, sponsam praedilectissimam omnino voluit mundanis eximi delusionibus'.

98 VM, *Mengeldichten*, 55–60, ll. 1–142. Putting it her own way, Beatrice said the same thing in the text referred to above, Chapter VI, n.268.

99 E. Gilson, *Mystical Theology*, 118.

We have already cited a selection of texts from Hadewijch, Beatrice and the three Idas to illustrate their desire for permanent union with Christ as man and as God.[100]

To conclude this chapter, we may quote a text from Bernard, and then, following it, one from Hadewijch to illustrate how she gave more concrete expression to the same concept. Bernard, having said that the soul's likeness to her Archetype has been restored by her conforming herself to God's will, then continues:

> Such conformity weds the soul to the Word, for one who is like the Word by nature shows herself like him too in will, loving as she is loved [she loves herself for God's sake even as God loves her for his own: the well-ordered charity, *caritas ordinata*]. When she loves perfectly she is wedded to the Word. What is lovelier than this conformity?.... Truly this is a spiritual contract, a holy marriage. I put it poorly: a contract? It is more than a contract, it is an embrace; an embrace where identity of will makes one of two spirits. There need be no fear that inequality of persons should impair the conformity of wills, for love is no respector of persons.... He and the soul are Bridegroom and bride. What other bond or compulsion do you look for between bridegroom and bride, except to love and to be loved? [101]

With the same belief as Bernard or any of their other mentors, the *mulieres religiosae* told through their visions and apparitions how they experienced their union with God. Hadewijch, the most outspoken of them, described in a majestic way her bridal union with her God. According to her twelfth vision, when she was taken out of herself in the spirit during Mass, she saw a vast and splendid city. In the midst of this city, Someone clothed with a robe whiter than white was sitting upon a round disk. His name was written on his breast: 'The most Beloved of all beloveds'. As a mystical bride, Hadewijch's soul, having arrived at the perfect

---

100 See above, chapter XI, pp. 338–39, nn. 126–133.
101. SC 83,3; SBOp 2: 299–300. The translation is partly taken from CF 40:182–83.

degree of virtue and having dispensed with the fear of God's
infinity, had become so free that she was worthy to be the partner
of the great Bridegroom.

There then came into the city a great crowd festively
dressed, each of them rich in her own works. They were all
the virtues, conducting a bride to her Beloved. They had
served her nobly and had kept her so nobly proud (*fier*) that
they could present her as worthy to be received by the
mighty great God as his bride .... The bride, in oneness of
will with the divine Nature [the conformity of the *caritas
ordinata*], was dressed in a robe decked with the symbols of
twelve virtues. Thus festively attired, the bride came forward with all the beautiful company [of virtues]. She bore
on her breast a broach with the divine seal,[102] indicating that
she had experiential knowledge of the undivided divine
Unity.... Accompanied by this party she came into the city,
in between the fruition of *minne* and the mandate to practice
the *virtues*: the *mandate* she brought with her, the *fruition*
she found there.... When she [Hadewijch] was then led to
the high seat, the eagle [who had earlier spoken to her] said:
'Now look through the Countenance and become the veritable bride of the great Bridegroom. And forthwith I saw
myself received in union with the One who sat there upon
the circling disk, and I became one with him in the certainty
of unity .... [The eagle spoke again and said] 'When previously you fell down before the Countenance [of God's
Majesty], you, like any ordinary soul, confessed it to be
frightening. When you stood up and grasped it [disregarding
the inequality between you two], you saw yourself perfectly
sealed as our veritable bride, by means of *Minne*...In that
abyss I saw myself swallowed up. Then I received the

---

102 J. Reynaert pointed out (*Beeldspraak*, 304, n.13) that for William the seal
is another image for union. See Nat am 31, PL 184: 399B. 'Tunc (sapientia)
apposito bonitatis Dei sigillo, omnia nostra pacata unctione illa et emollita
imprimit et conformat'.

certainty of being received in this form [as bride] in my
Beloved, and my Beloved also in me.[103]

What Hadewijch experienced in this vision seems to resonate in
her *Poem 12 in Stanzas*:

> What is this light burden of love
> And the sweet-tasting yoke?
> It is the noble fulness of love within
> With which Love affects the beloved
> And so makes her one with Her, in oneness
> Of will and being, united [in likeness] forever.[104]

---

103 VM, *Visioenen*, 1: 128–34, ll. 50–57; 140–60; 165–69; 172–74.
104 VM, *Strophische Gedichten*, 74, ll. 21–26: *Minne* leads the beloved to
oneness with her as she is, *sicuti est*.

CHAPTER SEVENTEEN

UNION FOREVER

W HEN HADEWIJCH SPOKE OF UNION FOREVER, she, like
the other *mulieres religiosae*, took it for granted that
there would be a *forever*, in the sense of a timeless,
eternal forever without, or rather beyond, time.[1] In the context of
their Christian belief and through their personal experiences,
which marked the spiritual development and maturation of their
lives, what else could they do but look forward intensely to a
union with God beyond time?[2] They knew very well that their

1 To speak of a 'timeless forever' does not express adequately the meaning of
an eternal forever, where any notion of time and duration is absent. The notions
of time, space, and matter as we experience them on earth do not apply in the
beyond, since 'there' these categories are transformed, i.e. transcended.

2 The *mulieres religiosae* could not have thought that science is more
convincing than a faith which is not subject to scientific proofs. Their strong
conviction that they were created by and for a God of whom they had at times a
foretaste would make them disagree with the opinion of some moderns that life
can be meaningful even without a belief in an afterlife. With regard to the latter
opinon, see Ambrose. M. Van de Walle, *From Darkness to the Dawn. How
Belief in the Afterlife Affects Living*, ET by John Bowden from the Flemish
(1981), (Mystic, CT, 1984) 6–9: Finding meaning in limitations. This work is
henceforth cited as *From Darkness to Dawn*. Various understandings
of this 'finding meaning in limitations' have been treated philosophically by
R.W. Hepburn, 'Questions about the meaning of life', *RSt* 1 (1965–66) 125–40.
It should, moreover, be noted that in the West peoples' belief is often influenced
too much by fear of a judging and punishing God and too little by the fear
of their own unreliability. The *mulieres religiosae* feared the latter more and
knew very well that God's love is incomparably much more important than
paralyzing fear.

concrete existence in the thirteenth century could last for only a short period, an *interim* as Bernard called it.[3]

The *mulieres religiosae* looked at the meaning of their lives from God's standpoint rather than their own.[4] It does not belong to the creature to tell the Creator what to do and how to do it. Being an infinitely loving God, he willed from all eternity to have man (*mensch*) as his love partner for all eternity. It is the duty of every human being to recognize and respect God's sovereignty, to listen reverently to God's inviting voice and faithfully respond to his love.[5]

To speak with some clarity about 'Union Forever' with this God, we will pay attention in the following pages to that inescapable passage through death which precedes any meaningful talk about a beyond. This includes the question of how this 'beyond' affects our notions and experience of time, space and matter. The insight we may gain from such an effort is certainly worth the price, especially when it refers to union forever with an incomprehensible God. For in the last analysis, it is he who is seen 'face to face', *sicuti est*, as he is, communicating himself to man (*mensch*) by letting him share forever in the fruition of his own ineffable and infinite glory and blessedness in an eternally ongoing sharing forever. To make this lengthy chapter more readable, five subtitles will be used, *viz* Death: Birth to Life; Christ the Mediator; Beatific Vision; *Regiratio* within the Triune God; and *Epectasis* or Eternally Ongoing Progress in Fruition. Contemporary theological considerations which would clutter the flow of this chapter, particularly in the footnotes, will

---

3 Bernard knows of another *interim*, see below, n. 64. Christine Mohrmann pointed out (SBOp2: xvi) that Bernard also used this term when he spoke of life on earth.

4 For the correctness of this stand, see Joseph Ratzinger, 'Auferstehung und ewiges Leben', *Liturgie und Mönchtum* 25 (1959) 92–103.

5 This duty applies to every human being, even those who, for one reason or another, do not believe in the Christian God. See, for instance, the penetrating and stimulating study by Piet Fransen, 'How can non-Christians find salvation in their own religion?', *Christian Revelation and World Religions*, J. Neuner ed. (London, 1967) 67–122, reprinted in P. Fransen's posthumous *Hermeneutics of the Councils and Other Studies*, H.E. Mertens and F. De Graeve eds, henceforth cited *Hermeneutics* (Leuven, 1985) 321–60.

be relegated to an appendix to the footnotes of this chapter, keeping the numerical sequence they have in the text. Although these notes do not strictly relate to the *mulieres religiosae*, and may quietly be left aside, some readers may desire to know more about the theological undergirding of what the *mulieres religiosae* said or alluded to.

A. DEATH: BIRTH TO LIFE

In his remarkable introduction to *Three Treatises on Man*, Bernard McGinn stated that 'the advice of the Delphic maxim that true wisdom was to know oneself was the cornerstone of Cistercian speculation on man'.[6] Beatrice, for instance, in order to grow in self-knowledge 'erected five mirrors before the eyes of her heart and strove to percieve the face of the inner man by constant meditation' (105,10). When she looked at the fifth mirror,

> She was frightened by the recollection of death[7] and the last judgment, and immediately girded herself to practice all patience, humility, obedience and constancy of behavior, knowing that she would then appear the more pleasing to the divine gaze as she would be found more outstanding in the radiance of virtues at the time of her call.[8]

The *mulieres religiosae* were well aware that death does not make one's life futile or purposeless; life is not a waste of time nor is death a sinking away into a meaningless void, a prospect which is totally incompatible with God's intention in creating

6 B. McGinn, *Three Treatises on Man. A Cistercian Anthropology*, CF 24, 29.

7 Between 1194 and 1197, Helinand of Froidmont (1160–after 1229), a troubadour turned Cistercian, wrote his famous 'Vers de la Mort' (Fr. Wulff and Em. Walberg eds: Paris 1895, rpt New York- London, 1965). This poetic work about death, written in vernacular French, made a deep impact in those and later times. It is not impossible that some of the *mulieres religiosae*, Hadewijch in particular, could have known it.

8 *Vita*, 110, 55. Her 'call' refers here to her own individual judgment at the time of her death, not to the general judgment of humankind at the end of time of which the Lateran Council of 1215 spoke.

humankind. When looked at properly,—as did the *mulieres reli-giosae*, i.e. with a religious and reflective mind—life is not a mere coming and going. Though man's life on earth has a begin-ning in time, he has existed in God's mind from all eternity. Death means only an ending in time, though not the end of the human person. As William says, death is only a crossing over, not the final end: 'The crossing over, which pitiable unbelievers call death, by what other name do believers call it but passover? In bodily death one dies perfectly to the world, that one may live perfectly for God'.[9] The promise to love 'till death do us part' made between marriage partners does not adequately apply to God and man. For man is loved by a faithful, eternal God, whose love has no beginning or end. The incarnation, death and resur-rection of Christ make God's plan plainly evident for anyone who cares to see it God's way:[10] He wills human beings to be with him forever.

Besides its enigmatic dark side, death has another aspect which has been called 'the heavenly side of death'.[11] For, as William wrote, 'our being does not die'.[12] Richard makes Christ say: 'be faithful unto death and I will give you after death, instead of death, eternity of life'.[13] For this reason, Gregory of Nyssa called death a good thing,[14] and Bernard did likewise: 'How good the death that does not take life away, but transforms it into some-

---

9 Nat am 15,44; PL 184,406D: 'Deinde venitur ad mortem. Hunc transitum miseri infideles mortem appellant; fideles autem quid, nisi Pascha? In morte igitur corporali perfecte moritur mundo, ut perfecte vivat Deo'.

10 Bernard, speaking of Christ's resurrection at Easter, calls it a passing over, a transmigration. See his Pasch 14; SBOp 5: 90: 'nempe resurrectio transitus, transmigratio'. In fact, man's trans migration is connected with and based upon Christ's transmigration.

11 Alois Haas, *Sermo mysticus*, 441: 'die himmlische Seite des Todes'.

12 Ep frat, PL 180: 353B; SCh 223: 382,295: 'in quo esse nostrum non moritur'.

13 *In Apocalypsim*, PL 196: 721D: 'Esto fidelis usque ad mortem, et dabo tibi, pro morte vitae aeternitatem'.

14 *Oratio de Pulcheria*; PG 46: 877A, cited by Hans von Balthasar, *Présence et pensée* (Paris, 1942) 50, and by Paul Evdokimov, *L'Orthodoxie*, (Neufchâtel-Paris, 1959) 326.

thing better'.[15] 'Thanks to Christ', wrote Yvo, 'death lost its sting and has become a shout of joy'.[16] Or, as Bernard has it: death ushers in 'the perpetual solstice, the day that will never decline into evening'.[17]

The *mulieres religiosae*, eager to know if their names were written in the 'book of life',[18] expressed not merely their desire to be remembered,[19] but above all also their hope of resting in this 'perpetual solstice'. We remember that Christ told Hadewijch that death meant her birth to life.[20] In a short sentence which recalls William's saying, Ida of Nivelles said: 'death is not death, but a crossing over to life'.[21] Death was for her, as it was for Beatrice (174,88), 'her migration'.[22] To the *mulieres religiosae* death was a one-way migration that ended their peregrination on earth once and for all. After this crossing over, Ida Lewis would then 'take up her residence with her Beloved'.[23] Beatrice's biographer wrote that by 'taking the shortcut of death', her mother 'migrated to the freedom of perpetual immortality'.[24] Hadewijch saw it as a festival,[25] 'where *Minne* shall never cease in all the unending ages to come'.[26]

When death comes knocking at the door of obdurate sinners, the crossing over leads to a very different end. To sinners

15 SC 52,4; SBOp 2: 92: 'Bona mors, quae vitam non aufert, sed transformat in melius'.

16 G. Dumeige, *Yves. Epître*, 49,4: 'Jam non stimulus [mors] sed jubilus'.

17 Bernard, SC 33,4; SBOp 1: 237: 'perenne solstitium, quando jam non inclinabitur dies'.

18 See above, Chapter III, pp. 88–89.

19 In fact, in some monastic communities the relation between the deceased and the living members of the community is kept vivid by reading the necrology aloud at the noon meal. Occasionally the memory of a departed member is also kept alive by an epitaph, as happened in the cases of Beatrice (Reypens, *Vita*, 187) and Ida of Nivelles (*Quinque*, 242). For a more developed treatment of this subject, see O.G. Oexle, 'Die Gegenwart der Toten', (Braet and Verbeke, eds), *Death in the Middle Ages*, (q.v.) 19–77.

20 See above, Chapter XV, p. 473.

21 *Quinque*, 278: 'mors non est mors, sed transitus ad vitam'.

22 *Ibid.*, 288: 'migratio ejus'.

23 AA SS Oct.13: 212,14: 'cum dilecto mansionem suscipere'.

24 *Vita*, 20,5.

25 Letter 6; VM, *Brieven*, 1: 69, ll. 353–54.

26 *Ibid.*, 1: 62, ll. 176–77.

stubbornly rejecting *caritas ordinata*, well-ordered charity, death
brings a curse with no end in sight. Since our subject is about the
mulieres religiosae, only one text from William need be quoted
by way of example:

> Although it [the obdurate sinner's soul] has completely lost
> its true essential virtue about which Wisdom says: 'Fear
> God and observe his commandments, for this is the whole of
> man' [Qo 12:13], yet by the most just judgment of God it is
> not permitted entirely to die. It remains passible but only for
> grief, excluded from all joy, separated from every hope,
> having no fear of sorrow but rather entirely enslaved to
> sorrow itself. Something living remains life-giving in it, but
> it lives only to suffer. It is possible to be punished and
> tortured, life-giving so as to give life again to the body to be
> tortured with it, with which it always wishes, if it could, to
> sin always. How much better it would have been for it if,
> like the soul of an animal, it had completely died with the
> body, so that it would be not punished forever! Only the
> difference in their loves makes the difference between the
> blessed soul and the damned. In the one love is the guardian
> of its natural dignity, in the other it degenerates into carnal
> bestiality.[27]

27 William, Nat corp 2,15; PL 180: 726 BC. The translation is taken from B.
McGinn, *Three Treatises on Man*, CF 24: 152. The text is remarkable for several
reasons: William uses the term 'obdurate sinners' to mean those who cling to sin
consciously and intentionally : two factors which determine their responsibility
to remain so selfishly in love with themselves that they refuse to love God
(P. Fransen, *Hermeneutics*, 347). William does not speak of hell as a 'place' nor
does he stress the physical sufferings in hell. Instead he emphasizes what an
unending torturing agony one undergoes, or rather inflicts upon oneself in body
and soul, when one is set on *caritas inordinata*, inordinate love for one's selfish
self, a stubborn clinging to isolation which freezes one in an aversion to God,
neighbor, and one's own true nature. This is basically what hell is. Richard, too,
knows of 'the book of life' for the saved. When he speaks of those in hell, he
calls this book their conscience which condemns their former living. See chapter
six of his sixth book *In Apocalypsim*, PL 196: 856C-858C. He admits that we
know little about hell, except that there one is prevented forever from seeing
God face to face: an indescribably painful penalty (*poena*). The opinion of
Origen, Gregory of Nyssa and others, that there is no eternal hell has been

Between these two extremes, there is another state, known as purgatory, for those who die truly penitent but have still to be purified before they can be admitted to union with God.[28] At the moment of their crossing over, they cannot look God straight in the face, to put it anthropomorphically, because the dust has first to be cleaned away, the dust of imperfections which still covers their resemblance to God and the nobility, dignity, and purity they naturally possess. They owe it to God and to themselves to go through this necessary purification, which is not meritorious, but only removes the residue of sin, that is, of former non-conformity with God.[29] A universal eschaton, or last judgment at the end of time, does not exclude a personal judgment when a person dies. As Robert Javelet observed, the doctrine of image and likeness is crowned by an eschatology, not at the end of time, but at the end of each person's life on earth.[30]

rejected by both the Eastern and Western branches of Christianity. See J. Ratzinger, *Eschatologie—Tod und ewiges Leben* [henceforth cited as *Eschatologie*], Kleine katholische Dogmatik 9 [J. Auer and J. Ratzinger eds], (Regensburg, 1977, 5th ed., 1978) 177. See also J. Gaïth, *La conception de la liberté*, 191–95.

28 Purgatory derives from *purgatio*, purification. See Philippe Ariès, 'Une conception ancienne de l'Au-delà', in Braet and Verbeke, eds, *Death and the Middle Ages*, (q.v.) 78–87, and the monograph by Jacques Le Goff, *La naissance du Purgatoire* (Paris, 1981), ET by A. Goldhammer, *The Birth of Purgatory* (Chicago, 1984), showing how the notion of purgatory came to be shaped and how it developed. See the pertinent review of this book and its inaccurracies by P. Dinzelbacher, in *OGE* 81 (1987) 278–282.

29 See J. Ratzinger, *Eschatologie*, 171–90. As has been mentioned (in Chapter VI, 176, n. 124), Beatrice's and Ida Lewis' great desire was to be so purified at the moment of their death that they would be admitted into heaven without any delay. Alice of Schaarbeek is said to have been stricken with leprosy in order to be totally purified from all stain of her earthly life. See above, Chapter VI, n. 179. Hadewijch and Beatrice strove with all possible zeal to be freed from all sin so that the primal dignity in which man was created would be restored, as was said above in Chapter V, p. 141, n. 102.

30 Javelet, *Image*, 1: 435: 'La doctrine de l'image et ressemblance ....se couronne par une eschatologie, non pas au bout du temps...mais au bout de l'homme tout simplement'. This statement is followed by the assertion that the personal eschatology points to a universal one (*ibid.*, 447–48, referring to a variant in Mss M and C of Bernard's SC 71,7; SBOp 2: 219). A. Van de Walle, *From Darkness to Dawn*, 115–23 came to the same conclusion as R. Javelet. See further the considerations about the *Communio Sanctorum* spoken of in n. 30 of the appendix to the footnotes of this Chapter (page 594).

Ida of Nivelles' 'crossing over into life', *transitus ad vitam*, has more meaning than a first glance might suggest. She called death a crossing over, but the addition *ad vitam* is very significant. Ida'a *ad* (to) is, in fact, the counterpart of another *ad*: man made to (*ad*) God's image and likeness. What has been said with regard to Augustine is equally valid for Ida: 'The *ad* [for Augustine] signifies at the same time a particular relationship of likeness to God...and an orientation, a movement of return to the Source'.[31] David Bell remarked that

> It is the rational soul or *mens* that is created *ad imaginem Dei*, and it is in the *memoria* that we carry the memory of our Creator. The memory may be vague and much obscured, but it is there, and it is there, because all that we are and all that we may be is a result of our participation in our Maker.... The memory therefore contains within itself that final term to which man should tend.... Through *memoria* God calls the soul back to himself and the soul has a natural tendency to return to its origin.[32]

William himself said: 'We were created for you by you, and to you is our *conversio*'.[33] Man is not God, but nevertheless there is something divine in man because God created him in time according to his image and likeness to exist necessarily for all eternity. William is quite explicit about this relation between man made to God's image and likeness and his final, eternal destiny.

31 Olivier du Roy, *L'Intelligence de la foi en la Trinité selon saint Augustin: Genèse de sa théologie trinitaire jusqu'en 391*, (Paris, 1966) 361. David Bell (*The Image*, 99, n. 48), pointed out that du Roy's observation applies to William as well.

32. D. Bell, *The Image*, 96–97 and notes.

33. Medit 1,3; PL 180: 206A. 'Ad te a te creati sumus, et ad te conversio nostra'. The Latin text is taken from R. Thomas, *Oraisons méditées*, vol. 1: 14 published *pro manuscripto* (Chambarand, 1964) according to MS 776 of the Mazarine Library. D. Bell (*The Image*, 91, n. 7) made the remark that *conversio* corresponds precisely to the 'epistrophè' of the Neo-Platonists. For the Christian use of epistrophè, see G.W. Lampe (ed.), *A Patristic Greek Lexicon* (Oxford, 1962) 536.

As he expresses it: 'For this alone were we created and live: to be like God, for we were created according to his image'.[34]

When William said that the soul has a natural tendency, *pondus*, to return to its origin, he meant that this *pondus*, like fire, has a natural tendency to rise upward.[35] According to Bernard the greatness of love is conditioned by its return to its source: 'Love is a great thing, provided that it returns to its beginning and goes back to its origin, that it flows back to its source, and draws from it the waters wherewith it may flow continually'.[36] Borrowing from Bernard, Yvo wrote that because 'God is love, whoever loves him loves Love', and consequently 'to love Love makes a circle'.[37] Though Bernard and William do not seem to use the term circle, the idea is there: the loving soul comes from deep within God, and after spending some time on earth is led back deeply into God.

In the present context the preposition *ad* (to) has been presented in two ways: as a natural tendency to turn back or to be led back to the origin, and as a flowing back to the source, thus completing the circle. In these expressions God's love appears as the beginning and the end, and the cooperative soul tends, flows, is led back to this source of life and love. The process of tending and flowing is technically known as *recursus* (return) or a *circulus* (a circular course). The term *regiratio* has the same meaning of return,[38] but is better reserved to express the flowing back and forth of the divine Persons within the one God, as well as the

34 Ep frat PL 180: 348C; SCh 221: 221,259: 'Propter hoc enim solum et creati sumus et vivimus ut Deo similes simus. Ad imaginem enim Dei creati sumus'.

35 D. Bell, *The Image*, 97, n. 40, says that the explanation of this *pondus* is partly provided by *memoria* and partly by love, as supported by William in his Spec fid, PL 180: 394A and especially in Cant PL 180: 516B-517A. *Pondus* had for William the same meaning it had for Augustine. See Bell, *The Image*, 37, n. 69.

36 The Latin text has been quoted in n. 51 of Chapter XV. Joris Reynaert, *Beeldspraak*, 43, n. 5, refers to Augustine's *Confessiones* (PL 32: 683) where he says the same thing.

37 G. Dumeige, *Yves. Epître*, 61, l. 22–23: 'Deus amor est, quem qui amat amorem amat. Amare autem amorem circulum facit'.

38 R. Vanneste, *Abstracta*, 26.

soul's participation in this movement, about which a word will have to be said below.

As Beatrice wrote: 'There are seven manners of loving which come down from on high and which return to the summit from which they come'. This opening sentence of her treatise *Seven Manieren van Minne* has been variously interpreted. According to Alcantara Mens the sentence refers to *regiratio*,[39] while Herman Vekeman argues convincingly that the accent lies not on *Minne* but on *manieren*, as the subtitle of this short treatise indicates. Beatrice intended to describe her own experience of Minne-mysticism as *recursus*.[40] In addition, the biographies of Beatrice and of Ida of Nivelles definitely mention *recursus*,[41] as does Hadewijch in her sixth letter.[42] *Recursus* has to do with passing through death into God's life and love. There is nothing new in the stand taken by the *mulieres religiosae*. Throughout history, at all times and in all cultures, man has refused to resign himself to physical death as the final end.[43]

In the *recursus*, the whole person—not just the soul or the body, but the soul and the body—is involved.[44] According to the *mulieres religiosae*, this return to their Source meant union for-ever, beyond time, space and matter. They talked or wrote about it in accordance with their mystical experiences, using images

39. A. Mens, *Oorsprong*, 130–31.

40. *Lexicografisch Onderzoek*, 1: 2 and 2: 384–85. Edm. Colledge's ET (*Medieval Netherlands Religious Literature*, Leiden-London-New York, 1965,19) runs: ' There are seven manners of loving, which come down from the heights and go back again far above.' In her turn M.J. Carton (*CSt* 19 [1984] 35) translated the text as: 'There are seven steps of loving coming from and returning to the Most High'. This sentence is good literary English, but cuts the text too short. Translating Latin into English is not always an easy task; each text needs to be situated in its context, which in this case requires the original language as its basis.

41. See above, Chapter III, p. 83, nn. 194–5.

42. Above, Chapter IV, p. 123, n. 175.

43 This has been amply proved by Mircea Eliade, in his *A History of Religious Ideas*. vol. I: *From the Stone Age to the Eleusian Mysteries*; vol. 2: *From Gautama Buddha to the Triumph of Christianity*, ET from the French by Williard Trask (Chicago, 1978 and 1982).

44 J. Ratzinger, *Eschatologie*, 149–50; A. Van de Walle, *From Darkness to Dawn*, 125–29.

and expressions which might not satisfy the discursive minds of some people. Commenting on Beatrice's first complete mystical experience her biographer wrote that Beatrice saw 'how almighty God is a Trinity of Persons and a Unity of substance, just as all the saints will see him in the fatherland after the general resurrection' (178,135). This interpretation calls for a closer attention to what the *mulieres religiosae* themselves had to say about a forever beyond time, space and matter.

Hadewijch wrote in her Letter 22 that 'God himself is eternal time',[45] while in her thirteenth vision she spoke of 'the full length of God's eternity'.[46] To express her desire to be with God forever, Hadewijch said in her eighteenth *Poem in Stanzas*:

> The time I continually long for
> Has robbed me of my heart.[47]

To express what she meant, an interpretative recasting would have to read:

> The [eternal] time I continually long for
> Has robbed me of my heart.

For her part, Beatrice says explicitly in her treatise that God's 'eternity is without time'.[48] The differences between these expressions are only minute when we consider that these women were not used to technical theological terminology. This fact makes it easier to accept that Hadewijch's 'full length of God's eternity' is, after all, not very different from what Beatrice called

---

45 VM, *Brieven*, 1: 192, l. 119. Hadewijch's expression reminds one of Bernard's saying: ' No reference to the "past" can deny that [God] is from all eternity, nor any reference to the "future" that he is for all eternity. In this way he proves that he truly *is*, that is, uncreatable, interminable, immutable': SC 31,1; SBOp 1: 219: 'Nec "fuit" sane tollit illi esse ab aeterno, nec "erit" esse in aeternum: ac per hoc sibi vindicat verum esse, id est increabile, interminabile, invariabile'.

46. VM, *Visioenen*, 1: 141, l. 27.

47. VM, *Strophische Gedichten*, 114, ll. 27–28.

48 R-VM, *Seven manieren*, 30–31, ll. 33–34: 'the eternity of *Minne* [here God] which is without time'.

God's 'eternity without time'. Both statements were intended to express the same thing: after death, they share in the timelessness of God's eternity.

Similarly, it does not make much sense logically to speak of a transformed space as a spaceless space. Nevertheless, by talking in human language, the *mulieres religiosae* could not escape the term space. What they intended to convey, however, refers to a state rather than to a space: an idea which also removes forever any danger of overpopulating heaven.[49]

One day, Ida of Nivelles, worried about Beatrice, asked Christ, who had appeared to her, to give her an indubitable sign of Beatrice's salvation. He responded: 'See, I show you the glorious and ineffable place of delight I will give her in the end without end'.[50] Whether this apparition really happened or not is of secondary importance to the meaning it was to express: the text says that death is followed by endlessness, in a 'place' of delight which refers to a state, not to a geographical place of glorious and ineffable delight. For the *mulieres religiosae* heaven was not a kind of theater or a place of entertainment. In the text just quoted, the intensity of the 'state' of delight without end is stressed, not the excitement of the 'place'. The state, not the place, is also stressed in Beatrice's biography. When she pleaded with God that she not be burdened by any sin at the moment of her death, she declared that for such an end she was ready to suffer anything gladly. She received then the news that her dear friend Ida of Nivelles had 'paid the penalty of death laid upon all flesh, and migrated to the state of immortality (*ad immortalitatis statum*) through the common passageway of death' (188,88). Beatrice's biography is still more instructive: when she was in her twenties she was afraid of the last judgment (110, 55), but later, after she had experienced an *excessus* in 1231, this fear disappeared and was completely replaced by *minne*. She was told then by the Holy Spirit that at the end of her life she would take the place of

---

49 Charles R. Meyer, 'The Life of the World to Come', *Chicago Studies* 24 (1985) 115–30; 119.

50 *Quinque*, 212: 'Ecce, inquit, ostendo tibi gloriosum ineffabilemque jucunditatis locum quam ei in fine sine fine daturus sum'.

beatitude prepared for her from the beginning.[51] Though the text speaks of a 'place of beatitude', this 'place' points as much to a state as did 'the place of delight' spoken of in the preceding quotation. Beatrice confirms this way of understanding these texts. In a passage of her *Seven manieren*, without mentioning the term, she speaks of heaven not as a place, but as a state of 'secure truth and pure clarity and noble sublimity and magnificent beauty'.[52]

When Alice of Schaarbeek died from excruciating leprosy, 'she took off the tunic of mortality and misery and put on the tunic of immortality and glory, full of happiness and delight'.[53] Ida of Nivelles certified to another nun that she knew from the Lord that, at her death this other nun would most certainly be taken up forever into the glory of God's immortality'.[54] Ida Lewis' biographer, contrasting grace and glory, ends her biography by saying that as she deserved to obtain God's grace when she was alive, so at her death she deserved to attain the glory of heaven.[55] Here too the stress is on glory as a state. In the thirteenth vision, when Hadewijch was enjoying a fruition, Our Lady told her: 'If you wish to have further fruition as I have, you must have your sweet body here'.[56]

---

51 *Vita*, 174,87: 'excurso praesentis vitae stadio...tunc demum ad eundem beatitudinis locum a Deo sibi perpetualiter ab initio praeparatum ...emigraret'. The explicitly mentioned 'place of beatitude' she had experienced during her *excessus* refers to a state rather than a place. *Excessus* has little to do with a space even if the word 'place' had to be used to express this spaceless experience. See further n. 85 below.

52. R-VM, *Seven manieren*, 31, ll. 38–40.

53 *AA SS* June 2: 482,32: 'Exuit tunicam mortalitatis et miseriae et induit tunicam immortalitatis et gloriae, plenam felicitatis et laetitiae'. The mortal body presented as a 'tunic of mortality' goes back at least to the Platonists and was also used by Origen and others. See Jean Pépin, 'Saint Augustin et le symbole néoplatonicien de la vêture', *AM* 2: 293–303.

54 *Quinque*, 218: 'Certissime scio te sine fine cum Domini immortalitatis gloria sublimandam'.

55 AA SS Oct. 13: 124,58: 'meruit ex operibus vivendo gratiam, et decedens coelorum gloriam adipisci'.

56 VM, *Visioenen*, I: 52, ll. 241–43. What Paul called a dilemma (Ph 1:23): his desire to be with Christ and the need to remain here for the sake of others is applicable to Hadewijch also. Notwithstanding her burning desire to be with Christ, she preferred to remain here for the sake of the *mulieres religiosae* under

Ida of Nivelles' biography provides a text which refers to the matter of the glorified body. At the end of her final illness, which lasted more than a year, and during her last night on earth Ida experienced an ecstasy. When she returned to herself, the abbess and the nurse who had been with her asked where she had been and she answered that she had been ushered into heaven. There she had seen herself glorified in body and soul; her body had seemed *altered in some manner*.[57] There is no compelling reason to think that the other *mulieres religiosae* were of a different opinion. To use a modern expression, they all lived on the same wave length. Moreover, Beatrice, Ida of Nivelles's best friend, and Ida Lewis, who lived in the same community as the first Ida, were acquainted with Ida of Nivelles' biography, and both were also among the witnesses whom the biographer, presumably Goswin of Villers, interviewed before he wrote the biography. This deduction should not be taken as a conclusive statement. The *mulieres religiosae* were not speaking as professionals. Moreover, there is the possibility that a study encompassing those equally pre-scholastic *mulieres religiosae* not considered in this work might show that the deduction proposed here is unconvincing.

When the *mulieres religiosae* experienced an *excessus*, (not a mere ecstasy), they were *buten den gheeste*, as Hadewijch used to say, beyond the spirit, i.e. beyond conceptualization; in this state their bodies played no part, except to bear the somatic repercussions. Although Ida of Nivelles said that she had seen herself in heaven, glorified in body and soul, the other biographies do not always make so clear a statement. Ida Lewis, for instance, as we have already mentioned in passing, asked insistently to become so purified that when she came to die the Lord would summon her

---

her guidance, as the text following this quotation indicates. See Fr. Willaert, 'Hadewijch und ihr Kreis in den Visionen'. Symposium Kloster Engelberg 1984, in *Religiöse Frauenbewegung* (P.Dinzelbacher and D.Bauer eds), q.v. 368–387.

57 *Quinque*, 289: 'Vidit se in anima et corpore glorificatam et quodam modo corpus suum alteratum'. This saying, not of the biographer, but of Ida, mentions the altered state of *her* body, which evidently she was unable to describe. She

soul to take up residence with him.[58] It is quite normal to speak of 'breathing one's last', or to use some similar expression, when dealing with the fact of dying. But does this allow us to conclude that Ida Lewis, who knew Ida of Nivelles' statement, was positive that only her soul and not her body would 'migrate' to heaven after death? Moreover, the biographer does not quote Ida's own words but describes in his way her desire and hope.

The above mentioned references to what the *mulieres religiosae* thought about time, space and matter in the state of glorification show that, when they spoke of their own experiences, they did not look for explanations or wonder how all this was to take place. They were not concerned about what would happen to their bodily remains,[59] or about the contemporary disputed question of the resurrection.[60] From the perspective of the *mulieres religiosae*, Christ's life, death and resurrection formed one unit, and similarly united was their own unrestrained determination to follow him all the way in his life, death and resurrection. As closely as possible they would live like him, die with him and rise with him, all as one unit.[61] At the end of her sixth letter, when she had written 'that man must offer *Minne* noble service in all works of virtue and the life in exile in obedience', Hadewijch concluded by saying in one breath: 'This is to be crucified with Christ, to die with him, and to rise again

made this clear by saying that her body was altered *quodam modo*, in some manner. See further n. 57 in the appendix (page 595).

58 *AA SS* Oct.13: 112,14: 'ut cum...vellet ipsius animam evocare, nulla obstaculis praepedita, cum dilecto mansionem suscipiens... libere evolaret'.

59. See n. 59 in the appendix (pages 595–96).

60 In relation to the resurrection modern theologians are divided on this point. See appendix, n. 60 (page 596).

61 In addition to what has been said in the last pages about time, space and matter according to the *mulieres religiosae*, other statements by the same women could be cited, statements reflecting the teaching of the IV Lateran Council (1215) which they accepted. We should, however, consider that they were unaffected by later councils, popes or theologians. Their strong desire 'to be with Christ', increased by their mystical experiences—certainly those of the *excessus*-type—, made them quite positive in perceiving their own destiny. They did not present their case as universal; they simply did not speak in universal terms.

with him. To this end he must always help us. I pray to him for this, calling upon his supreme goodness'.[62]

These women spent their lives in theopraxis, the concrete living of their belief — or, more accurately, their conviction — that a loving God called them to respond to his love in order to be united with him both here and there, without any hiatus in between. It is striking how often in the preceding pages the noun 'certainty', the adjective 'certain', or the verb 'to be certain' have been used by these women. There is no doubt that they were deeply affected by their own personal experiences, and in all their texts, both spoken or written,[63] there is clear evidence that in this matter, contrary to their normal practice, they did not follow their mentors who had quite another interpretation regarding entry into heaven. Stressing the solidarity of all humans at the expense of the individuality of each person, and following a literal interpretation of the book of Revelation (Rv 6: 9–11), these mentors thought that the purified souls must wait in a timeless abode, which they referred to as 'under the altar' - *viz.* under Christ's glorified humanity in heaven, — until the number of all the sanctified is completed. They believed that the general resurrection would then take place, and that the already glorified souls and their now glorified bodies would be reunited and pass into the heavenly glory of eternal felicity or its opposite.[64]

Whenever the resurrection happens, then every one passes into a timeless eternity where there is no more place for death. As Richard put it: Once there, 'death will be no more because there will be no longer any separation [in the sense of separability]

---

62 VM, *Brieven*, 1: 70, ll 374–78. The same idea, but in another context appears in her twelfth vision, VM, *Visioenen* 1: 131–32, ll. 112–34.

63 There could possibly be one case, though it is unlikely: when Ida of Nivelles asked the Lord to see him in his divinity, he told her to wait till he would make everything new (*Quinque*, 218: 'Cum nova fecero omnia') This sentence, taken from Rv 21:5, does not invalidate what she had said about her body 'being altered in some manner', for the scriptural text refers to the newness of the 'heavenly Jerusalem'.

64 To follow here the evolution of this theory would take us too far away from the *mulieres religiosae*. An explication can be found in n. 64 of the appendix (page 596–97).

between soul and body'.[65] In this eternity, there is no more ability to sin—*viz.* to be separated from God, as Augustine said,[66]—or to become bored by a timeless union in love with a loving God.[67] As Bernard wrote 'In this fatherland, no adversity or sorrow is allowed, and there will be no place for misery or time for mercy, for no misery will be there to inspire pity'.[68] Nor will there be any envy, because 'in the celestial city, they all will live as a most orderly and harmonious society, where they will enjoy fruition of God and, in him, of one another'.[69] This eternal life in heaven is expressed by means of images, metaphors and parables. Eternal life or heaven is a kingdom, the promised land, a paradise, wedding feast, treasure, glory and so forth.[70]

Admission to heaven is not the result of a bargain, not something one can claim, not a finality God *must* give, but one which he *will* give.[71] It is a gratuitous gift, albeit dependent also on man's cooperation during his lifetime on earth. Ida of Nivelles

---

65 *In Apocalypsim* 7.2; PL 196: 861C: 'Mors non erit, quia nulla erit animae corporisque separatio'. Augustine (*De genesi ad litteram* 36; PL 34: 354) said already that the possibility of dying [again] will be removed: 'non posse mori'.

66 *De corrreptione et gratia* , 35; PL 44: 938 and *ibid.* 38: 940.

67 A. Van de Walle, *From Darkness to Dawn*, 196–97: 'Eternity is not the same as all the time. Were that the case, then we could very well understand people who asked whether the constant vision of God would not ultimately become boring. Eternity is in no way a prologation of time.... Eternity is a particular kind, a particular mode of being by which we transcend time, i.e. are no longer subject to time'.

68 Bernard, Dil. 40; SBOp 3: 154: 'in illa autem patria nulla prorsus admittatur adversitas sive tristitia....Proinde ubi jam non erit miseriae locus aut misericordiae tempus, nullus profecto esse poterit miserationis affectus'.

69 Augustine, *De civitate Dei* 19,13,1; PL 41: 640: 'Pax coelestis civitatis, ordinatissima et concordissima societas fruendi Deo et invicem in Deo'.

70 Jean Leclercq, *L'Idée de la Royauté du Christ au Moyen Age*, (Paris, 1959) 29. The thirteenth century valued highly the idea of Christ's kingship and his many different titles as God, equal in power to his Father; as incarnate Word, as Redeemer who, through his passion, death and resurrection, triumphed over the devil, sin, and man. See also René Latourelle, *Théologie de la Résurrection*, 2nd ed.,(Bruges-Paris, 1966) 519. In the biographies and writings of the *mulieres religiosae* these representations are so frequent that references are superfluous.

71 As K. Rahner (*SM* 1: 152) put it: 'To say that the beatific vision is purely gratuitous is not to deny that in the *de facto* order of reality, the spiritual creature is freely willed by God *because* God willed to communicate himself freely. Hence nature is, because grace was to be'.

made this clear to the beguine whom she warned about her three hidden defects: she would have to correct them to the best of her ability, otherwise she would have less glory in heaven.[72] One of her favorite meditations focused on how saints enjoy a different degree of glory in accordance with what they have made of their lives.[73] In a different situation, Hadewijch exhorted a beguine under her guidance: It is man's duty to practice virtues not for any self-centered reason, but 'solely out of homage to the sublime dignity of God, who created and made human nature to this end: for *his* honor and for *his* glory, [resulting in] *our* bliss in eternal glory'.[74]

Heaven is not a giveaway, but a gift made 'giveable' because man responds to God's proffered love. Though Beatrice was convinced that she had to be 'consummated in virtue' if she was to 'emigrate to heaven' (174,85), she was no less convinced that basically it is God's will to give eternal life, as she said at the end of her sixth *maniere*: 'After which [a well-lived life on earth] comes eternal life. May God in his own goodness deign to grant it to all of us'.[75] Hadewijch thought similarly. At the end of her Letter 15, she wrote: 'Pass through this exile [on earth] so upright and so pure and so ardent that you may find God your Love at the end. May your help be God himself and his holy *Minne*'.[76]

To arrive at the felicity of heaven is to enter into God's reign. The Lord told Alice of Schaarbeek that he himself would 'establish her personally in his reign',[77] while Ida of Nivelles received

---

72 *Quinque*, 242: 'minorem gloriam habitura es in coelo, nisi eosdem pariter defectus quantum potueris studueris emendare'.

73 *Quinque*, 276: 'Sanctorum...diversam pro meritis gloriam speculando'. It should be kept in mind that recompense and merits always refer to God's free gift and, under God's activity or grace, to man's cooperation with this gift. As Bernard wrote: 'all things which are good, even those of which man is the agent, really come from God, not man'. SC 10,8; SBOp 1: 52: 'Omne bonum a Deo, non ab homine est, etiam ipsum quod per hominem ministratur'. D. Bell's interpretation of William's 'deserving' moves in the same direction. See *The Image*, 180–83.

74 Letter 6; VM, *Brieven*, 1: 67, ll. 319–23. Italics added.

75 R-VM, *Seven manieren*, 28, ll. 77–79.

76 VM, *Brieven*, 1: 129, ll. 119–22.

77 *AA SS* June 2: 480,16: 'te...in regno meo collocabo'.

the much appreciated assurance that she and several of her friends would arrive at the reign of supreme bliss.[78] Ida Lewis' biographer wrote 'that through death she reached the heavenly glory wherein she would reign',[79] while Beatrice's biography says that in heaven she would reign with Christ without end.[80]

These citations leave us in no doubt that the *mulieres religiosae* were very conscious that their lives on earth and their glory in heaven were an expression of God's love for them and of theirs for him. Whether here or there, their life was for his sake and by his grace. In living and loving for his sake, they would also live and love for their own sake,[81] and through death reach timeless union with him in love for all eternity.

B. Christ the Mediator

All that has been said so far, particularly in Part Two, points to the mediator between God and man: Jesus Christ.[82] The *mulieres religiosae* had a deeply rooted love for him, though they did not all put the same accent on his divinity. The biographer of Alice of Schaarbeek, for instance, shaken by the slow painful process of her decay, presented her against the background of the suffering Christ. When her right foot became so infected by leprosy that she could no longer walk, she cried out in pain, and all the more so because she would henceforth be unable to attend the celebration of the Eucharist. Christ told her not to be troubled, for

78 *Quinque*, 224: 'Quod ad summe beatitudinis regnum essent perventuri'.
79 *AA SS* Oct.13: 124,58: '...decedens coelorum gloriam adipisci. In qua regnans...'
80 *Vita*, 174,87: 'secum [Christ] sine fine regnatura'. For reigning as co-reigning, see Karl L. Schmidt. *TDNT* 1. 590–91 and M. De Jonge, 'The use of ὸ christós in the Apocalypse of John', *L'Apocalypse Johannique et l'Apocalyptique dans le Nouveau Testament*, henceforth cited as *L'Apocalypse Johannique* in Lambrecht (ed.), (q.v.) 267–281.
81 E. Gilson, *Mystical Theology*, 118: 'To love oneself, once one knows oneself to be a divine likeness, is to love God in oneself and to love oneself in God'.
82 As Bernard put it, quoting and combining scriptural texts as he often does: 'There is only one author of life, one mediator between God and man, the man Jesus Christ'; SC 48,6; SBOp 2: 70: 'unus est enim vitae auctor, unus mediator Dei et hominum, homo Jesus Christus.'

soon he would come to her. 'Tested and purified as she was, like gold in the furnace, he would very gladly receive her, carrying and placing her in heavenly repose'.[83] Ida Lewis's biographer, stressing bridal imagery, spoke in the same vein: 'She went to heaven, to enjoy the hoped-for embraces, and she will live with her beloved throughout all ages'.[84] Following the Christ event as described in the New Testament, Beatrice meditated upon all that Christ did for our redemption, from his incarnation till his ascension, when 'he placed the substance of our nature at the right hand of the divine Majesty'.[85]

The *mulieres religiosae* did not try to make 'theological investigations', reflections and deductions about Jesus of Nazareth as the God-Man. They spoke about their relations with the God-Man more experientially than theologically. 'When Beatrice had been in the office of prioress for a long time, she happened one day to hear one of the nuns reading that the blessed Bernard said there were many who suffer torments for Christ, but few who love themselves perfectly on account of Christ'.[86] While trying to understand this saying, she went into an ecstasy and when she came back to herself, 'she knew the meaning of the aforementioned words [of Bernard], not so much by understanding as by experience'.[87]

---

83 *AA SS*, June 2: 481,25: 'Unde in proximo est quod ego ad te venturus sum, et te probatam ac purgatam more auri in fornace, vehendam et locandam in coelesti requie'.

84 *AA SS* Oct.13: 124,58: 'et optatis fruens amplexibus, cum dilecto vivet per saecula saeculorum'.

85 *Vita*, 95,91. Augustine said: 'God is not in a place, nor has he a body with a right and with a left side' (*Ep.* 120,2,14; PL 38: 459). 'In regard to what is said about Christ sitting at the right hand of God', wrote William (Exp Rm, PL 180: 442D; CF 27: 179, from where the ET is taken) 'the divine power is shown through a human comparison. It is not that a throne is set up and God the Father sits on it and has his Son sitting with him, but that we cannot understand the Son judging and ruling, except by using our own language'. J. Ratzinger, *Eschatologie*, 192, calls it a figure of speech: 'Bildsprache'.

86 *Vita*, 234,4.

87 *Vita*, 237,52. Bernard's text referred to is found in Dil 10,27 and Dil 15,39; SBOp 3: 142 and 163, where he does indeed speak of love of oneself, but for God's sake (propter Deum), not only on account of Christ.

The experiences the *mulieres religiosae* had of God's Son led them through his humanity to his divinity. Bernard, who spoke so frequently and fluently of the human Christ,[88] himself looked for Christ on a higher level. He acutely felt the need to pass from Christ's humanity to his divinity. As he said: 'Although our whole hope rightly depends on God made Man, it is not because he is Man but because he is God'.[89] In Chapter Fourteen we met with several instances where certain *mulieres religiosae* spoke of their experiences of Christ as man and as God. To these texts some more may now be added to stress their concept of Christ in his divinity. One day, Ida of Nivelles 'went into an alienation of mind and was in a rapture raised up into heaven. There it seemed to her that she was standing next to her Beloved and Lover, the Lord of virtues and the King of kings', and she talked with him 'in a honeyed whisper'.[90] Much the same thing same happened to Beatrice: 'caught up beyond herself in ecstasy of mind—with the eyes of the mind, not of the flesh—she saw the heavens opened and Jesus standing at the right hand of the power of God'.[91] Hadewijch expressed it more explicitly: Near the end of her fourteenth vision, she wrote that 'taken up beyond the spirit, I

---

88 He confessed 'not without tears that he, a man, had to talk to men [his monks] about Christ, the man'. See his SC 22,3; SBOp 1: 131: 'Quod sine lacrymis non loquor...ipsum saltem hominem homo hominibus loquor'.

89 SC 10,8; SBOp 1: 52: ' Etsi spes nostra tota merito pendet ex homine Deo, non tamen quia homo, sed quia Deus est'.

90 *Quinque*, 211: 'In mentis transiens alienationem, sursum erecta raperetur in coelum. Ubi sicut sibi videbatur assistens dilecto et dilectori suo, Domino virtutum et Regi gloriae, coepit mellito susurrio rogare eum...' The honeyed whisper expresses Ida's loving intimacy with her Lord. The text cited refers to Christ as King. Though the expression *basileus* (king) had different meanings, several passages in the New Testament indicate that Christ's kingship was the same as God's: 'In ganzen gelten Basileia Gottes und Basilea Christi als identisch'. See R. Schnackenburg, *LThK*, vol. 2: (1958) 25–31. Schnackenburg is supported by G.R. Beasley-Murray, 'Jesus and the Apocalyptic: with Special Reference to Mark 14,62', in Lambrecht (ed.), *L'Apocalyptique Johannique* (q.v.) 414–429. Though the *mulieres religiosae* had no idea of twentieth-century exegesis, they knew the Scriptures well enough to grasp that Christ's kingship did not refer only to his divinity.

91 *Vita*, 149,80. Earlier (114,65) she also called him 'the Lord, the King of kings'.

saw that I had arrived at my choir [in heaven] for which I was
chosen in order that I might taste God and Man as One'.[92]

The risen Christ emphasized the sublimity of his glorified body
in opposition to the 'deformity' of his mortal body, at least
according to Bernard's commentary on the biblical scene where
Mary of Magdala touched the risen Christ. He put these words in
Christ's mouth:

> She will touch me worthily if she will accept me as seated
> with the Father, no longer in a lowly guise, but in my own
> flesh transformed with heaven's beauty. Why wish to touch
> what is ugly? Have patience that you may touch the beauti-
> ful.... Become beautiful and then touch me; live by faith
> and you are beautiful. In your beauty you will touch my
> beauty all the more worthily, with greater felicity. You will
> touch me with the hand of faith, the finger of desire, the
> embrace of love; you will touch me with the mind's eye.[93]

Christ, the man, equal to the Father in his divinity, is what
Bernard was looking for.[94]

What has been said of Bernard applies also to the *mulieres
religiosae*. This has been stated explicitly of Hadewijch.[95] At the
end of an *excessus*, Christ told Hadewijch: 'Chosen to conformity
with the God-Man, you I lead into the cruel world, where you
must taste every kind of death until you return hither in the
fulness of my fruition [*literally*: in the full name of my fruition —

92. VM, *Visioenen*, 1: 166, ll. 160–63.

93 SC 28,10; SBOp 1: 198–99: 'Illa igitur digne me tanget quae Patri
consedentem suscipiet, non iam in humili habitu, sed in caelesti carne ipsa, sed
altera specie. Quid deformem vis tangere? Expecta ut formosum tangas.... Esto
formosa, et tange me; esto fidelis, et formosa es. Formosa formosum et dignius
tanges, et felicius. Tanges manu fidei, desiderii digito, devotionis amplexu;
tanges oculo mentis'. The ET, not comparable in beauty to the original Latin
text, is taken from CF 7, 96. The same idea is expressed in different words in
Bernard's QH 9,9; SBOp 4: 442.

94 J.-Ch. Didier, 'L'ascension mystique et l'union mystique par l'humanité
du Christ selon saint Bernard', *SVS* 22 (1930) [140]-[155]; [147–50]: 'Par
l'humanité du Christ à sa divinité'.

95 P. Mommaers, *RAM* 49 (1973) 476: 'C'est l'*experience* du Christ, homme
et Dieu qui est centrale chez Hadewijch'.

as Man and God], baptized in the fulness in my depth'.[96] Hadewijch herself stated in her eleventh vision:

> I never felt love, except as an ever-new death—until the
> time of my consolation and until God would grant me the
> perfect pride (*fierheit*) of Minne, namely, how one should
> love the humanity [of Christ] leading to his divinity and
> [then I shall] rightly profess both in one person. This is the
> noblest life that can be lived in God's kingdom.[97]

To see Christ in his humanity and divinity was also the desire
of Ida of Nivelles. At first she dared not ask to see him in his
humanity, for she thought that her faith would prove to be
deficient: but when, despite this, she did see him in the Eucharist,
he told her then: 'If I show you my humanity, this is not because I
doubt your faith, but to show you the zeal of my love for you'.
Having received this assurance, she went a step further and
'expressed how very much she desired to see him in his divinity'.
But he answered: 'do not ask me that, daughter, because no one
alive on earth could come to know me as I am in my divinity'.[98]

A final word should be said here about seeing Christ's humanity and divinity. Though Bernard is certainly not the only one who
could be quoted, he may be allowed to speak once more, since
here he connects the pre-existence of man in God's mind with
man's 'post-existence' in heaven:

---

96 Vision 6; VM, *Visioenen*, 1: 70, ll. 99–103, where VM adds in a footnote
that 'depth' means here the oneness of Christ's being.

97 *Ibid.*, 1: 121–22, ll. 195–202. R. Vanneste [*Abstracta*, 41] observed that to
'profess both in one *nature*', as the original says, means here one person.

98 *Quinque*, 252–53: 'numquam eum [Christum] in specie humana videre
concupierat, reputans ne forte fides ejus minus integra quoddammodo defi-
ceret.... Dixitque ei: "Quod speciem humanitatis meae sub forma panis tibi, o
dulcis amica mea, visibilem ostendo, non hoc facio quasi de fidei tuae creduli-
tate ambigam, sed ut tibi notum faciam quanto amore, quamtave solicitudine
zelotus tui sim". Quibus auditis illa cogitatione tacita respondit ei dicens: "O
dulcissime, quam gratum haberem...si te in divinitate tua mihi ostenderes".
Dulcis autem puer cogitationi ejus respondens: "Ne quaeras hoc a me, filia,
quoniam nullus mortalium me in hac vita qualis in divinitate mea sum, cognoscere potest" '.

Heavenly birth is eternal predestination by which God loved
his chosen ones and endowed them with spiritual blessings
in his beloved Son before the world was made. Thus appearing before him in his holy [heaven], they will see his power
and glory and become sharers in the inheritance of the Son
in whose image they were to be conformed.[99]

Man is called to share in the Sonship of God's Son and in his
glory in heaven.[100] Sons do not fear, precisely because they are
sons, not servants. As Hadewijch wrote in her *Poem 12 in
Stanzas*:

> The servant's law is fear,
> But *Minne* is law to the sons.[101]

In her first *maniere*, Beatrice spoke of 'fear of our God's anger
and the judgment of the just judge'.[102] In her seventh *maniere* she
opposed this fear to her desire to be with Christ: 'not from fear of
future trouble, but only because of holy and eternal *Minne* does
the soul ardently and impetuously long and languish to arrive at
the eternal land'.[103]

99 SC 23,15; SBOp 1,149: 'Generatio caelestis aeterna praedestinatio est, qua
electos suos Deus dilexit et gratificavit in dilecto Filio suo ante mundi constitutionem, sic in sancto apparentes sibi, ut viderent virtutem suam et gloriam suam,
quo eius forent consortes hereditatis, cuius et apparerent conformes imaginis.'

100 At this point a portion of Bernard's famous eulogy for his brother Gerard
may be quoted: 'I saw him [when he was dying] look toward heaven and say:
"Father, into your hands I commend my spirit". Sighing frequently, he repeated
the same word: "Father, Father". Then turning to me, his face lit up with joy, he
said: 'How great the goodness of God, that he should become a father to men!
How great a glory for men, that they are the sons of God, heirs of God! For if
sons, then heirs too'. The translation is taken from CF 7,71; the Latin text can be
found in SBOp 1: 179.

101 VM, *Strophische Gedichten*, 74, ll. 19–20. These two verses reflect, as
J. Reynaert noted (*Beeldspraak*, 408, n. 8) what Bernard said in his Dil 14, 37;
SBOp 3: 151 about the law of fear for servants and the law of love and therefore
of liberty for sons.

102 R-VM, *Seven Manieren*, 6, ll. 56–57.

103 *Ibid.*, 33, ll. 82–87. In her biography Beatrice speaks several times of
sonship, which is also present in the *Seven Manieren*, but in a subordinate way
because in that treatise *minne* plays the predominant role, not the bride as is the
case in the biography.

Beatrice spoke of the eternal land she would arrive at when she had passed the gates of death. 'Eternal land' is only one of the many metaphors used by the *mulieres religiosae* to indicate their trajectory: piercing through the wall, the membrane of the body, the tunic of mortality, the prison, and similar terms also express their crossing over to an unending, eternal life. While Beatrice and Hadewijch spoke often of 'land', the Latin biographers used the term *patria*, fatherland. Explicitly or implicitly the *mulieres religiosae* considered this 'fatherland' as the togetherness of all glorified persons, united with God and with one another. The primary interest and supreme goal of these women 'in the fatherland' is what is called the beatific vision, their coming 'face to face' with their God. It is evident that this 'face' of God is an anthropomorphical expression, since God, a pure Spirit, does not have a face in our sense. Augustine had already pointed this out when he made the remark that God is said to be invisible in order to make it clear that he does not have a body as we do.[104]

C. BEATIFIC VISION

Human thought can never grasp the beyond and human language cannot adequately speak of God's 'face'. The term 'face' itself has a great variety of meanings in the Old Testament,[105] as it also does in the New.[106] In the opening phrase of the Vulgate version of Heb 1:1, vision of God and union with him in the beyond are spoken of as being *multifariam multisque modis*, in multiple and various ways, as for instance, the vision of God face to face (1 Cor 13:12), to see God as he is (1 Jn 3:2), to be with Christ (Ph 2:23), expressions often—though not always—emphasizing the individual's final beatitude. What all these expressions attempt to convey is oneness with a God who, para-

---

104 *Ep* 147,48; PL 38: 318: 'Deus invisibilis dicitur ne corpus esse creditur'. Et. Gilson elaborated on this is his 'L'Infinité divine chez saint Augustin', *AM* 1: 569–74.

105 A.S. van der Woudt, 'Angesicht', *Theologisches Handwörterbuch zum Alten Testament* (E. Jenni and Cl. Westermann eds), (Munich-Zurich, 1978) vol. 1: 432–60.

106 E.Lohse, 'Prosôpon', *TDNT* 6: 768–79.

doxically, remains incomprehensible. Their mentors hold this,[107] and so did the *mulieres religiosae*. Beatrice's biography mentions that the Trinity is totally incomprehensible to human understanding' (213,6). God 'escapes all human understanding' (217, 104). Her treatise says the same thing: 'the deep abyss of the Divinity… remains incomprehensible above all things'.[108] Hadewijch, in a sentence which reflects some of the texts of her mentors cited above, wrote in her twelfth Letter: 'All that man comes to in his thoughts about God, and all that he can understand of him or represent by any sense images, is not God. For if men could grasp him and know him with their sense images and with their thoughts, God would be less than man',[109] or as she put it in her Letter 22: 'in his highest height, he [God] is beyond our reach'.[110]

It is in God's incomprehensibility, not despite it, that one will forever find knowledge, union, and beatitude. As Karl Rahner says:

> It is not true that the 'deus absconditus' (the hidden God) is the sort of God who desires that we should not recognize him at all. He does not share one part of himself with us and conceal the other; rather he bestows his whole being upon

107 For Gregory of Nyssa, God's being remains ineffable, as W. Völker (*Gregor von Nyssa*, 198) put it: 'dass Gottes Wesen bleibt unsagbar'; — According to Augustine God cannot be comprehended (I. Bochet, *Augustin et de désir de Dieu*, 129, referring to *Sermo* 52,6,17; PL 38: 360: 'If you were able to understand, then you understood something else for God…. If you understood, it is not God ' (Si comprehendere potuisti, aliud pro Deo comprehendisti …. Hoc ergo non est, si comprehendisti). D. Bell, *The Image*, 76–77 and notes refers to other texts of the same vein; — William states that God as he is in himself, in his essence, can in no way be grasped by thought (Ep frat 2,3,23; PL 184: 353A; SCh 223: 378,292: 'Ipsum vero, idipsum quod est id quod est, cogitari omnino non potest'). This is echoed by Bernard in his *De consideratione*, where he states that 'God is incomprehensible, but you have learned a great deal if you have discovered this about him': Csi v,6,14; SBOp 3: 478: 'Incomprehensibilis est Deus, sed non parum apprehendisti, si hoc tibi compertum est'.

108 R-VM, *Seven manieren*, 29, l. 12.

109 VM, *Brieven*, 1: 102, ll. 31–37. Hadewijch could have read it also in Gregory the Great's *In primum Regum expositiones* (PL 79: 285C) as J. Reynaert indicated in *Beeldspraak*, 35. n. 79.

110 VM, *Brieven*, 1:189, l. 47.

us. In communicating himself as 'deus revelatus' (the
revealed God) he becomes radically open to man *as* the
'deus absconditus'. From this mystery man is no longer able
to escape: he accepts God as he is, as the mystery of
incomprehensibility who, once recognized, is the very truth
of man and, once loved, is his blessed fulfilment.[111]

We find in William a trustworthy guide who may lead us to
some understanding of this incomprehensibility of a God in
whom man mysteriously attains his ultimate perfection: 'When
reason has to step back [before God's incomprehensibility],
devout love steps in and will make its own understanding'.[112] It
should also be affirmed, as David Bell does, that

> the eye of reason was created in man so that through it he
> might see God. But such a vision is possible only with the
> help of illuminating grace.[113] Without the latter, *ratio* [rea-
> son] cannot achieve the contemplation of God, for although

111 This is the ending of K. Rahner's study of 'The Hiddenness of God',
Theological Investigations 16, ET by David Morland (New York, 1979, rpt
1983) 227–43. The mystery that man is to himself, his own incomprehensibility,
can only be understood in its relation to God's incomprehensibility. And, as we
will see below, it is when he finds his blessed fulfillment in loving God's
incomprehensibility, that he can paradoxically grasp the meaning of his own
incomprehensibility.

112 Cant, PL 180: 525A; SCh 82: 304,144: '...cum retroacta ratione amor
pius efficeretur intellectus suus'. See in this regard, Jean Déchanet, 'Amor ipse
intellectus', *RMAL* 1 (1945) 349–74, and D. Bell, *The Image*, 217–49, where he
dispels (248,n. 106) Déchanet's hesitation about the time of William's insight:
'William appears to have mentioned this intimate connection of love and
knowledge from his earlier years onwards, although the staightforward statement *amor ipse intellectus* does not appear before the time of the Canticles
commentary'. The text of William there quoted was used by Hadewijch in her
Letter 18. See VM, *Brieven*, 1: 155–56, ll. 80–111.

113 In contrast to creative grace by which God, in creating man to his own
image, gave him the *capacity* to participate in him, illuminating grace helps man
to *actualize* this capacity by which the likeness of the image is restored. See
William's Aenig, PL 180: 386C. How deeply the *mulieres religiosae* appreciated this illuminating grace and how sensitive to it they were, has been touched
upon in the last section of Part One dealing with unitive grace.

intelligentia rationis, a *ratio* operating at its own without
illuminating grace, might lead us to God, it cannot attain
him. It is love which is purer *intellectus* [understanding],
and which can provide us with the non-discursive and extra-
conceptual knowledge of God which William so earnestly
seeks.... The *amor -intellectus* [love-understanding] is true
knowledge *per connaturalitatem*, that is to say, a knowledge
and understanding which results from likeness, from participation.[114]

Jean-Marie Déchanet commented that the intervention of love-
understanding is not an abdication of the human intellect, but
rather compenetration of the two highest faculties of the soul,[115]
intellect and will/love, without sacrificing one to the other.[116]

In the paragraph above, William, Déchanet and Bell have
spoken of what happens in an ecstatic vision in which a new
dimension of consciousness is attained. But William's interpreta-

114 David Bell, *The Image*, 235–36 and 243.
115 Robert Javelet, *Image*, 1: 442, and Odo Brooke, 'Towards a Theology of
Connatural Knowledge', *Citeaux* 18 (1967) 275–90; 283 speak of interpenetration. As the latter explicitates it: 'This should be interpreted as an interpenetration and not as a formal identification of the faculties of love and intellect. See
also R. Javelet's 'Intelligence et amour chez les auteurs spirituels du XIIe
Siècle', *RAM* 37 (1961) 273–90; 429–50; 283–86, where he speaks of Hugh,
Richard, and Yvo (mistakenly considered to be Richard), who seem to say that
to love is to see, to love is to understand.
116 J. Déchanet, 'Amor ipse intellectus', *RMAL* 1 (1945) 360: 'On aurait tort
cependant d'imaginer que l'exercice du sens de l'amour entraîne l'abdication,
même sur le plan des choses divines, de l'intelligence humaine. Il y a assomp-
tion de l'intelligence, et surtout compénétration des deux facultés de l'âme, mais
non paralysie de l'une au profit de l'autre'. D. Bell, *The Image*, 239–40 is
insistent in stressing the needed differentiation between essential identity and
conceptual distinction [of love and knowledge], for 'unless we keep these two
quite separate we are doomed to confusion and misunderstanding', as he showed
before coming to this conclusion. Albert Deblaere, speaking of a mystical
experience, says that these two faculties [of love and reason] do not stay in their
proper domain, but converging in their common source, act together as one
dynamism', 'Témoignage mystique chrétien', *Studia Missionalia* 26 (1977) 117–
47; 117: 'Ces deux facultés cessent de s'exercer chacune dans son propre
domaine pour effluer vers leur source commune et ne se manifester que comme
un seul dynamisme'.

tion is also valid for the beatific vision because 'William leaves us in no doubt that the ecstatic vision is not different in *natura* from the beatific vision'.[117] According to Bernard, who always distinguishes a mystical *excessus* from the beatific vision,[118] knowledge (which comes from likeness) and love (which comes from vision) are always close to one another. In the beatific vision they fuse intimately together: 'It is assuredly a thing most marvellous and astonishing, that the likeness which accompanies the vision of God, is itself indeed this vision.... This vision is charity, and the likeness is charity'.[119] William, in agreement with Bernard,[120] expresses it even more clearly by saying that man was created to God's image and likeness in order to arrive at union in the vision of God.[121]

---

117 D. Bell, *The Image*, 223. The two visions, not different in *natura*, differ in *dignitas* (dignity). Bell here agrees with Javelet (*Psychologie*, 160, n. 572): 'L'ecstase est passagère; mais ce prélude est de même essence que le bonheur du ciel'.

118 E. Gilson, *Mystical Theology*, 235, n. 114.

119 SC 83,8; SBOp 2: 297: 'Admiranda prorsus et stupenda illa similitudo, quam Dei visio comitatur, immo quae Dei visio est.... Caritas illa visio, illa similitudo est'. For the likeness spoken of in this quoted passage, see Gilson, *Mystical Theology*, 11, where he cites a text from Cicero which says that 'the deepest cause of friendship lies in likeness, for nature loves nothing so much as that which resembles it'. C. Mohrmann, 'Le style de Saint Bernard', *Études sur le latin des Chrétiens*, vol.2: (Rome, 1961) 348–50 contests Gilson's opinion that Bernard is here dependent on Cicero, and refers to Ambrose's *De Officiis* as a more likely source. Though Mohrmann could not have mentioned Felix Claus' later study on this subject, the latter shows that Ambrose's treatise is not based on Cicero's *De Officiis*, but on his own commentary on Psalm 38. See F. Claus, 'De opvatting van Ambrosius over de navolging van de "De Officiis" ',in *HL* 26 (1972) 63–72. Claus refutes O. Hiltbrunner who supports Gilson in 'Die Schrift "De Officiis Ministrorum" ' des hl. Ambrosius und ihr ciceronisches Vorbild', *Gymnasium* 71 (1964) 174–89.

120 Some interesting insights in what Bernard and William have to say about beatific vision have been given by Joaquin Alonso in his 'Studios de teologia positiva en torno a la visión beata', *Estudios* 8 [Madrid] 1952, 535–47: San Bernardo y grupo cisterciense. Alonso stresses Augustine's influence on Bernard and William, rather than that of Maximus the Confessor and Scot Eriugena.

121 R. Javelet, referring to two texts of William, says (*Image* 1: 429; 2: 313, nn. 158–159) that for him 'the image is a dynamic medium of knowledge, precisely because, united with the Holy Spirit, one with him, invaded by his charity it has become likeness, has become vision (*regard*), vision capable of God'.

While on earth, the *mulieres religiosae* strove with all the determination of their loving hearts for the restoration of God's image and the recovery of the lost likeness. To be more precise, they cooperated with God who kneaded, molded, and shaped them into human beings able to respond to his divine love. This was God's way of making them ready for the realization of his final purpose in creating them: union with him in an undisturbed and undisturbable love-relationship, whereby they would see him, for, as they could have read in William: 'God created the soul to his image and for the vision of him'.[122]

The *mulieres religiosae* were deeply moved by God's love when they realized how their human littleness was destined to share in God's greatness. Their creation to God's image and likeness gave them a nobility and dignity which they appreciated highly and spoke of gratefully, as we noted above in Chapter Five. After Beatrice, for instance, expressed her determined desire 'to attain and to remain [here] in that purity and nobility in which it [the soul] was made by its creator to his image and likeness', she explicitly mentioned that she would 'ascend to a greater height of love and a closer knowledge of God, until it [the soul] reached [in heaven] that perfection for which it is fully made and called by God'.[123] She voiced in her own way what Bernard said earlier: 'He [God] will become visible to you in accordance with his image, renewed in you. And you, gazing confidently upon the glory of the Lord with unveiled face, will be transformed into that same image'.[124] Then

> will there be mutual vision [since each may know the other in knowing himself], and mutual dilection [like loving his like]. When that which is perfect is come [charity] then that which is in part [unlikeness] shall be done away; and between God and the soul shall be nought but a mutual

122 Nat corp, PL 180: 725C: 'anima ad ejus imaginem et visionem creata est'.
123 R-VM, *Seven manieren*, 4, ll. 21–24.
124 SC 36,6; SBOp 2: 8: 'et ex imagine tua, quae in te renovatur, ipse videbitur, dum tu quidem revelata facie gloriam Domini cum fiducia speculando, in eandem imaginem transformaris'.

dilection chaste and consummated, a full mutual recognition, a manifest vision, a firm conjunction, a society undivided, and a perfect likeness. Then shall the soul know God even as she is known; then shall she love as she is loved; and the Bridegroom shall rejoice over his bride, knowing and known, loving and beloved, Jesus Christ our Lord, who is forever over all things, God blessed forever. Amen.[125]

Equally important is a text from William:

There [in heaven], to be like God will be to see God or to know him. He who knows him or sees him does so insofar as he is like him, and to the extent that he is like him, so much he knows and sees him. For there, to see or know God is to be like God, and to be like him is to see or know him. This perfect knowledge will be eternal life.[126]

In his commentary on the Canticle, William goes on to say that in heaven 'the union of the Bridegroom and the bride will be full and eternal, in the fulness of likeness, when not only will the Bridegroom be seen as he is, but every [soul] that has deserved to be [called] a bride will be as he is'.[127]

125 SC 82,8; SBOp 2: 297–98: 'Facta igitur de medio iniquitate...erit unio spiritus, erit mutua visio mutuaque dilectio. Siquidem veniente quod perfectum est, evacuabitur quod ex parte est, eritque alterutrum casta et consummata dilectio, agnitio plena, visio manifesta, conjunctio firma, societas individua, similitudo perfecta. Tunc cognoscet anima sicut cognita est; tunc amabit sicut amata est; et gaudebit sponsus super sponsam, cognoscens et cognitus, diligens et dilectus, Jesus Christus Dominus noster, qui est super omnia Deus benedictus in saecula. Amen. The ET is taken from Gilson's *Mystical Theology*, 151–52. Bernard spoke often about God's vision, face to face. See, for instance, Csi v,13,27; SBOp 3: 490, or Div 42,7; SBOp 6/1: 260.
126 Spec fid, PL 180: 393C: 'Similem enim ibi esse Deo, videre Deum, sive cognoscere erit: quem in tantum videbit, sive cognoscet, qui cognoscet vel videbit, in quantum similis erit: in tantum erit ei similis, in quantum eum cognoscet vel videbit. Videre namque ibi seu cognoscere Deum, similem est esse Deo; et similem ei esse, videre seu cognoscere eum est. Haec cognitio perfecta vita erit aeterna.'
127 Cant, PL 180: 507B; SCh 82: 224,98: '...et tunc conjunctio Sponsi et Sponsae plena et perpetua fiet in plenitudine similitudinis, cum non solum

Texts as these must have made a deep impression on the *mulieres religiosae*, who strove with unabating zeal and through all kinds of vicissitudes to become *unus spiritus*, one spirit with God, as the right preparation to become *sicuti est*, as he is, in the beyond. Though the Latin biographies say little about this *sicuti est*, Hadewijch spoke of it explicitly in her fourteenth vision,[128] and Beatrice implicitly in her *Seven manieren*.[129]

To see God *sicuti est*, as he is, means—as Benedict XII would state officially a century later—an intuitive and direct vision of God's essence showing itself clearly and openly with no mediation of any finite being, ideas, images, or any other created medium whatsoever.[130] By this seeing, the glorified do not become *what* he is, but *sicuti est, as* he is, for the endlessness of God's incomprehensibility excludes any possibility of man becoming God, just as it excludes also a *complete* vision of God by man. If man could come to know God completely as he is in himself, he would have to be really and substantially the Son, who is *totally* involved in God's incomprehensibility.[131] Man can never become God, only *sicuti est*, as God is, i.e. by participation. In order to clarify what is meant by the *sicuti est*, only one pertinent text need be quoted. In his third meditation William

---

videbitur Sponsus sicuti est, sed et quaecumque Sponsa esse meruerit, erit sicut ipse est'. The ET is taken from D.Bell, *The Image*, 223.

128 See above, Chapter XIV, p. 423, and n. 117, or in her Letter 2 (VM, 1: 31, ll. 163–65) where she advises a friend: 'If you wish to have what is yours, trustingly abandon yourself completely to God to become what he is'.

129 At the end of her seventh *maniere* (R-VM, *Seven manieren*, 38, l. 165), she asserts that in heaven she will be wholly (*tota*) one spirit with him. For the meaning of this *tota*, as expressing the *sicuti est*, see below, n. 140.

130 H. Denziger and C. Bannwart, *Enchiridium Symbolorum*, 18–20th ed., (Freiburg/Br., 1932) 229–230. R. Forster expressed it by saying in *LThK*, vol.1 (1959) 590: 'Das primäre Objekt des Anschauung Gottes ist Gott der Dreieinige. Gottes Wesen wird unmittelbar geschaut'. In Div 19, 3; SBOp 6/1: 163, Bernard says that in heaven we will see 'with naked eyes, to put it this way, God's essence ....to enjoy at last happiness without end': 'nudis, ut ita dicam, oculis deitatis intuentur essentiam.... Ecce gaudium in fine, sed sine fine'.

131 J. Déchanet, 'Amor ipse intellectus', *RMAL* 1 (1945) 355. Déchanet's conclusion expresses what several mentors of the *mulieres religiosae* had frequently said before. There is no compelling need to list here the references.

himself asked the question: *Sicuti es*, as you [God] are: what does this mean? He then goes on to answer his own question:

It is beyond our powers to see you [totally], for to see what you are is to be what you are. And no one sees the Father but the Son, neither does anyone see the Son, except the Father [Mt 11:27]; for this is proper to the Father—to see the Son, and this is proper to the Son—to see the Father.[132]

If the *mulieres religiosae* were to see God *sicuti est in semetipso*, to see him completely as he is in himself, in his essence,[133] they would, of necessity, have to be what he is in the intimacy of his own infinite Being as Unity and Trinity: and this, clearly, is impossible if they were to avoid, as their mentors did, any pantheism. William obviously realized this, for the passage quoted above is followed by his affirmation that 'the text [Mt 11:27] continues saying: and to him to whom the Son shall choose to reveal him'.[134] In other words: God can be seen *sicuti est*, as he is, not totally as he is in himself, but by participation, always and only by participation. Referring to the beatific vision, Bernard often uses 1 Jn 3:2: 'when he [God] appears, we shall be like him, for we shall see him as he is'.[135] Here too, 'as he is',

---

132 Med 3,6; PL 180: 212D-213A, and Robert Thomas in his better edited text in *Oraisons méditées* 1:50: ' Quid ergo est "sicuti est"? Hoc videre supra nos est, quia videre quod tu es hoc est esse quod es. Nemo autem videt Patrem nisi Filius, et Filium nisi Pater; quia hoc est esse Patri, quod videre Filium, et hoc est esse Filio, quod videre Patrem'. William has more such expressions, but he made his point, and this is sufficient for this chapter.

133 In OS 4,3; SBOp 5: 357, Bernard says that we will see God *sicuti est in semetipso*. The context, however, indicates that he means to stress the vision of God *sicuti est*, in opposition to the way he is present within us and in other creatures: 'et videamus Deum sicuti est, id est non modo sicut inest nobis aut ceteris creaturis, sed sicut est in semetipso'.

134 Med 3,6, as in note 132: 'sed sequitur et dicit: et cui voluerit Filius revelare'.

135 In fact, Bernard herein follows Augustine. See I. Bochet, *Augustin et le désir de Dieu*, 293, n. 1, where several other instances are referred to. For Bernard's frequent use of this verse, see M. Standaert, 'La doctrine de l'image chez saint Bernard', *ETL* 23 (1947) 109 and n. 171. The 'he' in this verse does not refer to Christ as A. Michel has it in *DThC*, vol.7 (Paris, 1922) 2363, but to

means participation. To quote David Bell: 'participation, of necessity, excludes identity, and for William (and all the Cistercians [and we may add, and for all the *mulieres religiosae*]) the union of man and God is a union of likeness, not of essence'.[136]

Stating implicitly that all identity is excluded, Hadewijch once more used biblical imagery to say it. In her thirteenth vision she wrote that 'a new heaven was opened. There revealed itself that face of God with which he will satisfy all the saints and all men (*menschen*) for the full length of his eternity'.[137]

It should be noted that the *mulieres religiosae* had little, if any, knowledge of what the contemporary, professional theologians were discussing in their exclusive schools with regard to the beatific vision.[138] To explain how man's mind comes to an intuitive, open clear vision of God, Thomas Aquinas and Scholasticism had recourse to the *lumen gloriae*, the light of glory.[139] Before Thomas, Roland of Cremona, a Dominican contemporary of the *mulieres religiosae* coined the expression 'videbitur Deus

God. See J. Michl, *Die katholischen Briefe*, Regensburger Neues Testament 8/2, (O.Kuss ed.), (Regensburg 1968) 224 and Bruce Vawter, 'The Johannine Epistles', in *The Jerome Biblical Commentary* (R. Brown, J. Fitzmeyer, R. Murphy, eds), (Englewood, NJ., 1968) 409.

136 D. Bell, *The Image*, 177.

137 VM, *Visioenen*, 1: 141, ll. 24–28.

138 This subject has been thoroughly explained by H.F. Dondaine, 'L'Objet et le ''medium'' de la vision béatifique chez les théologiens du XIIIe siècle', *RTAM* 19 (1952) 60–99, and selected texts, *ibid.*, 100–130. These discussions took place before 1241/43, when the theologians and bishop William of Auvergne of Paris (at that time the 'magisterium', as J. Ratzinger simply called the parisian faculty in his *Eschatologie*, 116) stated: 'we firmly believe and affirm that God will be seen in his essence or substance by the angels and all the saints and by all the glorified souls': Firmiter credimus et asserimus quod Deus in sua essentia vel substantia videbitur ab angelis et omnibus sanctis et videbitur ab omnibus glorificatis (Dondaine, *ibid.*, 99). The unavoidable trouble with official statements is that when they are made in opposition to an error (as was the case when this so-called Parisian Magisterium spoke out), they become frozen when written down and later often acquire an interpretation which differs from what was originally intended. This process creates puzzles for anyone who tries to find his way through the maze of shifting interpretations.

139 A. Michel, 'Intuitive vision', *DThC*, vol.7: 2370 and ff: the *lumen gloriae* is a direct intervention by God himself, enabling the intellect of the glorified to see him intuitively and directly.

totus sed non totaliter', (God will be seen wholly but not totally).[140] Roland's dictum became successful mostly because of its assonance. The idea itself goes at least back to Augustine and Gregory the Great. The former said that God will be seen, not in his incomprehensibility, but as he is,[141] while the latter made a distinction between similar and equal.[142] The other mentors of the *mulieres religiosae* repeated Augustine.[143] Seeing God as he is, yet without attaining his incomprehensibility, may sound puzzling, but in fact it is not: we must keep in mind that to see God *sicuti est*, as he is, simply means that we shall see God or be God by participation, not by nature or essence.[144]

In this sense Hadewijch wrote in her Letter 13: 'He who loves passionately runs faster and attains more quickly to God's holiness which he is himself, and to God's totality, which is God himself'.[145] Although there is no sure way of knowing if her

140 Roland of Cremona was the first Dominican to become Master of theology at the University of Paris. See M.D. Chenu, *Nature, Man and Society in the Twelfth Century*, 15, n. 30. He seems to have been the first to have coined, before 1234, the straightforward expression which would become a classic in theological parlance. See Dondaine, 77, n. 69 in his publication mentioned above in n. 138. Without using the term *totaliter*, William spoke already in his Aenig (PL 180: 435B) of *totus* in the sense of *totaliter*. John Anderson understood this correctly when, in his ET (CF 9, 109), translating William's *totus* as 'totally', he puts the term within quotations marks to stress its meaning : 'you [God] are totally an unsearchable and inscrutable depth, "totally", however, in that you are to be understood, as you can be understood: as infinite'.

141 See several references in D. Bell's *The Image*, 26, n. 28.

142 *Moralia in Job* 18,93; PL 76: 96A: Our vision of God will be similar but not equal to God's own vision: 'Visio nostra...similis illius visionis, sed equalis non erit'; or, in the same commentary 19,13; PL 76: 928C: God's essence can be seen, but not perfectly; 'non tamen essentiam plene contuemur'.

143. Richard, *In Cantica Canticorum Explicatio*, PL 196: 421D; — William, Cant; PL 184: 379B; SCh 82: 92,20; — Bernard, SC 31,1; SBOp 1: 220.

144 What Thomas Aquinas said of God's essence as his quiddity [A. Michel, *DThC*, vol.5: 833], whereby he distanced himself from his master Albert the Great [H.F. Dondaine, 'Cognoscere de Deo "quid est"', *RTAM* 22 (1955) 72–77], had already been said by Christ to Hadewijch in her third vision. It was said, however, without any philosophical or theological explanation, which neither he nor she needed, for the language of the heart is more direct and penetratingly clear than that of a discursive mind. The text has been quoted in Chapter XV, 473–74. Note 83 refers to the text.

145 VM, *Brieven*, 1: 116, ll. 69–73.

Poem 20 in Stanzas was written before or after her thirteenth vision (referred to above in note 137), the latter seems to be the case, for there is a resonance in it of the former:

> When all things shall pass away,
> Noble *Minne* will remain
> And reveal her whole clarity
> Whereby you, in a new beginning
> Shall contemplate *Minne* with love:
> 'Behold' [she shall say] 'This is who I am'.[146]

It does not make much difference whether *Minne* in this poem refers to God or to Christ. When arriving in heaven the *mulieres religiosae* would 'be with Christ', or, as Beatrice put it now, 'to be [together] with Christ',[147] without any intermediary related to time, space or matter. In heaven, particularly in heaven, Christ is and remains 'their' Christ, God and Man, but now in his glorified humanity. How real and how dear Christ's glorified humanity was to them can be seen in Alice of Schaarbeek's biography. The description is doubtless the way popular piety pictured the meeting of Christ and Alice when she died, but it also indicates how the intimacy became enhanced by the glorification of them both. When, as has been mentioned above,[148] Alice took off the tunic of mortality and put on the tunic of immortality and glory, somebody, not present when she died, saw 'in the spirit', that Christ himself came to meet her at the head of a long procession, 'because he considered nobody else qualified to do so'. When they met, 'he took her in his arms and embraced her'.[149] Ida Lewis' biographer, mentioning her death, said that she went to

---

146 VM, *Strophische Gedichten*, 128, ll. 55–60. In the rephrasing by E. Rombauts and N. De Paepe in *Hadewijch. Strofische Gedichten*, 153, the last line runs: '[and you will understand] 'See, so am I', an interpretion suggested by VM. Hadewijch would see God (as *Minne*) *sicuti est*, as he is.

147 R-VM, *Seven manieren*, 33, l. 81: 'ende te wesene met kerste'.

148 See n. 53 of this Chapter.

149 AA SS June 2: 482,33: 'Ipse Dominus, neminem praeter ipsum ad eam recipiendam reputans idoneum, ut ipsam honorifice susciperet, ceteris praecedebat [et] brachiis suis ad amplexum' [recepit].

heaven 'to live forever with her beloved Christ, immersed in the flood of love, enjoying the delights of lovers and the hoped-for embraces forever and ever'.[150]

In the beyond the role of Christ as mediator is not suspended but brought to fulfilment.[151] The incomplete biography of Beatrice of Zwijveke expressed this mediating role of the glorified Christ in the following way: One day during Mass, she saw the heavens opened and the Son standing in front of the Father, the divinity radiating and shining through his whole humanity. From the Son this glory glittered upon Our Lady and all the saints.[152] Recalling what has been said in Chapter Ten about following Christ, and in the next one about the *mulieres religiosae* meeting him in the Eucharist, we need not elaborate here on the intensity of their encounter with Christ in his glorified humanity.[153]

In their all pervading love for Christ, the *muliéres religiosae* desired above all to see him in his divinity. As Robert Javelet has pointed out, once union with Christ is attained, participation in God's trinitarian life becomes emphasized: from being the end,

---

150 *AA SS* Oct.13: 124,58: 'in amoris mersa diluvio, amantium gaudens deliciis et optatis fruens amplexibus, cum dilecto Christo vivat in saecula saeculorum.

151 In his lengthy paper 'Cristo glorioso, Revelador del Padre', *Gregorianum* 39 (1959) 222–70, Juan Alfaro studies first John's gospel, particularly the prologue, and then elaborates in scholastic terminology on what the incarnation of God's Son and the glorification of his humanity mean as mediation for man's own glorification and beatitude in the beatific vision.

152 L. Reypens, 'Nog een dertiendeeuwse mystieke Cisterciënsernon', *OGE* 23 (1949) 245, l. 93–96: 'vidit in spiritu celum apertum et filium ante patrem, et divinitatem totam irradiantem et perlucentem ipsius filii humanitatem, et a filio resplendentem in beatam virginem et in omnes sanctos'. In this Beatrice could have been influenced by miniatures or other pictorial representations. The *Illuminations of Hildegard of Bingen (1098–1179)*, M. Fox ed., (Santa Fe, NM, 1985), 110 shows just such a picture as Beatrice of Zwijveke claimed to have seen in her vision.

153 We take note of what K. Rahner wrote about the predominant role Christ, God's incarnate Son, plays in the beatific vision. In his study 'The Body in the Order of Salvation', *Theological Investigations* 17, 71–89; 80, he wrote that 'the beatific vision, the direct contemplation of God, is based on a grace which would not exist, and probably could not exist, unless the divine Logos had taken, and remained, flesh'. Or as Rahner says elsewhere: 'the *personal* Absolute can be truly *found* only in him, in whom dwells the fulness of the Godhead in the earthly vessel of his humanity. Without him every absolute of which we speak

Christ becomes the principle.[154] Ida of Nivelles is a case in point. When Christ appeared to her in his human form, she asked to see him is his divinity and he answered her: 'O friend of peace, have peace in me, because when I will...gather you to myself, you will know the glory of my divinity, face to face'.[155] Christ did not explain to Ida all that is contained in the simple words he used. Here, the *mulieres religiosae* had in mind and heart the God whom they knew not so much philosophically or theologically as experientially and phenomenologically. Never do we hear them asking if the term 'person' has identically the same meaning on the human and the divine level, and if not, what difference may exist between the two.[156] If we hope to understand what the *mulieres religiosae* were talking about, we must look more closely at what is implied in Christ's divinity, the divinity of the One God in three Persons, the relations among them and between them and us.

Being incomprehensible, God cannot be grasped by the human mind. But to gain some understanding, one has to 'humanize' him, thereby inevitably running into seemingly contradictory

or which we imagine we attain by mystical flight is in the last analysis merely the never attained, objective correlative of that empty and hollow, dark and despairingly self-consuming infinity which we are ourselves: the infinity of dissatisfied finiteness, but not the blessed infinity of truly limitless fullness. This, however, can be found only where Jesus of Nazareth is, this finite concrete being, this contingent being, who remains in all eternity': *Theological Investigations*, vol.3, ET by Karl and Boniface Kruger, (London, 1967, New York, 1982):' The eternal significance of the humanity of Jesus for our relationship with God', 35–46; 43–44.

154 R. Javelet, *Image*, 2: 230, n. 245: ' Une fois l'union accomplie, c'est la participation à la vie trinitaire. De fin le Verbe est devenu principe'.

155 *Quinque*, 253: 'Habete igitur, o pacis amica, pacem in me, quoniam cum...collegero te ad me, divinitatis meae gloriam facie ad faciem cognoscere poteris'.

156 Any interested reader can find pertinent definitions, distinctions and explanations in John Walgrave's *Person and Society. A Christian View*, Duquesne Studies. Theological Series 5 (Philadelphia, PA, 1965) 90–116: 'Personalism: Metaphysics and the General Ethics of the Person'; in K. Rahner, *The Trinity*, ET by Joseph Donceel (New York, 1970) 103–15: 'The Problem of the Concept of "Person" '; in R. Javelet, *Psychologie*, 86–91; and particularly in C. Kiesling's 'On Relating to the Persons in the Trinity', *TS* 47 (1986) 599–616, where he explains that when we speak of 'Person' in God, we use the term analogically.

statements.[157] The terminology of the *mulieres religiosae* and that of their mentors, which had not yet been systematized, does not favor an easy understanding.[158] On the other hand, if they are interpreted along the lines of scholastic or post-scholastic authors,[159] it is equally difficult to avoid misunderstandings and confusion. This is all the more obvious since, to give one example, the term *substantia* in pre-scholastic Latin can refer to essence, person, or nature, the context alone indicating what is meant.[160]

D. *REGIRATIO* WITHIN THE TRIUNE GOD

How cautious and attentive one has to be is seen in Christ's response to Ida's request to see him in his divinity: 'when I will gather you to myself, then you will know the glory of my divinity, face to face'. This answer suggests two interpretations. The first is clear enough: she would have to wait till she entered the beyond before she could see him in his divinity. Centuries earlier, Augustine had already made the observation that the vision of Christ in his divine form is reserved for the future.[161] Bernard

157 When talking about the Persons in the Trinity, for instance, one cannot simply identify person with consciousness as we do in relation to a human person. If we were to do so it would mean that there are three consciousnesses and consequently three free wills and three Gods. In the One God, however, there is only one consciousness, which in its totality is equally present in the three Persons, each in his own and proper way, as Father, Son and Holy Spirit.

158 J. de Ghellinck studied precisely this topic in his paper: 'L'Entrée d'essentia, substantia et autres mots apparentés dans le latin médiéval', *Archivum Latinitatis Medii Aevi* 16 (1941) 77–112. There he shows the vageries of the terms essence, substance, subsistence in their Latin terminology, reluctant to take over the more refined Greek vocabulary.

159 J. L. Thomas, 'The Identity of Being and Essence in God' *HJ* 27 (1986) 394–408; 398, objects to A. Kenny who considered the identity of God's Being and his Essence as 'manifest nonsense'. However, J. Thomas' recourse to 'transference' to explain the identification is not too convincing either.

160 E. Gilson, *Introduction*, 297–98; R. Vanneste, *Abstracta*, 30. This is why works written by pre-scholastic authors need translators competent in the terminology of the time. If they are not, their translations will inevitably suffer from linguistic and conceptual leukemia which, unfortunately, occurs all too often.

161 D. Bell, *The Image*, 80, n. 49 lists several instances where Augustine repeatedly said so.

said so too: 'The Son will show you himself, as he promised, not [as now] in the form of a servant, but [then] in the form of God'.[162] The second thing is the indivisibility of the Father, the Son, and the Holy Spirit. As Augustine said: 'When the one God is seen, the Trinity is seen'.[163] For 'where the nature or substance of God cannot be divided, the vision of the Father and of the Son cannot be separated'.[164]

Christ promised Ida of Nivelles that she would know not 'my divinity', but 'the glory of my divinity', for Christ does not have a divinity exclusively his own. As Bernard explains it: 'He [the Son] will also reveal to us the Father and the Holy Spirit, since without that vision nothing could satisfy us; for this is eternal life: that we may know the Father, and Jesus Christ whom he has sent, and in them also and undoubtedly the Spirit of them both'.[165]

Hadewijch says as much in her third vision. Taken up in the spirit, 'He [God, *lit.* gode, though the context refers to Christ] brought me before the Countenance of the Holy Spirit, who possesses the Father and the Son in one Essence'.[166] She is even more explicit in her twelfth vision, where she, as a bride,

one with him [the Son] ascended to the Father, and there with him she acknowledged the Father as Father, and she acknowledged him [the Son] with him as Son, and with him

162 OS 4,2; SBOp 5: 356: 'Ostendit enim nobis Filius, ut pollicitus est, semetipsum, non in forma servi, sed in forma Dei'.

163 *Ennarationes in Psalmum* 84,9; PL 37: 1095: ' Cum unus Deus videtur, Trinitas videtur'.

164 *Ibid.*, 85,21; PL 37: 1097: 'Patris et Filii separari non potest visio: ubi non separatur natura et substantia, visio separari non potest'.

165 OS 4,2; SBOp 5: 356: 'Ostendet etiam nobis Patrem et Spiritum Sanctum, sine qua nimirum visione nihil sufficeret nobis, quoniam haec est vita aeterna, ut cognoscamus Patrem et quem misit Jesum Christum, et in eis, quod non est dubium, etiam Spiritum utriusque'.

166 VM, *Visioenen*, 1: 42, ll. 3–6. She expresses here what Bernard had also said: 'in the supreme Unity which is in God and is God...there the three Persons are one essence': Csi v, 9, 20; SBOp 3: 484: '[in] summa, quae in Deo est et Deus est, unitate...ibi tres personae [sunt] una essentia'. Gilbert of Hoyland, who continued Bernard's commentary on the Songs, said equally: 'in the unity of the divine Essence, there are three Persons': Cant 21,3; PL 184: 116C: 'In unitate divinae essentiae tres esse personas'.

she acknowledged the Holy Spirit as Holy Spirit, and with him [the Son], like him, she [Hadewijch] knew all [Persons] as One, and the Essence in which they are One.[167]

Without repeating what has been said earlier on pages 48–65 of Chapter Three and in Chapter Eleven, we may refer to the several texts quoted there. They clearly indicate that these *mulieres religiosae* shared Hadewijch's conviction: to see God as he is, *sicuti est*, is to see him as the triune God: One and Three at the same time. Ida of Nivelles' biography gives us a clear glimpse of her experience of God as Trinity. Enraptured in the Trinity, she had tasted and perceived 'what was unveiled to her: how the essence of the Father is in the Son, and the Son's in the Father's, and the essence of them both in the Holy Spirit. The One God as Trinity had talked to her as with his beloved, and she herself had conversed with the Trinity'.[168] Her intimacy with the One God in three Persons was even mentioned on her epitaph: 'The Three and the One allowed her to see him as Triune'.[169]

William, in using a figure of speech called 'antimetabole', stressed this vision of God as Unity and Trinity all at once and at the same time, but without the logical succession which appears in the passage from Hadewijch just quoted:

In the next life...with a single glance they [the blessed] will perceive all their knowledge, which will be only about you, o true God. The vision of that contemplation and the contemplation of that vision will not pass from the Father to the Son, from the Son to the Father, from the Son to the Holy Spirit; it will not be divided into three, nor will it be gathered into one; but in blessed perpetuity and a perpetual

---

167 VM, *Visioenen*, 1: 131–32, ll. 127–31.
168 The text has been quoted above in n. 129 of Chapter XI. In that short sentence, Ida too refers to the Unity of God in his essence and the threeness of the Persons in the Trinity, but—and this should once again be taken into account—Ida did not speak from a merely conceptual, but from an experiential level, just as the other *mulieres religiosae* had done.
169 *Quinque*, 292: 'Qui se concessit spectandum Trinus et Unus'.

blessedness men, no longer seeking but enjoying (*fruentes*), they will contemplate you the One true God, Father, Son, and Holy Spirit living forever and ever.[170]

Robert Javelet's comment on *excessus* can also be applied to William's saying. The otherness of God's transcendence is tempered by the intimacy between 'Thou and I'.[171] In his essence, where he is what he is, God is one. Since he is pure spirit, totally above the categories of time, space and matter, he is an eternal now, from all eternity to all eternity. Hadewijch expressed this in her Letter 22 in the following way: 'What God has is identical with what he is [*literally* he himself is what he has].[172] His own eternity attends his Being (*Wesen*) without end'.[173] This sentence is followed by the very important statement that God 'within his Being is [also and simultaneously] engaged without beginning in one fruition in accordance with his own [eternal] *Minne*'.[174] Hadewijch spoke of God's essence,

---

170 Aenig, PL 180: 435C: 'Ibi qui te vibebunt...uno simul cernent intuitu. Non enim visio illius contemplationis, seu contemplatio illius visionis, a Patre transibit ad Filium, a Filio ad Spiritum Sanctum; non in tres dividetur, nec colligetur in unum. Sed beata perpetuitate et perpetua beatitudine, non jam quaerentes sed fruentes contemplabuntur te unum et verum Deum, Patrem et Filium et Spiritum Sanctum viventem in saecula saeculorum. The ET is taken from CF 9, 107. K. Forster confirms what William said when he wrote (*LThK* vol.1 [1957] 589) that the vision of God implies participation in his intra-trinitarian life: 'Die Anschauung Gottes...bedingt die Teilnahme des Seligen am innertrinitärischen Lebensaustausch, der sich wesentlich in der Weise des Erkennens vollzieht'. M. Schmaus, *Katholische Dogmatik*, Bd 4/2, 5th ed., (Munich 1959) 620–21, calls it a participation in the dialogue between the three divine Persons.

171 R. Javelet, *Psychologie*, 193: 'La transcendence se tempère d'altérité avec un "Toi et moi".'

172 Hadewijch follows here Augustine, who said in his *De Trinitate* 1, 26; PL 42: 839 'est id quod habet', God is that what he has.

173 VM, *Brieven*, 1: 189, ll. 28–31. Hadewijch stresses here God's Unity as did Bernard when he said that God's 'unique and supreme Unity is not brought about by an act of uniting but exists from all eternity': SC 71, 4, 9; SBOp 2: 220: 'Singularis ac summa illa unitas, quae non unitione existit, sed est ex aeternitate'.

174 VM, *Brieven*, 1: 189, ll. 32–33. This sentence implies that God is dynamically active within himself. God being eternal and atemporal, the Father is (to our human way of thinking) continually—i.e. from all eternity and to all

without beginning and without end, and of God being 'engaged' within himself, without beginning and without end. Each time, she used the verb *oefent*, which means 'to attend to' or 'to apply to', and 'to be engaged in'. God's 'attending to his Being' indicates that in the oneness of his Being, God affirms himself eternally as one God. But, while the term 'essence' emphasizes God's Being, the term 'nature' stresses the engagement, the activity within the one God, expressed in the threeness of Persons, who from all eternity and to all eternity are three in their one nature, as they are simultaneously one in their essence.[175]

The term 'essence' expresses particularly the Oneness, whereas the term 'nature' has a greater compass. Nature means the

eternity—begetting the Son and breathing or spirating with his Son, the Holy Spirit; the Son is continually being begotten by the Father and, with him, continually breathing or spirating the Holy Spirit; the Holy Spirit is continually from all eternity and to all eternity being breathed or spirated by the Father and the Son. William expressed the idea by saying that: 'the Father did not diminish himself that he might have a Son; rather, he begets from himself another self so that he remains complete in himself, and is as much in the Son as he is in himself.... Now, for the Son to be from the Father and to be that which he is, is always to be born; likewise, for the Holy Spirit to be from the Father and from the Son and to be that which they are, is an eternal procession from both', cf CF 9: 92. The Latin text from Aenig, PL 180: 427D runs: 'Neque Pater ut haberet Filium minuit semetipsum, sed ita genuit de se alterum se, ut totus maneret; et tantus esset in Filio, quantus in se.... Sicut Filio a Patre esse, et hoc esse quod est ille, natum semper esse est; sic Spiritui Sancto a Patre esse et a Filio, et hoc esse quod illi sunt, aeterna processio est'. Bernard himself says little in metaphysical terms about the intratrinitarian relations within God. See A. Van den Bosch, 'Présupoposés à la Christologie bernardine', *Citeaux* 9 (1958) 98–99: 'Saint Bernard parle très peu des relations intratrinitaires en termes métaphysiques'.

175 In our handicapped human terminology, Hadewijch said more simply what theologians say more elaborately, more abstractly and in a more refined way. Forced to pay attention to a correct understanding and expression, and also to avoid misunderstandings, they are, nevertheless, as far removed from comprehending the incomprehensible as Hadewijch was. Moreover, when it comes to God as the Trinity, the begetting by the Father, the being begotten of the Son, and the spiration of the Spirit can be rendered by other terms with the same meaning. Human speech relating to the Triune God possesses other verbs in their active and passive forms, such as to generate, to proceed, to stream from and to, to flow in and out, to go out and to return, to be swallowed up, or similar verbs. One finds such expressions in Beatrice's treatise, and many more in Hadewijch's extensive writings. The latter, for instance, speaks in one place of her Letter 22 of 'God bringing the Persons out of his Unity' (VM, *Brieven*, 1: 192, l. 117 'vte gheven'), in another of 'pouring out' (*ibid.*: 198, l. 257: 'vte ghieten') and at another place of 'gushing out' (*ibid.*, 199, l. 269: 'vte storten').

undivided unity of the divine essence and, at the same time, this essence as the source of activity; it is the source, the *terminus a quo*, resulting in the three Persons, and it is the goal, the *terminus ad quem*, the 'flowing back' of the three Persons into the Oneness of the Unity. Hadewijch expressed this in Letter 17 where she wrote that 'this pouring out [in Persons] and the returning [*lit.* the holding back, i.e. in the Unity] are the pure Divinity and the entire nature of *Minne*'.[176]

Being perhaps more deeply moved by the depth, length and strength of God's endless love, Hadewijch uses still stronger, almost juridical, expressions in Letter 30, where she talks of summons and claims made by the divine persons to be united in the fruition of their Unity:

> The Father summons the Son and the Holy Spirit into the eternal fruition within the Unity; and the Son and the Holy Spirit claim the debt [of return] which the Son and the Holy Spirit demand from the Father to [have] fruition [in the Unity] of the Holy Trinity. This summons is eternally ever new in one possesion and in one Being (*Wesene*).[177]

Augustine had said twice in his *Confessiones* that 'God is always active, always quiescent'.[178] The dialectical opposition between being always active and always quiescent, or to use Hadewijch's terminology, between pouring out and bringing back is the continual *regiratio* in God of his nature as *Minne*. In Letter

176 VM, *Brieven*, 1: 140, ll. 21–23. In regard to the Trinity as Unity, William made the remark that 'although in God there is Trinity which is Unity and Unity which is Trinity, nevertheless, in no way does the name Unity signify here under the name of Trinity some sort of numerical union of triplicity, but the inseparable simplicity of the divine essence'. The ET is taken from CF 9: 95, a passage from Aenig, PL 180: 429AB: 'Licet enim ipsa ibi sit Trinitas quae Unitas, et Unitas quae Trinitas, nequaquam tamen significat ibi nomen Unitatis sub nomine Trinitatis, quasi numerosam triplicitatis conjunctionem, sed inseparabiliter divinae essentiae unitatem'.

177 Letter 30, VM, *Brieven*, 1: 253–54, ll. 49–55.

178 'Semper agens, semper quiescens', and 'Tu autem Domine, semper operaris et semper quiesceris'. See I. Bochet, *Augustin et le désir de Dieu*, 185–86.

28, Hadewijch used water symbolism to refer to the *regiratio*: 'He [God] rests in nothing but in the tempestuous nature of his profusely overflowing flood [of love], which flows in and out, back and forth'.[179]

In Letter 17 Hadewijch stated explicitly that for God the fruition of himself is primary and basic: 'The singularly just nature [of God] in which *Minne* is *Minne* and perfect fruition of herself [is] not drawn or inclined toward virtue or to [any] particular work'.[180] When the Persons 'return' — in accordance with our human way of expressing it[181] — into the unity of God's essence (which in God himself happens simultaneously since he is atemporal), God has fruition of himself and in himself, with no attention to any other activity outside his Triunity. He enjoys himself infinitely; he has immeasurable fruition in the Oneness of the perfectly identical divine nature of the three Persons. As Hadewijch said in the same Letter: 'In that fruition of love, there never was and never can there be any other work than that one fruition in which the one almighty Deity is *Minne*'.[182]

---

179 VM, *Brieven*, 1: 198, ll. 252–55. Hadewijch here joins Richard: 'One could speak of this wave of the Divine and the overflow of the Supreme Love [the Father], flowing out without being poured into, in the other [the Son] flowing out and being poured into as well; in the third [the Holy Spirit] not flowing out but only poured into while, nevertheless, there is one and the same wave in all of them'. The Latin text is in Richard's *De Trinitate*, PL 196: 99A; SCh 63: 360: 'Dicatur itaque illa divinitatis unda et summi amoris affluentia, in alio tamen effluens nec infusa, in alio tam effluens quam infusa, in tertio non effluens sed solum infusa, cum sit tamen in omnibus una et eadem unda'.

180 VM, *Brieven*, 1: 142, ll. 67–71.

181 In Csi v,13, 29; SBOp 3: 490 Bernard says that the divisions or distinctions exist only in our understanding, not in God: 'Divisus hic est, non illic'.

182 VM, *Brieven*, 1: 143, ll. 74–77. An observation by Paul Mommaers may be quoted here. In 'Bulletin d'histoire de la spiritualité: L'École néerlandaise', *RAM* 49 (1973) 465–92; 474–75, he wrote: When the Flemish mystics [i.e. Hadewijch and Ruusbroec] speak of God, they emphatically affirm...that God is at one and the same time repose and activity, Essence and Persons. He is at all times both these aspects.... Repose is not only the 'perfection' of activity, activity is just as much the 'perfection' of repose.... These mystics who have a sharp phenomenological consciousness, intend to stress that 'to repose' as such is not identical with 'to be active' and, nevertheless, these two concepts coexist, form and *are* God. The activity never 'enters' the fruition of repose because as Hadewijch said [and here Mommaers cites the text this note refers to]: 'In that fruition of love, there never was and never can there be any other work than that

In the unlimited perfection of his essence, God rests in complete quescence and enjoys infinite, everlasting fruition of himself. There 'God's love is self-sufficient', says Hadewijch: 'were no one to love [God as] *Minne*, her being [*lit*. her name] would give her enough lovableness in the splendid glory of herself',[183] for the Persons 'are all simultaneously one love and nothing else'.[184]

It is the same God as *Minne* who in the infinite superabundance of his love from all eternity willed a relationship in love with a human partner. As has been noted in Part One, when God drew man (*mensch*) out of his pre-existence in his divine Exemplar and put him on earth, creating him to his own image and likeness, he had to endow him with freedom. When man failed to use his freedom, or to put it in another way, when man failed in *caritas ordinata*, the well-ordered love spoken of in Chapter Fifteen, God sent his Son and subsequently the Holy Spirit to show man how much he is loved by this God, and what man has to do to respond to this love. By following Christ and cooperating with the purifying, sanctifying activity of the Holy Spirit, men can move in the direction in which they were invited to go. The *mulieres religiosae* were well aware, as has already been pointed out,[185] that their creation, recreation and consummation were an integral part of an immensely vaster plan: God extending his *Minne* to all the human beings he created in order that they might live with him in a reciprocal love-relationship forever, even if they had to be redeemed to do so.

For the *mulieres religiosae* this meant a relationship not just with anybody but with the absolute and infinitely loving God who willed to have them with him, and who would bring his plan to its completion by letting them share in the unity of his Oneness and

one fruition in which the one almighty Deity is *Minne*'. This is a correct observation, not only because Hadewijch or Ruusbroec said so, but because in his Oneness God has within himself quiescence or repose (*otium*) and, being atemporal, simultaneously activity within himself.

183 Letter 20; VM, *Brieven*, 1: 174, ll. 127–30.

184 Letter 17; VM, *Brieven*, 1: 141, ll. 46–47. The translation follows VM's suggested interpretation in *Brieven*, 2: 88.

185 Chapter XVI, n. 2.

in the Trinity of the Persons. The first has already been spoken of above,[186] and refers to the attributes or characteristics of God which are, in fact, common to the three Persons in their Unity, but are attributed by us to a single Person. In a passage of Letter 17, however, Hadewijch spoke of a second kind of attribute, that related to the extra-trinitarian relations between God and man. Summarizing what she had said earlier in this letter, she wrote: 'Each Person [of the Trinity] has separately given out what is proper to him, as I have said already '.[187] In the order of salvation there are, indeed, three 'manifestations' or attributes which reflect the relation of each Person in this salvific work. Referring to the second kind of attributes, Hadewijch said: 'to be generous and zealous is [attributed to] the nature of the Holy Spirit; that is what his proper Person is [in the order of salvation]. And not to apply himself to a particular task is [attributed to] the Father; in this way [as unoriginated] he is the unique Father.... And to have kindness and compassion for every need: this was the Son in what is proper [properly attributed] to his Person'.[188]

Beatrice too attributes a sphere of operations to the individual Persons. In relation to herself, 'she looked up at the all-powerful [one] God, offering with devotion to the Father the necessary weakness of human nature to be strengthened and lifted up... to the wisdom of the Son... to have the darkness of her blindness and ignorance enlightened, and to the Holy Spirit... to have the intimate affections of her heart moderated and ordered'.[189]

186 Chapter V, 128–31: analogical implications.
187 VM, *Brieven*, 1: 142, ll. 66–67.
188 Letter 17; VM, *Brieven*, 1: 140–41, ll. 16–21; 49–51. In 'Hadewijchs eerste ontwerp van de wezensmystiek (Br. XVII)', *HL* 26 (1972) 5–57; 24, n. 1, Albert Brounts corrected VM's incorrect understanding of the attributes spoken of here. He also rectified (*ibid.*, 48) one inexact interpretation by R. Vanneste. Hadewijch's text has been theologically expressed by L. Scheffczyk [*SM* 2: 390]: 'It is the mystery of the perfect redemption in which the mysterious "God above us" (the Father) becomes "God with us" (the incarnate Son) and "God in us" (the Holy Spirit in grace).
189 *Vita*, 43,40. When the biographer describes how 'from the fire of love with which she was burning inside, a spiritual fire arose also to her bodily eyes, and emitted from both eyes a ray of wonderful brightness for those sitting around her to see', he continues by saying (*Vita*, 241,31) 'In that heavenly

What has been said in Chapter Five, pp. 126–31, about the analogical implications of the image and likeness and in Chapter Eleven about the Eucharist shows sufficiently how the other *mulieres religiosae* were also aware of this second kind of attributes, even if they were not as articulate as Hadewijch. Both kinds of attributes are important because they relate to man's participation in God's Unity and Trinity in the beyond, a participation begun here and achieved there.[190] Paul Mommaers, referring to Bernard Spaapen,[191] says that in a complete mystical experience, repose and activity, while maintaining their distinction, coexist as they do in God. According to Hadewijch and Ruusbroec, one and the same person lives these two complementary aspects.[192] Both Mommaers and Spaapen make extensive use of texts from Hadewijch and Ruusbroec to show how the more systematic Ruusbroec (1293–1381) has been influenced by Hadewijch,[193] and sometimes clarifies some difficult passages of Hadewijch, who was one of his sources.[194] Hadewijch herself, who had a less

brightness she penetrated with the marvellous keenness of contemplation things both visible and invisible, corporeal and spiritual. In this kindling of her spirit Beatrice wished to consecrate to almighty God some pleasing oblation and acceptable sacrifice. It was divinely answered her that she should offer the Son to the Father, and her soul to the Son, and that she should consecrate the whole affection of her heart and sacrifice of love to the Holy Spirit'.

190 This aspect has been well treated by C. Kiesling in his paper mentioned above in n. 156, 'On Relating to the Persons of the Trinity', *TS* 47 (1986) 599–616.

191 'Hadewijch en het vijfde visioen', *OGE* 44 (1970) 370–77. See n. 182.

192 'Lorsque Hadewijch et Ruusbroec parlent de l'expérience accomplie, ils visent un état d'âme complexe, où, à l'example de ce qui se passe en Dieu, repos et activité, jouissance et recherche coexistent, ne *font* qu'un tout en étant, en tant que repos ou activité, des aspects différents. Un seul et même homme vit les deux éléments complémentaires'. (See P. Mommaers, p. 475 of his paper mentioned above in n. 182). In her sixth *maniere* [R-VM, 27, ll. 58–61], Beatrice says that 'then love makes the soul so bold and free that... it truly feels that love is as lively and operative in bodily rest as in many actions'.

193 This has been penetratingly studied by J. Reynaert, 'Ruusbroec en Hadewijch', *OGE* 55 (1981) 193–232.

194 It is remarkable how Hadewijch and Ruusbroec moved in the same direction by maintaining that the distinction between repose and activity should be kept without separating the two. The several quotations from Ruusbroec to support what Hadewijch said or meant to say are certainly admissible, but they call for the most delicate care. Albert Ampe, for instance, has shown in his

methodical mind than Ruusbroec, made a distinction between living on earth with the Trinity and, in the beyond, in God's Unity.[195] In Letter 17, she speaks of her relation with God as *Minne*, whereby the singularity within her is like that of the three Persons within their Unity: 'As long as one is in union with *Minne*, one is Godlike, mighty and just. Will, work and might are then single in our singularity as the three Persons are in the one God'.[196] In a passage of *Poem 16 in Couplets*, Hadewijch exposes in imagery both expressive and impressive how she participated mystically in God's *regiratio* here on earth.

> This bliss and madness of love (*orewoet*)
> Cast them into the abysmal flood,
> Which is bottomless and ever living

'Bernardus en Ruusbroec', *OGE* 27 (1953) 143–79, that Ruusbroec in his own well-structured synthesis integrated several of Bernard's ideas, transferring to the here and now what the latter had applied to the beyond. The stress on the simultaneity of activity and repose spoken of could be partly due also to a needed correction of the exaggerated interpretations of some who spoke of the contemplative Mary who had chosen 'the better part' (Lk 10:42) as opposed to the overly concerned busy Martha. Apart from what has been said in this note, it would be inexcusable not to refer the reader to the excellent introduction and ET of four of Ruusbroec's works by James Wiseman in the series of 'The Classics of Western Spirituality': *John Ruusbroec. The Spiritual Espousals and Other Works* (New York-Toronto, 1985). The 'select bibliography' deserves a special mention. The bibliography is complete, or nearly so, and very informative. To be recommended also is the projected ten-volume critical edition of Ruusbroec's works, with the original text, Surius' Latin translation, and the ET in 'American English' by Helen Rolfson, professor at St. John's University, Collegeville, MN. The first three volumes are already in print (Brepols, Turnhout, Belgium), 1981, and the next is on its way.

195 Letter 30; VM, *Brieven*, 1: 255, ll. 107–08: 'There are three things through which one lives for *Minne* in the Trinity and, in the beyond, in the Unity'. The three things are to live with the Son, the Holy Spirit and the Father. At times, Hadewijch shows certain monistic tendencies (J. Reynaert, *Beeldspraak*, 447), and we must care not to give her sayings an elasticity which exceeds what she meant. This may be seen in some of the unacceptable deductions made by Albert Brounts in his posthumously published paper cited above, n. 188. Some sayings of Hadewijch could be interpreted as pantheistic or quietistic, but only when taken out of context.

196 VM, *Brieven*, 1: 144, ll. 96–100. The translation follows VM's suggested interpretation of this unclear passage of a letter which is one of the most difficult of her 31 Letters.

God and man in one single love
Taken up in the life of the Three in Unity:
This is Trinity beyond all thought.[197]

Though Hadewijch, at times, does not mince her words, no one could reasonably call her reckless. At the end of Letter 17, aware of her incapacity to put the fulness of God's love into human words, she simply confessed that God, not she, had to teach her friend to put into practice what Hadewijch advised her to do,[198] and in Letter 30, faced with the reality of human littleness, she admitted in plain words: 'How this is, I do not dare to tell you, for I am not grown up enough and my love is too small'.[199] Aware that God is the primary mover, she ended that same letter by saying: 'May God correct us and grant us such perfection that we may live in conformity with the Trinity and we may become 'oned' with the Unity of the Deity. Amen'.[200]

After these quotations from Hadewijch, the question could be asked: what did the other *mulieres religiosae* think? As Hadewijch spoke from her most intimate relations with God which she experienced in her ecstasies, so too did some of the others, even if they are not as informative as Hadewijch.

197 VM, *Mengeldichten*, 84–85, ll. 191–96. Other texts could be quoted, for she speaks about this topic in Letters 17,18, 20, 22, 30 and in her *Poem 16 in Couplets*. In her Letter 22, she spoke of God who is above, beyond, within and underneath everything. To what VM (*Brieven*, 1: 179–87) and J. Reynaert (*Beeldspraak*, 237–41, who calls this letter her masterpiece in prose) said about the curious and difficult to understand paradoxes she used, could be added the observations made by Jean Leclercq and Robert Dresser in regard to Bernard. See the former's 'L'Art de composition dans les traités de S.Bernard', *RBén* 76 (1966) 87–115, reproduced in his *Recueil d'études sur saint Bernard et ses écrits* (Rome, 1969) vol.3: 105–35, and the latter's 'Gradation: Rhetoric and Substance in Saint Bernard', in Elder (ed.), *Goad and Nail*, CS 80, (q.v.) 71–85. See also Ch. Dumont, *Aelred de Rievaulx, La vie de recluse*, SCh 76 (Paris, 1961) 22, n. 1.

198 VM, *Brieven*, 1: 145, l. 135.

199 *Ibid.*, 1: 258, ll. 177–78. P. Mommaers and Fr. Willaert made a remarkable attempt to show why Hadewijch spoke the way she did. See their in 1986 delivered paper 'Mystisches Erlebnis und sprachliche Vermittlung in den Briefen Hadewijchs', in *Religiöse Frauenbewegung und mystische Frömmigkeit im Mittelalter*, P. Dinzelbacher and D. D. Bauer eds, 117–151.

200 VM, *Brieven*, 1: 261, ll. 245–48.

The Trinity held as prominent a place in Beatrice's thought as in that of Hadewijch and the others. It is unfortunate that her auto-biography did not reach us in its original vernacular form, for in it we could have heard Beatrice speaking for herself. Her biographer, leaving out what he thought to be above the level of the simple-minded for whom he wrote, mentions that Beatrice 'investigated with the lively clear understanding of her purified mind, the Son eternally born of the Father, the Spirit proceeding from both of them, the distinction of the Persons, the Unity of the divine essence and the other holy mysteries of the Trinity' (164,63). In fact, during the five years before she moved to Nazareth in 1236, the Trinity seemed to have engaged her whole attention. Around Christmas 1231,

She conceived a great desire to know the holy and undivided Trinity. Although the Trinity itself is totally incomprehensible to human understanding, she aspired to the unattainable...with humble heart, devout mind and fervent love.... Sometimes, when she was diligently and keenly inquiring after what she sought, using books on the Holy Trinity of which she kept a supply at hand, and sometimes when she was alertly attending to meditation and prayer, it happened that the light of heavenly truth rushed in like lightning into her opened heart. There, in a moment of time she deserved to lay hold of what she sought; what she could not explore by vigor of mind, the divine Spirit breathed into her through heavenly grace, not to store away in her mind, but to enjoy for the briefest moment.[201]

Shortly thereafter, in January 1232, two months after her first *excessus*, it seemed to her that she could pass to the everlasting fruition of the Trinity in heaven as easily as a thin membrane could burst or as a little cloud could evaporate in the radiance of

---

201 *Vita*, 213,4. Interesting as this text may be, it is a description by the biographer, and does not equal the warmth of Beatrice's heart, which we miss here.

a sunbeam. She realized, as the biographer tells us in a tortuous Latin sentence, that:

> restrained by its mortality, her affection could not attain the everlasting fruition of the Supreme Good which it [her spirit] sought. Her body like a thin membrane which is easily broken, or like a shining cloud which is easily penetrated by the clear radiance of the sun, but still seemed to obstruct her spirit which was always aspiring upward. Once the cloud was dispelled there was nothing by which any sort of obstacle could keep her spirit from being perpetually illuminated by the eternal sun. Therefore she sought in prayer that this thin membrane be speedily broken, and with fervent desire of her heart she persistently desired that the light little cloud be driven away by the ray of the eternal sun.[202]

When she wrote her treatise many years later, the passing of time had dissipated her hope, not to say her illusion, of an early death, but had not mellowed her desire. She did not speak any more of a thin membrane easily broken or of a light little cloud to be dispelled: the fervor of her desire had increased dramatically and she used a strongly-worded sentence to express the pertinacity and voracity of her burning desire to have fruition of God.

> The blessed soul is so sweetly immersed in love and so vehemently attracted by desire that its heart rages and becomes fidgety impatient within; its soul melts and languishes in love; its mind is madly lifted up with vehement desire and all its senses draw it thither so that it wills to be in fruition of love. This it desires from God insistently, and it seeks it ardently from God and it must necessarily desire it intensely. For love does not allow it to be appeased or rest or enjoy peace.[203]

202 *Vita*, 198,49.
203 R-VM., *Seven manieren*, 29–30, ll. 15–25.

It should be noted that her desire for God not only increased over the years, but it impelled her more strongly toward fruition, while at the same time she became more deeply convinced that no abatement was possible until God should grant it. An inward force compelled her to desire fruition with increasing passion, while postponement purified this craving desire from the residue of any Beatrice-centered ardor for fruition. She had to learn to strive ardently for fruition of God for the sake of him who is infinitely perfect. Only in him can fruition find its purest and fullest form. With God's help, and by fulfilling the demands laid upon her to cooperate satisfactorily with his love, she would become an acceptable partner, sharing copiously in God's fruition.

During an ecstasy, 'she investigated what she had desired to understand of the mystery of the Holy Trinity'. Beatrice's soul 'understood more fully at that instant of time, by revelation of the divine Spirit, namely the Lord, the Son eternally born of the Father,...the Holy Spirit proceeding equally from the Father and the Son, also the difference of Persons existing in the [unity of the] one Essence of the eternal divine Majesty, and the other sacrosanct mysteries of the divine Trinity' (217,90).

When she had been in office for a long time as prioress, she was one day taken up in ecstasy: 'fixing her contemplative gaze on the incomprehensible essence of the divinity [she] wonderfully beheld with her mind's eye the very supreme and uncreated, eternal and true God and Lord in the substance of his Majesty' (236,32). The biographer's mention of 'the distinction of the Persons, the Unity of the divine Essence and the other holy mysteries of the Trinity' (164,63) and of 'the difference of Persons existing in the [Unity of the] one Essence of the eternal divine Majesty and the other sacrosanct mysteries of the divine Trinity' (217,90) seems to infer agreement with what we have seen in Hadewijch, whose writings did not pass through the hands of a censoring editor, about God's Trinity and Unity in himself and in his relations with man. But given the fact that the biographer presumably left out the more extensive descriptions of Beatrice's experiences, there is no way of knowing what she wrote.

Any hope of finding the original autobiography is nil, and speculation cannot substitute for the missing information.

Evidently one has to look at Beatrice's treatise to see whether she gives us more than the few crumbs the biographer left us. However, as Herman Vekeman has correctly pointed out,[204] in her *Seven manieren* she leaves metaphysical considerations aside. She speaks about how she experienced God's love here on earth, and how she realized that in becoming thoroughly purified she had to strive toward a profuse, flaming reciprocal love, in order to be admitted to an unending participation in God's love and fruition as God had planned. Her biographer wrote that shortly before her father went to Nazareth in November 1235 to erect the buildings, she did not seem to have had any doubt about the realization of her expectation of heaven. She ends her treatise by saying that 'having worshipped [the Lord] in the time of grace, it [her soul] will have fruition of him in eternal glory'.[205]

As we have already seen, when Ida Lewis was taken to task for not taking a sip from the ablution cup, she affirmed that she could not do so, for how could she drink from this cup, 'when the Trinity rejoices in me and the [Unity] of the Godhead delights in me and my own spirit becomes one spirit with the Beloved?'[206] Her biographer informs us that right after this incident, something greater and more extraordinary occurred to her, but he preferred, as did Beatrice's biographer, not to mention it because of unsophisticated, simpleminded people.[207]

We also catch a glimpse of Ida of Nivelles' experience: enraptured in the Trinity, she tasted and perceived, as we mentioned earlier, 'what was unveiled to her: how the essence of the Father is in the Son, and the Son's essence in the Father's, and she herself had conversed with the Trinity'.[208]

---

204 H. Vekeman, *Lexicografisch Onderzoek*, 2: 384.

205 R-VM., *Seven manieren*, 38, ll. 167–68.

206 The Latin text has been quoted in n. 132 of Chapter XI.

207 *AA SS* Oct.13: 121,48 : 'Alterum etiam aliud dixit ei mirabile quod ei contingebat, sed propter simplices intellectus provide dignum duximus non scribendum'.

208 In this short sentence, Ida too refers to the unity of God and the threeness of Persons in the Trinity. She spoke not from a merely intellectual but from an

In his *Speculum fidei*, William says that in creating man, God gave him the potential to have fruition of him, the goal for which he made him: man's 'mind [was] created for eternity, that it might through its intelligence be capable of it and by its fruition share in it'.[209] And in his *Commentary on the Song of Songs* he again refers to man's creation to God's image and likeness in view of man's participation forever in God's fruition: 'O Lord our God, you did create us to your image and likeness, i.e. to contemplate you and have fruition of you. No one contemplates you with fruition, save insofar as he becomes like you'.[210]

It is God who effects it, for '[God's] wisdom disposes of all things, both the adversities and prosperities, arranging and composing all things unto good, until it leads the soul back to its origin in and hides it in the hiddenness of God's face'.[211] He effects it, but with the indispensable free cooperation of man: 'Even if nature has from creating grace a hunger for these [heavenly things], still it cannot tell them apart perfectly except by illuminating grace, nor does it apprehend them unless God grants them'.[212] William referred more than once to God as the primary mover of the grace-filled relationship between him and man. He puts it in the mouth of the Son to make his point:

> And this is the prayer of the Son to the Father: 'I will, (that is, I effect by the strength of my will which is the Holy Spirit) that as you and I are one in substance, so also they may be one in us by grace, one in love, one in beatitude, one

experiential level, just as the others had done. The experiences of the other *mulieres religosae* are in most cases related to the one God who is Trinity. The texts have been quoted above in Chapter XVII, p. 551, n. 168.

209 Spec fid, PL 180: 386B: 'Menti siquidem ad aeternum creatae, ut per ejus intelligentiam sit capax, per fruitionem particeps'.

210 Cant. PL 180: 473C: 'Domine Deus noster, qui ad imaginem et similitudinem creasti nos scilicet ad te contemplandum teque fruendum; quem nemo usque ad fruendum contemplatur, nisi in quantum similis tibi efficitur'.

211 Nat an, PL 184: 408A: 'Sapientia suaviter disponens omnia, et adversa et prospera, omnia ei in bonum modificans et componens, donec animam ad principium suum reducat, et abscondat in abscondito faciei Dei'.

212 Spec fid, 24; PL 180: 386C: 'in quibus [bonis aeternis] tametsi habet natura appetitum ex gratia creante, non tamen ea perfecte dignoscit nisi ex gratia illuminante, nec apprehendit nisi Deo donante'.

in immortality and incorruption, and even in some way one in divinity itself.[213]

In a sermon Bernard describes what this fruition consists of:

In the everlasting and blissful beatitude we shall have fruition in three different ways: we shall see him in all his
creatures, we shall possess him in ourselves, and — what is
ineffably more delightful than either of these, — we shall
contemplate the Trinity in Itself, gazing upon that supreme
glory with the eye of a pure heart, without any riddle.[214]

While they greatly desired to have fruition of God here on
earth, the *mulieres religiosae*, like their mentors, were even more
desirous of having fruition of him in the beyond. Beatrice's
biographer tells us that with the foretaste of fruition she had in her
first *excessus* in 1231, she was told that she could look forward
for a sempiternal taste:

---

213 Nat corp, PL 180: 722D: 'Et haec est oratio Filii ad Patrem: "Volo, i.e.
voluntatis meae virtute, qui Spiritus Sanctus est, efficio ut sicut ego et te unum
sumus in substantia, sic et ipsi in nobis unum sint ex gratia" (Jn 17:21). Unum
amore, unum beatitudine, unum immortalitate et incorruptione, unum etiam
quodammodo ipsa divinitate'. William refers here to man's participation in the
beyond in God's Unity and the *regiratio* in love of the Trinity. D. Bell, referring
to this passage, rightly comments (*The Image*, 231): 'Our divinity and unity is a
derived divinity and unity, and so, too, our joy and blessedness. In other words,
we can become God by participation, not by substance, and when our participation is actualized and we realize that all we are and have is from God and in God,
then, as William says, we become what God is (*quod Deus est*), but we do not
become God'.

214 OS 4,3; SBOp 5: 357: 'Triplicem in aeterna illa beatitudine fruemur Deo,
videntes eum in omnibus creaturis, habentes eum in nobis ipsis et, quod his
omnibus ineffabiliter iucundius et beatius, ipsam quoque in semetipsa Trini-
tatem et gloriam illam sine ullo aenigmate mundo cordis oculo contemplantes'.
To 'see the Trinity Itself and its glory', seems to refer to God as Trinity and the
glory of the three Persons in their Unity. Indeed, in SC 72,2; SBOp 2: 226,
Bernard says paradoxically that 'in heaven the only activity is quiescence': 'Ubi
omne negotium otium'. Augustine spoke already of a *negotium otiosum*. See I.
Bochet, *Augustin et le désir de Dieu*, 131, n. 1. Some similar or nearly similar
expressions can be found in Jean Leclercq, *Otia Monastica. Études sur le
vocabulaire de la contemplation au Moyen Age*, Studia Anselmiana 51, (Rome,
1963).

She knew by revelation of the Holy Spirit that... when she had finished the course of her present life... being consummated in virtue, then she would emigrate to heaven to the blessed place prepared by God for her perpetually from the beginning, here...to enjoy (*fruitura*) everlasting life.[215]

In fact, she finished 'the course of the present life' in 1268, some thirty seven years after the promise was made. She could say, as Hadewijch did, that 'Love rewards to the full, though it often comes late'.[216] Beatrice knew very well that life here takes its value and meaning from God, who willed that she participate in his fruition for all eternity, and, as has been clearly indicated in Part Three of this study, this convinction was held by the other *mulieres religiosae*. Beatrice herself wrote in the seventh *maniere* of her treatise:

that the soul wills to proceed to the fatherland... where it rests in love, for it well knows that there every impediment will be removed from it and that it will be received with love by its Beloved: there to gaze with eagerness upon what it so tenderly loved, and it will possess for its own blessedness him whom it has faithfully served, and it will with full delight have fruition of him whom she has often embraced in her soul with love.[217]

As for Hadewijch, she is at this point as communicative as ever: mind, reason, wisdom or anything else, she says, 'cannot penetrate the wonderful fathomlessness hidden to all things: this is reserved [in heaven] for the fruition of *Minne*'.[218] Nothing outside God can tell him to share or how much to share his fruition. It is completely up to him, as Hadewijch said in her fifth

---

215 *Vita*, 178,81. This text is another instance where the migration to heaven right after death is implied.

216 Letter 7; VM, *Brieven*, 1: 72, l. 18–19. This text has already been referred to above in n. 54 of Chapter XV, p. 467.

217 R-VM, *Seven manieren*, 37–38, ll. 145–57.

218 Letter 18; VM, *Brieven*, 1: 156, ll. 101–03.

vision. While she was taken up in the spirit, 'there revealed itself
the Countenance of God with which *he* will satisfy all the saints
and all men for the full length of his eternity'.[219] Sharing in
God's fruition necessarily has a character of its own. This participation can never become tainted by any form of greediness on
man's side. No ego can be involved in such an experience, for
only with a creature who has the necessary openness can God
wholly share his fruition. This is why Hadewijch wrote in her
eleventh vision: 'I loved the saints in what they mean to God.
This stimulated my desire for blessedness in which God within
them has fruition of himself'.[220] God gave her the firm, unshakable hope that some day she would be ready and wholly prepared
for such sharing. One day, after an *excessus*, she was brought
back 'in the spirit' by the Triune [*lit.* 'I who am in three Persons':
ben ic in .iij.personen] who said to her: 'As you [now] have
fruition of me, so shall you have fruition eternally'.[221] One can
still feel how strongly her anticipation of this participation
vibrated in her first *Poem in Couplets*:

> With ardor shall we have fruition of *Minne*
> And perfectly taste and know
> *Her* glory and *her* splendor
> *Our* gladness and *our* blessedness
> In the eternally new time.[222]

219 VM, *Visioenen*, 1: 141, ll. 425–28.
220 *Ibid.*, 1: 118, ll. 134–38. This text indicates clearly that fruition takes
place by participation, a degree of participation Hadewijch was not ready for
when she wrote these lines. In the next sentence after the one quoted here, she
expressed how hurt she felt because she was not yet able to enjoy it herself.
221 Vision 5; VM, *Visioenen*, 1: 62, ll. 67–68.
222 VM, *Mengeldichten*, 13, ll. 275–80 (italics added). In this whole stanza
Hadewijch says in her own way what K. Rahner wrote in the text referred to
above in n. 111 of this Chapter: 'by accepting God as he is, as the mystery of
incomprehensibility, once [this is] recognized it is the very truth of man and,
once loved, is his blessed fulfilment'. At the end of the summary of an address
('Divertimento op het "nieuwheids"-motief in het werk van Hadewijch', *Handelingen van het XXIXe Vlaams filologencongres* [Antwerp, 1973], 255–57),
Bernard Spaapen quoting Hadewijch (without any reference to Rahner), said
that 'the love wherewith Hadewijch loves is ever [*lit.* at all hours] new, because
the *Minne* [here God] who is loved, is ever [*lit.* at all hours] new'. J. Reynaert

Hadewijch refers also to fruition in heaven in her twelfth
Letter: 'All the saints [*lit.* the inhabitants of heaven] shall eternally blaze with love to give *Minne* satisfaction to the full'.[223] In
her *Poem 16 in Couplets*, speaking of man's participation in
God's fruition, she uses the image of the kiss to express the
deepest and most blessed union between them, comparing this
kiss with the one within the Trinity itself.

When the loved one will receive from the Beloved
The kisses that truly belong to *Minne*,
When he takes possession of her in every way,
Love draws in and tastes these kisses through and through.
When *Minne* thus bestirs the loved soul,
She eats its flesh and drinks its blood.
When *Minne* dissolves her thus, [and]
Sweetly seduces them both
To one undivided kiss;
That same kiss which fully unites
The three Persons in one sole Being.[224]

E. *Epectasis* or Eternally Ongoing Progress in Fruition

What we have in the preceding pages seen most *mulieres
religiosae* describe sparingly and Hadewijch profusely, is analo-
gous to what several of their mentors had spoken of; it is usually
known as *epectasis*[225] or infinite progress which affects not God
himself but the *hemelingen*, the inhabitants of heaven, as Hadewijch called them. Their beatific vision not only goes on forever,
but eternally expands in depth and degree for each person in
accordance with one's balance sheet at the moment of death.

confirmed Spaapen's interpretation in *Beeldspraak*, 392–401; 394–95:
'nuweheit', in relation to the ever newness of God's and Hadewijch's love, as
Fr. Willaert, *De Poëtica van Hadewijch*, 165–67 did in relation to the ever
newness of Hadewijch's love in her *Poems in Stanzas*.

223 VM, *Brieven*, 1: 102, ll. 23–25.

224 VM, *Mengeldichten*, 82. ll. 114–24.

225 The Latin writers seem not to use Gregory of Nyssa's term *epectasis*. In
fact, they did not have a technical word for it, but spoke of the balance between
satiation and weariness, as we will see below.

Though *epectasis* is primarily a pure gift, God does not discount man's contribution. Man's life should be a freely willed response to God's love, a response which one cannot render without God's assistance.

Epectasis is a very important aspect of the beatific vision, as we may see from a number of thorough studies. [226] The first to have spoken of it repeatedly and discussed it extensively is Gregory of Nyssa. Before we look at the Latin mentors of the *mulieres religiosae*, therefore, Gregory's view of *epectasis* deserves closer attention. When enjoyment is experienced on the human level, he wrote, one has to draw the line somewhere, otherwise satiation sets in, thereby postponing the moment when the enjoyment can be fully experienced again.[227] In the beyond, things happen differently. In his *Contra Eunomium*, Gregory wrote that:

> since the First Good [God] is by nature infinite, it follows of necessity that the participation of that which enjoys it will be also infinite, grasping forever more, yet always discovering something beyond that which has been already grasped, and being never able to equal it (*viz.* the object of its desire) because neither that which is participated (the First Good) ends nor the one which increases by participation stops.[228]

God's infinity is infinity in act and therefore incapable of movement. When finite man shares in God's infinity, this shared infinity is infinite-in-becoming: a progressive, dynamic movement which never reaches the non-existent limit. In this shared

---

226 To name the most important studies in chronological order, Hans von Balthasar. *Présence et Pensée*; Jean Daniélou, *Platonisme*, especially 309–26; Walther Völker, *Gregor von Nyssa*, particularly 186–95; Jerome Gaïth, *La conception de la liberté*, 196–206 and David Balás, *Man's Participation*.

227 Gregory and several others pointed this out. Charles Dumont, for instance, has listed several references in the writings of Aelred and Bernard. See his introduction of *La vie de recluse*, SCh 76, 32, n. 2.

228 The translation is taken from D. Balás' *Man's Participation*, 59, as is the following text from Gregory in *De vita Moysi* (*ibid.*, 154): 'It is absolutely impossible to attain perfection, for perfection is not confined within limits, and the only determination of virtue is infinity. How could then one reach the limit he is looking for, if no limit can be found?' This sentence hints that perfectionism has absolutely nothing to do with *epectasis* nor with perfection.

infinity, God fulfils the soul's desire—instilled by him at creation,[229] —to participate in his infinite perfection and the fruition thereof. Looking not for spectators but for partakers, God also, on his own initiative, dilates the soul's capacity with a more intense desire for increased participation. As a result, the desire is continually satiated by what it participates in and simultaneously remains insatiate because it can never attain the infinity of God's own love and fruition. For this is proper to seeing God's face: to be always intensely satiated by the fruition experienced in this vision, and at the same time spared any possibility of weariness.[230] While ever experiencing more ardent and renewed desires to be satiated by the fruition of God's *Totality*, the participant finds that these desires will never be and can never be totally satiated. It is in this complementary combination of continuously satiated desires and the continuously increasing desires without end and without ever becoming satiated with God's totality that the paradox of man's simultaneous satiation and insatiation consists.

Nor is there any danger of fusion, since the distance between the finite and the infinite always remains the same, never threatened by whatever degree of participation the finite might attain. Hadewijch expressed this by saying in Letter 22: 'The deepest of God's depth and the very highest of his height have the same [infinite] length';[231] 'his elevation escapes us eternally and his highest height is beyond our reach'.[232] As God is within himself simultaneously active and quiescent, so are all participants in God's fruition simultaneously active in desiring more of him and quiescent in the fruition they enjoy according to the degree of their participation. The movement of man's divinization, begun at the incarnation, is infinitely and with ever greater intensity

229 This is the equivalent, says Daniélou (*Platonisme*, 315) of the *pondus* of Augustine [and of William] spoken of above in n. 35 of this Chapter.

230 Weariness is a time-related experience which cannot happen in a timeless situation, as has been well explained by D. Balás, in *Man's Participation*, 157–58: 'Participation and Eschatology', and still better by J. Gaïth, *La conception de la liberté*, 203–06: 'Béatitude ou désespoir?'.

231 Letter 22; VM, *Brieven*, 1: 191, ll. 88–90.

232 Ibid., 1, 189, ll. 46–47.

prolonged for all eternity. In heaven, man exists not in a prepara-
tory stage as he does here, but definitively. Or as Sirach 18:6 has
it in the Vulgate: 'cum consummaverit homo, tunc incipit': when
a man finishes [his earthly life], then he really begins to exist, 'as
Gregory of Nyssa, Augustine, Bernard and many others would
interpret this biblical sentence'.[233]

The *mulieres religiosae* could not have read Gregory of
Nyssa's works in their original Greek. How far they might have
known him in Latin translations has still to be explored. But they
knew or could have known the Latin authors who wrote about
epectasis. Augustine is chronologically one of the first and certainly the most influential of the Latin Fathers to treat it, even if
he did not write on this subject as extensively as did the Cappado-
cian Gregory. The fact that glorified man can be satiated derives
from his being made to God's image and thus having the capacity
for participating in God's satiation.[234] In his Commentary on
John Augustine wrote:

> Do not fear that [in heaven] weariness will take hold of you.
> The enjoyment of this Beauty [God] will be such that it will
> always be present to you without you ever becoming sati-
> ated; yes, you will always be satiated and you will never be
> [totally] satiated. If I say to you that you will not be satiated
> this would mean hunger; if I say that you will be [totally]
> satiated, I fear weariness. Where there will be neither hun-
> ger nor satiety, I do not know what to say. But God has the
> power to grant it to those who do not know how to phrase it,
> and see to it that believers receive it.[235]

---

233 Henri de Lubac, *The Supernatural*, 263.
234 *De Trinitate* 14, 8, 11; PL 42: 1044: 'Eo quippe ipso imago ejus est, quo
ejus capax est, ejusque particeps esse potest'.
235 *Tractatus in Johannis Evangelium* 3,21; PL 35: 1405D: 'Noli timere ne
fastidio deficias: talis erit illa delectatio pulchritudinis, ut semper tibi praesens
sit, et numquam satieris; imo semper satieris et numquam satieris. Si enim
dixero quia non satiaberis, fames erit; si dixero quia satiaberis, fastidium timeo:
ubi nec fastidium erit, nec fames, quid dicam nescio. Sed Deus habet quod
exhibebat non invenientibus quomodo dicant, et credentibus quod accipiant'.

Though Augustine had trouble in phrasing it, nevertheless, he stood by his paradoxes:

He [God] will satiate you and not satiate you [totally]. What I am saying is astonishing. If I say that he will [totally] satiate you, I am afraid that you will wish to withdraw as if satiated by a meal or a repast. What shall I say then? That he will not satiate you? Again, I am afraid that if I say that he will not satiate you, you will seem to be in want.... What shall I say then, except what can be said, though hardly be thought? He will satiate you and he will not satiate you [totally], for I find both in Scripture.[236]

In one of his sermons he repeated his teaching, saying: 'You will always be satiated and never be [totally] satiated,...there will be no weariness, or hunger'.[237]

Gregory the Great, having stated that satiety on earth is usually followed by weariness, goes on to affirm that in the beatific vision the opposite happens to the angels and the blessed:

In order not to have anxiety [of weariness] in their desire, they [the angels] are satiated while desiring, and so too, in order not to experience weariness in their satiety, they desire while being satiated. They desire without effort because desire and satiety go together; they are satiated without weariness because satiety is ever inflamed by desire. So too will it be for us when we arrive at the very fountain of life; we will delightfully be full of both thirst and satiety. But the need [to be quenched] is far away from this thirst, and

236 *Ennarationes in Psalmum 85*,24; PL 37: 1099: ' Et satiat te et non te satiat. Mirum est quod dico. Si dicam quia satiat te, timeo ne quasi satiatus velis abscedere, quomodo de prandio, quomodo de caena. Ergo quid dicam? Non te satiat? Timeo rursus ne si dixero: non te satiat, indiges videaris; quid ergo dicam, nisi quod dici potest, cogitari vix potest? Et satiat te, et non te satiat, quia utrumque invenio in scriptura'.

237 *Sermo* 369,29; PL 39: 1633A: ' Semper satieris, et numquam satieris,... nec fastidum erit, nec fames'.

weariness from satiety, because, while thirsting we will be satiated, and satiated, thirsting. Indeed, we shall see God.[238]

Sometimes mention is made in this connection of Rhabanus Maurus, a Benedictine abbot, who died in 856 as bishop of Mainz. His contribution, however, can be neglected, for he merely repeated what Gregory the Great had said.[239] The ongoing process of simultaneous satiation and insatiation apparently passed unemphasised through the Dark Ages till it received a renewed interest in the Renaissance of the twelfth century. One of the first to speak of it was Peter Damian (d.1072), closely linked with the Gregorian Reform of his time.[240] He too is in line with Gregory the Great. Describing what the saints will experience in heaven, he says that 'there they will drink from the fountain of life, and drinking still remain thirsty, for there the avidity of want cannot arise, nor does satiety cause weariness'.[241]. In his Rhythm on the Glory of Heaven he put it succintly and pointedly:

Avidi et semper pleni,	Avidly longing they are always full,
Quod habent desiderant:	What they have they desire:

---

238 *Moralia in Job* 18,54,91; PL 76: 94 BC: 'Satietatem solet fastidium subsequi.... Ne enim sit in desiderio anxietas, desiderantes satiantur; ne autem sit in satietate fastidium, satiati desiderant. Et desiderant igitur sine labore, quia desiderium satietas comitatur; et satiantur sine fastidio, quia ipsa satietas ex desiderio semper accenditur. Sic quoque et nos erimus quando ad ipsum fontem vitae venerimus. Erit nobis delectabiliter impressa sitis simul atque satietas. Sed longe abest ab ista siti necessitas, longe a satietate fastidium, quia et sitientes satiabimur, et satiati sitiemus. Videbimus igitur Deum'. Gregory repeats the same description in nearly the same words in his *Homilia in Ezechielem* 1,8,15.

239 Rhabanus Maurus, *De videndo Deum*, PL 112: 1282B.

240 Fridolin Dressler, *Petrus Damiani. Leben und Werk*, Studia Anselmiana 34, (Rome, 1954) and Jean Leclercq, *St. Pierre Damien, ermite et homme d'Église*, (Rome, 1960).

241 *Institutio Monialis* 15, PL 145: 748D: 'Illic vitae fontem et sitientes hauriunt, et haurientes sitiunt; quia ibi non potest, vel aviditas passionum gignere, vel satietas fastidire'.

Neque satietas fastidit,	Satiety is not loathsome,
Neque fames cruciat:	Nor does hunger torment:
Inhiantes semper edunt,	With appetite they continually eat,
Et edentes inhiant.	And eating they long for more.[242]

Jean Leclercq's *The Love of Learning and the Desire of God*,[243] makes it clear that monastic writers were especially interested in and intent on enjoying the felicity of heaven. The first to attract attention was the influential Bernard, who accentuated the relationship between God's Son, his Word, the Bridegroom, and man's soul, his bride. According to Bernard, God from all eternity willed the incarnation of his Son, which did not take place only in view of man's re-creation. Man was created primarily in view of the incarnation which points to God's glorification by man's participation in Christ's Sonship.[244]

The heavenly birth of which Bernard spoke, must be seen, not in opposition to birth on earth, but relative to the end of time:

A time will come when the shadows will wane and even entirely fade away with the advance of dawn, and a vision as clear as it is everlasting will steal upon her [the bride], bringing not only sweetness to the taste but satisfaction to the heart [*lit.* to the belly], yet without surfeit.[245]

Recalling that on earth, Christ compared himself to a shepherd, Bernard applied this figure to Christ's pastoral care in heaven:

Who would not vehemently desire to be fed there [in heaven] on account of its peace, its nourishment, and satiation? Nothing is feared, nothing is distasteful, nothing lacking. Paradise is a safe dwelling-place, the Word a sweet

---

242 *De gloria paradisi rythmus*, PL 145: 863–64.
243 Chapter 4, 57–86: 'Devotion to heaven'.
244 Bernard's text has been quoted above in n. 99 of this chapter.
245 SC 48,6; SBOp 2: 72–73: 'Eritque, cum declinaverunt umbrae, crescente lumine, immo penitus disparuerint, et subintrabit sicut perspicua, ita et perpetua visio, eritque non modo suavis gutturi, sed et satietas ventri, sine fastidio tamen'.

nourishment, eternity a wealth beyond calculation.... Let us
make haste to live [there] where we may dwell without fear,
may abound without want, may feast without satiation. You,
Lord,... feed there all in security, you who are the shepherd
of the sheep.[246]

In accordance with the promise made by God's Son:

The just are already feasting and rejoicing in the sight of
God, delighting in their gladness [Ps 67:4]. Hence this
satiety without weariness; hence this insatiable curiosity
without restlessness; hence that eternal, inexplicable desire
knowing no want; hence finally that sober inebriation, not
from sheer overdrinking, not reeking with wine, but burning
for God.[247]

Addressing his monks, Bernard assured them that heaven's
horn of plenty will never become empty; its abundance will go on
forever and ever:

when the soul happily finds him [God], its holy desire is not
quenched but kindled. Does not the consummation of joy
bring about the consuming of desire? It is rather oil poured
upon the flames, for he himself is the flame. So it is. Joy will
be fulfilled, but there will be no end to desire nor therefore
of seeking. Conceive, if you can, the fervor of seeking

246 SC 33,2–4; SBOp 1: 235–36: ' Quis non illic vehementer cupiat pasci, et
propter pacem, et propter adipem, et propter satietatem? Nihil ibi formidatur,
nihil fastidium, nihil deficit. Tuta habitatio paradisus, dulce pabulum Verbum,
opulentia multa nimis aeternitas... Festinemus ut habitemus sine metu, abun-
demus sine defectu, epulemur sine satietate. Tu enim, Domine,...cum securitate
omnia ibi pascis, idem ipse...pastor ovium'.
247 Dil 11,32; SBOp 3: 147: 'Quemadmodum Dei Filium promisit..."justi
epulentur et exsultent in conspectu Dei, et delectentur in laetitia''. Hinc illa
satietas sine fastidio; hinc insatiabilis illa sine inquietudine curiositas; hinc
aeternum illud atque inexplicabile desiderium, nesciens egestatem, hinc denique
sobria illa ebrietas, vero, non mero ingurgitans, non madens vino, sed ardens
Deo'.

eagerly without want, and desire without anxiousness: for presence excludes the one, abundance the other.[248]

Everyone will share in this heavenly felicity, but each one in accordance with the dimensions his desire acquired during his lifetime on earth. This already noted belief is here repeated in Bernard's words:

He who hungers, let him hunger still more, and he who desires, let him desire more abundantly, because as much as one will be able to desire, just so much shall one receive.... O truly happy and glorious satiety! O holy feast! O most desirable banquet, where there never will be any anxiety, never any weariness, because satiety will be full and have from within plenty of desire.[249]

William, at the time still a Benedictine abbot, wrote that in heaven all share in God's love for his absolute, all-perfect Self: all love him in themselves and themselves in him, all love one another in his love for all. There is no place for ambition or competition since the present human condition is gone and the sovereignty of divine love permeates and saturates all. In a sentence in which he relies on Gregory the Great's Commentary on Ezechiel (1,8,15), and uses human terminology, William wrote that this union with God, who is 'an ocean of love', begins here with exacting demands and is fulfilled there where satiety cannot be disturbed by weariness, nor desire by anxiety.

---

248 SC 84,1; SBOp 2: 303: ' Utique non extundit desiderium sanctum felix inventio, sed extendit. Numquid consummatio gaudii, desiderii consumptio est? Oleum magis est illi: nam ipse flamma. Sic est. Adimplebitur laetitia; sed desiderii non erit finis, ac per hoc nec quaerendi. Tu vero cogita, si potes, quaeritandi hoc studium sine indigentia, et desiderium sine anxietate: alterum profecto praesentia, alterum copia excludit'.

249 OS 1,11; SBOp 5: 336: 'Qui esurit, esuriet amplius, et qui desiderat, abundantius desideret, quoniam quantumcumque desiderare potuerit, tantum est accepturus.... O felix et gloriosa satietas! O sanctum convivium! O desiderabiles epulae, ubi nimirum anxietas nulla, nullum potuit esse fastidium, quoniam satietas summa et summum inerit desiderium!'.

It is, indeed [God who is] Love who is loved. Out of the abundance and the nature of its goodness, Love fills with the same grace but in different measure those who love and co-love, those who rejoice and co-rejoice. And the more plentifully he [God as Love] pours himself into the faculties of those who love him, the more he dilates their capacity to receive him. He provides them with satiety but without weariness; this satiation itself does not diminish their desire, but rather increases it, although it removes any worrying distress. For, as was said, it is Love which is loved. It is he [God as Love] who, by the flood of his delights, repels any weariness in satiety from the one who loves him, any anxiety in the desire or any resentment or envy [of those who have a higher degree of love or more encompassing amplitude of satiation]. He enlightens them, as the Apostle says 'from clarity to clarity' (2 Cor 3:18), that in the light they see light and draw in love from Love. For here is the fountain of life that always flows and never runs dry... here, he who desires finds forthwith what he wants, and he who loves finds what he loves. Therefore, he who desires loves always to desire, and he who loves desires to love always. And for him who desires and loves, O Lord, you make what he desires so to abound, that satiety does not vex the one who desires, nor does weariness afflict his abundance of satiety.... This is perfection: to keep always moving [forward], this is to arrive.[250]

---

250 Contempl 8; PL 184: 371B-D; R. Thomas, *Contemplation de Dieu*, (Chambarand, 1965) 64–68, where the Latin text can be found and the reference to Gregory the Great is mentioned: 'Nimirum amor est qui amatur, quia est magna bonitatis suae affluentia et natura amantes et coamantes, gaudentes et cogaudentes, pari implet gratia, licet dispari mensura; et quantum se amantium sensibus largius infundit, tanto eos sui capaciores efficit, satietatem faciens, sed sine fastidio; et ipsa satietate non minuens desiderium, sed augens, sed remota omni anxietudinis miseria. Amor enim est, ut dictum est, qui amatur, qui ex voluptatis suae torrente omnem ab amatore suo repellit vel in satietate fastidii, vel in desiderio anxietudinis, vel in zelando invidiae miseriam. Illuminans eos, ut dicit Apostolus, "a claritate in claritatem", ut in lumine videant lumen, et in

As a Cistercian monk in Signy William wrote in his *Commentary on the Song of Songs* that satiety in heavenly delights is the equivalent of being [within limits] satiated with the vision of God, where: 'in eternal beatitude he [God] feeds with himself both angels and saints [who are] ever satiated by the perfection of blessedness, ever desirous of contemplating him because of the tenderness and sweetness of love'.[251]

Aelred too says that the vision of God causes desire to become satiated but never wearied: 'We will see [God] always and always desire to see [him], so that the vision will satiate the aspiring desire, while the desire will do away with weariness'.[252] In a treatise Aelred wrote for his sister, a recluse, he said that in heaven the fruition born of seeing the trinitarian God will never be totally satiated nor will the desire to see him ever be diminished:

The Father will be seen in the Son, the Son in the Father, and the Holy Spirit in them both. He will be seen... face to face. He will be seen as he is, when his promise will be fulfilled: 'Who loves me will be loved by my Father, and I shall love him and show myself to him' (Jn 14:21) .... Of all this is born such an affection, such an abundance of fruition,

---

amore concipiant amorem. Hic est fons vitae qui semper fluit, et numquam effluit...quia praesto est desideranti quod desiderat, et amanti quod amat. Ideoque et qui desiderat, semper amat desiderare, et qui amat, semper desiderat amare, et desideranti et amanti quod desiderat et amat, sic facis abundare, O Domine, ut nec anxietas desiderantem, nec fastidium affligat abundantem.... Haec est perfectio; sic semper ire, hoc est pervenire'. Monique Simon's paper: 'Le "face à face" dans les méditations de Guillaume de Saint-Thierry', *Coll* 35 (1973) 12–36, pointed out how often William used this expression is his meditations, mostly connected—as can be expected—with a biblical text.

251 Cant, PL 180: 491C; SCh 82: 150,56: 'Ubi in aeterna beatitudine pascit de seipso tam angelorum quam sanctorum hominum satietatem, semper plenam ob perfectionem beatitudinis; semperque in eum respicere desiderantem, ob pietatem et dulcedinem amoris'.

252 C.H. Talbot, *Sermones inediti*, 36: 'Semper igitur videbimus, et semper videre desiderabimus, ut et visio satiet affectum, desiderium vero tollat fastidium'.

such a vehemence of desire, that satiety will not diminish the desire, nor will desire obstruct satiety.[253]

Baldwin, another English Cistercian, abbot of Ford and later archbishop of Canterbury (d.1190), is not less explicit than Aelred. In his treatise on the Eucharist he wrote that in heaven one who remains insatiated finds, nevertheless, eternal satiety:

> In the eternal satiety there is some hunger, not one of need but of felicity; there they never refuse to eat who desire always to eat, and are never weary in satiety. Indeed, there is satiety without weariness and desire without a sigh.... He [God] is always sought because he is loved that he may be held forever: And so, those who find, still search, and those who eat are still hungry, as those who drink are still thirsty. This searching removes all anxiety, and this hunger drives away all hunger; this thirst quenches all thirst. For this [thirst] is not one of need but of consummated felicity.[254]

Adam of Perseigne also knew of this insatiating satiety and desire.[255] Not unimportant is Yvo's 'Letter to Severin', a short

253 C.H. Talbot, 'The "De Institutione Inclusarum" of Ailred of Rievaulx', *AC* 7 (1951) 167–217; 216, ll. 9–17; rpt in modern spelling in CCCM 1 (A. Hoste and C.H. Talbot eds), (Turnhout, 1971) 681, ll. 1506–1516: 'Videbitur Pater in Filio, Filius in Patre, Spiritus Sanctus in utroque. Videbitur...facie ad faciem. Videbitur enim sicuti est, impleta illa promissione qua dixit: " Qui diligit me, diligetur a Patre meo, et ego diligam eum, et manifestabo ei meipsum" .... Ex his tanta nascitur dilectio, tantus ardor pii amoris, tanta dulcedo caritatis, tanta fruendi copia, tanta desiderii vehementia, ut nec satietas desiderium minuat, nec desiderium satietatem impediat'. See also A. Hallier, *Un éducateur*, 168–169.

254 Baldwin of Ford, *Liber de Sacramento altaris*; PL 204: 690B–691A: 'Est enim in illa aeterna satietate quasi quaedam esuries, non egestatis, sed felicitatis; ubi semper manducare appetunt, qui manducare numquam nolunt, et in satietate numquam fastidiunt. Est enim satietas sine fastidio, et desiderium sine suspirio.... Semper enim quaeritur, qui ad hoc diligitur, ut semper habeatur. Itaque et qui inveniunt, adhuc quaerunt; et qui edunt, adhuc esuriunt; et qui bibunt, adhuc sitiunt. Sed haec inquisitio omnem sollicitudinem tollit, sed haec esuries omnem esuriem pellit, sed haec sitis omnem sitim extinguit. Non est egestatis, sed consummatae felicitatis.'

255 Adam, Cistercian abbot of Perseigne (1188–1221) in Champagne, wrote in one of his letters that he feared to talk about the marvels of heaven 'where no

treatise where, borrowing copiously from Bernard, he also speaks of satiety and desire. The text may be quoted, since the writings of Beatrice and Hadewijch's show some familiarity with this letter.[256]

The end of desire, as someone has said, is satiety. In fact, it is evident that those who are always hungry are not satiated. But very happy the hunger which hungers only for what it has and has only what it hungers for... Be convinced, therefore, that no one in the future [life] can be [totally] satiated with the sweetness of divine love, just as no one will be filled with it in the present life.[257]

Mention might be made of the treatise *De spiritu et anima* written by an anonymous Cistercian, briefly referred to above.[258] Chapters 57–65, which were added by an unknown hand in the early thirteenth century, describe the joys and blessings of life in heaven, yet has only a few incomplete and vague references to satiety and desire.[259] The mentors of the *mulieres religiosae* had during their lifetime as little experience of fruition in heaven as the *mulieres religiosae* themselves. But whereas the former with their brilliant minds and their theological expertise could aptly speculate about it, the *mulieres religiosae*, not having their pastoral responsibilities or their theological training, were not prepared to talk about it in a methodical way. But they tried with all

---

weariness is begotten from satiety. In full satiety there is still full desire, and in the fulness of desire, satiety in all good (things)'. See PL 211: 607D. Apparently Adam remembered what he had read somewhere.

256 For references, see above, Chapter IV, n. 163.

257 G. Dumeige, *Yves. Epître*, 63, ll. 17–22: 'Finis autem desiderii, ut ait quidam, satietas est. Qui vero semper esuriunt liquet quod satiati non sunt. Sed vere beata esuries que esurit solum quod habet et solum habet quod esurit. His itaque persuasum sit... quod dulcedine divini amoris nemo in futuro satiari potest, nemo in praesenti impleri'.

258 See above, Chapter IV, n. 70.

259 In CF 24, 67, B. McGinn calls the whole treatise 'an admirable textbook or *vade mecum*'. The later added third part, chapters 57–65, could be called 'an admirable hodgepodge' about heaven, though in the Middle Ages many readers did not share this view, as can be deduced from the many extant manuscripts of

their hearts and actions to strive toward heavenly satiation. Most
of the biographies were written by men who had not known the
mulieres religiosae personally, and so are less than helpful in this
matter. But each one of these women went courageously and
wholeheartedly through the process of painful purification, a
growing attachment to God and an increasing love for him and for
his sake. In fact, as can be seen in their mentors' writings, this is
itself the best preparation for the progress of *epectasis*. However
inclined the biographers may have been to accept, at times too
credulously, what they had gathered from witnesses, no one was
bold enough to fantasize about *epectasis*.

This leaves us with Hadewijch, of whom no biography was
written but whose writings survive, and Beatrice, whose auto-
biography covering twenty years of her life (1215–35 with some
additions) was turned into a not always satisfactory biography.
But these writings, together with Beatrice's treatise, enable us to
know to some extent what they did and said in this world, while
expecting, as did the other *mulieres religiosae*, unhindered fruition in the next.

For instance, in a passage of *Poem 30 in Stanzas*, Hadewijch
expressed the intensity of her desire when, as so often happened,
reason brought her down to cold, harsh reality:

> Would that *Minne* might fully be mine! [so I wished]
> Thereto I so exerted myself
> That all my veins exulted;
> Then came reason and made me realize:
> 'Look at what you want to share in already
> And all what must still happen to you beforehand.[260]

Not only reason, but Christ too told her what she had to do:

> Since you are a human being, live in [the] misery [of exile
> on earth] as man (*mensch*). I wish that on earth my life in
> you should be so fully lived in all virtues that you in no

this *vade mecum*. Many of them, however, lack this third part, as is shown by L.
Norpoth in the publication mentioned above in n.70 of Chapter IV.
260 VM, *Strophische Gedichten*, 195, ll. 37–42.

point fail me in myself. Have then the gifts of the Spirit and the power and help of my Father in the perfect works of virtue with which one becomes and remains [like] God eternally.[261]

In other words, Christ told her that in order to have fruition, she had to pay the tuition. As she said in her *Poem 24 in Stanzas*:

> He who wishes to conquer *Minne*
> Must not neglect
> To give himself continually to Love.
> And he must take pains
> Incessantly
> For what his heart has chosen,
> And surrender himself in pain and disgrace,
> In sorrow, in joy, in *Minne*'s chains:
> Thus shall he come to know
> The noblest Being in the depth of *Minne*.[262]

She realized in her first vision that this was the way to arrive at fruition in the hereafter: 'Beyond the multiplicity of virtues be always steadfastly and wholly with love, in the totally unique Virtue [God] that engulfs the two lovers in one and casts them into the abyss where they shall seek and find eternal fruition'.[263]

She encouraged a friend of hers to stand steadfastly turned toward *minne* in the midst of the flow of human life on earth: 'O my dear,... sink wholly into him with all your soul, for our adversities are many, but if we stand firm, we shall reach our full growth'.[264]

261 Vision one; VM, *Visioenen*, 1: 30, ll. 350–57. The last part of this sentence has already been referred to above, n.170 of Chapter VI, 'Liberating grace'.

262 VM, *Strophische Gedichten*, 157, ll. 81–90.

263 Vision one; VM, *Visioenen*, 1: 20, ll. 171–76. In her third letter, she spoke of 'Virtue,...which is God himself' (VM, *Brieven* 1: 32, l. 2). Centuries earlier, Gregory of Nyssa had said exactly the same in his *De vita Moysi*, see J. Daniélou, *La vie de Moïse*, SCh 1 bis, (Paris, 1955) 3–4, with Greek text and French translation.

264 Letter 5; VM, *Brieven*, 1: 43, ll. 9–11.

Hadewijch considered this process of becoming *volwassen*, fully grown up, very important.[265] She knew, as she wrote in her Letter 6, that 'before *Minne* burst her dikes, and before she ravishes man out of himself and so touches him with herself that he is one spirit and one being with her and in her, he must offer people noble service and the life of exile'.[266] How understandable is her complaint when she said: 'This desire for unattainable fruition which *Minne* has always given me for the sake of fruition of *Minne*, has injured and wounded me in the breast and in the heart'.[267]

The unattainable fruition! Hadewijch was stopped not by a removable temporary roadblock, but by the fact that God in his totality can never be reached. God's totality could never become hers, as she said in Letter 12:

> Those who strive to content *Minne*, are also [like *Minne*] eternal and unfathomable, for their conversation is in heaven and their souls take after their Beloved who is unfathomable. But even if they also were loved with eternal love, they also could never attain [the totality of] *Minne*'s depth, just as they cannot attain the One they love and content him [in his totality]. And nevertheless they will nothing else.[268]

With her keen sense of God's unattainable Allness, Hadewijch was well aware that her union with God would be a joining of Creator and the creature, between God and man: the one being unlimited and the other limited, and both unable to bridge the immeasurable gap between them, yet still united in the oneness of love:

> They who strive and desire to please God in love, begin here on earth that eternal life by which God lives eternally. For to

---

265 This has already been shown above in Chapter X, p. 280, n. 37.
266 VM, *Brieven*, 1: 69, ll. 361–66.
267 Letter 29; VM, *Brieven*, 1: 244, ll. 52–55.
268 *Ibid.*, 1: 103, ll. 43–51.

give him love to the full, and to please him according to his
dignity, heaven and earth are busy every moment in new
service, and this they will never perfectly fulfill. Indeed, the
sublime *Minne* and the grandeur that God is, are never
satisfied or acknowledged by all that man can accomplish.
And all the inhabitants of heaven shall blaze eternally in
love in order to give *Minne* satisfaction to the full. So he
who here on earth accepts no other pleasure or alien consolation but strives at every moment to please *Minne*, begins
here on earth that eternal life in which all the inhabitants of
heaven are with God in fruitive love.[269]

With the keenness of her intelligence, and the longing of her
heart, Hadewijch accepted his Allness. She resigned herself
lovingly and respectfully to the unattainable infinity, knowing
that she would never have fruition of God in his totality. She
understood that she would find the totality of her own fruition
precisely and only by her own eternally ongoing progress toward
the unattainable fruition God has of himself in his totality:

It is in contenting him [God] with that love [with which the
triune God loves himself] that all the inhabitants of heaven
are and shall be eternally engaged. This is their occupation
which never is accomplished. And the wanting [*ghebreken*]
of this fruition [*ghebruken*] of God [in his totality] is yet the
sweetest fruition.[270]

For her part, Ida Lewis, as her biography mentions:

understanding the readings of blessed Augustine, who in his
treatises spoke so wonderfully about the marvels of the
Trinity, her spirit became so excited and her soul was
suddenly filled with such delight, steeped in such over-

269 Letter 12; VM, *Brieven*, 1: 101–02, ll. 13–20.
270 Letter 16; *ibid.*, 1: 131–32, ll. 14–19.

whelming gladness of heart, that she was almost afraid of losing her senses and slipping into madness.[271]

This passage claims that Ida was acquainted with Augustine's writings, at least with his *De Trinitate* (*On the Trinity*). She did not merely read it, but let it drop down into her mind and heart to be digested and absorbed. Her reaction intimates that, as the balanced and mature woman she showed herself to have been, her feelings did not suddenly overtake her. Her soul became so inundated with delight, so fascinated with the insight into the *mirabilia Trinitatis*, that she became almost afraid of losing her mind. Though *regiratio* and fruition are not mentioned, when this passage is put in the context of this chapter, it seems likely that this no-nonsense woman was very taken by the astonishing *regiratio* of the three divine persons into the fruition of God's Unity and her participation in it. This text of her biography evokes another question: what kind of written or spoken information did the biographer have at hand to write as he did? Ida was a trained and qualified copyist of manuscripts. Did the biographer have at his disposal some account of her mystical experiences she had written down on parchment, or is his text based on an oral communication made to some confidant of hers?

When we turn to Beatrice, we find that her biography and her treatise give us detailed information on how she lived her whole life—as did the other *mulieres religiosae*—as a preparation for *epectasis*, even if this term does not appear in her or in the others' biographies. Beatrice knew from Ida of Nivelles that the Lord had shown the latter 'the glorious, ineffable, happy place I [the Lord] shall give her [Beatrice] in the end beyond an end'.[272] Accordingly, Beatrice 'aspired to the rest in the fatherland, refusing to be consoled with earthly and transitory things' (125,5), knowing

---

271 *AA SS* Oct.13: 122,52: 'lectiones intelligens de beati tractatibus Augustini loquentis mirabiliter de mirabilibus Trinitatis, tantis repente gaudiis, exaestuante spiritu, fuit ipsius anima delibuta, quod pene timuit ne sensum perderet, et prae mirabili cordis laetitia semet amittens penitus insaniret'. This was equally said by Hadewijch in Letter 25. See VM, *Brieven*, 1: 216, ll. 34–39.

272 *Quinque*, 212.

very well 'that her affection could not [here] attain the everlasting fruition of the Supreme Good which she sought' (198,4). As her mentors had said and done themselves, she too 'forgetting the things that were behind stretched forth with the Apostle (Ph 3:13) to those that were ahead by the steady exercise of the virtues' (166,39). Her biographer did mention that 'to arrive at that happiness [in heaven] she found this shortcut: she would let her mind dwell only on heavenly desires, and henceforth she would cling through pure contemplation of heavenly joys with more gracious service of devotion according to the purity of her mind's eye' (183b,19).

In her biography as well as in her treatise the term desire took second place after the so-frequently mentioned *amor* or *Minne*: 'Since she could not find in present things what she desired, the more her insatiable appetite increased its [the soul's] desire, her appetite continually hungry and famished sought the satiety of eternal refection' (203,65). Her insatiable appetite for *Minne*, 'sighing for eternal things [was] unable to...attain what she insatiably desired' (221,73). Around New Year 1236, before she went in June of that year to Nazareth, the biographer describes how she strove for heavenly fruition:

> Although she had kept her will conformed to this desire [for fruition in heaven] all her life long, at this time the desire thrived more vigorously than usual in the blessed woman's mind. It so grew beyond the possibilities of human strength that Beatrice would [paradoxically] most willingly have supported in her body the very pains of hell for a time, as long as she could arrive at the fulfilment of this insatiable desire after the fires of hell.[273]

The pain caused by her insatiable desire, was seen as an indispensable ticket for admittance to the greatest possible participation in the glory of heaven. In her treatise, she writes that

[273] *Vita*, 222,15.

the soul often refuses all consolation from God himself and from his creatures, for every consolation that would come to her from them [God and his creatures] would strengthen its [the soul's] love still more, drawing its desire to a higher state, and this renews the soul's desire to foster love, and to stay in the fruition of *Minne*, and to live in exile without joy. And thus in all these gifts the soul remains unsatisfied and unpacified until it shall attain what it so incessantly seeks.[274]

Striving for the perfection [*lit.* for the supremely best], being based on the restoration of her likeness to God,

the soul always wills to foster *Minne*, to know *Minne*, and to have fruition of *Minne*, which cannot happen to it in this exile. Therefore, the soul wills to proceed to the fatherland where it has built its home and directed its whole desire, and where it rests in love, for it well knows that there every impediment will be removed from it, and that it will be received with love by its Beloved. There [in heaven] it will gaze with eagerness upon what it has so tenderly loved, and it will possess for its own blessedness him whom it has faithfully served; it will with full delight have fruition of him whom it has often embraced in her soul with love. There it will enter into the joy of the Lord as saint Augustine says: 'He who enters into you, enters into the joy of the Lord etc.' and he will not fear. In him, who is all-perfect, she shall have all perfection.[275]

Using other imagery, Beatrice refers in the seventh of her *Seven manieren* to God's Unity and Trinity: 'Its [the soul's] delightful rest and enjoyable dwelling is with [the Unity of] the great Godhead and [the ongoing activity of] the lofty Trinity'.[276] Her real fatherland was heaven and, though she says it only

274 R-VM, *Seven manieren*, 34–35, ll. 108–117.
275 *Ibid.*, 37–38, ll. 143–62.
276 *Ibid.*, 31, ll. 47–49.

implicitly, to be in this fatherland is to participate in God's eternally ongoing fruition. Her whole biography and treatise could be summed up in a few sentences: she went deliberately through all the demanding efforts, all the 'pining' as she called it, to be wholly purified, to restore the image and to recuperate the likeness in which she was made by and for God. While remaining unsatiated by not attaining God's fruition, God would grant her to be drawn [*lit.* to be pulled, *getrect*] to this eternal fatherland to enjoy the 'glory of [ongoing] fruition'.[277]

> It [the soul] is lifted up above its human mode into *Minne*, and above its own nature in the desire of transcending it. All that the soul is, all its will, its desire, its love are all there in that secure truth and pure clarity and noble sublimity and magnificent beauty and in that sweet society of the heavenly spirits who overflow with superabundant love and who are in the knowledge, possession and fruition of their *Minne*.[278]

As Herman Vekeman said: 'In [*Seven manieren*] *Minne* as a concept contains the totality of Beatrice's experience of divine love. Next to its ability to express the existential value of divine love, this concept excels in flexibility to explain intelligibly the whole phenomenon of divine love'.[279]

The biographer tells us about the insatiability of her desire and how she sought—to use her own words—'satiety of eternal refection in the fatherland where with her insatiable desire she had built her home', where Beatrice expected satiation through participation in God's fruition and simultaneous insatiation of the totality of God's own fruition, as all her mentors had told her, no matter who most influenced her.

The last sentence of her treatise seems to corroborate this, for she wrote: 'Having worshipped him in the time of grace, it [the soul] will have fruition of him in eternal glory where the only

277 *Ibid.*, 33, l. 87: 'glorie der gebrukelicheit'.
278 *Ibid.*, 31, ll. 34–44.
279 H. Vekeman, 'Minne in "Seven manieren" van Beatrijs van Nazareth', *Citeaux* 19 (1968) 284–316, at the end of the summary in English.

activity will be praising and loving'.[280] This saying calls for two
comments: while in her treatise 'the soul' stands seemingly for
her own soul, in the last words of the treatise Beatrice took care to
extend her range. She now points at every soul, not hers alone.
The final words state clearly: 'May God lead us all there.
Amen.'[281] Though this ending is close to a much used *topos*, it is
significant that here 'the' soul has become 'us', as the 'there' has
likewise grown into a 'where'—where the two lovers, God and
man, the infinite and the finite meet and embrace one another.
Such a meeting cannot be expressed except in paradoxes: for the
meeting is going on eternally, as is the fruition of both, each in his
own way. God is infinitely satiated by the fruition of his own
unlimited loveliness. Man created by him to his image and likeness will be satiated by the participated fruition he has. Lovingly
respecting God's infinity, man (*mensch*) remains eternally satiated without being satiated with God's unlimited satiety, finding
in this limitation the culmination of his own satiation, in which
his only activity, as Beatrice put it, is praising and loving.

The last words of Beatrice's treatise, that in heaven 'the only
activity is praising and loving', are quite similar to what Augustine had said: 'This will be our activity [in heaven], the praise of
God. You love him and you praise him'.[282] The bishop of Hippo
also said: '[God] himself will be the haven of our labors: to see
him and to praise him'.[283] Aelred, seemingly inspired by

---

280 R-VM, *Seven Manieren*, 38–39, ll. 167–70.

281 *Ibid.*, 39, ll. 170–71. She ended her sixth *maniere*, which also is one of
'higher *minne*', using nearly the same words. See R-VM, *Seven Manieren*, 28, ll.
78–79.

282 *Ennarationes in Psalmum* 85,24; PL 37: 1099: ' Haec erit actio nostra,
laus Dei. Amas et laudas'. J. N. D. Kelly (*Early Christian Doctrines*, 489),
referring to Augustine's *De civitate Dei*, thus summarizes his teaching: 'The
chief enjoyment of heaven, or the city of God, will lie in praising God: "He
shall be the end of our desires who shall be contemplated without ceasing, loved
without cloy, and praised without weariness". There will be degrees of honour
there,...but there will be no jealousy; and free will will not only continue to be
exercised by the saints, but will be the more truly liberated from delight in
sinning. In fact, for the redeemed eternal life will be a perpetual sabbath, when
they will be filled with God's blessings and sanctification'.

283 *Sermo* 37, 20; PL 38: 270: 'Ipse erit portus laborum nostrorum, videre et
laudare Deum'.

Augustine, wrote that in heaven, 'we will see our Creator, love him and praise him. From vision comes love and from love, praise'.[284] Of the several others who could be quoted,[285] a sentence from Bernard may be cited, for he made the praise reciprocal when he wrote:

> The blessed in heaven feast and find their happiness in unending praise and exultation.... Then, he (Paul in I Cor 4:5) says, 'shall every man have praise'. From whom? From God. A great Eulogist and a eulogy most ardently to be desired. Happy interchange of praise, where to praise and to be praised is blessedness.[286]

What Bernard means is that praise welling out of love cannot be a one-way affair. It is, of necessity, the expression of *caritas ordinata*, well-ordered love, which must flow both ways. Union with God forever is a pure gift, given when the human receiver is freely and willingly open to it. By cooperating with God's grace or with God's love (for they are the same thing), one is made roomy enough for such a gratuitously bestowed gift. As Hadewijch put it in her twelfth Letter: 'All men (*menschen*) praise him according to his supreme loftiness which is *Minne*, and nothing less. They love him also in his eternal nature without beginning, with which he will eternally satisfy all those who become [by participation] God with God[287] forever.

284 C.H. Talbot, *Sermones inediti*, 37: ' Ergo, creatorem nostrum videbimus, amabimus, laudabimus. Erit amor ex visione, laus ex amore'.

285 See A. Michel, 'Gloire des élus', *DThC*, vol. 6: 1393–1426; M.Schmaus, *Katholische Dogmatik*, Bd 4/2, 659–90, and H. Bouëssé, 'God, Glory of —, *SM* 2: 401–03, all with bibliography.

286 OS 5, 3–4; SBOp 5: 363–64: 'festivitas...illorum magis in exsultatione et laude versatur.... Tunc, inquit, unicuique laus erit. A quo? A Deo. Magnus laudator et vehementer ambienda laudatio. Felix commutatio laudis, ubi et amare beatum est, et laudari.'

287 VM, *Brieven*, 1: 191, ll. 90–95.

SUMMARY

God showed the *mulieres religiosae* how much he loves each
person individually and all persons collectively by creating them
to his own image and likeness. He sent his Son to teach them
what they had to do to love him in return, as he expected and
commanded them to do for his and their sake. The *mulieres
religiosae* did not spare themselves. Intrepidly they went through
many trials, including the ups and downs of daily life and their
even more demanding mystical experiences, which made them so
sharply aware of God's Allness and their own insignificance.
They had to be and wanted fervently to be purified in order to
become responsible and responsive partners in a deep, lasting
love-relationship, accepted undeservedly and responded to unre-
servedly.

Tasting and taking the bitter and the sweet inherent in *caritas
ordinata*, well-ordered love, they learned how to love their God,
their neighbor and themselves. Realizing what they meant to God,
they became by the same fact aware of what this God intended to
be for them: the source of life and the flaming hearth of love
without end. Hence their burning desire turned into a desired
burning to empty themselves of the last residue of self-
centeredness and self-complacency, in order to make more room
for God as *Minne*.

Union with God implies more than simply being united with
him. It means union with a God who is, from all eternity and for
all eternity, a God of never ending love. If the *mulieres religiosae*
were to become his partners in love as he willed them to be, they
had to give themselves wholly to him and be 'oned' with him.
Without ever becoming God, their vehement longing for him
propelled them to become—by his grace—*sicuti est*, as he is. His
incomprehensibility challenged them to face the mystery they
were to themselves. They struggled indefatigably as they moved
through the dreadful tunnel which opens into participation in the
mysterious *regiratio* of the three divine Persons within the Unity
of the One God.

Supported by their mystical experiences, life became so dear to
them that they desired it to the full as God willed it to be. Death,

therefore, became not a dreaded event but a longed-for passage to this fullness of life. After death, free of time, space and matter, they would in accordance with their capacity, so taxingly acquired, have fruitive satiation of him, and simultaneously would remain eternally unsatiated by the unattainable satiation of God himself. There they found what they so eagerly sought and so unremittingly fought for, what they steadily suffered and lovingly longed for on earth: union with God forever.

Appendices to footnotes of Chapter XVII

30 Joseph Bonsirven, *Palestinian Judaism in the Time of Jesus*, (ET from the French by William Wolf, New York-San Francisco, 1964) chapter eight: 163–68), said that 'according to all views mentioned above [in his book], man's fate is determined immediately after death'. See also the excellent study of Joseph Plevnik, 'The Taking up of the Faithful and the Resurrection of the Dead in 1 Thessalonians 4: 13–18', *CBQ* 46 (1984) 274–83. On p. 282, the author asked the question: 'is there no hint in the presentation in 1 Thessalonians 4 that the reunion with Christ at his parousia involves at the same time a transformation, which implies a change in the physical constitution of a person?'. He answered that 'Paul, of course, does not talk directly about this in 1 Thessalonians 4. Yet the structure of assumption can express something like this in its own terms. Through the assumption, wrought by the power of God, the faithful are taken out of the world in which they live and are brought into the exalted world of the risen Lord. This is the world of heaven, eternal life with Christ in the presence of God'. Reviewing many publications of the last hundred years on this topic, Ben J.Meyer asks and answers two questions in his study: 'Did Paul's View of the Resurrection Undergo Development?, *TS* 47 (1986) 363–87, 381: 'Apropos of 2 Cor 5, do vv. 2–4 refer to the Parousia or the acquisition of a resurrection-body immediately after death? Linguistic and conceptual indices point to the Parousia. Are vv. 6–9 concerned with the parousia or with an intermediate state after death? They bear on an intermediate state, just as Phil 1: 23 does'. André Feuillet, who is not mentioned by Ben Meyer, devoted a lengthy study to Paul's eschatology: 'La demeure céleste et la destinée des chrétiens. Exégèse de II Cor V, 1–10 et contribution à l'étude des fondements de l'eschatologie paulinienne', *RSR* 44 (1956) 161–92; 360–402. His conclusion is that Paul probably knew of a personal eschatology, though not surprisingly (il n'y a pas lieu de s'en étonner) says little about it in his Epistles. His principal concern here was Christ's ultimate and definitive triumph over sin and death, and our participation in the life of the risen Christ, participation inaugurated at baptism and completed at the parousia. As Hadewijch pointed out in her twelfth vision, 'all who were multiple and manifold become one in that [God's] Countenance' (VM, *Visioenen*, 1: 126, ll. 28–29). Most *mulieres religiosae*, however, felt no special need to speculate about the relationships among the glorified. Being together implies necessarily the *Communio Sanctorum*, the communion of saints as it is technically called, because *caritas ordinata*, the well-ordered love or charity, attains there its highest and most intense expression. Since this work is about the *mulieres religiosae* themselves and not about theological speculations related to 'The Last Things', we need not supply information about things they did not explicitly mention or question. As we tried to show in Chapter X, the way they lived their relations with their fellow-pilgrims and their concern for their spiritual needs, make it sufficiently clear that they were affectively and effectively involved in the salvation of their neighbors. The subtitle of J. Ratzinger's *Eschatologie: Tod und ewiges Leben* (Death and Eternal Life) would have appealed to the *mulieres religiosae*. However, the 193 pages of this book, some of them really moving, speak of death, last judgment and general resurrection, while only four pages are devoted to *Himmel* (Heaven). The distance, or better

perhaps, the difference between between mystics and theologians has been talked about in favor of the former by Ernst Benz, *Die Vision*, 493, and by Albert De Blaere, 'Témoignage mystique chrétien', *Studia missionalia* 26 (1977) 117–47, though it would not be difficult to refer to authors, including Ratzinger, who are of an opposite opinion, which is correct as far as *some* mystics are concerned. See above, n.167 of Chapter XIV.

57 The altered state of the same or identical body spoken of is most important, if the individual is to be the same here and there without loss of identity. For a philosophical look at this question, see Louis Dupré, *Transcendent Selfhood. The Loss and Discovery of the Inner Life*, (New York, 1976) 79–91: 'The Self Immortal', where he concludes that 'all we possess beyond the mere absence of evidence to the contrary is one indication: certain phenomena show that the mind is not in all its functions directly dependent upon the contributions from the senses. This conclusion, however modest, still requires a notion of selfhood expanded beyond its ordinary empirical restrictions. But such an expansion is truly warranted by the findings of depth psychology and the experiences of mystics. Without asking full account of them, the very conditions for meaningfully asking the question of immortality are lacking'. C.F.Moulde, 'St Paul and Dualism', *NTS* 12 (1965–66) 106–23 came to the conclusion that in referring to the *sōma pneumatikòn* (I Cor.15:44) Paul is consistent in holding that 'man dies mortal and corruptible and is raised a glorious body; he dies animal and is raised spiritual. But always it is the same individual'. It is only by means of the body, says Bernard, that we gain ascent and access to a life of blessedness (SC 5,1; SBOp 1: 21: 'ad ea quibus beate vivitur nullus nobis ascensus vel accessus patet, nisi per corpus'). Bernard follows the lead of Augustine: man is a whole, a body-soul person. A resurrected body, not a bodiless soul, appealed to Augustine. Augustine's stand has been carefully studied in E. Hendrikx's 'Platonisches und biblisches Denken bei Augustinus', *AM* 1: 285–92, and by Charles Journet, 'Saint Augustin et l'exégèse traditionnelle du "corps spirituel" ', *AM* 2: 879–94, wherein he insists upon the deep meaning of the incarnation of the Son, which is concerned with the salvation of the whole man, soul and body, both destined to be glorified. Maurice Carrez, asking 'With what body do the dead arise again?', *Concilium* 10,6, (London, 1970) 92–102 pointed out 'that God respects the identity of the body in its transformations and that it is the *same person* who is in glory. *Glory* confers an existence to the *sōma*, the body, the ego, the person... provided one does not consider the continuity of the *soma*, the 'body' in a purely biological sense'.

59 According to X. Léon-Dufour, *Resurrection and the Message of Easter*, ET from the French (1971) by R.N. Wilson, (New York, 1975) 239–41, a dead body 'returns to the undifferentiated universe of matter.... Far from reducing the resurrection to the reanimation of a dead body, we must affirm that the whole of the historical body, including the corpse, has now been transformed into the Christ. This does not mean the dissolution of the personality into an undifferentiated world. The continuity which unites the risen Christ to the man who lived on earth is therefore not determined by the taking on of some chemical or organic particle of what was his body, but by two associated factors. First of all, and essentially, it is guaranteed by the same God who brought it into existence and brings it back to life; secondly it is maintained in being because the object of the divine action is not a 'spiritual soul' and a 'material body' in turn, but a being

who was a living body, a person who was previously maintained in being throughout a continual transformation of the parts which composed him'. As William [Exp Rm, PL 180: 442; CF 27: 178, from which the ET is taken] says: 'the body will be wholly subject to the spirit and endowed with sufficient life so that it will need no nourishment, for it will not be a natural body but a spiritual one, truly possessing the substance of flesh without the corruption of flesh'.

60 Resurrection of the body will not take place before the 'general resurrection' at the end of time, according to J.Ratzinger, (*Eschatologie*, 95–96; 134–35) who rejects the opposite opinion of Gisbert Greshake and Gerhard Lohfink, who argue for an individual's resurrection right after death. See their *Naherstehung — Auferstehung — Unsterblichkeit*, Questiones Disputatae 71 (Freiburg, 1975). They are supported therein by A. Van de Walle's *From Darkness to Dawn*, 123–131. In *Hoffnung und Vollendung: Aufriss der Eschatologie*, Quaestiones Disputatae, 91 (Freiburg 1980, 2nd ed. 1984) Herbert Vorgrimler has some counter arguments against Ratzinger (*ibid.*, 154–55) as he has against G. Lohfink (*ibid.*, 81 and n. 188). In the 3rd ed. of the above mentioned book (1978), 156–84, Greshake justified himself against Ratzinger and other critics as did Lohfink (*ibid.*,131–55). Mention could be made of H. Haag, *Bibellexikon*, (Einsiedeln-Zurich-Cologne, 1951) 'Besonderes Gericht', 553–54, and 'Vergeltung', 1671–77. See also M. Schmaus, *Katholische Dogmatik* Bd 4/2, 5th ed., (Munich, 1959) 'Das besondere Gericht', 432–55. For an interesting overview of this whole question, see Vorgrimler's *Hoffnung*, 141–55 and, in English, Zachary Hayes who published a general survey in the series 'What Are They Saying', in this case: '*About the End of the World?*, (New York, 1983) On pp. 48–49, Z. Hayes admits that 'it would not be true to say that the authors who espouse various forms of this theory [of Gershake and Lohfink] focus on the individual to the detriment of the collective dimension of eschatology'. Philosophers do no better than theologians. John Morreal in his paper 'Happiness and the Resurrection of the Body', *RSt* 16 (1980) 29–35, arrives at the conclusion that 'the resurrection of our bodies would be simply otiose'. In a reply to Morreal, 'Happiness and Resurrection', *RSt* 17 (1981) 387–93, Richard Creel says that 'the resurrected saints will not be *happier* because of the resurrection, but because of it they will be happy in more things'.

64 The following publications should prove helpful for an interested reader: J.N.D. Kelly, *Early Christian Doctrines* 459–85 for the early Christian centuries; for the East: M. Lot-Borodine, 'La béatitude dans l'Orient chrétien', *Maison-Dieu* 15 (1950) 85–115. Of special importance for the West is Bernard de Vrégille's study: 'L'Attente des saints d'après saint Bernard', *NRT* 70 (1948) 225–44, where the position of Bernard, Ambrose, Augustine, Gregory the Great—each one in his own way—is explained, as well as Bernard's other meaning of *interim*. Though Richard is not mentioned, a reading of his *In Apocalypsim*: PL 196: 683–888 (see, for instance 768D; 816A etc.) shows that he too, like Aelred (C. Talbot, *Sermones inediti*, 213) and most theologians of his time, shared the same view. John XXII, pushing Bernard's opinion to the limit, (see M. Dykmans' *Les sermons de Jean XXII sur la Vision béatifique*, Miscellanea Historiae Pontificae 34 [Rome, 1973], provoked the intervention of his successor, the Cistercian pope Benedict XII, who in 1336 stated that the souls of the deceased, when freed from their sins and their need of purification, enjoy at once the unmediated vision of God's essence, even before the general resurrection

(see Friedrich Wetter, *Die Lehre Benedikts XII. vom intensiven Wachstum der Gottesschau*. Analecta Gregoriana 92, (Rome, 1958). An overview in English of this position and its evolution can be found in H. de Lubac's *Catholicism. A Study of Dogma in Relation to the Corporate Destiny of Mankind*, ET by Lancelot Shepperd (London 1950, rpt 1958 of the French edition, Paris 1947) 51–63, or in Karl Rahner's essay 'The Intermediate State', *Theological Investigations* 17, ET by M. Kohl, (London-New York, 1981) 114–24. For Bernard in particular P. Delfgaauw,'La nature et le degré de l'Amour selon saint Bernard', *AC* 9 (1953) 234–67; 249–51; ET in *MnS* 1 (1963) 85–110; 106–08. N. De Paepe treated this topic in relation to Hadewijch in his paper: 'Hadewijchs vijfde visioen en de Apocalyps. Dood is niet dood', *Uut goeder jongster*, Festschrift Prof. Dr. L. Roose, (K. Parteman ed.), (Leuven-Amersfoort, 1984) 13–21.

GENERAL CONCLUSIONS

A book such as this is customarily followed by a general conclusion presenting an overall view of what the author intended to communicate and to share. The two last volumes dealing with 'Beatrice in her Context' have three parts: 'God, and Man Made to God's Image and Likeness'; 'The *Mulieres religiosae* and Christ'; [their striving] 'Toward Unification with God'; and since each of these three parts has its own conclusion, and since these three are sufficient to form a general conclusion. There is no need to reiterate what has already been said.

Beatrice is not a lonely star, but part of a movement which flourished in Belgium in the thirteenth-century. Of the several outstanding women of that movement, six have been given special attention here: Beatrice herself, Hadewijch, Alice of Schaarbeek, and the three Idas: Ida of Nivelles, Ida Lewis and Ida of Leuven. To focus on these six seemed to be sufficient to locate Beatrice in her context.

The movement of the *mulieres religiosae*, described to some extent in this work, occurred between about 1180 and 1270, though the dates are by no means rigid. At the beginning the movement included unmarried women: nuns, many small groups of pious women staying together, and women living alone as solitaries or as recluses. But as the beguines became grouped in beguinages, the term *mulieres religiosae* gradually lost its all-embracing meaning, and eventually disappeared. Nuns were now spoken of only in relation to the religious Orders to which they belonged, and the name 'beguines' was applied to all the others. Some of the later beguines did not live in beguinages and a number of them went off in various heterodox directions, as can be seen in *The Beguines* by Ernest McDonnell, and *The Heresy of the Free Spirit* by Robert Lerner.

'Free Spirit' is a designation with a usually heterodox content, contrary to what this expression meant when, in earlier days, it was used by the *mulieres religiosae* including Hadewijch.[1] Ruusbroec, in his last book *Vanden XII. Beghinen* (*On the Twelve Beguines*), written for Marguerite of Meerbeek, a nun in a convent of Poor Claires in Brussels, spoke of the beguines of 'the good old days', referring to the thirteenth-century *mulieres religiosae*.[2] At the same time he castigated some contemporary beguines who had moved in the direction of the 'Free Spirit' of his time.[3]

The biographies of the five Cistercian nuns studied here were published by Chrysostomus Henriquez in his *Quinque Prudentes Virgines*.[4] Henriquez, a monk of Huerta in Spain, sent a copy of his *Quinque* to his abbot Angelus Manrique, himself an historian. In his *Cistercium Annalium Tomus Quartus*,[5] A. Manrique quoted many long extracts of the biographies of Beatrice, Ida of Nivelles and Ida of Leuven.[6] Of Hadewijch we have no biography, only some vague data. We do not know if she had personal contact with the five Cistercian nuns we have studied. In a small country with so many Cistercian communities it is almost impossible to believe that she had no contact with them, but apart from some

1. See Chapter VI, n. 251 and the substantial work of R. Guarnieri spoken of there. H. Grundmann, *Religiöse Bewegungen*, 38–39, made the correct observation that some forms of heterodoxy, at least in the twelfth century, were linked not primarily with belief, but rather with a way of life.
2. G. Epiney-Burgard, 'L'influence des béguines sur Ruusbroec', in Mommaers and De Paepe (eds), *Jan van Ruusbroec* 65–85; 69.
3. Gerard Grote, a friend and admirer of Ruusbroec, criticized this work, not in relation to the 'Free Spirit', but because Ruusbroec spoke of the planets symbolically, while Grote looked at them scientifically. See G. Epiney-Burgard, *Gerard Grote (1340–1384) et les débuts de la dévotion moderne*, Abendländische Religionsgeschichte 54, J. Lortz ed., (Wiesbaden, 1970) 133–35.
4. Though he was only thirty-eight years old when he died in 1632, Henriquez published numerous books, all on Cistercian topics. Like his contemporaries he is superficial and often inaccurate. Abbots who gave him a grant to finance his publications were nearly sure to find a laudatory mention in his *Menologium Cisterciense*, as happened, for instance, to Bernard de Montgaillard, then abbot of Orval.
5. Lyons, 1649, rpt Westmead, England, 1970.
6. The accounts *de rebus Cisterciensibus*, On Cistercian Affairs, are spread out chronologically in his *Annales* till 1237. This could explain why he did not mention Ida Lewis or Alice of Schaarbeek. He did however make great use of Caesarius of Heisterbach, of the biographies by Thomas of Cantimpré, and of the superficial *Chronicon Cisterciensis Ordinis* by Autbertus Miraeus, (Cologne, 1614).

not yet identified names, nothing in her writings gives any explicit indication that she did, nor does any of the five biographies. This is all the more striking since one encounters so many parallelisms in the five biographies and in the writings of Hadewijch and Beatrice's *Seven manieren*. It cannot be purely coincidental that all six experienced such an exceptionally blazing love for Christ, the God-Man, and such an enormous attraction for God as Trinity. Moreover, each one went in her own way through the inexpressibly painful vicissitudes which accompany the experience of God in the infinity of his allness and the indescriptability of his love. Hadewijch was undoubtebly the first to have been so frequently outspoken about Christ as the God-Man and about God as *Minne*. The fact that Beatrice wrote her *Seven Manieren* some twenty years after she closed her diary in 1236 (with a few additional entries from a later time) does not exclude *a priori* some influence of Hadewijch on Beatrice, though this is far from proven, if it ever can be.

The attentive reader may have noticed that certain texts of or about these *mulieres religiosae* have been quoted more than once. These texts often have great density and depth of meaning, deserving attention, despite the risk of repetitiveness. For example, Ida of Leuven said in a prayer: 'You, my Lord, you know that my heart's only trouble is simply that fire of love seething to approach you, the excessive desire for fruition of you, the sweet dwelling together drawing the interior appetite to spiritual embraces'.[7] This seemingly simple sentence is one in which nearly every word begs for a closer look, for each indicates a different aspect of Ida's desire to be united with God.

This work is not a monograph on Beatrice, but considers her in the context of five other outstanding *mulieres religiosae*. Each of them talked or wrote about the manifold aspects of their common spiritual journey. This journey is marked not only by their own experiences and by their personalities but also by those of their biographers. The common themes have also been illustrated by many quotations, particularly from Richard, Bernard and William, their favorite mentors.

7. The Latin text has been quoted in n. 76 of Chapter XVI.

These women were rooted in a tradition coming partly from Gregory of Nyssa, but much more from Augustine and a number of other Latin authors known in the form their teachings had taken by the thirteenth century. This does not mean that the *mulieres religiosae* always had the actual texts of their mentors in mind, but only that they moved along the same lines and in the same direction. Familiarity came either from reading their writings or from hearing them read aloud. This applies not only to their mentors' authentic works, but also to the writings erroneously attributed to them. For example, in the thirteenth century William's *De contemplando Deo*, his *Epistola ad Fratres de Monte Dei*, and his *De natura et dignitate amoris* were attributed in many manuscripts to Bernard.[8]

With regard to Bernard himself, Ulrich Köpf made the well-founded observation that in the fourteenth and fifteenth centuries the copying by hand of Bernard's treatises and his lengthy *Sermons on the Canticle of Canticles* cost more time, energy and expense than ordinary readers in Germany could afford. But, a whole string of pious tracts were in circulation in the vernacular. Excerpts from Bernard found their way into these extracts with the result that only the most striking sayings of Bernard reached the general public.[9] The same could also be said of some of the other mentors.

The *mulieres religiosae* did not have at their disposal series of patristic writings such as those published in Migne's *Patrologiae cursus completus*, *Sources chrétiennes*, *Corpus Christianorum* and its *Continuatio mediaevalis*, or *Cistercian Publications*, to cite only these. They could, however, have borrowed and copied some of their mentors' works from the libraries of Villers, Aulne, Ter Doest, Ter Duinen or other Cistercian houses, which were usually well stocked.[10]

---

8. See Chapter IV, n. 92.
9. Ulrich Köpf, 'Bernhard von Clairvaux in der Frauenmystik', in Dinzelbacher and Bauer (eds), *Frauenmystik im Mittelalter* 48–77.
10. See Simone Roisin, 'Réflexions sur la culture intellectuelle en nos abbayes cisterciennes', *Miscellanea L. Van der Essen*, (Leuven, 1947) 245–56.

The writings and biographies of the *mulieres religiosae* are no small contribution to the development and evolution of Christian spirituality. If Van Mierlo were to write his paper on 'The Origins of Germanic Mysticism' today,[11] then—given the many thorough studies published since his time—he would certainly reformulate it, but his basic affirmation still holds true, that the mysticism of the *mulieres religiosae*, of Ruusbroec, and of the *Imitatio Christi*, all from the Low Countries, had a profound impact on Western culture and spirituality in their own and later times.

The *mulieres religiosae* learned much from their mentors, but did not follow them blindly. These women stood on their own feet, uncompromisingly dedicated to Christ, their greatest Mentor of all. He taught them how to live courageously and lovingly, how to hope firmly, and what to expect with certainty. This certainty was confirmed by mystical experiences, in which they saw their God at work.

They grasped clearly the implications of the incarnation of God's Son, and what God intended *ab aeterno*, from all eternity, by creating man (*mensch*) according to his image and likeness. They tried their best to be docile to *amor illuminatus*, enlightened love, listening attentively to the guidance of the Holy Spirit, meeting Christ in the Eucharist, following him intrepidly throughout life, to attain after death full union with God. The *mulieres religiosae* would certainly agree with Étienne Gilson's conclusion that Cistercian mysticism is totally trinitarian,[12] a statement which applies fully also to Hadewijch.

Commenting on a text of Bernard,[13] Robert Javelet put it pointedly: 'the *epectasis* is enfolded in the divine prevision. By striving after perfection, we move toward that purpose which God

---

11. Joseph Van Mierlo, 'Over het ontstaan der Germaansche Mystiek', *OGE* 1 (1927) 11–37.

12. Et. Gilson, *L'Ésprit de la philosophie médiévale*, 2nd ed., (Paris 1944) vol.1: 93 : 'La mystique cistercienne est tout entière suspendue à une théologie de la Trinité '.

13. Quoted above, Chapter XVIII, n. 99.

envisioned from all eternity by creating us'.[14]. If the *mulieres religiosae* did not know the term *epectasis*, they knew very well what it meant: God as *Minne* desired to have them share in the fullness of his own fruition, as far and as much as they made themselves 'roomy' for such participation with the help of illuminating grace. The absolute priority of an infinitely loving and lovable God made them realize the all-demanding necessity of loving God and all the consequences that such love implied.

Imbued with the fear of the devil at an early stage of their lives and without the more scientific knowledge of the complexity of the human psychè reached in the twentieth century, the *mulieres religiosae* and their contemporaries, not surprisingly, easily and too often project their psychological problems on to the devil's influence. This made their sincere search for self-knowledge and self-acceptance and their determined striving toward virtuous living all the more difficult and valuable. Biographers in particular excelled in stressing the interference of 'the enemy of the human race', as Beatrice's biographer so repeatedly and annoyingly did. Fear, no doubt, is a forceful means of keeping people in line, but when it is overdone, it becomes an unwarranted and even harmful pressure. Happily, the *mulieres religiosae* were able to counterbalance this unhealthy approach by their penetrating and growing insight into God's love for them and by their elicited and whole-heartedly given love in return.

Instead of overestimating what was ascribed to devilish whisperings, the *mulieres religiosae* learned to look at their human limitations in the light of God's unlimited Allness, and to use it as a springboard to become grounded in his love for them and their love for him. Love indeed is stronger than death and stronger than fear.

God as *Minne* transformed their existence by a painfully purifying and gracefully sanctifying process, which made them beautiful human persons, giving themselves wholly to the ineffable beauty of God's totality. In their demanding upward struggle to

---

14. R. Javelet, *Image*, 1:116: 'L'épectase est dans la prévision divine. En allant vers la perfection, nous allons vers ce dessein que Dieu s'est proposé de toute éternité en nous créant'.

become what God willed them to become, they had, at times, a foretaste of God as *Minne*. And when they passed through the gates of physical death, they became by participation involved and integrated in the fruition of the one God as Trinity, united with him in an unperturbed, continually growing union forever.

BIBLIOGRAPHY

Section A: *Primary Sources*
       A.1 Beatrice of Nazareth
       A.2 Hadewijch
       A.3 Biographies of mulieres religiosae
       A.4 The Mentors of the mulieres religiosae

Section B: *Secondary Sources*

607

SECTION A

A.1 BEATRICE OF NAZARETH

The biography in its latin form is reproduced in the first volume of this work from the critical edition of Dr Leonce Reypens: *Vita Beatricis: Autobiographie van de Z. Beatrijs van Tienen, O. Cist., 1200–1268*, Studiën en textuitgaven van Ons Geestelijk Erf 15, Antwerp, 1964. The English translation by Roger De Ganck is printed on facing pages.

Beatrice's treatise is quoted according to the critical edition of Leonce Reypens and Joseph Van Mierlo: *Beatrijs van Nazareth: Seven Manieren van Minne*, Leuven, 1926. Occasionally mention is made of *Beatrijs van Nazareth: Van Seuen Manieren van heiliger Minnen*, according to manuscript B of the Royal Library in Brussels, edited by H.W.J. Vekeman and J.J.Th. Tersteeg, Zutfen, 1970.

A.2 HADEWIJCH

All citations to Hadewijch's works are made from the critical edition by Joseph van Mierlo in *Leuvense Studiën en tekstuitgaven:*

1. *Brieven*, 1. Tekst en commentaar; 2. Inleiding, 2nd rev. ed. 1947. Two volumes.
2. *Visioenen*, 1. Tekst en commentaar; 2. Inleiding, 2nd rev. ed. 1924–1925. Two volumes.
3. *Strophische Gedichten*, 1. Tekst en commentaar; 2. Inleiding, 2nd rev. ed. 1942. Two volumes.
4. *Mengeldichten*, 2nd rev. ed. 1952.

A.3 BIOGRAPHIES OF *MULIERES RELIGIOSAE*

1. *Vita* of Ida of Nivelles by Goswin Bossut (?), edited by Chrysostome Henriquez, *Quinque prudentes virgines*. Antwerp, 1630: 199–298. The prologue and additional excerpts from Ida's *Vita* are published in *CCH*, volume 2. Brussels, 1889: 222–228.
2. *Vita* of Alice of Schaarbeek, ed. G. Henschen, *AA SS* June 2. Antwerp, 1698: 476–483.
3. *Vita* of Ida Lewis, ed. R. De Buck, *AA SS* October 13. Paris, 1883: 100–124.

4. *Vita* of Ida of Leuven, ed D. Papebrouck, AA SS April 2. Paris, 1886: 155–189.
5. The incomplete *Vita* of Beatrice of Zwijveke is cited according to the published work of Leonce Reypens in *OGE* 26 (1952) 244–246.
6. Thomas of Cantimpré's *Vita* of Lutgard, ed. G. Henschen, *AA SS* June 4. Paris, 1867: 187–210. G. Hendrix, 'Primitive Versions of Thomas of Cantimpré's *Vita Lutgardis'*. *Citeaux* 29 (1979) 153-206.
7. *Vita* of Mary of Oignies by James of Vitry, and Thomas of Cantimpré's *supplementum* are both edited by D. Papebrouck, *AA SS* June 5. Paris, 1867: 542–572; 572–581.

A.4 THE MENTORS OF THE *MULIERES RELIGIOSAE*

All quotations of the works of Bernard of Clairvaux are taken from the critical edition, *Sancti Bernardi Opera*, edd. Jean Leclercq, C.H. Talbot, and H.M. Rochais. Rome, 1957–1979. Ten volumes. The latin texts of Augustine and all other mentors are cited according to the *Patrologia Latina*. Occasionally use has been made of critical or at least better editions when these have been available, either separately or in such series as Sources chrétiennes, Corpus Christianorum Continuatio Mediaevalis, or others.

SECTION B

This bibliography is restricted to works cited in the three volumes of this work: The *Life of Beatrice*, and *Beatrice of Nazareth in Her Context*, two volumes. Studies in collective publications are followed by the title of the book(s) in which they appeared. The place and the year of such publications are given only at the name of the editor(s).

Adnès, Pierre. 'Goût spirituel', *DSp* 6: 626–644.

_____. 'Larmes', *DSp* 9: 287–303.

_____. 'Mariage mystique', *DSp* 10:388–408.

Alaerts, Joseph. 'La terminologie "essentielle" dans *Die Gheestelike Brulocht* et *Dat Rijcke der Ghelieven*', *OGE* 49 (1975) 337–365.

Albrecht, Carl. *Psychologie des mystischen Bewusstseins*. Bremen, 1951.

_____. *Das mystische Erkennen*. Bremen, 1958.

Alfaro, Juan. 'Cristo glorioso. Revelador del Padre', *Gregorianum* 39 (1959) 222–270.

Alonso, Joaquin. 'Studios de teologia positiva en torno a la visión beata', *Estudios* (Madrid) 8 (1952) 535–547.

Altermatt, Alberich. 'Die Christologie Bernhards von Clairvaux', *AC* 33 (1977) 3–176.

Altmann, Alexander. *Studies in Religious Philosophy and Mysticism*. London, 1969.

Ampe, Albert (ed.). *Dr. Reypens Album*. Antwerp, 1964.

_____. 'Bernardus en Ruusbroec', *OGE* 27 (1953) 143–179.

Anderson, John D. 'Introduction', The Enigma of Faith, CF 9. Washington, D.C., 1974.

_____. 'The Use of Greek Sources by William of St. Thierry, especially in the *Enigma fidei*'. *One Yet Two*. Ed. M. B. Pennington (q.v.): 242–253.

Arbesmann, Rudolph, 'Christ the *medicus humilis* in St. Augustine', *AM* 2: 623–629.

Arbman, Ernst. *Ecstasy or Religious Trance*. Uppsala, 1963–1970. Three volumes.

Ariès, Phillippe. 'Une conception ancienne de l'Au delà'. *Death and the Middle Ages. Edd. H. Braet and W. Verbeke* (q.v.): 78–87.

Attfield, Robin. 'The Lord is God: There is no Other', *RS* 13 (1977) 73–84.

Auberger, Jean-Baptiste. *L'Unanimité cistercienne primitive: Mythe ou réalité?* Achel, 1986.

Auden, W.H. 'Four Kinds of Mystical Experience'. *Understanding Mysticism.* Ed. R. Woods (q.v.): 379–399.

Augustinus Magister: Congrès international augustinien. Paris 21–24 Septembre 1954 (F. Cayré, ed.). Paris, 1954. Three volumes.

Axters, Stephanus A. *Inleiding tot een Geschiedenis van de Mystiek in de Nederlanden.* Verslagen en Handelingen van de Koninklijke Academie voor Taal-en Letterkunde. Ghent, 1967.

_____. 'De "Unio mystica" voor de Brabants-Rijnlandse mystiek van de dertiende eeuw'. *Mededelingen van de Koninklijke Academic voor Wetenschappen, Letteren en Schone Kunsten van België.* Klasse der Letteren 11, n. 6 (1949) 3–27.

Balás, David. *Methousia Theou: Man's Participation in God's Perfection according to Saint Gregory of Nyssa.* Studia Anselmiana 55. Rome, 1966.

Baldwin, John. *Masters, Princes and Merchants.* Princeton, NJ, 1970. Two volumes.

Baron, Roger. *Hugues de Saint-Victor: La contemplation et ses espèces.* Tournai-Paris, 1955.

_____. *Études sur Hugues de Saint-Victor.* Paris, 1963.

_____. 'L'influence de Hugues de Saint-Victor', *RTAM* 22 (1955) 56–71.

Barré, Henri. 'Haymo d'Auxerre', *DSp* 7:91–97.

Bavaud, Georges. 'Les rapports de la grâce et du libre arbitre: Un dialogue entre saint Bernard, saint Thomas d'Aquin et Calvin', *Verbum Caro* 14 (1960) 328–338.

Baxter, Anthony. 'The term "archetype" and its application to Jesus Christ', *HJ* 25 (1984) 19–38.

Beasly-Murray, G.R. 'Jesus and the Apocalyptic: with Special Reference to Mark 14:62'. *L'Apocalypse Johannique.* Ed. J. Lambrecht (q.v.): 415–429.

Bell, David N. *The Image and Likeness: The Augustinian Spirituality of William of Saint Thierry.* CS 78. Kalamazoo, MI 1984.

_____. 'The Vision of the World and the Archetypes in the Latin Spirituality of the Middle Ages' *AHDL* 44 (1977) 7–31.

_____. 'The Commentary on the Song of Songs of Thomas the Cistercian and his Conception of the Image of God', *Citeaux* 27 (1977) 5–25.

_____. 'Love and Charity in the Commentary on the Song of Songs of Thomas the Cistercian', *Citeaux* 28 (1977) 249–267.

_____. 'Contemplation and the Vision of God in the Commentary on the Song of Songs by Thomas the Cistercian', *Citeaux* 29 (1978) 207–227.

_____. 'Greek, Plotinus and the Education of William of St Thierry', *Citeaux* 30 (1979) 221–248.

_____. 'The Alleged Greek Sources of William of St Thierry'. *Noble Piety.... Ed. R. Elder* (q.v.) 109–122.

_____. 'The Background and the Teaching of the Nature and Dignity of Love', introduction to the ET of Thomas X. Davis, *William of St Thierry: The Nature and Dignity of Love.* CF 30. Kalamazoo, 1981: 5–43.

_____. 'A Doctrine of Ignorance: The Annihiliation of Individuality in Christian and Muslim Mysticism' in Elder (ed.), *Benedictus* (q.v.): 30–52.

_____. 'William of St Thierry and John Scot Eriugena', *Citeaux* 33 (1982) 5–28.

_____. 'Esse, Vivere, Intelligere: The Noetic Triad of the Image of God', *RTAM* 52 (1985) 5–43.

Bell, Rudolph. *Holy Anorexia.* Chicago-London, 1985.

Benoit, Pierre. 'Préexistence et Incarnation'. *RBibl* 77 (1970) 5–29.

Benz, Ernst. *Die Vision: Erfahrungsformen und Bilderwelt.* Stuttgart, 1969.

_____. 'Uber den Adel in der deutschen Mystik', *Deutsche Vierteljahrschrift für Literaturwissenschaften und Geistesgeschichte* 14 (1936) 505–555.

Bergson, Henri. *The Two Sources of Morality and Religion*, ET by J. Audra and Cl. Brereton. Garden City, New York, 1935.

Berkhout, Carl and Jeffry Burton Russell, *Medieval Heresies: A Bibliography, 1960–1979*. Toronto, 1981.

Berlière, Ursmer. 'Écoles claustrales au Moyen Age'. *Académie Royale de Belgique. Bulletin de la classe des Lettres et des Sciences morales et politiques* 12 (1921) 550–572.

Berlioz, J. 'Le récit efficace: l'"exemplum" au service de la prédication (XIIIe - XVe siècles)', *Mélanges de l'École française de Rome: Moyen Age-Temps modernes* 92 (1980) 113–146.

Bernard of Clairvaux. *On the Christian Year*, ET by A Religious of CSMV. London, 1954.

Bernards, Matthäus. *Speculum Virginum: Geistigkeit und Seelenleben der Frau im Hochmittelalter*. Forschungen zur Volkskunde 36/38. Cologne-Graz, 1955.

_____. 'Nudus nudum Christum sequi', *Wissenschaft und Weisheit* 14 (1951) 148–151.

Bernhardt, Joseph. 'Heiligkeit und Krankheit', GL 23 (1950) 172–195.

Bertaud, Emile. 'Efflorescence du culte eucharistique', *DSp* 4:1622–1638.

Bertholet, H.R. *Histoire de l'Institution de la Fête-Dieu avec la vie des bienheureuses Julienne et Eve*, 3rd ed. Liège, 1846.

Bets, P.V. 'Preface inédite de la B. Béatrice de Tirlemont', *AHEB* 7 (1970) 77–82.

Bett, Henry. *Johannes Scotus Eriugena: A Study in Medieval Philosophy*. New York, 1964.

Blanpain, Jacques. 'Langage mystique, expression de désir dans les Sermons sur le Cantique des Cantiques de Bernard de Clairvaux', *Coll* 36 (1974) 45–68.

Bochet, Isabelle. *Saint Augustin et le désir de Dieu*. Paris, 1983.

Boissard, Edmond. 'La doctrine des anges chez St. Bernard', *AC* 9 (1953) 114–135.

Bolton, Brenda. 'Fulk of Toulouse. The Escape That Failed'. *Church, Society and Politics*. Ed. Derek Baker. London, 1975: 83–93.

_____. 'Some thirteenth-century Women in the Low Countries', *Nederlands Archief voor Kerkgeschiedenis* 61 (1981) 7–29.

Bonsirven, Joseph. *Palestinian Judaism in the Times of Jesus*. ET by W. Wolf. New York-San Francisco, 1964.

Borst, Arno. *Die Katharer*, Schriften der Monumenta Germaniae Historica 12. Stuttgart, 1953.

Boüessé, Humbert. 'God, Glory of', *DSp* 2:401–403.

Boyer, Regis. 'An Attempt to Define the Typology of Medieval Hagiography'. *Hagiography and Medieval Literature. A Symposium*. Odense, 1981:27–36.

Braceland, Lawrence C. *Gilbert of Hoyland: Sermons on the Song of Songs*, CF 20. Kalamazoo, 1979.

_____. 'The Soul's Pilgrimage in the Planned City of God', *CSt* 13 (1978) 228–243.

Bracke, Joseph A. 'The Holy Trinity as a Communty of Divine Persons', *HJ* 15 (1974) 166–182.

Braet, Herman and Werner Verbeke (eds.), *Death in the Middle Ages*. Mediaevalia Lovaniensia. Series I, Studia 9. Leuven, 1983.

Brauns, Marcel. 'Fierheid in de religieuse beleving', *Bijdragen* 6 (1943–45) 185–246; 7 (1946) 73–139. In book form: Bruges, 1959.

Bredero, Adriaan. 'Le Moyen Age et le purgatoire', *RHE* 78 (1983) 429–452.

Brémond, Clément, Jacques Le Goff, Jean-Claude Schmitt. *Les 'Exempla'*. Typologie des sources du Moyen Age occidental, 40. Turnhout, 1982.

Breuer, Wilhelm. 'Mystik als alternative Lebensform: Das 37. Strophische Gedicht der Suster Hadewijch', *Zeitschrift für deutsche Philologie* 103 (1984) 103–115.

Brody, Saul Nathaniel. *The Disease of the Soul: Leprosy in Medieval Literature*. Ithaca-London, 1974.

Brooke, Odo. 'The Trinitarian Aspect of the Ascent of the Soul to God in the Theology of William of St. Thierry', *RTAM* 26 (1959) 85–127.

_____. 'Towards a Theology of Connatural Knowledge', *Citeaux* 18 (1967) 275–290.

_____. *Studies in Monastic Theology*, CS 37. Kalamazoo, 1980.

Brouette, Emile. 'La cistercienne Cathérine de Louvain fut-elle abbesse de Parc-les-Dames?', *AB* 78 (1960) 84–91.

Brounts, Albert. 'Hadewijch en de ketterij naar het vijfde visioen', *HL* 26 (1968) 73–139.

——————. 'Hadewijch's eerste ontwerp van de wesenmystiek (Br. xvii)', (A. Lievens, ed.) *HL* 26 (1972) 5–57.

Browe, P. *Die eucharistischen Wunder des Mitttelalters.* Breslauer Studien zur historischer Theologie, N.S. 4. Breslau, 1938.

——————. *Die häufige Kommunion im Mittelalter.* Munster/ W., 1938.

——————. 'Wann fing man an die Kommunion ausserhalb der Messe auszuteilen?'. *Theologie und Glaube* 23 (1931) 757–763.

Brown, Raymond E., Joseph A. Fitzmeyer, Roland E. Murphy (eds.), *The Jerome Biblical Commentary.* Englewood, NJ, 1968.

Brugge (City of). *Vlaamse Kunst op Perkament.* Bruges, 1981.

Bücher, C. 'Die Frauenfrage im Mittelalter', *Zeitschrift für die gesammte Staatswissenschaften* 38 (1882) 344–397.

Bultot, Robert. *La doctrine du mépris du monde: Christianisme et valeurs humaines:* Le XIe siècle. Leuven-Paris, 1963–64. Two volumes.

——————. 'Cosmologie et "contemptus mundi"', *Sapientiae Doctrina: Mélanges...offerts à D. Hildebrand Bascour.* Leuven, 1980: 1–23.

Burch, George Boswell. *Bernard Abbot of Clairvaux: The Steps of Humility.* ET with Introduction and Notes, as a Study of his Epistomology. Notre Dame, 1963.

Bussels, Amandus. 'Het hart van Sinte Lutgart', *Coll* 8 (1946) 257–283.

——————. 'Was Elisabeth van Spaalbeek Cisterciënserin in Herkenrode?' *Citeaux* 2 (1951) 43–54.

Caesarius of Heisterbach. *Dialogus miraculorum.* Ed. Joseph Strange. Cologne, 1851. Two volumes.

Cames, G. *Allégories et symboles dans l'Hortus deliciarum.* Leiden, 1971.

Canivez, J. M. *Statuta Capitulorum Generalium Ordinis Cisterciensis 1116–1786.* Leuven, 1933–1941. Eight volumes.

Cappuyns, Maïeul. 'Le "de imagine" de Grégoire de Mysse traduit par Jean Scot Erigène', *RTAM* 33 (1965) 205–262.

Carol, J. B. *Why Jesus Christ?* Manassas, VA., 1986.

Carrez, Maurice. 'With What Body do the Dead Arise?', *Concilium* 10, no. 6. London, 1970: 92–102.

Carton, Mary Josepha. 'The Seven Steps of Love by Beatrice of Nazareth', *CSt* 19 (1984) 31–42.

Casey, Michael. 'In Pursuit of Ecstasy: Reflections on Bernard of Clairvaux' "De diligendo Deo"', *MnS* 16 (1985) 139–156.

Catry, Patrick. 'Amour du monde et amour de Dieu chez saint Grégoire le Grand', *StM* 15 (1973) 253–275.

Ceglar, Stanislaus. *William of Saint Thierry. The Chronology of His Life with a Study of His treatise* On the Nature and Dignity of Love, *His Authorship of the* Brevis Commentatio, *the* In Lacu, *and the* Reply to Cardinal Matthew. Ann Arbor: University Microfilms, 1971.

Chadwick, Owen. *John Cassian.* 2nd ed. Cambridge, 1960.

Chatillon, Jean. *Théologie, Spiritualité et Métaphysique dans l'oeuvre oratoire d'Achard de Saint-Victor,* Études de Philosophie Médiévale 58. Paris, 1969.

_____. 'Les quatre degrés de la Charité d'après Richard de Saint-Victor', RAM 20 (1939) 237-264.

_____. 'Les trois modes de la contemplation selon Richard de Saint-Victor', *Bulletin de Littérature Ecclésiastique* 41 (1940) 3–26.

_____. 'Dulcedo, Dulcedo Dei', *DSp* 4: 1777–1795.

Chauvin, Benoît (ed.). *Mélanges à la mémoire du Père Anselme Dimier.* Pupille, 1982–1987. Six volumes.

Chenu, Marie-Dominique. *Nature, Man and Society in the Twelfth Century,* ET by Jerome Taylor and Lester K. Little. Chicago-London, 1968.

_____. 'Erigène à Citeaux', *La Philosophie et ses problèmes: Festschrift R. Jolivet.* Paris, 1960: 99–107.

_____. '*Spiritus,* le vocabulaire de l'âme au XIIe siècle', *Revue des Sciences philosophiques et théologiques* 41 (1957) 209–232.

Cirlot, J.E. *A Dictionary of Symbols.* ET by J. Sage. New York, 1962.

Claus, Felix. 'De opvatting van Ambrosius over de navolging van de "De Officiis"', *HL* 26 (1972) 63–72.

Clifford, Richard J. 'The Hebrew Scriptures and the Theology of Creation', TS 46 (1985) 607–623.

Cocheril, Maur. 'Graal', DSp 6:672–700.

Colledge, Edmund. *Medieval Netherlands Religious Literature.* Leiden-London-New York, 1965.

—————, and James Walsh. *Guigo II le Chartreux: Lettre sur la vie contemplative.* Douze Méditations, SCh 163. Paris, 1970. ET *Guigo II the Carthusian: The Ladder of Monks and Twelve Meditations.* CS 48. Kalamazoo, 1981).

Conn, Walter E. 'Morality, Religion and Kohlberg's Stage 7', IPQ 21 (1981) 379–389.

Conrad of Ebrach, *Exordium Magnum Cisterciense sive narratio de initio Cisterciensis Ordinis.* Series Scriptorum S. Ordinis Cisterciensis 2. Ed. Bruno Griesser. Rome, 1961.

Copleston, Frederick. *A History of Philosophy*, 6th ed. Westminster, Md., 1980. Eight volumes.

Corsini, E. 'Plérôme cosmique chez Grégoire de Nysse', Harl (ed.), *Écriture et culture philosophique*(q.v.): 111–126.

Courclle, Pierre. *Connais-toi toi-même: de Socrate à saint Bernard.* Paris, 1974–1975. Three volumes.

—————. 'La première expérience augustinienne de l'extase', *AM* 1: 53–57.

—————. 'Tradition Néo-Platonicienne et traditions chrétiennes de la "région de dissemblance"'. *AHDL* 32 (1958) 5–33.

—————. 'Témoignages nouveaux de la "région de dissemblance"', *Bibliothèque de l''École des Chartes* 118 (1960) 20–36.

—————. '"Nosce teipsum" du Bas-Empire au Haut Moyen Age: L'Héritage profane et les développements chrétiens', *Settimana di Studi del Centro italiano di studi nell'alto medievo, Spoleto,* 9 (1962) 265–295.

Courtès, J. 'Saint Augustin et la médicine', *AM* 1:43–51.

Couturier, Charles. 'La structure métaphysique de l'homme d'après saint Augustin', *AM* 1:543–550.

Crane, Thomas. *The Exempla or Illustrative Stories from the 'Sermones Vulgares' of Jacques de Vitry*. New York, 1890, rpt 1971.

Creel, Richard. 'Happiness and Resurrection: A Reply', *RSt* 17 (1981) 387–393.

Dahood, Mitchell. *Psalms 1–50*. The Anchor Bible 16. Garden City, New York, 1966.

Dalarun, Jacques. *L'Impossible Sainteté: La vie retrouvée de Robert d'Abrissel*. Paris, 1985.

Dalmau, J.M. 'Predestinatio, electio en el libro "De praedestinatione Sanctorum"', *AM* 1: 127–136.

d'Alverny, Marie-Thérère. *Alain de Lille; Textes inédités*. Études de psychologie médivale 42. Paris, 1965.

Daniélou, Jean. *Platonisme et Théologie mystique: Essai sur la doctrine spirituelle de saint Grégoire de Nysse*. Théologie 2. Paris, 1944.

_____. *La vie de Moïse*. SCh 1bis. Paris, 1955.

_____. 'Bernard et les Pères grecs', *AC* 9 (1953) 46–55.

Daoust, J. 'Fontevrault', *DHGE* 17: 961–971.

Davis, Thomas X. (trans.). *William of Saint Thierry: The Mirror of Faith*. CF 15. Kalamazoo, 1979.

Davy, Marie-Madeleine. 'Le rôle de la connaissance de soi dans l'École Cistercienne du XIIe siècle', *VS* 64 (1984) 118–141.

Deblaere, Albert. 'Témoignage mystique chrétien', *Studia missionalia* 26 (1977) 117–147.

Deboutte, Alfred. 'Saint Lutgarde et sa spiritualité': *Coll* 44 (1982) 73-85.

De Bruyn, Cebus C. 'De prologen van de eerste Historiebijbel geplaatst in het raam van hun tijd'. *The Bible and Medieval Culture. Edd. Lourdaux and Verhelst* (q.v.): 190–219.

Déchanet, Jean-Marie. *Oeuvres choisies de Guillaume de Saint-Thierry*. Paris, 1943.

_____. *Aux sources de la spiritualité de Guillaume de Saint-Thierry*. Paris, 1944.

_____. *Guillaume de Saint-Thierry: Exposé sur le Cantique des Cantiques*. SCh 82. Paris, 1962. ET by Columba Hart, *William of Saint Thierry: Exposition on the Song of Songs*. CF 6. Spencer, 1970.

——————. *William of St. Thierry: The Man and His Work.* ET by Richard Strachen. CS 10. Spencer, 1962.

——————(trans.). *Guillaume de Saint Thierry: Lettre aux Frères du Mont-Dieu (Lettre d'Or).* SCh 223. Paris, 1975. ET by Theodore Berkeley, *The Golden Epistle,* CF 12. Spencer, 1971.

——————. '"Amor ipse intellectus est": La doctrine de l'amour chez Guillaume de Saint-Thierry', *RMAL* 1 (1945) 349–374.

——————. 'Études critiques du texte de la Lettre auz Fréres du Mont-Dieu', *Scriptorium* 6 (1952) 196–212; 8 (1954) 236–271.

——————. 'Les fondements et les bases de la spiritualité bernardine', *Citeaux* 4 (1953) 292–313.

——————. 'Le pseudo-prologue de *De contemplando Deo*', *Citeaux* 8 (1957) 5–12.

——————. Introduction to William of St Thierry, *Exposition on the Song of Songs,* CF 6. Spencer 1970: vii-xlviii.

De Fontette, Micheline. *Les Religieuses à l'âge classique du Droit Canon.* Paris, 1967.

De Ganck, Roger. 'Het kloosterslot der Bijloke in het gedrang', *Citeaux* 3 (1952) 90–111.

——————. 'Nederigheid uit waarheidsdwang en uit liefdedrang bij Bernardus', *Sint Bernardus van Clairvaux.* Achel, 1953: 165–194.

——————. 'Over de benoeming van een nieuwe rector te Nazareth in 1448', *Citeaux* 7 (1956) 102–123.

——————. 'Het "placet" voor buitenlandse Cisterciënser-visitators in de 16e eeuw', *Citeaux* 5 (1954) 45–541.

——————. 'De Stichting van Cisterciënser-monialenabdijen in de Zuidelijke Nederlanden in de 12e en 13e eeuwen'. *De Monialen van de Orde van Citeaux.* Westmalle, *pro manuscripto,* 1961: 21–32.

——————. 'The Cistercian Nuns of Belgium in the Thirteenth-Century', *CSt* 5 (1970) 169–187.

——————. 'Les pouvoirs de l'Abbé de Cîteaux, de la bulle *Parvus Fons* (1265) à la Révolution française', *AC* 27 (1971) 3–63.

_____. 'Chronological Data in the Lives of Ida of Nivelles and Beatrice of Nazareth' *OGE* 57 (1983) 14–28.

_____. 'The Three Foundations of Bartholomew of Tienen', *Citeaux* 37 (1986) 49–75.

de Gandillac, Maurice. 'Note sur le 13e siècle', *DSp* 3:357.

de Ghellinck, Joseph. *L'Essor de la littérature latine du Moyen-Age*, 2nd ed. Brussels-Paris, 1954.

_____. 'L'Entrée d'essentia, substantia et autres mots apparentés dan le latin médiéval', *Archivum Latinitatis Medii Aevi* 16 (1941) 77–112.

Degler-Spengler, Brigitte. 'Dis Zistercienserinnen im 12. Jahrhundert'. *Helvetia Sacra*, Part 3, vol. 3: *Die Zistercienser und Zistercienserinnen...in der Schweiz*. Bern, 1982: 510–519.

De Jonge, Marinus. 'The Use of *ò christós* in the Apocalypse of John'. *L'Apocalypse Johannique*. Ed. Lambrecht (q.v.): 267–281.

de la Peza, E. *El significado de 'Cor' en San Agustin*. Paris, 1962.

Delaruelle, Étienne. *La Piété populaire au Moyen Age*. Turin, 1975.

_____, E.R. Labande, Paul Ourliac. *L'Église au temps du Grand Schisme et de la crise conciliaire 1378–1449)*. Paris, 1964. *Histoire de l'Église depuis les origines jusqu'à nos jours,* 14. Edd. Fliche and Martin. Twenty-one volumes.

Delfgaauw, Pacifique. *Saint Bernard: Maître de l'amour divin*. Diss., Rome, 1952.

_____. 'La nature et les degrés de l'amour selon S. Bernard', *AC* 9 (1953) 234–252. ET in *MnS* 1 (1963) 85–110.

Delhaye, Philippe. 'Dans le sillage de S. Bernard: Trois petits traîtés', *Citeaux* 5 (1954) 92–105.

Delort, Robert. *Life in the Middle Ages* ET by R. Allen. New York, 1983.

de Lubac, Henri. *Catholicism: A Study of Dogma in Relation to the Corporate Destiny of Mankind*. ET by L. Shepperd. London, 1950, rpt. 1958.

_____. *Exégèse Médiévale: Les quatre sens de l'Écriture*. Paris, 1959–1964. Four volumes.

_____. *The Mystery of the Supernatural*. ET by R. Sheed. London-New York, 1967.

_____. 'La rencontre de *supperadditum* et *supernaturale* dans la théologie médiévale', *RMAL* 1 (1945) 27–34.

Delumeau, Jean. *Le péché et la peur: La culpabilisation en Occident (XIIIe -XVIIIe siècles'*. Paris, 1983.

de Margerie, Bertrand. *La Trinité chrétienne dans l'Histoire*. Théologie Historique 31. Paris, 1975.

De Martel, Gérard. 'Un nouveau témoin de la liste des vices au moyen âge', *RTAM* 44 (1977) 65–79.

de Moreau, Edouard. *L'Histoire de l'Abbaye de Villers-en-Brabant aux XIIe et XIIIe siècles*. Brussels, 1909.

Denis, E. *Saint Julienne de Cornillon*. Liège, 1927.

Denis-Boulet, Noële-Maurice. 'Analyse des rites et des prières de la Messe', in Martimort (ed.), *l'Église en prière (q.v.)*, *323–434*.

Denziger, Henricus and Clemens Bannwart (eds.). *Enchiridium Symbolorum*. 18th–20th ed. Freiburg/Br., 1932.

De Paepe, Norbert. *Hadewijch: Een studie van de Minne in het kader der 12e en 13e eeuwse mystiek en profane minnelyriek*. Ghent, 1967.

_____. 'Hadewijchs vijfde visioen en de Apocalypse. Dood is niet dood', in R. Parteman (ed.), *Uut goeder jongster*. Festschrift L. Roose. Leuven-Amersfoort, 1984: 13–21.

De Raeymaeker, Louis. *The Philogophy of Being*. ET by E. Ziegelmeier. 2nd ed. Saint Louis-London, 1957.

Despy, Georges. 'Les débuts de l'Inquisition dans les anciens Pays-Bas au XIIIe siècles'. *Problèmes du Christianisme* 9. Hommages Jean Hadot. Brussels, 1980: 71–104.

de Vogüé, Adalbert. 'La paternité du Christ dans la règle de saint Benoît', *VS* fasc 105 (1964) 55–67. ET in *MnS* 5 (1968) 45–57.

De Vooys, C.G.N. *Middelnederlandse Legenden en Exempelen: Bijdragen tot de kennis van de prozaliteratuur en het volksgeloof der Middeleeuwen*. 2nd rev. ed. Groningen-Amsterdam, 1974.

de Vrégille, Bernard. 'L'Attente des Saints d'après Saint Bernard', *NRT* 70 (1948) 225–244.

d'Haenens, Albert. 'Femmes excédentaires et vocation religieuse. Le cas d'Ide de Nivelles (1200–1231)'. *Hommages à la Wal-*

lonie. Festschrift honoring M. A. Arnould and P. Ruelle. Brussels, 1981: 217–234.

Didier, J.-Ch. 'L'Ascension mystique et l'union mystique par l'humanité du Christ selon saint Bernard', *SVS* 22 (1930) [140]-[155].

Dimier, Anselme. *Saint Louis et Cîteaux.* Paris, 1954.

_____. 'Mourir à Clairvaux', *Coll* 17 (1959) 272–284.

_____. 'Chapitres généraux d'abbesses cisterciennes', *Cîteaux* 11 (1960) 268–275.

_____. 'Folquet ou Foulques de Marseille', *DGHE* 7: 777–780.

Dinzelbacher, Peter. *Vision und Visionsliterature im Mittelalter.* Monographien zur Geschichte des Mittelalters 23. Stuttgart, 1981.

_____ and D. D. Bauer (eds.). *Frauenmystik im Mittelalter.* Ostfildern, 1985.

_____ and D. D. Bauer (eds.). *Religiöse Frauenbewegung und mystische Frömmigkeit im Mittelalter.* Paderborn, 1988.

_____. 'Ida von Nijvels Brückenvision', *OGE* 52 (1978) 179–194.

_____. 'Hadewijchs mystische Erfahrungen in neuer Interpretation', *OGE* 54 (1980) 267–279.

_____. 'Das Christusbild der heiligen Lutgard von Tongeren im Rahmen der Passionsmystik und Bildkunst des 12. und 13. Jahrhunderts', *OGE* 56 (1982) 217–277.

_____. 'Körperliche und seelische Vorbedingungen religiöser Träume und Visionen'. *I Sogni del Medioevo. Seminario Internazionale Roma, 2–4 ottobre 1983.* Ed. T. Gregory. Pp. 57–86.

_____. Review of Jacques Le Goff, *La naissance du purgatoire* (Paris, 1981) in *OGE* 61 (1987) 278–282.

Dondaine, H.F. 'L'Objet de le "medium" de la vision béatifique chez les théologiens du XIIIe siècle', *RTAM* 19 (1952) 60–130.

_____. 'Cognoscere de Deo "Quid est"', *RTAM* 22 (1955) 7–77.

Dresser, Robert. 'Gradation: Rhetoric and Substance in Saint Bernard'. *Goad and Nail.* Ed. E. R. Elder (q.v.): *71–85.*

Dressler, Fridolin. *Petrus Damiani. Leben und Werk.* Studia

Anselmiana 34. Rome, 1954.

Dreyfus, P. 'L'Actualisation de l'Écriture', *RBibl* 86 (1979) 161–193.

Dronke, Peter. *Medieval Latin and the Rise of European Love Lyric*. Two volumes. Oxford, 1968.

Dubois, Gérard. 'Spiritual Inebriation', *Liturgy* (Gethsemani Abbey) 12/2 (1978) 3–24.

Ducange, Ursinus. *Glossarium Novum ad Scriptores Medii Aevi*. Ed. D. P. Carpentier. Paris, 1766. Four volumes.

Duggan Charles. 'Equity and Compassion in Papal Marriage Decretals in England'. *Love and Marriage in the Twelfth Century*. Edd. Van Hoecke and Welkenhuysen (q.v.): 59–87.

du Halgouët, Jérôme. 'Poètes oubliés', *Coll* 20 (1958) 128–144; 227–242.

Dumeige, Gervais. *Ives: Epître à Séverin sur la charité. Richard de Saint Victor: Les quatre degrés de la violente charité*. Paris, 1955.

—————. (ed.) *Histoire des Conciles Oecuméniques*. Paris, 1963–1964.Twelve volumes.

—————. 'L'Influence de Denys l'Aréopagite sur Richard de Saint-Victor', *DSp* 3: 324–329.

—————. 'Médecin (le Christ)', *DSp* 10:891–901.

Dumont, Charles. *Aelred de Rievaulx: La vie de recluse*. SCh 76. Paris, 1961.

Dumontier, Maurice. *Saint Bernard et le Bible*. Bruges-Paris, 1953.

Dumoutet, Edouard. *Le désir de voir l'Hostie et les origines de la dévotion au Saint-Sacrement*. Paris, 1962.

Dupré, Louis. *Transcendent Selfhood: The Loss and Rediscovery of the Inner Life*. New York, 1976.

—————. *The Deeper Life: An Introduction to Christian Mysticism*. New York, 1981.

—————. *The Common Life*. New York, 1984.

—————. 'The Mystical Knowlege of the Self and its Philosophical Significance', *IPQ* 14 (1974) 495–511.

de Roy, Olivier. *L'Intelligence de la foi en la Trinité selon Saint Augustin: Genèse de sa théologie trinitaire jusqu'en 391*. Paris, 1966.

Dykmans, M. *Les Sermons de Jean XXII sur la vision béatifique.* Miscellanea Historiae Pontificae 34. Rome, 1973.

Ehman, Robert R. 'Two Basic Concepts of the Self', *IPQ* 6 (1965) 594–611.

Elder, E. Rozanne (ed.). *Noble Piety and Reformed Monasticism.* Studies in Medieval Cistercian History 7. CS 65. Kalamazoo, 1981.

—————— (ed.). *Benedictus: Studies in Honor of St. Benedict of Nursia.* Studies in Medieval Cistercian History 8. CS 67. Kalamazoo, 1981.

—————— (ed.). *Goad and Nail.* Studies in Medieval Cistercian History 10. CS 84. Kalamazoo, 1985.

——————. 'William of St. Thierry and the Greek Fathers: Evidence from Christology'. *One Yet Two.* Ed. M. B. Pennington (q.v.): 254–266.

Eliade, Mircea. *A History of Religious Ideas*, Vol. 1: *From the Stone Age to Eleusian Mysteries*; Vol. 2: *From Gautama Buddha to the Triumph of Christianity.* ET by W.R. Trask. Chicago, 1978 and 1982.

Endepols, H.J.E. 'Bijdragen tot de eschatologische voorstellingen in de Middeleeuwen', *TNTL* 28 (1909) 49–111.

Epiney-Burgard, Georgette. *Gerard Grote et les débuts de la Dévotion Moderne.* Abendländische Religionsgeschichte 54. Wiesbaden, 1970.

——————. 'L'Influence des béguines sur Ruusbroec', *Jan van Ruusbroec.* Edd. P. Mommers and N. De Paepe (q.v.): 65-85.

Ernst. Cornelius. 'De kennis van Jesus vaar middeleeuwse interpretatie', *TT* 10 (1970) 151–178.

Escherich, Mela. 'Das Visionwesen in den mittelalterlichen Frauenklöster', *Deutsche Psychologie* 1 (1916) 153–166.

Ethier, A.M. *Le 'De Trinitate' de Richard de Saint-Victor.* Paris-Ottawa, 1939.

Evans, Gillian R. 'The Place of Peter the Chanter's *De tropibus loquendis*', *AC* 38 (1983) 231–253.

Evans, Robert F. *Pelagius: Inquiries and Reappraisals.* London, 1968.

Evdokimov, Paul. *L'Orthodoxie.* Neuchâtel-Paris, 1955.

Ewer, M.A. *A Survey of Mystical Symbolism.* London-New York, 1933.

Farkasfalvy, Denis. *L'Inspiration de l'Écriture Sainte dans la théologie de saint Bernard.* Studia Anselmiana 53, Rome, 1964.

Faust, Ulrich. 'Bernhards "Liber de gratia et libero arbitrio". Bedeutung, Quellen und Einfluss'. *Studia Anselmiana 50. Rome, 1962: 35–51.*

Festugière, A.-J. *L'Idéal religieux des Grecs et l'Evangile.* Paris, 1932.

──────. *Contemplation et vie contemplative selon Platon.* Bibliothèque de Philosophie 2. 3rd ed., Paris, 1967.

Feuillet, André. 'Le demeure céleste de l'eschatologie paulinienne', *RSR* 44 (1956) 161–192; 360–402.

──────. 'La création de l'Univers d'après l'Epître aux Colossiens (1:16a)', *NTS* 12 (1966) 1–9.

Fischer, Balthasar. 'Jesus, unsere Mutter', *GL* 59 (1985) 147–156.

Fitzmeyer, Joseph A. 'The Ascension of Christ and Pentecost', *TS* 45 (1984) 409–440.

Fletcher, Angus. *Allegory: The Theory of a Symbolic Mode,* 4th ed. Ithaca-London, 1975.

Fontenrose, Joseph. *Python: A Study of Delphic Myth and its Origin.* Berkeley-Los Angeles-London, 1959. Paperback edition, 1980.

──────. *The Delphic Oracle: Its Responses and Operations with a Catalogue of Responses.* Berkeley-Los Angeles-London, 1978.

Forest, Aimé. 'Das Erlebnis des consensus voluntatis beim heiligen Bernhard', in J. Lortz (ed.), *Bernhard von Clairvaux* (q.v.) 120–127.

──────. 'La synthèse de Jean Scot Erigène'. *Histoire de l'Église*, 3. Edd. A. Fliche and A. Martin. Paris, 1965: 9–32.

Foreville, Raymonde, *Latran I, II, III, et IV.* Histoire des Conciles Oecuméniques, 6. Ed. G. Dumeige. Paris, 1964.

Forster, K. 'Anschauung Gottes', *LThK* 1: 585–591.

Fox, Matthew. *Illuminations of Hildegard of Bingen (1098–1179).* Santa Fe, New Mexico, 1985.

Franklin, J.C. *Mystical Transformations: The Imagery of Liquids in the Works of Mechtild of Magdeburg*. Madison, New York-London, 1978.

Fransen, Piet. *Hermeneutics of the Councils and Other Studies*. Bibliotheca Ephemeridum Theologicarum Lovaniensium 69. Edd. H. E. Mertens and F. De Graeve. Leuven, 1985.

Fredericq, Paul. *Corpus documentorum Inquisitonis haereticae pravitatis Neerlandicae*. Geschiedenis der inquisitie in de Nederlanden tot aan hare herinrichting onde Keizer Karel V (1025–1520). Ghent-The Hague, 1892–1899. Two volumes.

Frend, W.H.C. *The Donatist Church*. Oxford, 1952.

Frenken, A.M. 'The *Vita* van Abundus van Hoei', *Citeaux* 10 (1959) 5–33.

Frenken, Goswin. *Die Exempla des Jacob von Vitry: Ein Beitrag zur Geschichte der Erzählungsliteratur des Mittelalters*. Quellen und Untersuchungen zur lateinischen Philologie des Mittelalters. Munich, 1914.

Fromm, Erich. *The Fear of Freedom*. London, 1942. Rpt 1966.

Fürkotter, Adelgundis, and Angela Carlevaris. *Hildegardis: Scivias*. CCCM 43–43A. Turnhout, 1978. Two volumes.

Gaïth, Jérôme. *La conception de la liberté chez Grégoire de Nysse*. Études de philosophie médiévale 43. Paris, 1953.

García, Maria Columbas. *Paradis et vie angélique*. Trans. C.Caron. Paris, 1961.

Garnier, François. *Le langage de l'Image au Moyen Age: Signification et Symbolique*. Paris, 1982.

Gauthier, René-Antoine. *Magnanimité: L'Idéal de la grandeur dans la Philosophie païnne et dans la théologie chrétienne*. Bibliothèque Thomiste 28. Paris, 1951.

Gilson, Étienne. *The Mystical Theology of Saint Bernard*. ET by A.H. C. Downes. London, 1940, rpt. Kalamazoo, 1990.

_____. *L'Esprit de la Philosophie médiévale*, 2nd ed. Paris, 1944. Two volumes. ET by A.H. C. Downes, *The Spirit of Medieval Philosophy*. London, 1950.

_____. *Introduction à l'étude de saint Augustin*. Études de philosophie médiévale 11. 3rd ed. Paris, 1949.

_____. 'Maxime, Erigène, S. Bernard'. *Aus der Geisteswelt des Mittelalters*, Studien und Texte Martin Grabmann zur Vollendung des 60. Lebensjahres von Freunden und Schulern gewidmet. Edd. A. Lang, J. Lechner and M. Schmaus. Munich, 1935. Vol. 1: 188–195.

_____. ' L'Infinité chez saint Augustin', *AM* 1: 569–574.

Gimpel, John. *The Medieval Machine: The Industrial Revolution of the Middle Ages.* New York, 1976.

Goetstouwers, Adriaan. 'De Oorsprong der Abdij Roosendaal', *Bulletin de la Commission Royale d'Histoire* 119 (1949) 257–298.

Gold, Penny Schine. 'Male/Female Cooperation: The Example of Fontevrault'. *Distant Echoes.* Medieval Religious Women 1. CS 71. Edd. L.T. Shank and J.A. Nichols. Kalamazoo, 1984: 151–168.

Gooday, Frances. 'Mechtild of Magdeburg and Hadewijch of Antwerp. A Comparison', *OGE* 48 (1974) 305–362.

Grabmann, Martin. *Mittelalterliches Geistesleben.* Munich, 1926–1966. Three volumes.

Grant, Robert M. *The Apostolic Fathers.* Camden-New York-Toronto, 1964–1968. Six volumes.

Graves, Coburn V. 'The Organization of an English Nunnery in Lincolnshire', *Citeaux* 33 (1982) 333–350.

Grégoire, Réginald. 'A saeculi actibus se facere alienum': Le 'Mépris du monde dans la littérature monastique latine médiévale', RAM 41 (1965) 231—240. *StM* 8 (1966) 313–328.

_____. 'Introduction à une étude théologique du "Mépris du monde"', *StM*8 (1966) 313–328.

_____. 'Il matrimonio mistico', *Settimane di studio del centro italiano sull'alto medioevo* 24/2 (1977) 701–817.

Greshake, Gisbert and Gerhard Lohfink. *Naherstehung-Auferstehung-Unsterblichkeit.* Quaestiones disputatae 71. Freiburg/ Br, 1975; rpt 1978,

Greven, Joseph. *Die Anfänge der Beginen: Ein Beitrag zur Geschichte der Volksfrommigkeit und des Ordenswesen im Hochmittelalter.* Vorreformationsgeschichtliche Forschungen 9. Munich, 1912.

Griesser, Bruno (ed.). *Exordium Magnum Cisterciense sive Narratio de Initio Cisterciensis Ordinis.* Series Scriptorum S. Ordinis Cisterciensis 2. Rome, 1961.

_____. 'Die Officia ecclesiastica Cisterciensis Ordinis des Cod. 1171 von Trient', *AC* 12 (1956) 153–288.

Grillmeier, Aloys and Heinrich Bacht. *Das Konzil von Chalkedon*. 3rd revised edition. Würzburg, 1951–1954. Three volumes.

Grundmann, Herbert. *Religiöse Bewegungen im Mittelalter*. Historische Studien 267. Berlin, 1935; rpt Hildesheim, 1961.

_____. 'Die geschichtliche Grundlagen der deutschen Mystik', *Deutsche Vierteljahrschrift für Literaturwissenschaften und Geistesgeschichte* 12 (1934) 405–429.

_____. 'Jubel', in B. Von Wiese and K. Borck (eds.), *Festschrift für Jost Trier*. Meisenheim, 1954: 477–511.

Guarnieri, Romana. 'Il movimento del libero spiritu dalle origini al secolo XVI', *Archivio italiano per la storia delle pietà, 4. Rome, 1964*.

_____. 'Frères du Libre Esprit', *DSp* 5:1241–1268.

Guest, T.M. 'Hadewijch and Minne'. *European Context. Edd. King and Vincent*. (q.v.): 14–29.

Guignard, Philippe. *Les monuments primitifs de la Règle cistercienne*. Dijon, 1878.

Guimet, Fernand. '*Caritas ordinata* et *amor discretus* dans la théologie trinitaire de Richard de Saint-Victor', *RMAL* 4 (1948) 225–236.

Guy, Jean-Claude. 'La place du *contemptus mundi* dans le monachisme ancien', *RAM* 41 (1965) 237–249.

Haacke, Hrabanus. *Ruperti Tuitensis Liber de divinis officiis*. CCCM 7. Turnhout, 1967.

Haag, Herbert. *Bibellexikon*. Einsiedeln-Zurich-Cologne, 1951.

Haas, Alois M. *Sermo mysticus: Studien zur Theologie und Sprache der Deutschen Mystik*. Dokimion 4. Fribourg/Sw., 1979.

_____. 'Mort mystique', *DSp* 10:1777–1790.

Hallier, Amédée. *Un éducateur monastique: Aelred de Rievaulx*. Paris, 1959. ET by Columban Heaney, *The Monastic Theology of Aelred of Rievaulx*. CS 2. Spencer-Shannon, 1969.

Hammerstein, R. *Die Musik der Engel. Untersuchungen zur musikanschauung des Mittelalters*. Bern, 1962.

Hamon, Auguste. *Histoire de la dévotion au Sacré-Coeur*. Paris, 1921–1940. Five volumes.

—————. 'Coeur (Sacré)', *DSp* 2: 1023–1049.

Häring, Nicholas. 'Der Literaturkatalog von Affligem', *RBén* 80 (1970) 64–96.

Harl, Marguerite (ed.). *Écriture et culture philosophique dans la pensée de Grégoire de Nysse. Colloque de Chevretogne, 1969*. Leiden, 1971.

Hart, Columba. *Hadewijch: The Complete Works*. New York-Toronto, 1980.

—————. 'Consecratio virginum: Thirteenth-Century Witnesses', *The American Benedictine Review* 23 (1972) 258–274.

Haskins, Charles Homer. *Studies in Medieval Culture*. 2nd ed. New York, 1965.

Hauréau, B. *Notices et extraits de quelques mss latins de la B.N.*. Paris, 1890.

Hausherr, Irénée. *Penthos: The Doctrine of Compunction in the Christian East*, ET by Anselm Hufstader. CS 53. Kalamazoo, 1982.

Hautcoeur, Edouard. *Histoire de l'Abbaye de Flines*. 2nd ed. Lille, 1909.

Hayes, Zachary. *What Are They Saying About the End of the World*. New York, 1983.

Hedwig. Klaus. *Sphaera Lucis: Studien zur Intelligität des Seienden im Kontext der mittelalterlichen Lichtspekulation*. Beiträge zur Geschichte und Theologie des Mittelalters, N.S.18. Munster/W., 1980.

Heine, Ronald E. *Perfection in the Virtuous Life: A Study in the Relationship between Edification and Polemical Theology in Gregory of Nyssa's 'De Vita Moysi'*. Patristic Monograph, Series 2. Cambridge, MA, 1975.

Heinz, Andreas. 'Die Zisterzienser und die Anfänge des Rosenkranzes', *AC* 33 (1977) 269–309.

Helinand of Froidmont, *Les vers de la mort*. Edd. Fr. Wulff and Em. Walberg. Paris, 1895; rpt New York-London, 1965.

Hendrikx, Ephraim. *Augustinus Verhältniss zur Mystik*. Würzburg, 1936.

_____. 'Platonisches und biblisches Denken bei Augustinus', *AM* 1:285–292.

Hendrix, Guido. 'Cistercian Sympathies in the 14th-century *Catalogus Virorum Illustrium*', *Citeaux* 27 (1976) 267–278.

_____. 'Primitive Versions of Thomas of Cantimpré's "Vita Lutgardis"', *Citeaux* 29 (1978) 153–206.

Henriquez, Chrysostom. *Quinque Prudentes Virgines*. Antwerp, 1630.

Hepburn, R. W. 'Questions about the Meaning of Life', *RSt* 1 (1965–66) 125–140.

Herbert, R. 'Saint Augustin et la virginité de la foi', *AM* 2: 645–655.

Herlihy, David. *The Social History of Italy and Western Europe, 700–1500*. London, 1979.

Heszler, Esther. 'Stufen der Minne bei Hadewijch'. *Frauenmystik im Mittelalter*. Edd. Dinzelbacher and Bauer (q.v.): 99–122.

Hick, John. *Death and Eternal Life*. London, 1976; rpt. 1985.

Hickey, Leo. *Saint Bernard: The Nativity*. Chicago-Dublin-London, 1959.

Hilka, Alfons. 'Altfranzösische Mystik und Beginentum', *Zeitschrift für romanische Philologie* 47 (1927) 121–170.

Hiltbrunner, O. 'Die Schrift "De Officiis Ministrorum" des hl. Ambrosius und ihr ciceronisches Vorbild', *Gymnasium* 71 (1864) 174–189.

Hiss, Wilhelm. *Die Anthropologie in der Theologie Bernhards von Clairvaux*. Quellen zur Geschichte der Philosophie, 7. Berlin, 1964.

Höld, Ludwig. 'Der Transsubstantionsbegriff in der scholastischen Theologie des 12. Jahrhunderts', *RTAM* 31 (1964) 230–259.

Holmes, Urban T. *Daily Living in the Twelfth Century Based on the Observations of Alexander Neckam (1157–1217) in London and Paris*. Madison-Milwaukee-London, 1966.

Honecker, M. 'Christus medicus'. *Der kranke Mensch im Mittelalter und Renaissance*. Ed. von Wunderli. Studia humaniora, 5. Düsseldorf, 1986: 27–43.

Honemann, Volker. *Die 'Epistola ad fratres de Monte Dei' des Wilhelms von Saint-Thierry: Lateinische Überlieferung und mittelalterliche Übersetzungen*. Münchener Texte und Untersuchungen zur deutschen Literatur des Mittelalters, 61. Zurich-Munich, 1978.

Hontoir, Camille. 'La dévotion au Saint-Sacrement chez les premiers cisterciens', *Studia Eucharistica*. Antwerp, 1964: 133–155.

Hoste, Anselme and C.H. Talbot. *Aelredi Rievallensis: Opera omnia*. CCCM 1. Turnhout, 1971.

Hourlier, Jacques. *Guillaume de Saint-Thierry: La contemplation de Dieu: L'Oraison de Dom Guillaume*. SCh 61. Paris, 1959. ET by Penelope Lawson. *William of Saint Thierry: On Contemplating God, Prayer, and Meditations*. CF 3. Spencer, 1971.

——————. 'La Doctrine des anges chez s. Bernard' *AC* 9 (1953) 114–135.

Huftier, M. 'Libre arbitre, liberté et péché chez saint Augustin', *RTAM* 33 (1966) 187–286.

Hughes, Philip. *The Church in Crisis: History of the Twelve Great Councils*. London, 1963.

Huyben, J. 'Le movement spirituel dans les Pays-Bas au XIIIe siècle', *SVS* (1947) 29–45.

Huyghe, Gérard. *La clôture des moniales des origines à la fin du XIIIe siècle: Étude historique et juridique*. Roubaix, 1944.

Institut Catholique de Paris. *Les Visions mystiques*. Nouvelles de l'Institut Catholique de Paris, N.1. Paris, 1977.

Jackson, Stanley W. 'Acedia the Sin and its Relationship to Sorrow and Melancholia in Medieval Times', *Bulletin of the History of Medicine* 55 (1981) 172–185.

Jaeger, Werner. *Gregor von Nyssa's Lehre vom Heiligen Geist*. Ed. H. Dörries. Leiden, 1966.

Javelet, Robert. *Image et Ressemblance au douzième siècle: de saint Anselme à Alain de Lille*. Paris, 1967. Two volumes.

——————. *Psychologie des auteurs spirituels du XIIe siècle*. Strasbourg, 1959.

——————. 'Intelligence et amour chez les auteurs spirituels du XIIe siècle' *RAM* 37 (1961) 273–290, 429–450.

——————. 'Thomas Gallus et Richard de Saint-Victor mystiques', RTAM 29 (1962) 206–233; 30 (1963) 89–121.

_____. 'Image de Dieu et nature au XIIe siècle', *La filosofia della natura nel Medioevo. Atti del III Congresso internazionale di filosofia medioevale. Mendola (Tente) 31 agosto– 5 settembre 1964.* Milan, 1964: 286–296.

_____. 'La Réintroduction de la liberté dans les notions d'image et de ressemblance conçus comme dynamisme'. *Miscellanea Medievalia: Der Begriff der Repräsentation im Mittelalter. Stellvertretung. Symbol. Zeichen. Bild.* Ed. A. Zimmermann. Berlin-New York, 1971: 1–34.

_____. 'Sens et réalité ultime chez Hugues de Saint-Victor', *Ultimate Reality and Meaning* 3 (1980) 84–106.

_____. 'Sens et réalité ultime selon Richard de Saint-Victor', *Ultimate Reality and Meaning* 6 (1983) 221–243.

_____. 'Exstase au 12e siècle', *DSp* 4:2113–2130.

Jean-Nesmy, Claude. 'La dévotion au Sacré-Coeur est-elle une dévotion particulière? Jalons pour une recherche méthodique des thèmes et de leur portée'. *Dr. Reypens Album.* Ed. A. Ampe (q.v.): 241–256.

Jenni, E. and Chr. Westermann (eds.). *Theologisches Handwörterbuch zum Altem Testament.* Munich-Zurich, 1979.

Jetté, Fernard. 'Exstase: tradition spiritelle du 13e au 15e siècle', *DSp* 4: 2131–2133.

Jolivet, Régis. *The God of Reason.* ET by M. Pontifex. London, 1959.

Journet, Charles. 'Saint Augustin et l'exégèse traditionnelle du "corps spirituel"', *AM* 2: 879–894.

Jungmann, Josef. *Missarum Solemnia.* Vienna, 1949. ET by F. A. Brenner and C.K. Riepe, new abridged edition in one volume. New York, 1959.

_____. *The Place of Christ in Liturgical Prayer.* ET by A. Peeler, 2nd ed. London, 1965.

Kaufmann, Alexander. *Caesarius von Heisterback: Ein Beitrag zur Culturgeschichte des zwölften und dreizehnten Jahrhunderts.* 2nd ed. mit einem Bruckstück aus des Caesarius *VIII Libri miraculorum.* Cologne, 1862.

Kazemier, G. 'Hadewijch en de minne in de Strofische Gedichten', *TNTL* 87 (1971) 241–259.

Kelly, J.N.D. *Early Christian Doctrines*, 2nd ed. London, 1960.

Kennedy, V.L. 'The Moment of the Consecration and the Elevation of the Host', *MS* 6 (1944) 121–150.

Kereszty, Rochus. 'Die Weisheit in der mystischen Erfahrung beim hl. Bernhard von Clairvaux', *Citeaux* 14 (1963) 6–24; 105–143; 185–201.

Kerstens, Christilla. 'De wazige spiegel van Hadewijch. Het onuitsprekelijk Diets gemaakt in beelden', *OGE* 47 (1973) 347–385.

Kiesling, Christopher. 'On Relating to the Persons in the Trinity', *TS* 47 (1986) 599–616.

King, Archdale. *Citeaux and its Oldest Daughters*. London, 1974.

——————. 'Eucharistic Reservation in Cistercian Churches', *Coll* 20 (1950) 114–127.

King, P. K. and P. F. Vincent (eds.). *European Context: Studies in the History and Literature of the Netherlands presented to Theodor Weevers*. Cambridge, 1971.

Kirchmeyer, Jean. 'L'Église grecque.... L'Archétype de l'Image', *DSp* 6: 814–815.

Kirschbaum. Engelbert *et al. Lexikon der christlichen Ikonographie*. Rome-Freiburg-Basel-Vienna, 1968–1976. Eight volumes.

Kleinknecht, Hermann, Gottfried Quell, Ethelbert Stauffer and Karl Kuhn. 'Theos', *TDNT* 3: 65–139.

Kleineidan, Erich. 'Wissen, Wissenschaft, Theologie bei Bernhard von Clairvaux'. *Bernhard von Clairvaux. Mönch und Mystiker*. Ed. Josef Lortz (q.v.): 128–167.

Knotzinger, K. 'Hohes Lied und bräutliche Christusliebe bei Bernhard von Clairvaux', *Jahrbuch für mystische Theologie* 7 (1961) 9–90.

Knowles, David. *The Evolution of Medieval Thought*. London, 1962.

——————. *The English Mystical Tradition*. 2nd ed. London, 1964.

——————. *The Nature of Mysticism*. New York, 1966.

Koepplin, Dieter. 'Interzession', *Lexikon der christlichen Ikonographie*, vol. 2: 346–352.

Konstantinou, Evangelos. *Die Tugendlehre Gregors von Nyssa im Verhältnis zu der Antik-Philosophischen und Jüdisch-Christlichen Tradition.* Würzburg, 1966.

Koorn, F. W. 'Ongebonden Vrouwen. Overeenkomsten en verschillen tussen Begijnen en Zusters des Gemenen Levens', *OGE* 59 (1985) 392–401.

Köpf, Ulrich. *Religiöse Erfahrung in der Theologie Bernhards von Clairvaux.* Beiträge zur historischen Theologie, 61. Tübingen, 1980.

_____. 'Bernhard von Clairvaux in der Frauenmystik', in Dinzelbacher and Bauer (eds.), *Frauenmystik im Mittelalter* (q.v.): 48–77.

Korger, M. 'Grundproblemen der Augustinischen Erkenntnislehre', *Recherches Augustiniennes* 2 (1962) 33–57.

Krenig, Ernst. 'Mittelalterliche Frauenklöster nach den Konstitutionen von Citeaux, unter besonderer Berücksichtigung fränkischer Nonnen-Konventen', *AC* 10 (1954) 1–105.

Kroll, Jerome. 'Carol Houselander's Childhood Neurosis', *Vox Benedictina* 2 (1985) 74–80.

_____ and Roger De Ganck. The Adolescence of a Thirteenth-century Visionary Nun', *Psychological Medicine* 16 (1986) 745–756.

Kuhn, Reinhard. *The Demon of the Noontide: Ennui in Western Literature.* Princeton, 1976.

Küsters, U. *Der verschlossene Garten: Volkssprachliche Hohelied-Auslegung und monastische Lebensform im 12. Jahrhundert.* Studia humaniora 2. Düsseldorf, 1985.

Lachance, Paul. *The Spiritual Journey of the Blessed Angela de Foligno according to the Memorial of Frater A.* Studia Antoniana, 24. Rome, 1984.

Lackner, Bede K. 'Early Citeaux and the Care of Souls'. *Noble Piety and Reformed Monasticism.* Ed. E. R. Elder (q.v.): 52–67.

Ladner, Gerhard B. 'St Augustine's Conception of Man to the Image of God', *AM* 2: 867–878.

Lambot, C. 'La Fête-Dieu à Fosses en 1246', *RBén* 79 (1969) 215–222.

_____. 'Un précieux manuscrit de la Vie de Sainte Julienne de Mont-Cornillon', *RBén* 79 (1969) 223–231.

_____. 'Eve de Saint-Martin et les premiers historiens liégeois de la Fête-Dieu', *RBén* 79 (1969) 232–254.

_____. 'Les anciennes peintures de l'église de Cornillon représentant l'histoire de Sainte Julienne', *RBén* 79 (1969) 255–260.

_____. La bulle d'Urbain IV à Eve de Saint-Martin sur l'Institution de la Fête-Dieu', *RBén* 79 (1969) 261–290.

_____. 'Une oeuvre liégeoise inédite de Jacques de Troyes, le futur pape Urbain IV', *RBén* 79 (1969) 304-315.

Lambrecht, Daniel. *De Synode in het oude bisdom Doornik gesitueerd in de Europese ontwikkeling.* Diss. Ghent, 1976.

_____. *De parochiale Synode in het oude bisdom Doornik gesitueerd in de Europese ontwikkeling. 11de eeuw–1559.* Verhandelingen van de Koninklijke Academie voor Wetenschappen, Letteren en Schone Kunsten. Klasse der Letteren 113. Brussels, 1984.

Lambrecht, Jan (ed). *L'Apocalype Johannique et L'Apocalyptique dans le Nouveau Testament.* Leuven-Gembloux, 1980.

Lampe, G.W.H. (ed.). *A Patristic Greek Lexicon.* Oxford, 1962.

Latourelle, René. *Théologie de la Résurrection.* Bruges-Paris, 1966.

Laurent, Jacques. 'Un opuscule ascétique inédit attribué à saint Bernard: "meditatio secundum septem Horas Diei"', *Saint Bernard et son temps.* Dijon, 1929. Volume 2:111–114.

Lazzari, Francisco. M*istica e ideologia tra XI e XIII secolo.* Milan, 1972.

_____. 'Le "contemptus mundi" chez saint Bernard', *RAM* 41 (1965) 291-304.

Leclerc, Joseph. *Vienne,* Histoire des conciles oecuméniques. Ed G. Dumeige. Vol. 8 (Paris 1964).

Leclercq, Jean. *L'Idée de la Royauté du Christ au Moyen Age.* Paris, 1959.

_____. *The Love of Learning and the Desire for God.* ET by Catherine Misrahi. London, 1978.

_____. *St. Pierre Damien, ermite et homme d'Église.* Rome, 1960.

_____. *Otia Monastica. Études sur le vocabulaire de la contemplation au Moyen Age.* Studia Anselmiana 51. Rome, 1963.

_____, François Vandenbroucke and Louis Bouyer. *The Spirituality of the Middle Ages.* A History of Christian Spirituality, 2. ET by the Benedictines of Holme Abbey, Carlisle. New York, 1968.

_____. 'Études sur saint Bernard et le texte de ses écrits', AC 9 (1953) 9–247.

_____. 'Drogon et saint Bernard', *RBén* 63 (1953) 11-31.

_____. 'La plus ancienne collection d'oeuvres de saint Bernard', *AC* 9 (1953) 124–133.

_____. 'Aspects littéraires de l'oeuvre de s. Bernard', *Cahiers de civilisation médiévale* 1 (1958) 425–450; 8 (1965) 299-326.

_____. 'Psycho-history and Medieval People', *CSt* 11 (1976) 269–289.

_____. 'Monachisme et pérégrination du IXe au XIIe siècle', *StM* 3 (1961) 33–52.

_____. 'Caelestinus de Caritate', *Citeaux* 14 (1963) 202–217.

_____. 'De quelques procédés du style biblique de S. Bernard', *Citeaux* 15 (1964) 330—349.

_____. 'L'Art de composition dans les traités de S. Bernard', *RBén* 76 (1966) 87–115.

_____. 'Autour de la correspondance de S. Bernard', *Sapientia doctrina* offerts à D. Bascour. Leuven, 1980: 185–198.

_____. 'Les Traductions de la Bible et la Spiritualité médiévale'. *The Bible and Medieval Culture.* Edd. W. Lourdaux and D. Verhelst (q.v.): 263–277.

_____. 'L'Amour et le mariage vus par des clerc et des religieux au XIIe siècle'. Love and Marriage in the Twelfth Century. Edd. Van Hoecke and Welkenhuysen (q.v.): 102–115.

_____. *Receuil d'Études sur saint Bernard et ses écrits.* Rome, 1962–1987. Four Volumes. [Several of the articles cited above are also contained in these volumes.]

Lefebvre, Charles. 'Formation du Droit canonique'. *Histoire du Droit et des Institutions de l'Église en Occident.I. L'Age classique, 1140–1378.* Paris, 1965: 133-345.

Le Goff, Jacques. *La naissance du purgatoire.* Paris, 1981. ET by A. Goldhammer, *The Birth of Purgatory.* Chicago, 1984.

Lejeune, R. 'L'évêque de Toulouse, Foulques de Marseille', *Mélanges F. Roossen.* Brussels, 1958: 433–448.

Lekai, Louis J. *The Cistercians. Ideals and Reality.* Kent, Ohio, 1962.

―――――― and A. Schneider. *Geschichte und Wirke des Weissen Mönche.* Cologne, 1958.

Léonard, Augustin. 'Recherches phénoménologiques autour de l'expérience mystique', *SVS* 54 (1952) 430–494.

Leonardi, Cl. *Conciliorum Oecumenorum Decreta.* Freiburg/Br., 1962.

Léon-Dufour, Xavier. *Resurrection and the Message of Easter.* ET by R. N. Wilson. New York, 1975.

―――――――. 'Grâce et liberté chez S. Augustin', *RSR* 33 (1946) 126–163.

Lerner, Robert E. *The Heresy of the Free Spirit in the Later Middle Ages.* Berkeley-Los Angeles-London, 1972.

Lewis, Gertrud Jaron. 'Christus als Frau. Eine Vision Elisabeths von Schönau', *Jarhbuch für Internationale Germanistik* 15 (1983) 70–80.

Lewy, H. *Sobria ebrietas. Untersuchungen zur Geschichte der antiken Mystik.* Giessen, 1929.

Leys, Roger. *L'Image de Dieu chez Grégoire de Nysse: Esquisse d'une doctrine.* Museum Lessianum, section théologique 49. Brussels-Paris, 1951.

Lohse, Eduard. 'Prosōpon', *TDNT* 6:768–779.

Longère, Jean. *Le prédication médiévale.* Paris, 1983.

Lorié, L.T. *Spiritual Terminology in the Latin Translations of the Vita Antonii.* Latinitas Christianorum Primaeva. Nijmegen, 1955.

Lortz, Josef (ed.). *Bernhard von Clairvaux. Mönch und Mystiker. Internationales Bernhardskongress Mainz 1953.* Wiesbaden, 1953.

Lossky, Vladimir. 'Études sur la terminology de saint Bernard', *Archivum latinitatis Medii Aevi* 17 (1942) 79–95.

——————. *In the Image and Likeness of God*. ET by John Erickson and Th. Bird. London-Oxford-Crestwood, 1975.

——————. *The Mystical Theology of the Eastern Church*. Crestwood, NY, 1976.

——————. *Orthodox Theology. An Introduction*. ET by J. Kesarcodi and I. Watson. Crestwood, New York, 1978.

Lot-Borodine, Myrrha. 'La doctrine de la "déification" dans l'Église grecque jusqu'au XIe siècle', *Revue d'Histoire des Religions*, 105–106 (1932) 5–43; 525–574; 107 (1933) 8–55.

——————. 'La béatitude dans l'Orient Chrétien', *Maison-Dieu* 15 (1950) 85–115.

Lottin, Odon. *Psychologie et morale au XIIe et XIIIe siècles*. Leuven-Gembloux, 1957–1960. Six volumes.

Lourdaux, Willem and Daniel Verhelst (eds.). *The Bible and Medieval Culture*. Mediaevalia Lovaniensia, Series I, Studia 7. Leuven, 1979.

Lucchesi-Palli, Elisabeth. 'Himmlischer Liturgie', *Lexikon der christlichen Ikonographie*, 3:103–106. Rome, 1971.

Lucet, Bernard. *La codification de 1212 et son évolution ultérieure*. Bibliotheca Cisterciensis 2. Rome, 1964.

Luchaire, Achille. *Innocent III*. Paris, 1905; rpt. 1969. Three volumes.

Luyckx, Theo. *Johanna van Vlaanderen en Henegouwen (1205–1244)*. Antwerp-Utrecht, 1946.

Luypen, William. *Existential Phenomenology*.Duquesne Studies. Philosophical Series 12, 3rd ed. Pittsburgh-Leuven, 1963.

Mahn, Jean-Berthold. *L'Ordre Cistercien et son Gouvernement dès origines au milieu du XIII siècles* (1098–1265). Paris, 1945.

Maiorino, Anna. 'La connaissance de soi chez Guillaume de Saint-Thierry', *RAM* 44 (1970) 145–160.

Mâle, Emile. *Religious Art in France: The Twelfth Century. A Study on the Origins of Medieval Iconography*. Bollingen Series 90,1. ET by E. Matthews. Princeton, 1978.

_____. *Religious Art in France: The Thirteenth Century. A Study on the Origins of Mediveal Iconography*. Bollingen Series 90,2. ET by E. Matthews. Princeton, 1985.

Malevez, Louis. 'La doctrine de l'image et de la connaissance mystique chez Guillaume de Saint-Thierry', *RSR* 22 (1932) 175–205, 257–279.

Malmberg, Felix. 'The Human Existence of Christ'. *A New Look of the Church: Readings in Theology*. 2nd ed. New York, 1963: 221–242.

Maloney, Raymond. 'The Mind of Christ in Transcendental Theology: Rahner, Lonergan and Crowe', *HJ* 25 (1984) 288-300.

Mandouze, André. 'L'Exstase d'Ostie', *AM* 1: 67–84.

Mann, William E. 'Simplicity and Immutability in God', *IPQ 23 (1983) 267–276.*

Manrique, Angelus. *Annales Cistercienses*. Lyons, 1642; rpt. Westmead, 1970. Four volumes.

Marchal, Jean. *Le 'Droit d'Oblat': Essai sur une variété de pensionnés monastiques*. Archives de la France monastique 49. Ligugé-Paris, 1955.

Maréchal, Joseph. *Studies in the Psychology of the Mystics*. ET by A. Thorold. London, 1927; rpt. Albany, New York, 1964.

Marenbon, J. 'A Florilegium from the *Periphyseon*', *RTAM* 47 (1980) 271–277.

Martelet, Gustave. 'Sur le motif de l'Incarnation'. *Problèmes de Christologie*. Edd. H. Bouëssé and J. Latour. Bruges-Paris, 1965: 35–80.

Martène, Edmundus and Ursinus Durand. *Thesaurus novus Anecdotorum*. Paris, 1717. Six volumes.

Martimort, Aimé-Georges (ed.). *L'Église en Prière: Introduction à la liturgie*. Paris-New York, 1961.

Mathon, Gérard. 'Un florilège érigénien à l'abbaye de Saint-Amand au temps d'Hucbald', RTAM 20 (1953) 302-311.

Mayeski, Mary Ann. 'Aelred of Rievaulx (1109–1167) and the Spiritual Life: A Study of the Influence of Anthropology on Theology'. Diss. Fordham University, 1974. Ann Arbor: University Microfilms, 1974.

Maxsein, Anton. '''Philosophia cordis'' bei Augustinus', AM 1: 357-371.

McDonnell, Ernest. *The Beguines and Beghards in Medieval Culture: With Special Emphasis on the Belgian Scene.* New Brunswick, New Jersey, 1954.

McEnvoy, James. 'The Absolute Predestination of Christ in the Theology of Robert Grosseteste'. *Sapientiae Doctrina.* Mélanges D. Bascourt. Leuven, 1980: 212–230.

McGinn, Bernard. *The Golden Chain. A Study in the Theological Anthropology of Isaac of Stella.* CS 15. Washington C.D., 1972.

——————. *Three Treatises on Man. A Cistercian Anthropology.* CS 24. Kalamazoo, 1977.

——————. 'Isaac of Stella and the Divine Nature', *AC* 29 (1973) 3–56.

——————. 'Pseudo-Dionysius and the Early Cistercians'. *One Yet Two.* Ed. M. B. Pennington (q.v.): 200–241.

——————. Introduction to *Bernard of Clairvaux: On Grace and Free Choice.* CS 19. Kalamazoo, 1977: 3–50.

——————. 'Resurrection and Ascension in the Christology of the Early Cistercians', *Citeaux* 30 (1979) 5–22.

McGuire, Brian Patrick. 'A Lost Clairvaux Exemplum Found: The *Liber visionum et miraculorum* compiled under Prior John of Clairvaux (1177–1179)', *AC* 39 (1983) 27–62.

Mechtild of Hackeborn. *Sanctae Mechtildis Virginis Ordinis Sancti Benedicti 'Liber specialis gratiae', accedit Sororis Mechtildis ejusdem ordinis 'Lux divinitatis',* Solesmensium monachorum cura et opera. Paris-Poitiers, 1877.

Meersseman, Gillis. 'Les Frères Prêcheurs et le mouvement dévot en Flandre au XIIIe siècle', *AFP* 18 (1948) 69–130.

Megivern, J.J. *Concomitance and Communion: A Study in Eucharistic Doctrine and Practice.* Studia Friburgensia, N.S. 33. Freiburg, 1963.

Mellinkoff, Ruth. *The Horned Moses in Medieval Art and Thought.* Berkeley-Los Angeles-London, 1970.

Mens, Alcantara. *Oorsprong en betekenis van de Nederlandse Begijnen-en Begardenbeweging.* Antwerp, 1947.

Metz, René. *La consécration des vierges dans l'Église romaine: Étude d'Histoire et de Liturgie.* Paris, 1954.

Meyer, Benjamin J. 'Did Paul's View of the Resurrection Undergo Development?', *TS* 47 (1986) 363-387.

Meyer, Charles R. 'The Life of the World to Come', *Chicago Studies* 24 (1985) 115-130.

Michel, Albert. 'Essence', *DThC* 5: 831-850.

—————. 'Gloire des élus', *DThC* 6: 1393-1426.

—————. 'Intuitive (Vision)', *DThC* 7: 2351-2394.

Michl, Johann. *Die katholischen Briefe*. Regensburger Neues Testament 8/2. Regensburg, 1968.

Mikkers, Edmund. 'Deux lettres inédites de Thomas chantre de Villers', *Coll* 10 (1948) 161-173.

—————. 'De Kerk als bruid in de hoogliedcommentaar van Sint Bernardus', *Sint Bernardus van Clairvaux*. Achel, 1953: 221-242.

Milis, Ludo. 'Guillaume de St. Thierry. Son origine, sa formation et ses premières expériences monastiques'. *Saint-Thierry: Une Abbaye du VIe au XXe siècle*. Saint Thierry, 1979: 261-279. ET by Jerry Carfantan, 'William of Saint Thierry, His Birth, His Formation, and His First Monastic Experiences'. *William Abbot of Saint Thierry*. Kalamazoo, 1987: 9-33.

Miller, John W. 'Depatriarchalizing God in Biblical Interpretation: A Critique', *CBQ* 48 (1986) 609-616.

Miraeus, Aubertus. *Chronicon Cisterciensis Ordinis*. Cologne, 1614.

Mohrmann, Christine. *Études sur le Latin des Chrétiens*. Rome, 1961-1977. Four volumes.

—————. 'Observations sur la langue et le style de saint Bernard', *SBOp* 2: ix-xxxiii.

Mols, Roger. 'Burgundio de Pise', *DGHE* 2: 1336-1339.

Mommaers, Paul. *Hadewijch: Visoenen: Vertaling en kommentaar. Tekstuitgave*. Spiritualiteit 15-15 supplement. Nijmegen-Bruges, 1979. Two volumes.

————— and N. De Paepe (eds.). *Jan van Ruusbroec. The Sources, Content and Sequels of His Mysticism*. Medievalia Lovaniensia, Series I, Studia 12. Leuven, 1984.

—————. 'Bulletin de l'histoire de spiritualité: L'École néerlandaise', *RAM* 49 (1973) 465-492.

_____. 'Het VIIe en VIIIe visioen van Hadewijch. Affectie in de mystieke beleving', *OGE* 49 (1975) 105–131.

_____. 'Der Mystiker und das Wort. Ein Einblick auf Hadewijch und Ruusbroec', *GL* 57 (1984) 4–12.

_____ and Frank Willaert. 'Mystisches Erlebnis und sprachliche Vermittlung in den Briefen Hadewijchs'. *Religiöse Frauenbewegung*. Edd. Dinzelbacher and Bauer (q.v.): 117–151.

Monti, Dominic. 'The Way Within: Grace in the Mystical Theology of William of Saint-Thierry', *Citeaux* 26 (1975) 31-47.

Moorman, J.R.H. *A History of the Franciscan Order from its Origin to the Year 1517*. Oxford, 1968.

Morel, G. *Offenbarungen der Schwester Mechtild von Magdeburg oder Das Fliessende Licht der Gottheit*. Regensburg, 1879; rpt. Darmstadt, 1963.

Morreal, John. 'Happiness and the Resurrection of the Body', *RSt* 16 (1980) 29-35.

Morris, Colin. *The Discovery of the Individual 1050-1200*. London, 1972.

Morson, John and Hilary Costello. 'The *liber amoris*', *Citeaux* 16 (1965) 114-135.

Moule, C. F. D. 'St Paul and Dualism', *NTS* 12 (1965-66) 106-123.

Müller, Gregor. 'Das Beguinenwesen, eine Abzweigung von den Cistercienserinnen?' *Cistercienser Chronik* 27 (1913) 33-41.

Neumann, Hans. 'Beiträge zur Text des "Fliessenden Licht des Gottheit" und zur Lebensgeschichte Mechtilds von Magdeburg'. *Altdeutsche und Altniederländische Mystik*. Ed. K. Ruh (q.v.): 175-239.

_____. 'Mechtild von Magdeburg und die mittelniederländische Frauenmystik', *Medieval German Studies: Festschrift für Frederic Norman*. London, 1965: 231-246.

Neuner, J. and J. Dupuis. *The Christian Faith in the Doctrinal Documents of the Catholic Church*. Westminster, Md, 1975.

Nichols, Aidan. *The Art of God Incarnate: Theology and Image in Christian Tradition*. London-New York, 1980.

Noonan, John T. *Contraception: A History of its Treatment by the Catholic Theologians and Canonists*. Cambridge, MA, 1966.

Norpoth, Leo. *Der Pseudo-augustinische Traktat de Spiritu et Anima: Erstmals gedruckt und anstelle einer Festschrift dem Autor zu seinem 70. Geburtstag am 14. April 1971 überreicht.* Cologne-Bochum, 1971.

Noschitzka, Canisius. 'Codex manuscriptus 31 universitatis Labacensis' *AC* 6 (1950) 1-124.

Nübel, O. *Mittelalterliche Beginen-und Sozialsiedlungen in den Niederlanden.* Tübingen, 1970.

Oexle, Otto Gerhard. 'Die Gegenwart der Toten'. *Death in the Middle Ages.* Edd. Braet and Verbeke (q.v.): 19-77.

O'Donovan, Daniel (trans.). *Bernard of Clairvaux: On Grace and Free Choice.* CF 19. Kalamazoo, 1977.

Ohly, Friedrich. *Hohelied-Studien: Grundzüge einer Geschichte des Hoheliedauslegung des Abendlandes bis um 1200.* Wiesbaden, 1958.

——————. 'Geistige Süse bei Gotfried', *Typologia Litterarum: Festschrift für Max Mehrly.* Zurich, 1969: 85-124.

Oppenheim, Philipp. *Die consecratio virginum as Geistesgeschichtliches Problem: Eine Studie zu ihrem Aufbau, ihrem Wert und ihrer Geschichte.* Rome, 1943.

Ortiz de Urbina, Ignacio. *Nicée et Constantinople.* Histoire des Conciles oecuméniques. Ed. G.Dumeige. Vol. 1. Paris, 1963.

—————— . 'Das Symbol von Chalkedon. Sein Text, sein Werden, seine Dogmatische Bedeutung'. *Das Konzil von Chalkedon. Edd. Grillmeyer and Bacht* (q.v): vol. 1: 873-923.

Ott, Ludwig. 'Das Konzil von Chalkedon in der Frühscholastik'. *Das Konzil von Chalkedon.* Edd. Grillmeier and Bacht (q.v.): vol. 2: 873-923.

Otto, St. *Gottes Ebenbild im Geschichtlichkeit.* Munich-Paderborn -Vienna, 1964.

Paris, Juliano. *Nomasticon Cisterciense.* Paris, 1664.

Partridge, Eric. *Origins: Etymological Dictionary of Modern English,* 2nd rev. ed. New York, 1959.

Pennington, M. Basil (ed.). *One Yet Two: Monastic Tradition East and West.* CS 29. Kalamazoo, 1976.

Pépin, Jean. '''Stilla aquae modica multo vino, ferrum ignitum, luce perfusa aer''. L'Origine de trois comparaisons familières à la théologie médiévale', *Divinitas* 11 (1967) 331-375.

_____. 'Saint Augustin et le symbole néoplatonicien de la vêture', *AM* 2: 293-303.

Perella, Nicolas J. *The Kiss Sacred and Profane: An Interpretative History of the Kiss Symbolism and Related Religio-Erotic Themes.* Berkeley-Los Angeles, 1969.

Peterson, Robert T. *The Art of Ecstasy.* London, 1970.

Philippart, Guy. 'L'Edition médiévale des legendiers latins dans le cadre d'une hagiographie générale', *Hagiography and Medieval Literature: A Symposium.* Odense, 1981: 127-165.

Philippen, L.J.M. *De Begijnhoven. Oorsprong, Geschiedenis, Inrichting.* Antwerp, 1918.

Phillips, Dayton. *Beguines in Medieval Strasbourg.* Stanford, CA, 1941.

Philomena, Mary. 'St.Edmund of Abingdon's Meditations before the Canonical Hours', *Ephemerides Liturgicae* 78 (1964) 33-57.

Picard, Michel-Jean. 'Croix (Chemin de)', *DSp* 2: 2575-2606.

Pieper, Josef. *About Love,* ET by A. and C. Winston. Chicago, 1974.

Pirenne, Henri. *Economic and Social History of Medieval Europe,* ET by E. G. Gregg. New York-London, 1937.

_____. *Histoire économique de l'Occident Médiéval.* Bruges, 1951.

Platelle, Henri. 'Le receuil de miracles de Thomas de Cantimpré et la vie religieuse dans les Pays-Bas et le Nord de la France au XIIIe siècle', *Actes du 97e Congrès National des Sociétés Savantes, Nantes 1972.* Paris, 1979: 469-498.

Plevnik, Joseph. 'The Taking up of the Faithful and the Resurrection of the Dead in I Thessalonians 4: 13-18', *CBQ* 46 (1984) 274-283.

Pollmann, Leo. *Die Liebe in der Hochmittelalterlichen Literatur Frankreichs: Versuch einer historischen Phänomenologie.* Analecta Romania 18. Frankfurt/M, 1966.

P[orion] Jean-Baptiste. *Hadewijch: Lettres Spirituelles. Béatrice: Sept degrés d'amour.* Geneva, 1972.

Powicke, F. M. *Walter Daniel's Life of Ailred, Abbot of Rievaulx, with the Letter to Maurice.* London-Toronto-New York, 1950.

Preuss, Hans D. 'Demuth', ET by J. Willis and G. Bromiley, TDOT 3: 257-260. Grand Rapids, MI, 1978.

Quasten, Johannes. *Patrology*. Utrecht-Antwerp-Westminster, MD, 1960. Three volumes.

Raciti, Gaetano. 'L'Autore del "De Spiritu et anima"', *Rivista di Filosofia Neo-Scholastica* 53 (1961) 392–394.

——————. 'Un opuscule inédit d'Adam de Perseigne: le Livre de l'Amour mutuel', *Citeaux* 31 (1981) 296-341.

Rahner, Hugo. *Greek Myths and Christian Mystery*, ET by E. James. London-New York, 1963.

——————. 'Die Gottesgeburt: Die Lehre der Kirchenväter von der Geburt Christi im Herzen des Gläubigen', *ZKT* 59 (1935) 33-418.

——————. 'Dreifaltigkeit', *LThK* 3: 548-554.

Rahner, Karl. 'Theos in the New Testament', *Theological Investigations,* vol. 1, ET by C. Ernst. London-Baltimore, 1961: 79-148.

——————. 'The Eternal Significance of the Humanity of Jesus for our Relationship with God'. *Theological Investigations*, 3, ET by K. and B. Kruger. London, 1967; rpt. New York, 1982: 35-46.

——————. 'Remarks on the Dogmatic Treatise *De Trinitate*'. *Theological Investigations*, 4, ET by K. Smyth. Baltimore-London, 1966: 77-102.

——————. 'On the Theology of the Incarnation'. *Theological Investigations* 4: 105-120.

——————. 'On the Duration of the Presence of Christ after Communion'. *Theological Investigations* 4: 312-320.

——————. 'Dogmatic Reflections on the Knowledge and Self-Consciousness of Christ'. *Theological Investigations*, 5, ET by H. Kruger. London-Baltimore, 1966: 193-215.

——————. 'The Hiddenness of God'. *Theological Investigations*, 16, ET by D. Morland. New York, 1979; rpt. 1983: 227-243.

——————. 'The Body in the Order of Salvation'. *Theological Investigations*, 17, ET by M. Kohl. London-New York, 1981: 71-89.

_____. 'The Intermediate State'. *Theological Investigations*, 17: 114-124.

_____. *The Christian Commitment*. ET by C. Hastings. New York, 1963.

_____. *Visions and Prophesies*. Quaestiones Disputatae 10. ET by Ch. Henckey and Richard Strachan. 3rd ed. New York, 1964.

_____. *The Trinity*, ET by J. Donceel. New York, 1970.

_____. 'Über Visionen und Verwandte Erscheinungen', *GL* 21 (1948) 179-213.

_____. 'Beatific Vision', *SM* 1: 151-153.

_____. 'Jesus Christ', *SM* 3: 192-209.

_____. 'Trinity, Divine', *SM* 6: 295-303.

Randall, Lillian. *Images in the Margins of Gothic Manuscripts*. Berkeley-Los Angeles-London, 1966.

Ratzinger, Joseph. *Eschatologie: Tod und ewiges Leben*. Kleine katholische Dogmatik 9. Edd. J.Auer and J.Ratzinger. 5th ed. Regensburg, 1978.

_____. 'Auferstehung und ewiges Leben', *Liturgie und Mönchtum* 25 (1959) 92-103.

_____. 'Is the Eucharist a Sacrifice?', *Concilium* 24. New York, 1967: 66-77.

Rayez, André. 'Influence du pseudo-Denys en Occident', *DSp* 3: 318-429.

Renckens, H. *The Religion of Israel*. ET by N. B. Smith. New York, 1966.

Renna, Thomas. 'The City in Early Cistercian Thought', *Citeaux* 34 (1983) 5-19.

_____. 'Virginité and Chastity in Early Cistercian Thought', *StM* 26 (1984) 43-54.

Reynaert, J[oris]. *Beeldspraak van Hadewijch*. Studiën en textuitgaven van Ons Geestelijk Erf 21. Tielt-Bussum, 1981.

_____. 'Attributie-problemen in verband met de ''Brieven van Hadewijch''', *OGE* 49 (1975) 225-247.

_____. 'Over Hadewijch naar aanleiding van drie recente publikaties', *OGE* 54 (1980) 280-292.

_____. 'Ruusbroec en Hadewijch', *OGE* 55 (1981) 193-232.

——————. 'Hoogheid en devotie in de Middeleeuwse Maatschappelijk'.*Handelingen van het wetenschappelijk colloquium te Brussel 21-24 oktober 1981.* Ed. J. D. Janssens. Brussels, 1982: 156-173.

Reypens, Leonce, and Joseph Van Mierlo. *Beatrijs van Nazareth: Seven Manieren van Minne.* Leuven, 1926.

——————. *Vita Beatricis: De Autobiografie van de Z. Beatrijs van Tienen O.Cist., 1200-1268.* Studiën en textuitgaven van Ons Geestelijk Erf 15. Antwerp, 1964.

——————. 'Ruusbroec-Studiën. Het mystieke "Gherinen"', *OGE* 12 (1938) 157-186.

——————. 'Sint Lutgards mystieke opgang', *OGE* 20 (1946) 7-49.

——————. 'Nog een dertiendeeuwse mystieke Cisterciënsernon', *OGE* 23 (1949) 225-246.

——————. 'Nieuws over Beatrijs van Nazareth: Ging Beatrijs school te Leuven?', *OGE* 26 (1952) 54-60.

——————. Een derde Beatrijs in onze dertiendeeuwse Letteren? Beatrijs van Dendermonde', *OGE* 37 (1963) 419-422.

Richstätter, Carl. *Die Herz-Jesu-Verehrung des deutschen Mittelalter.* Paderborn, 1919. Two volumes.

Riedlinger, Helmut. *Die Makellosigkeit der Kirche in den lateinischen Hoheliedkommentaren des Mittelalters.* Beiträge zur Geschichte der Philosophie und Theologie des Mittelalters 38/3. Munster/W, 1958.

——————. 'Von Weg des Glaubens zum Herrn der Zukunft'. *Jesus: Orte der Erfahrung Gottes.* Ed. B.Casper. Freiburg-Basel-Vienna, 1976: 237-247.

Ringler, Siegfried. *Viten-nd Offenbarungsliteratur in Frauenklöstern des Mittelalters: Quellen und Studien.* Münchener Texte und Untersuchungen zur deutschen Literatur des Mittelalters 72. Zurich-Munich, 1980.

——————. 'Die rezeption mittelalterlicher Frauenmystik als wissenschaftliches Problem, dargestelt am Werk der Christine Ebner'. *Frauenmystik im Mittelalter.* Edd. Dinzelbacher and Bauer (q.v.): 178-200.

Riou, Alain. *Le monde et l'Église selon Maxime le Confesseur.* Théologie historique 22. Paris, 1973.

Rode, Rosemarie. *Studien zu den mittelalterlichen Kind-Jesu-Visionen.* Diss. Frankfurt/M, 1957.

Rodriguez Lopez, L. *El Real Monasterio de Las Huelgas.* Burgos, 1907.

Roisin, Simone. *L'Hagiographie cistercienne dans le diocèse de Liége au XIIIe siècle.* Recueil de Travaux d'Histoire et de Philosophie. Series 3, fasc. 27. Leuven-Brussels, 1947.

_____. 'L'Efflorescence cistercienne et le courant féminin de piété au XIIIe siècle' *RHE* 39 (1943) 432-478.

_____. 'Réflexions sur la culture intellectuelle en nos abbayes Cisterciennes'. *Miscellanea L.Van der Essen.* Leuven-Brussels, 1947. 245-256.

Rombouts, E. and Norbert De Paepe. *Hadewijch. Strofische Gedichten.* Zwolle, 1961.

Rondet, H. 'Predestination', *SM* 5: 88-90.

Roques, René. 'Contemplation, exstase et ténèbres chez le pseudo-Denys', *DSp* 2: 1885-1911.

_____. 'Denys l'Aréopagite (Pseudo-)' *DSp* 2: 246-286.

Rousselot, Pierre. *Pour l'histoire du problème de l'Amour au Moyen Age.* Münster/W; rpt. Paris, 1933.

Ruh, K. *Altdeutsche und Altniederländische Mystik.* Darmstadt, 1964.

_____. *Abendländische Mystik im Mittelater: Symposium im Kloster Engelberg.* Stuttgart, 1986.

Russel, J. B. and Carl T. Berkhout. *Medieval Heresies: A Bibliography: 1960-1979.* Toronto, 1981.

Salet, Gaston. *Richard de Saint-Victor. La Trinité.* SCh 63. Paris, 1959.

Sartorius, Augustinus. *Verteutschtes Cistercium bis-tertium.* Prague, 1708.

Saward, John. *Perfect Fools: Folly for Christ's Sake in Catholic and Orthodox Spirituality.* Oxford-New York, 1980. [French translation: *Histoire des Saints fous pour le Christ.* Paris, 1983.]

Schaffner, Otto. 'Die "nobilis creatura" des hl. Bernhard von Clairvaux', *GL* 23 (1950) 43-53.

Schalij, J. M. 'Richard van St.Victor en Hadewijchs 10de brief', *TNTL* 62 (1943) 219-228.

Scheffczyk, Leo. 'God', *SM* 2: 381-390.

Schillebeeckx, Edward. 'Het Bewustzijnsleven van Christus', T*T* 1 (1961) 227-251.

Schiltz Edward. 'Aux sources de la théologie du mystère de l'incarnation. La Christologie de saint Augustin', *NRT* 12 (1936) 789-813.

Schmaus, Michael. *Katholische Dogmatiek*. Munich, 1953-1958. Eight volumes.

Schmidt. Karl. L. 'Basileia', *TDNT* 1: 578-591.

Schnackenburg, Rudolf. 'Basileia', *LThK* 2: 25-31.

Schneider, Bruno. 'Citeaux und die benediktinische Tradition' *AC* 16 (1960) 169-254; 17 (1961) 73-114.

Schneider, Fulgence. *L'Ancienne Messe Cistercienne*. Tilburg, 1929.

Scholem, Gershom. *Major Trends in Jewish Mysticism*. 8th ed. New York, 1974.

Schoonenberg, Piet. 'Continuïteit en herinterpretatie der Drieëenheidsleer', *TT* 14 (1974) 54-72.

Schreiber, Georg. 'Studien zur Exemptionsgeschichte der Zisterzienser, zugleich ein Beitrag zur Veronese Synode vom Jahre 1184', *Zeitschrift der Savigny-Stiftung für Rechtsgeschichte*, Kanonistische Abteilung 4 (1914) 74-116.

Schubart, Walter. *Religion und Eros*, 2nd ed. Munich, 1966.

Schultze, Bernhard. 'Zum Ursprung des Filioque' *OXP* 84 (1982) 5-18.

Schwartz, E. *Acta Conciliorum Oecumenorum*. Berlin-Leipzig, 1927-1940. Fourteen volumes.

Schweitzer, F. J. *Der Freiheitsbegriff der deutschen Mystik*. Frankfurt/M-Bonn, 1981).

Séjalon, Hugo. *Nomasticon Cisterciense*. Solesmes, 1892.

Senn, Frank C. 'The Lord's Supper, not the Passover Seder', *Worship* 60 (1986) 362-368.

Shahar, S. *Die Frau im Mittelalter*. ET by C. Galai. *The Fourth Estate. A History of Women in the Middle Ages*. London-New York, 1983.

Sherwood, Polycarpe. and André Rayez. 'L'Influence du Pseudo-Denys en Occident', *DSp* 3: 286-318.

Shoemaker, Sydney. *Self-knowledge and Self-Identity*. Ithaca-New York, 1963.

Simon, Monique. 'Le "face à face" dans les méditations de Guillaume de Saint-Thierry', *Coll* 35 (1973) 12-36.

Smalley, Beryl. 'Ecclesiastical Attitudes to Novelty, c.1100-1250'. *Church Society and Politics*. Ed. Derek Baker. Studies in Church History. London, 1975: 113-131.

Smelik, K. A. (ed.) *Jodendom: Bibliografie over het Jodendom en Israel voor het Nederlandse taalgebied*. The Hague, 1983.

Smith, Mark S. 'God Male and Female in the Old Testament: Yahweh and his "asherah" ', *TS* 48 (1987) 333-340.

Solignac, Aimé. 'Image et ressemblance dans la Patristique Latine', D*Sp* 7: 1406-1425.

_____. 'Ivresse spirituelle', D*Sp* 7: 2322-2337.

Somers, Herman. 'Image de Dieu et illumination divine: Sources historiques et élaboration augustinienne', A*M* 1: 450-462.

Southern, R. W. *Western Society and the Church in the Middle Ages*. The Pelican History of the Church. Harmondsworth, 1970.

Spaapen, Bernard. 'Hadewijch en het vijfde visioen' *OGE* 44 (1970) 7-44; 113-141; 353-404; 45 (1971) 129-178; 46 (1972) 113-196.

_____. 'Le mouvement des "Frères du libre esprit" et les mystiques flamands du XIIIe siècle', *RAM* 42 (1966) 423-439.

_____. 'Hebben onze 13de-eeuwse mystieken iets gemeen met de Broeders en Zusters van de vrije geest?', *OGE* 40 (1966) 369-431.

_____. 'Divertimento op het "nieuwheids"-motief in het werk van Hadewijch', *Handelingen van het XXIXe Vlaamse filologencongres*. Antwerp, 1973: 225-257.

_____. L'Imitation du Christ', D*Sp* 7: 2355-2368.

Spidlík, Thomas. 'Fous pour Dieu...en Orient', *DSp* 5: 751-761.

Staals, Frits. *Exploring Mysticism: A Methodological Essay*. Berkeley-Los Angeles-London, 1975.

Standaert, Maur. 'La doctrine de l'image chez St Bernard', E*TL* 23 (1947) 70-129.

_____. 'Le principe de l'ordination dans la théologie spirituelle de Saint Bernard', *Coll* 8 (1946) 178-216.

Stanks, Thomas D. 'The Eucharist: Christ's Self-communication in a Revelatory Event', TS 28 (1967) 27-50.

Stauffer, Ethelbert. 'Theos', in *TDNT*, vol.3, 94-119.

Steenwegen, Anton. 'De gelukz. Ida de Lewis of Ida van Gorsleeuw', OGE 57 (1983) 105-133; 209-244; 305-322.

Stracke, Désiré A. 'Arnulf van Leuven, O.Cist versus Gelukz. Hermann Jozef, O.Praem.', OGE 24 (1950) 27-90.

Strange, L. *Caesarii Heisterbachensis Monachi Dialogus Miraculorum.* Cologne-Bonn-Brussels, 1851. Two volumes.

Strätter, C. 'Het geheim van God: Drie personen, een natuur', *Bijdragen* 18 (1957) 243-259.

Stroick, Autbert. 'Der Verfasser und Quellen der *collectio de scandalis ecclesiae*', *Archivum Franciscanum Historicum* 23 (1930) 3-41; 273-299; 433-466.

_____. 'Ausgabe der Collectio', *Archivum Franciscanum Historicum* 24 (1931) 33-62.

Sullivan, J. E. *The Image of God : The Doctrine of S.Augustine and its Influence.* Dubuque, IA, 1963.

Szarmak, Paul. *Introduction to the Medieval Mystics of Europe.* Albany, NY, 1984.

Talbot, C. H. *Sermones inediti B. Aelredi Abbatis Rievallis.* Rome, 1952.

_____. 'The "De Institutione Inclusarum" of Ailred of Ricvaulx', AC 7 (1957) 167-217, rpt. CCCM 1, 637-682.

Taymans d'Eypernon, Fr. *Le mystère primordial: La Trinité dans sa vivante Image.* Museum Lessianum. Section théologique 41. Brussels-Paris, 1950.

Thomas, A. H. *De oudste constituties van de Dominicanen.* Leuven, 1965.

Thomas of Cantimpré, *Bonum universale de apibus.* Douai, 1605.

Thomas, J. L.H. 'The Identity of Being and Essence in God', HJ 27 (1986) 394-408.

Thomas, Robert. *Guillaume de S.Thierry: Oraisons méditées, pro manuscripto.* Chambarand, 1964. Two volumes.

_____. *Prière de Guillaume, pro manuscripto.* Chambarand, 1965.

_____. *Contemplation de Dieu, pro manuscripto.* Chambarand, 1965.

Thompson, Sally. 'The Problem of Cistercian Nuns in the Twelfth and Early Thirteenth Centuries'. *Medieval Women. Festschrift Rosalind M. Hill.* Ed. Derek Baker. Studies in Church History 7. Oxford, 1978: 227-252.

Thouzellier, Christine. *Cathérisme et Valdéisme en Languedoc à la fin du XIIe et au XIIIe siècle*, 2nd ed. Leuven-Paris, 1969.

Thurston, Herbert. *The Physical Phenomena of Mysticism* (J. H. Crehan, ed.). London, 1952.

Tissier, Bertrand. *Bibliotheca Patrum Cisterciensium*. Bellefontaine, 1660-1669. Eight volumes.

Tobey, J. L. *The History of Ideas: A Bibliographical Introduction*. Santa Barbara, CA-London, 1977.

Tomasic, Thomas M. 'Neoplatonism and the Mysticism of William of St.-Thierry', in P. Szarmack (ed.), *Introduction to the Medieval Mystics of Europe* (q.v.) 53-75.

Tribble, Phyllis. 'Depatriarchalizing in Biblical Interpretation', *Journal of the American Academy of Religion* 41 (1973) 30-44.

Tuozzi, Anna M. *La conoscenza di sè' nella scuola cistercense*. Naples, 1976.

Underhill, Evelyn. *Mysticism: A Study in the Nature and Development of Man's Spiritual Consciousness*, 10th ed. Cleveland-New York, 1963.

Unger, Dominic G.. 'Robert Grosseteste, Bishop of Lincoln (1235-1253): On the Reason for the Incarnation', *Franciscan Studies* 16 (1956) 1-36.

Vadjà, G. *L'Amour de Dieu dans la théologie juive du moyen-âge*. Paris, 1957.

Van Baest, M. J. *"Fiere herte doelt na minnen gronde"*: *De fierheid als kernmoment in het zelfverstaan van Hadewijch*. Tilburg, 1984.

Van Caster, G. 'Notice historique sur Waelhem et de l'ancienne abbaye de Roosendaal', *Bulletin du Cercle Archéologique de Malines* 2 (1891) 249-270.

van Cranenburgh, Henri. 'Hadewijchs twaalfde visoen en negende strofisch gedicht: Een proeve van tekstverklaring', *OGE* 36 (1961) 361-384.

Van Damme, Jean-Baptiste. 'Les pouvoirs de l'Abbé de Cîteaux au XIIe et XIIIe siècles', *AC* 24 (1968) 47-85.

Van den Bosch, Amatus. 'Pourquoi l'Incarnation du Fils, non d'une autre personne de la Trinité?' *Citeaux* 9 (1958) 99-104.

_____. 'Présupposés à la Christologie bernardine', *Citeaux* 9 (1958) 5-17; 85-105.

_____. 'Le Mystère de l'Incarnation chez Saint Bernard', *Citeaux* 10 (1959) 85-92; 165-177; 245-267.

Vandenbroucke, François. 'Fous pour le Christ...en Occident', *DSp* 5: 761-770.

Van der Vet, W. A. *Het Biënboek van Thomas van Cantimpré en zijn Exempelen*. The Hague, 1902.

Van der Woudt, A. S. 'Angesicht'. *Theologisches Handwörterbuch zum Alten Testament*. Edd. Jenni and Westermann. Vol. 1: 432-460.

van der Zeyde, Marie-Héléne. *Hadewijch: Een studie van de mens en de schrijfster*. Groningen-The Hague-Batavia, 1934.

Van de Walle, Ambrose Remy. *From Darkness to the Dawn: How Belief in the Afterlife Affects Living*, ET by John Bowden. Mystic, Ct. 1984.

Van Doninck, Benedict. *Obituarium Monasterii Loci Sancti Bernardi S.Ord.Cister. 1231-1900*. Lérins, 1901.

Van Engen, John. 'Rupert of Deutz and William of St. Thierry', *RBén* 93 (1983) 327-336.

Van Hoecke, William and Andries Welkenhuyse (eds). *Love and Marriage in the Twelfth Century*. Mediaevalia Lovaniensia. Series I, Studia 8. Leuven, 1981.

Van Mierlo, Joseph. 'Hadewijch. Une mystique flamande du treizième siècle, *RAM* 5 (1924) 269-289; 380-404.

_____. 'Béguines. Histoire du mot', *DSp*. 1: 1341-1343.

_____. 'Over het ontstaan der Germaansche Mystiek', *OGE* 1 (1927) 11-37.

_____. 'Hadewijch en Willem van St.-Thierry', *OGE* 3 (1929) 45-59.

_____. 'De "Minne" in de Strophische Gedichten van Hadewijch,' *VMKVA* 1941, 687-705.

_____. His critical edition of Hadewijch's writings is cited in this Bibliography under: Primary Sources A.2.

Vanneste, Jan. 'La théologie mystique du Pseudo-Denys l'Aréopagite'. *Studia Patristica*, 5: 401–415. Berlin, 1962.

————————. 'Is the Mysticism of Pseudo-Dionysius genuine?' *IPQ* 3 (1963) 286-303.

Vanneste, R. 'Over de betekenis van enkele abstracta in de taal van Hadewijch', *Studia Germanica* 1 (1959) 9-95.

Van Parijs, Moral. 'Exégèse et théologie dans les livres contre Eunome de Grégoire de Nysse' in Harl (ed.), *Ecriture et culture* (q.v.) 111-126.

van Schaick, Peter S. 'Le coeur et la tête. Une pédagogie par l'image populaire', RAM 50 (1974) 457-478.

Van Schoors, J. *Ida van Leuven*. Diss., Leuven, 1983.

Vawter, Bruce. *On Genesis: A New Reading*. Garden City, NY, 1977.

————————. 'The Johannine Epistles'. *The Jerome Biblical Commentary*. Edd. Brown, Fitzmeyer, Murphy (q.v.): 404-413.

Vekeman, Hermann W. *Seuen Manieren van Minne: Lexicografisch Onderzoek*. Diss. Leuven, 1967. Two volumes.

————————. and J. J. Tersteeg. Th. *Beatrijs van Nazareth. Van Seuen Manieren van Heiliger Minne*. Zutfen, 1970.

————————. *Visioenenboek van Hadewijch*. Nijmegen-Bruges, 1980.

————————. 'Minne in de "Seuen manieren van Minne" van Beatrijs van Nazareth', *Citeaux* 19 (1968) 284-316.

————————. 'Vita Beatricis en Seuen Manieren van Minne. Een vergelijkende studie', *OGE* 46 (1972) 3-54.

————————. 'Van seuen Manieren van heiliger Minne. Exstase en traditie in een cultus van de Minne', *TNTL* 88 (1972) 172-199.

————————. 'Hadewijch. Een interpretatie van de Brieven I, II, XXVIII, XXIX als dokumenten over de strijd rond de wezensmystiek', *TNTL* 91 (1975) 337-366.

————————. 'De Ontrouwe maakt ze diep. Een nieuwe interpretatie van het vijfde visioen van Hadewijch', *De Nieuwe Taalgids* 71 (1978) 385-409.

————————. 'Panorama du mysticisme moyen-néerlandais', *Septentrion* 10 (1981) 24-31.

Verbeke, Gérard. 'Connaissance de soi et connaissance de Dieu chez Saint Augustin', *Augustiniana* 4 (1954) 495-515.

Verdeyen, Paul. 'La Théologie mystique de Guillaume de Saint-Thierry', *OGE* 51 (1977) 327-366; 52 (1978) 152-178; 257-295; 53 (1979) 129-220; 321-404.

_____. 'De invloed van Willem van St. Thierry op Hadewijch en Ruusbroec', *OGE* 51 (1977) 3-19.

Verdon, Jean. 'Les moniales dans la France de l'Ouest aux XIe et XIIe siècles. Étude d'histoire sociale', *Cahiers de Civilisation médiévale* 19 (1976) 247-263.

Vicaire, M. D. *Saint Dominique and his Time*. New York-Toronto-London, 1964.

Völker, Walther. *Gregor von Nyssa as Mystiker*. Wiesbaden, 1955.

Von Balthasar, Hans. *Présence et pensée: Essai sur la philosophie religieuse de Grégoire de Nysse*. Paris, 1942.

Von E. Scott, H. and C. C. Swinton Bland. *The Dialogue on Miracles: Caesarius of Heisterbach (1220-1235)*. London, 1929. Two volumes.

Von Ivánka, Endre. *Plato christianus*. Einsiedeln, 1964.

Von Rad, Gerhard. *Genesis*, ET by J.H. Marks. London, 1961.

Von Wiese, B and H. Borck (eds.). *Festschrift für Jost Trier*. Meisenheim, 1954.

Von Wunderli, P. (ed.). *Der kranke Mensch im Mittelalter und Renaissance*. Studia humaniora 5. Düsseldorf, 1986.

Vorgrimmler, Herbert. *Hoffnung und Vollendung: Aufriss der Eschatologie*. Quaestiones disputatae 91. Freiburg, 1980; 2nd ed. Freiburg, 1984.

Walgrave, Jan. *Person and Society: A Christian View*. Duquesne Studies. Theological Series 5. Philadelphia, PA, 1965.

Walker Bynum, Caroline. *Jesus as Mother: Studies in the Spirituality of the High Middle Ages*. Berkeley-Los Angeles-London, 1982.

_____. 'Maternal Imagery in the Twelfth-century Cistercian Writings'. *Noble Piety and Reformed Monasticism*. Ed. E. R. Elder (q.v.): 183-199.

_____. 'Women Mystics and Eucharistic Devotion in the Thirteenth Century', *Women's Studies* 11 (1984) 179-214.

Walsh, James. 'Guillaume de Saint-Thierry et les sens spirituels' *RAM* 35 (1959) 27-42.

Walther, Gerda. *Die Phänomenologie der Mystic*, 2nd rev.ed. Olten-Freiburg/Br., 1955.

Wapnick, Kenneth. 'Mysticism and Schizophrenia', *Journal of Transpersonal Psychology* 1 (1969) 49-68.

Ward, Benedicta. 'The Desert Myth: Reflections on the Desert Ideal in Early Cistercian Monasticism'. *One Yet Two*. Ed. M. B. Pennington (q.v.): 183-199.

Warnach, Victor. 'Symbol and Reality in the Eucharist', *Concilium* 40 (New York, 1969) 82-106.

Wasselynck, René. 'La présence des *Moralia* de saint Grégoire le Grand dans les ouvrages de morale du XIIe siècle', *RTAM* 35 (1968) 197-240; 36 (1969) 31-45.

Webb, Geoffrey. *An Introduction to the Cistercian* De Anima. London, 1932, rpt. 1971.

Weinand, Heinz G. *Tränen: Untersuchungen über das Weinen in der deutschen Sprache und Literatur des Mittelalters*. Bonn, 1958.

Weisweiler, Henry. 'Die Ps.-Dionysiuskommentare "In Coelestem Hierarchiam" des Scotus Eriugena und Hugos von St. Viktor', *RTAM* 19 (1952) 26-47.

Wenzel, Siegfried. *The Sin of Sloth: Acedia in Medieval Thought and Literature*. Chapel Hill, NC, 1960.

Wetter, Friedrich. *Die Lehre Benedikts XII. von intensiven Wachstum der Gottesschau*. Analecta Gregoriana 92. Rome, 1958.

White, Victor. *God and the Unconscious*. London, 1952.

──────────. (ed.). *The Highest State of Consciousness*. New York, 1972.

Wilbers, Kenneth. 'The Developmental Spectrum and Psychiatry', *Journal of Transpersonal Psychology* 16 (1984) 137-166.

Wildiers, N. Max. *Wereldbeeld en Teologie: Van de Middeleeuwen tot Nu*. Antwerp-Amsterdam, 1977. ET by P. Dumphy, *The Theologian and his Universe: Theology and Cosmology from the Middle Ages to the Present*. New York, 1982.

Willaert, Frank. *De Poëtica van Hadewijch in de Strofische Gedichten*. Utrecht, 1984.

──────────. 'Is Hadewijch de auteur van de XXVIIIe Brief?, *OGE* 54 (1980) 26-38.

_____. 'Hadewijch und ihr Kreis in den "Visionen" '. *Religiöse Frauenbewegung.* Edd. Dinzelbacher and Bauer (q.v.): 368-387.

Williams, D. H. 'The Seal in Cistercian Usage with Special Reference to Wales'. *Mélanges Anselme Dimier.* Ed. B. Chauvin (*q.v.*). Vol. 3: 249-257.

Williams, Watkin. *Monastic Studies.* Manchester, 1938.

Wilmart, André. *Auteurs spirituels et textes dévots du Moyen Age latin.* Paris, 1932, rpt., 1971.

Winkler, Klaus. 'La théorie augustinienne de la mémoire à son point de départ', *AM* 1: 511-519.

Winter, Gabriele. 'Die Herz-Jesu-Mystik bei Mechtild von Magdeburg, Mechtild von Hackeborn and Gertrud von Helfta', *Jahrbuch für salesianische Studien* 17 (1984) 72-82.

Wiseman, James. *'Minne' in 'Die Gheestelicke Brulocht' of Jan van Ruusbroec.* Diss. Washington D.C. -Microfilms International, Ann Arbor, MI-London, 1981.

_____. John Ruusbroec: *The Spiritual Espousals and Other Works.* New York-Toronto, 1985.

Wolfskeel, C. W. 'Some Remarks with Regard to Augustine's Concept of Man as the Image of God', *Vigiliae Christianae* 30 (1976) 63-71.

Woods, Richard (ed.). *Understanding Mysticism.* Garden City, NY, 1980.

Wulff, Fredrich. and Emmanuel Walberg (eds.). *Vers de la mort par Hélinand, moine de Froidmont.* Paris, 1895, rpt. New York-London, 1965.

Zimmermann, Gerd. *Ordensleben und Lebensstandard: Die Cura corporis in den Ordensvorschriften des Abendländischen Hochmittelalters.* Beiträge zur Geschichte des alten Mönchtums und des Benediktinerordens 33. Münster/W, 1973.

Zwingmann, Wolfgang. *'Ex affectu mentis.* Über die vollkommenheit menschlichen Handelns und menschlicher Hingabe nach William von St. Thierry', *Citeaux* 18 (1967) 5-37.

_____. *'Affectus illuminati amoris.* Über das Offenbarwerden der Gnade und die Erfahrung von Gottes beseligender Gegenwart', *Citeaux* 18 (1967) 353-369.

INDEX OF NAMES

ANALYTICAL INDEX

252, to remember his passion stirs pain 253–54, brings joy 265, 267, his humanity created by Trinity 67, called creator 67, his grace 162–64, his heart 413, to be loved for his sake 530, preferably looked at in his divinity 531–32, which prevails 532–35 (*see* Blood, Eucharist, Following Christ, Hypostatic Union, Incarnation, Lamb, Marks)

Christlike: 290, 293, 470, 483

Cistercian nuns: density in Belgium and Germany 10–20, 184, 317, 326–27, protected by Citeaux' strength 184, are fond of freed will 196, some are mediocre nuns 317, receiving Communion 326- 27 (*see* Mulieres religiosae)

Christianity: a difficult religion 226

City: C of love 375, the supreme C 508–09, the heavenly C 527, 591

Clairvoyance: 303–04, 449

Clerics: 350–51

Compassion/ com-passion: 261–65, 296–97, 412

Completion of fulfillment: found in God alone 467

Confessors: 350

Confidence: (*see* Trust)

Conformity: C to Christ necessary in everything 183, 293, how to arrive at C.? 197, perfect C only in heaven 208, to live and to suffer in C with Christ 274, C leads to trans formation 373–74, 481, through C of will arrive at union with God 485–86, C weds to God 508

Consciousness: as creature man has C 74–75, makes him great 75, brings soul to C of her dignity 109, its voice is Christ's vicar 116, is present to God's image 124, religious C 132- 33, 138–39, total purification of C 146, God's glance penetrates C 157, 160, the house of pure C 164, 176, 179, widening of C 179, free C in harmony with God 203, C of Christ's passion 254, expanded C 383, 404, ecstasy in spirit is radical change of C 408

Consecration: 318–19 (*see* Eucharist)

Consent: helps to judge oneself 110, and *liberum arbitirum* 118, to C to God's grace is to be saved 63, 114, 205, cooperative receptivity 403, C needed for rapture at least in beginning 406

Consummation: 358 (*see* Fulfillment)

Contemplation: 58, 99, 129, memory as seat of C 132–34, 153, 217, sleep of C 242, 412–14, C of God's love 272, of God's perfection 359–60, ecstasy of C 407, 411–14, infused C 436, contemplative heart 458–59, to insist on C 493

Contempt: 32–39, to suffer C 274, 290, requested for love's sake 377

Covenant: of faithfulness 45

Creation: reflects God's beauty 37, man central in C 65, C is orderly, 69–76; care for C is man's service 69–72, C of the human body 72–74; C of man 74–76, his archetype 77–78, C provides man's analogical knowledge of God 126, man's C by Trinity 269–70 (*see* Archetype)

Cura animarum: 18–21

Dancing: 373 (*see* Tripudium)

Darkness: D of God's incomprehensibility 56, D of unconsciousness 175, total D 280, finding consolation in D of adversity 291, D of death 382, D and light as opposites 116, D way to light 386

Death: God wants conversion of sinner, not his D 140, protest against D 152, 173, gates of D 190, not feared 178–90, agony of bitter D 273, shudder of D 273, dreaded sleep 411, D frees from body 283, D hailed 171, as liberation and entrance into glory 145, 170–72, 173, 176, 176, 178, desire for D is not escape 271–72, is happy migration to life 171, 172, 514–15, D is immediate union with God 178, birth to life 513–29, D alters body 524–25

Deification: 97, 99, process of D 107, Eucharist and D 313, 490

Delight: Desire is source of suffering and D 363, heavenly D 500, 504, flood of D 578, 363, 578

Depression: integration of D. needed 377–78, D of dark night 386

Desert: as metaphor of exile 282 (*see* Exile)

Desire: D for peace 153, for fulfillment 155, D to increase God's grace 163, in classical Latin 355, burning D 358–70, sentimentality in D is frivolous 350, illuminating 358, dimensions of D 55, 58–59, 358, leads to love 359, is test for loving God 359, affects the whole person 360, wounds 362, is required 362, D of heart 363, hunger and thirst for God 363–66, burns for God 367, for union with God 368, affects body 368–71, desired burning 371–96, is long process 375–76, a heavy burden 377–79, distrusted 383, fever of D 394, is impetuous flight to God 476, with 'wings' 476, purified D 492, D to have fruition 562, seeks consumation 576, insatiable D 387–89 (*see* Orewoet)

Despair: 144, 168, 280, 389, utter D 386, D caused by unlikeness 193, 383

Devil: D cannot stand a woman re-acting 36, is wicked 113, strives to become as God 113, uses ingeniousness and whispers 176, is not feared 178, D is as cruel as *Minne* 379, 449, 604

Diem festum agere (=celebration) 135, 500

Dignity: man's intellect and freedom are his D 34, his upright posture shows his D 73, his D is created 75, 135, 139–41, equivalents 139, his D is his free will 195, its core 210, to share in the Son's sonship 223 (*see* Consciousness)

Dilation: 404

Distress: 182–83, 376

Distrust: unintegrated D 178, noble D 383

Donatists: 97

Drugs: 404

Ecstasy: 111, 165, 208, 239, coming back from E is distressing 284–85, 330, 393, related to Eucharist 317–18, 224, 327, 330, 383, 393, E and visions 397–452, 12th cent. E 401–02, E and *excessus* 404–05, samples of E and *excessus* 406–07, Two kinds: in or beyond the spirit 408–09, E in the spirit leaves room for imagination 409–10, the bride's E 411, 414–15, is curious type of sleep 411, E of contemplation 417–18, age of ecstatics 427–28, duration of E 432, 524, 531, 563 (*see* Beatific vision, E and visions)

Ecstatic movement: 429–32

Egocentricity: 180, E excluded from *Minne* 385, 427, 486–87 (*see* self-centeredness)

Elevation: as *sublevatio* 404

Elevation of Eucharist: 318–21, 324

Elongation: 258, 370

Embraces: Confidently to approach the E of the Word 115, E are sweet 148, 160, 206, 237–42, 266, to suffer is to experience Christ's E 291, to E all 296, E in Eucharist 324–25, 484, E express comfort and confidence 500, other verbs used to express E 503, E of love 504, 567 (*see* Kisses, Eroticism)

Enclosure: 10, 15–15, E of the heart 179, 327

Enlightenment: 166–67, 423, 502

Epecstasis: What E is 569–70, E and Gregory of Nyssa 570–72, Augustine 572–74, Bernard 575–77, William 577–79, Hadewijch 582–85, *Mulieres religiosae* 585–90

Eroticism: 237–40, 483, 500–01

Eucharist: 154–55, 238–39, 247, 253, the Eucharist 307–42 is memorial 307, Christ's true presence in E 308, is aqueduct of love 308–09, transsubstantiation done by Trinity 309–10, is sacrament, price of redemption, treasure, food, refuge 310, is medicinal 313, Christ's true humanity and divinity 312–13, mutual eating 313, every week in communitarian meal 314, a com-union 315, instituted primarily to be consumed, not to be contemplated 316, E and feminism 317–18, highpoints of eucharistic celebration: consecration 318–21, and reception 321–32, 491, pschosomatic phenomena 327–32, stories about receiving Communion 332–33, recieving the E ceremoniously 335–36, E and Trinity 338–39, mysticum sacramentum 349 (*see* anorexia, pyx)

Eye: of the heart 33, love is an E 62, Love and reason, the two E 63–64, E of reason 537, E of the soul 116, is censor and arbiter 116, memory as E 134, focused E 198, the inner E 451, naked E 542, of pure heart 566, the mind's E 587

Excessus: 403–05, difference between ecstasy and E. 406–07, is beyond the spirit 408–09, E compared to sleep 412, interpreted as vision 418–27, is beyond conceptualization 418–27, 488, 493, 522, 524, 532, 539, is not beatific vision 552, 561 (*see* ecstasy)

Exemplar: 82, 99, 103, 556 (*see* Archetype)

Exemplum: as literary genre 119

Exile: to be on earth is E 177, 272, 279, 280–81, metaphors with similar meanings 282–83, state of E 388, 433, life is passing through E 628, 588 (*see* Sufferings)

Exinariri (empty oneself): 205, 209

Experience: of God's darkness and light 50, of God 58, 64 of God's grace 155

Fainting: 326–31, 368, 412–13

Faculties: Three F of reason, will, memory 126–31, 464, 538 (*see* trinity (analogical)

Faith: F in God's transcendence 44, anchored in God's love as Trinity 48, support of reason 60, to rely on F 168, strength of F 207, Christianity requires F 226, strong F 272, 294, 324, leads to knowledge 359, is understanding, 359, 501, not subject to scientific proofs 511, deficient F 533

Faithful: to self and God 93, 155, 158, 199–200, faithful in every service 362, 465, 501, 576, F received from God 386

Fall of Christ: into humanity 227, 269 (*see* Incarnation)

Fall of man: 96, 101, 112

Fear: 168, desire to die but not of F 373, why F of God? 177–78, neurotic F of dying without union with God 178, 202, when all F is gone 188, F of God 193, 199, F driven away by love 193, 199, 201–02, F of death 262, F after ecstasy 285, F of emotions 356, burdened with F 386, law of servants 531, unwarranted F 202, 511, 604

Feminine touch: 185–86

Fever: 382, F of desire 316, 394, 417

Fidelity: 137–38, 183

Filioque: 49

Fire: love sets afire 367, God is inextinguishable F 391, F of love 394, 502–03

Following Christ: 40, 94, till the likeness becomes restored 106, F X entreaded 183, 185, 250, Following Christ 269–306: brings union with God 270, is done in humility, obedience and love 271–72, X as the way 273–74, reason stresses inequality 275, X humanized the human miseries 276, they now bear his stamp 278, F X in exile and service 279, negligence in F X 286, F X in insults 287–88, F X in his love 293, implies to care for neighbor's needs 294–403 (*see* Christ, vicissitudes)

Foretaste: of celestial sweetness 363, 511, F of fruition 566, 605

Frauenfrage: 2–3

Freedom: is gift and risk 47, needed for salvation 84, makes one God's collaborator or partner 86, misuse of F looses God's likeness 96, man can use or misuse his F 109, his consent determines his responsibility 110, as does his use of *liberum arbitrium* 110, free choice defines his responsibility 110, Root of dialogue in love lies in God 110–15, three states of F 112–14, free choice makes us willers 113, free willing merely capable of receiving salvation 114, liberty is linked with rational nature of the soul 118, man can obtain F from sin 141, use of F leads to increase of grace 160, metaphysical F respected by God 168, F from and F for 169–70, 172, F in heaven desired 170–72, inner purification is important for F 175–76, keeping free from sin 176, F from fear 178–79, pure heart is F for 179, loftiness of mind frees one from oneself 186, total F requested 186, to accept totally and freely God's will 188, F leads to common will 194–97, a freed will opens gate for recovery of lost likeness 196, love frees 202-04, F at times maltreated in ecclesiastical circles 204, longing to be freed from exile on earth 282–83, F from within 283; F of love for oneself's sake 457 (*see* conscience, self-will)

Frugality: 24–26, 174

Fruition: 145, 155, desired 359, 363, 416, 469, to be here without F 375, 368, 375, F in union with God 416, 422, 425, 327, 460–61, 474, 495, F cannot be explained 500, 505, 532, God's F 552–56, 583–90 (*see* Epecstasis)

Frustration: feeling of God's absence is F 356–57, love of desire causes F 359, 363

man his free choice 110, L is God's birthplace and nobility 136, God is L but not necessarily only God 142, L practiced by virtues 195, what God is 202, his L consumes and unites 206, cannot be completely enjoyed in exile 281 (*see* Minne)

Love (human): true L more related to heart than body 27, L conquers body 61–63, is mutual 47, cannot be forced 104, can stand suffering 137, 207, 278, is hell 178, 189, L is without fear 201–03, L is stronger than fear 202, L does not fear God 202, has no fear of God's judgments 202–03, is knowledge 207, total L for God required 276, to love oneself for God's sake 189, gratuitous and enjoined L 462–64, to court God 464, soul is daughter of L 475, falling asleep in L 504, burning desire 355–70, desired burning in L 371–91 (*see* Love [divine], *Minne*, *Orewoet*)

Madness: feigned M 264, suspected of M 322, M and Eucharist 322, 331, to be demented as part of purification 378, 383, 389, M of love 391, unfamiliar M 394, spiritual or holy M 395, almost mad 586

Man: paradisiacal M 93, 138, created out of love 34, M's intellect and freedom give him greatness and make him precious, wonderful and miserable 31–35, *mensch* includes both sexes 37–37, his human condition 39, M's centrality in creation 65, creation of M 74–76, is reasonable animal 77, 93, created to God's image and likeness 76–124, his nobility, dignity, purity 135–46, not all men similarly gifted 136, natural and gratuitous gifts 151–211, man only a man 375, shares in the Son's Sonship 96, 534, his pre-existence 533, his incomprehensibility 537 (*see* freedom, hunman condition, image, identity with God, likeness)

Marks of passion (*stigmata*): 252, 256–59, 262, 399, 406, 440, crucifixion complex 259

Marriage: 27 (*see* spiritual marriage)

Meditation: 58, 89, 217, 229, 235, 242, M on Christ's passion 255, 260–61, fervent M 440, constant M 513, attending to M 561 (*see* privacy)

Melting: (*see* liquefactio)

Memory: 126–28, attending M 131–35, M of Christ's passion 253–54, 518

Migrate: from exile to fatherland 284, 525, 528, M to heaven right after death 567 (*see* death)

Minne (Love): frugality out of M 24, drives fear away 201, M is unchangeable and astonishing 369, M acts riotously in body also 369, fulfillment by M impossible here 372, M for God alone 375, M scrubs thoroughly 374–75, M requires all 376–79, is more cruel than the devil 379, M's highest name: hell 179, 188, 202, 384–85, M 453–

Stigmata: 200 (*see* marks)

Struggle: gift from God 179, 187, to be disturbed by S 387

Sublevatio: inferior to *alienatio* 401, 404

Suicide: 383

Suffering: of all things with equal love 186, 188, S obedience 145, as Christ did 241, 263, 266, 276, S from weariness in present life 281, as Christ exprienced 286, S sought 288–89, to endure S is gift to Christ 291, spiritual S 297–98, S for neighbor 300, vicarious S 301, S needed for *Minne's* sake 375–77, S purifies 393, desire is source of S and delight 363, 368, S many a night by day as Christ did 385–86, S for the deceased 503, S 583 (*see* exile, vicissitudes)

Surrender: Christ did it in all things and at all times 137, 272–73, *Minne* requests ultimate S 385

Sweetness (dulcedo, *suavitas*): 323–24, does not always come from God 355–56

Sword: S of love 300 (*see* arrow, javelin)

Tears: 242, 285, 296, 324, 362, 388, T of joy 501, 531

Television (charism): 305–06

Temptation: part of human condition 39, gift from God 39, purifies 168, 386, T requested 376–77, T remedied by Eucharist 311, *Excessus* cuts T off 411, T a blessing in disguise 488

Terminology: fluidity in T 82, 99, 102–03, 103, 124, 155, 241, 402, 509

Thanksgiving: for graces received 159–60, 124, 178, 235–36, for Eucharist 312, to love God if only by desire 358, 388 (*see* praise)

Thunder: T is incarnation of Son 229, signifies human condition 166, *Minne's* voice is T 458

Time: T flows by when love is dominant 201, eschatological end of T 225, Christ's incarnation 'relaxed' T 227, timelessness after death 514–15, 518–22

Touches: God T man's interior senses 404, T of the Holy Spirit 417, 478

Transformation: (*see* restoration)

Transsubstantiation: effected by Trinity 30–9, when? 318

Trichotomy: 103, 403

Trinity: One God in three Persons 45–48, 126–27, all three equal 51–52, T is absolute Being 48, hard to define 49–51, formulation of Lateran Council IV (1215) 52, best known by unknowing 53, T and Mulieres religiosae 57–65, is Mystery 60–61, its veil partially lifted by incarnation 61, is always and unchangeable 67–68, 76, made the incarnation to happen 126–27, 221, also the transsubstantiation 309, visions of the T 424–27, not seen directly 439–40, *regiratio* 563–64. (*see* Minne)

Trinity (analogical) Augustine's psychological T 95, 126, is metaphor or analogy? 127, created T 127, 132, and *Mulieres religiosae* 129–32

Tripudium (dance): 266, 323–24, 373, 389–90

Troubadours: 69, 473, 498

Trust: T in God's promise 168, 292–93, T God who has the last word 377, to T in God 383, vested T 383–84, T when in deep waters 388, T in loving God without reward 467, complete T 505

Truth: enlightens the mind 145, 367, the way of T 155, the path of T 167, enjoyment of T 273, 367, light of T 377, sweetness of T 479, heavenly T 561

Union with God: desired at moment of death 171, 186–90, to become one spirit with God 195, 205–06, 208, realizable through Christ 211, 233, 239, 247, Christ's humanity and passion show way to U 269–70, the human situation and the Creator point to U 276, U is the other-in-me 211, desire for U 368, arriving at U 383, experienced as *excessus* 418–27, love of God is the uniting factor 474, brings forgetfulness of everything else 478, is *minne's* objective 480, U now 481–510, exemplified in the God-man 482, is communion of wills and accord in charity 486–87, 495, expressed by embraces and kisses 501–08, great vision of U 508–10, U forever 511–97, *recursus* 519–20, timeless U 529 (*see* Bond, Christ as mediator, *regiratio*, *epecstasis*)

Unitas spiritus: 107, 123, sought by *Mulieres religiosae* 137, 207, includes impossibility of slightest unlikeness 208, 210, U of likeness 487, 496, 507–10, 540

Unlikeness: dissimitude of likeness to God 105, the land of U is foreign country 114, U 116–17, 190, 508, return from U 127, U made by sin 193, U is what is only in part 508, 540 (*see proprium, unitas spiritus*)

Unus spiritus: from 1 Cor 6:17 derived 485, to see God *sicuti est* 542–44

Vainglory: 180, 288, 329, 442

Valley: 285, 438 (*see* humility, misery)

Veins: 322–3, 369, 383, 393, 475, 582

Vices: 153, 175, pride the queen of all V 175, 298, seeds of V 474

Vicissitudes: 176, 185, 187, 199, V of Christ 273, 278–79, 289- 91, 294, V needed and desired 375–82, the experience of alternate presences and absenses of God creates V 382, 386- 87, 388–95, 416, 457, 583, 601

Virginity: 26–30, 484

Virtues: V required by liberty of grace/counsel 111, V undergird growth toward likeness 122, 124, V are the way to *unitas spiritus* 123,

equal with escaping from the W 171–72, W profane, and ecclesiastic 184, misery of life not in opposition to W 281–82, the W cannot calm and satisfy the soul 282, W is a squalid prison 263, the W's customary way of acting 294, to embrace the W 295, why die to the W? 514, cruelty of W (as as opposed to heaven) 532

ABBREVIATIONS

Abbreviations of Journals and Series

AA SS	*Acta Sanctorum*
AB	*Acta Bollandiana.* Brussels.
AC	*Analecta Sacri Ordinis Cisterciensis* (1945–64); *Analecta Cisterciensia* (1966 –). Rome.
AFP	*Archivum Patrum Praedicatorum.* Rome.
AHDL	*Archives d'Histoire doctrinale et littéraire du moyen âge.* Paris.
AHEB	*Analectes pour servir à l'Histoire Ecclésiastique de la Belgique.* Leuven.
BGHB	*Bijdragen tot de geschiedenis van het aloude Hertogdom Brabant.* Leuven.
Bijdragen	*Bijdragen. Tijdschrift voor Filosofie en Theologie.* Maastricht.
CBQ	*Catholic Biblical Quarterly.* Washington, D.C.
CCCM	Corpus Christianorum. Continuatio Mediaevalis. Turnhout.
CCH	*Catalogus Codicum Hagiographorum Bibliothecae Regiae Bruxellensis.* Brussels.
CF	Cistercian Fathers Series. Spencer, Kalamazoo.
Cîteaux.	Cîteaux *Cîteaux in de Nederlanden* (1950–1958); *Cîteaux* (1959–). Westmalle. Achel. Cîteaux.
Coll	*Collectanea Ordinis Cisterciensium Reformatorum* (1934–64); *Collectanea Cisterciensia* (1966–). Scourmont.
CS	Cistercian Studies Series. Kalamazoo, Michigan.
CSt	*Cistercian Studies.* Gethsemani, Kentucky.
DHGE	*Dictionnaire d'Histoire et de Géographie ecclésiastique.* Paris.
DSp	*Dictionnaire de Spiritualité.* Paris.
DThC	*Dictionnaire de Théologie catholique.* Paris.
ETL	*Ephemerides Theologicae Lovanienses.* Leuven.

GL	*Geist und Leben. Zeitschrift für Aszese und Mystik.* Munich/Würzburg.
HJ	*Heythrop Journal.* London.
HL	*Handelingen. Koninklijke Zuidnederlandse Maatschappij voor Taal- en Letterkunde en Geschiedenis.* Brussels.
IPQ	*International Philosophical Quarterly.* Fordham, New York-Namur.
LThK	*Lexikon für Theologie und Kirche.* Freiburg im Breisgau.
LV	*Lumière et Vie.* Savoie/Paris.
MnS	*Monastic Studies.* Pine City, New York. Montreal.
MS	*Medieval Studies.* Toronto.
MSR	*Mélanges de science religieuse.* Lille.
NRT	*Nouvelle Revue Théologique.* Tournai.
NTS	*New Testament Studies.* Cambridge.
OGE	*Ons Geestelijk Erf.* Antwerp.
OXP	*Orientalia Christiana Periodica.* Rome.
PL	*Patrologiae cursus completus, Series Latina.* Paris.
RAM	*Revue d'ascétique et de mystique.* Toulouse.
RBén	*Revue Bénédictine.* Maredsous.
RBibl	*Revue Biblique.* Paris.
RechSR	*Recherches de science religieuse.* Paris/ Strasbourg.
RHE	*Revue d'Histoire Ecclésiastique.* Leuven.
RMAL	*Revue du moyen-âge latin.* Strasbourg.
RSR	*Revue des sciences religieuses.* Paris.
RSt	*Religious Studies.* Cambridge.
RTAM	*Recherches de Théologie anncienne et médiévale.* Leuven.
SCh	Sources chrétiennes. Paris.
StM	*Studia Monastica.* Barcelona.
SVS	*Supplément à la Vie Spirituelle.* Paris.
TDNT	*Theological Dictionary of the New Testament.* Grand Rapids, Michigan.

TDOT	*Theological Dictionary of the Old Testament.* Grand Rapids, Michigan.
TNTL	*Tijdschrift voor Nederlandse Taal- en Letterkunde.* Leiden.
TS	*Theological Studies.* Baltimore, Maryland.
TT	*Tijdschrift voor theologie.* Nijmegen/Leuven.
VMKVA	*Verslagen en Mededelingen van de Koninklijke Vlaamse Academie voor Taal- en Letterkunde.* Brussels.
VS	*La Vie Spirituelle.* Paris.
ZKT	*Zeitschrift für katholische Theologie.* Innsbruck.

Abbreviations for Books

AM	*Augustinus Magister. Congrès international augustinien, Paris 21–24 Septembre 1954.* Three volumes. F. Cayré, ed.. Paris. 1954.
ET	English translation (or) English text.
Quinque	*Quinque prudentes virgines.* Chrysostom Henriquez, ed. Antwerp, 1630. (199–298: *Vita Idae Nivellensis)*
R-VM	*Beatrijs van Nazareth. Seven Manieren van Minne.* L. Reypens and J. Van Mierlo, edd. Leuven, 1926.
SBOp	*Sancti Bernardi Opera.* Ten volumes. Jean Leclercq, C.H. Talbot, H.M. Rochais, edd. Rome. 1957–1977.
SM	*Sacramentum Mundi.* Six volumes. Karl Rahner, C. Ernst, K. Smyth, edd., New York. 1968–1970.
Statuta	*Statuta Capitulorum Generalium Ordinis Cisterciensis ab anno 1116 ad annum 1786.* Eight volumes. J.M. Canivez, ed. Leuven. 1933–1941.

VM   Van Mierlo, Joseph, editor of the works of
            Hadewijch:
            Hadewijch: Visioenen. Two volumes. Leuven.
            1924–1925. *Hadewijch: Strophische Gedichten.*
            Two volumes. Antwerp. 1942. *Hadewijch:*
            Brieven. Two volumes. Antwerp. 1947.
            Hadewijch: Mengeldichten. Antwerp. 1952.

Abbreviations for the Works of Bernard of Clarivaux and William
of Saint Thierry

The abbreviations used in this study are those recommended by
the Board of Editors of Cistercian Publications.

Abbreviations for the Works of Bernard of Clairvaux

Adv   *Sermo in adventu Domini*
And   *Sermo in natali sancti Andreae*
Ann   *Sermo in annuntiatione dominica*
Asc   *Sermo in ascensione Domini*
Conv   *Sermo de conversione ad clericos*
Csi   *De consideratione libri v*
Ded   *Sermo in dedicatione ecclesiae*
Dil   *Liber de diligendo Deo*
Div   *Sermones de diversis*
Ep   *Epistola*
Gra   *Liber de gratia et libero arbitrio*
IV HM   *Sermo in feria iv hebdomadae sanctae*
Hum   *Liber de gradibus humilitatis et superbiae*
Miss   *Homelia super* missus est *in laudibus Virginis*
             Mater
Nat   *Sermon in nativitate domini*
I Nov   *Sermo in dominica I novembris*
O Pasc   *Sermo in octava Paschae*
OS   *Sermo in festivitate Omnium Sanctorum*
Par   *Parabolae*
Pasc   *Sermo in die Paschae*
Pent   *Sermo in die pentecostes*
Pre   *Liber de praecepto et dispensatione*

QH	*Sermo super psalmum* Qui habitat
SC	*Sermon super Cantica canticorum*
V Nat	*Sermo in vigilia nativitatis domini*

Abbreviations for the Works of William of Saint Thierry

Adv Abl	*Disputatio adversus Petrum Abaelardum*
Aenig	*Aenigma fidei*
Cant	*Expositio super Cantica canticorum*
Contemp	*De contemplando Deo*
Ep frat	*Epistola [aurea] ad fratres de Monte Dei*
Exp Rm	*Expositio in epistolam Pauli ad Romanos*
Med	*Meditativae orationes*
Nat am	*De natura et dignitate amoris*
Nat corp	*De natura corporis et animae*
Sacr altar	*De sacramento altaris liber*
Spec fid	*Speculum fidei*

A NOTE
ON THE REFERENCES USED

1. All patristic and medieval works are referred to according to the printed editions contained in Migne's *Patrologia Latina*, except when more recent and better editions were available to me.
2. The titles of all other books and articles are given in full in the bibliography contained in volume three.
3. All biblical references follow the enumeration of the Vulgate text.

CISTERCIAN PUBLICATIONS INC.
Kalamazoo, Michigan

TITLES LISTING

CISTERCIAN TEXTS

THE WORKS OF BERNARD OF CLAIRVAUX

Apologia to Abbot William
Five Books on Consideration: Advice to a
  Pope
Grace and Free Choice
Homilies in Praise of the Blessed Virgin
  Mary
The Life and Death of Saint Malachy the
  Irishman
Parables
Sermons on the Song of Songs I-IV
Steps of Humility and Pride

THE WORKS OF WILLIAM OF SAINT THIERRY

The Enigma of Faith
Exposition on the Epistle to the Romans
The Golden Epistle
The Mirror of Faith
The Nature and Dignity of Love

THE WORKS OF AELRED OF RIEVAULX

Dialogue on the Soul
The Mirror of Charity
Spiritual Friendship
Treatises I: On Jesus at the Age of Twelve,
  Rule for a Recluse, The Pastoral Prayer

THE WORKS OF JOHN OF FORD

Sermons on the Final Verses of the Song of
Songs I-VII

THE WORKS OF GILBERT OF HOYLAND

Sermons on the Songs of Songs I, II, III
Treatises, Sermons and Epistles

OTHER EARLY CISTERCIAN WRITERS

The Letters of Adam of Perseigne I
Baldwin of Ford: Spiritual Tractates
Guerric of Igny: Liturgical Sermons I-II
Idung of Prüfening: Cistercians and Cluniacs:
  The Case for Citeaux
Isaac of Stella: Sermons on the Christian Year
Serlo of Wilton & Serlo of Savigny
Stephen of Lexington: Letters from Ireland
Stephen of Sawley: Treatises

MONASTIC TEXTS

EASTERN CHRISTIAN TRADITION

Besa: The Life of Shenoute
Cyril of Scythopolis: Lives of the Monks of
  Palestine
Dorotheos of Gaza: Discourses
Evagrius Ponticus: Praktikos and Chapters
  on Prayer
The Harlots of the Desert
Iosif Volotsky: Monastic Rule
The Lives of the Desert Fathers
Menas of Nikiou: Isaac of Alexandra & St
  Macrobius
Pachomian Koinonia I-III
The Sayings of the Desert Fathers
Spiritual Direction in the Early Christian East
  (I. Hausherr)
The Syriac Fathers on Prayer and the Spiritual
  Life

WESTERN CHRISTIAN TRADITION

Anselm of Canterbury: Letters I-[II]
Bede: Commentary on the even Catholic
  Epistles
Bede: Commentary on Acts
Bede: Gospel Homilies
Gregory the Great: Forty Gospel Homilies
Guigo II the Carthusian: Ladder of Monks
  and Twelve Meditations
Peter of Celle: Selected Works
The Letters of Armand-Jean de Rance I-II
The Rule of the Master

CHRISTIAN SPIRITUALITY

Abba: Guides to Wholeness and Holiness
  East and West
Athirst for God: Spiritual Desire in Bernard
  of Clairvaux's Sermons on the Song of Songs
  (M. Casey)
Cistercian Way (A. Louf)
Fathers Talking (A. Squire)
Friendship and Community (B. McGuire)
From Cloister to Classroom
Herald of Unity: The Life of Maria Gabrielle
  Sagheddu (M. Driscoll)
Life of St Mary Magdalene... (D. Mycoff)
Rancé and the Trappist Legacy (A.J.
  Krailsheimer)
Roots of the Modern Christian Tradition
Russian Mystics (S. Bolshakoff)
Spirituality of Western Christendom
Spirituality of the Christian East
  (T. Spidlék)

MONASTIC STUDIES

Community and Abbot in the Rule of St
Benedict I-II (Adalbert De Vogüé)
Consider Your Call: A Theology of the
Monastic Life (Daniel Rees et al.)
The Finances of the Cistercian Order in the
Fourteenth Century (Peter King)

Fountains Abbey and Its Benefactors
(Joan Wardrop)
The Hermit Monks of Grandmont
(Carole A. Hutchison)
In the Unity of the Holy Spirit
(Sighard Kleiner)
Monastic Practices (Charles Cummings)
The Occupation of Celtic Sites in Ireland by
the Canons Regular of St Augustine and the
Cistercians (Geraldine Carville)
The Rule of St Benedict: A Doctrinal and
Spiritual Commentary (Adalbert de Vogüé)
The Rule of St Benedict (Br. Pinocchio)
St Hugh of Lincoln (D. H. Farmer)
Serving God First (Sighard Kleiner)

CISTERCIAN STUDIES

A Second Look at Saint Bernard (Jean Leclercq)
Bernard of Clairvaux and the Cistercian
Spirit (Jean Leclercq)
Bernard of Clairvaux: Studies Presented to
Dom Jean Leclercq
Christ the Way: The Christology of Guerric
of Igny (John Morson)
Cistercian Sign Language
The Cistercian Spirit
The Cistercians in Denmark (Brian McGuire)
Eleventh-century Background of Citeaux
(Bede K. Lackner)
The Golden Chain: Theological Anthropology of
Isaac of Stella (Bernard McGinn)
Image and Likeness: The Augustinian
Spirituality of William of St Thierry   (David
N. Bell)
The Mystical Theology of St Bernard
(Étienne Gilson)
Nicholas Cotheret's Annals of Citeaux
(Louis J. Lekai)
William, Abbot of St Thierry
Women and St Bernard of Clairvaux
(Jean Leclercq)

MEDIEVAL RELIGIOUS WOMEN

Distant Echoes (Shank-Nichols)
Gertrud the Great of Helfta: Spiritual Exercises
(Gertrud J. Lewis-Jack Lewis)
Peace Weavers (Nichols-Shank)

STUDIES IN CISTERCIAN ART AND ARCHITECTURE
Meredith Parsons Lillich, editor

Studies I, II, III now available
Studies IV scheduled for 1991

THOMAS MERTON

The Climate of Monastic Prayer (T. Merton)
The Legacy of Thomas Merton (Patrick Hart)
The Message of Thomas Merton (Patrick Hart)
Solitude in the Writings of Thomas Merton
(Richard Cashen)
Thomas Merton Monk (Patrick Hart)
Thomas Merton Monk and Artist
(Victor Kramer)
Thomas Merton on St Bernard
Toward an Integrated Humanity
(M.Basil Pennington et al.)

CISTERCIAN LITURGICAL DOCUMENTS SERIES
Chrysogonus Waddell, ocso, editor

Cistercian Hymnal: Text & Commentary
(2 volumes)
Hymn Collection of the Abbey of the Paraclete
Molesme Summer-Season Breviary
(4 volumes)
Institutiones nostrae: The Paraclete Statutes
Old French Ordinary and Breviary of the
Abbey of the Paraclete: Text and
Commentary (5 volumes)

STUDIA PATRISTICA

Papers of the 1983 Oxford Patristics Conference
Edited by Elizabeth A. Livingstone

XVIII/1 Historica-Gnostica-Biblica
XVIII/2 Critica-Classica-Ascetica-Liturgica
XVIII/3 Second Century-Clement & Origen-
Cappodician Fathers
XVIII/4 available from Peeters, Leuven

TEXTS AND STUDIES
IN THE
MONASTIC TRADITION

North American customers may order these books
through booksellers or directly from the warehouse:

Cistercian Publications
St Joseph's Abbey
Spencer, Massachusetts 01562
(508) 885-7011

Editorial queries and advance book information
should be directed to the Editorial Offices:

Cistercian Publications
Institute of Cistercian Studies
Western Michigan University
Kalamazoo, Michigan 49008
(616) 387-5090

A complete catalogue of texts in translation and
studies on early, medieval, and modern monasticism
is available at no cost from Cistercian Publications.